EARLY CHRISTIANITY IN CONTEXT

Editor
John M.G. Barclay

Editorial Board
Loveday Alexander, Troccls Engberg-Pedersen, Bart Ehrman,
Joel Marcus, John Riches

Published under
LIBRARY OF NEW TESTAMENT STUDIES
286

Formerly Journal for the Study of the New Testament Supplement Series

Editor
Mark Goodacre

Editorial Board
John M.G. Barclay, Craig Blomberg, Kathleen E. Corley,
R. Alan Culpepper, James D.G. Dunn, Craig A. Evans, Stephen Fowl,
Robert Fowler, Simon J. Gathercole, John S. Kloppenborg, Michael Labahn,
Robert Wall, Robert L. Webb, Catrin H. Williams

To my *Großdoktorvater*

Gilles Quispel

Recovering the Original *Gospel of Thomas*

A History of the Gospel and its Growth

April D. DeConick

t&t clark

Copyright © April D. DeConick, 2005
A Continuum imprint

Published by T&T Clark International
The Tower Building,   15 East 26th Street,
11 York Road,   Suite 1703,
London SE1 7NX   New York, NY 10010

www.tandtclark.com

British Library Cataloguing-in-Publication Data
A catalogue record for this book is available from the British Library

Library of Congress Cataloging-in-Publication Data

De Conick, April D.
  Recovering the original Gospel of Thomas : a history of the gospel and its growth / April D. De Conick.
    p. cm. -- (Early Christianity in context) (LIBRARY OF NEW TESTAMENT STUDIES; 286)
  Includes bibliographical references and index.
  ISBN 0-567-04342-8
  1. Gospel of Thomas (Coptic Gospel)--Criticism, interpretation, etc. I. Title. II. Series. III. Series: Journal for the study of the New Testament. Supplement series ; 286

  BS2860.T52D42 2005
  229'.8--dc22

                                                           2005045758

Typeset by Tradespools, Frome, Somerset
Printed on acid-free paper in Great Britain by, MPG Books Ltd, Bodmin, Cornwall

CONTENTS

PREFACE

Writing this book has been a joy from beginning to end. It was not written in isolation but is the result of generous conversations and interactions with many people who have inspired and influenced me along the way. It would not have been possible to write this book without them. I am grateful for each and every person who took time to listen to me or to question me, to think with me or argue with me, to read drafts of my work or to provide comments. I wish to thank as many as I can, recognizing that my acknowledgment of them does not necessarily mean the endorsement of my opinions.

The initial inspiration to sort out the unresolved problems of the *Gospel of Thomas* came to me one memorable moment in my classroom when my student Mark Lamie asked me why the Gospel contained a saying condemning circumcision while at the same time revering James the leader of the Jerusalem Church. That was in the autumn of 1998. I went back to my office after class and decided that the time had come to provide a reasonable answer to that question.

I began drafting my ideas immediately and proposed preliminary remarks on the subject to the Thomasine Traditions Group in 2000 at the Nashville convention for the Society of Biblical Literature. The paper was called, '"Go to James the Righteous" (Thomas 12): A Reconstruction of the History of a Christian Jewish Community from Jerusalem.' The following year in Denver, I spoke about my continuing work on the problem, 'The Gospel of Thomas and Jewish Traditions.' In these sessions, many Group members provided me with valuable questions and comments which helped to inspire and consolidate my position. I would especially like to thank Risto Uro, Jon Asgeirsson, and Phil Sellew for their friendship and support. I wish to thank Vernon Robbins in particular for the time he took to meet with me over coffee to continue to discuss rhetorical criticism and my idea about a 'collapsed apocalypse.'

After the Denver convention, I realized that I should write and publish a preliminary article on the subject. It appeared subsequently in 2002 in *Vigiliae Christianae* 56 under the title, 'The Original *Gospel of Thomas*.' I wish to thank J. den Boeft for his editorial advice and support. As I prepared the final manuscript of that article, at a conference at New York University, I met Bill Arnal who had been working on his own stratification of the Gospel. It was Bill who convinced me that we needed to discuss the history of the text in terms of literary method, and he gave me the word 'accretions' when I told him how much I disliked 'layers' because it did not get across the 'rolling' compositional process I was envisioning. His opinion influenced the language I used in that article and in this monograph to discuss the principles for discerning later sayings from earlier, although I was unwilling then, and remain unwilling today, to use literary method without reference to tradition history. It was this conviction that made me forge ahead, concentrating on developing a 'new' *traditionsgeschichtliche* approach which I now describe in Chapter 1.

A few months after 'The Original *Gospel of Thomas*' appeared in print, Tom Thatcher contacted me because he and Alan Kirk wanted to put together a volume for *Semeia* that applied Social Memory Theory to early Christian literature: *Memory, Tradition, and Text: Uses of the Past in Early Christianity*. Would I contribute? Since I knew nothing about Social Memory Theory, I was hesitant, especially because I wanted to finish this monograph and thought that a new project would divert my energy and time. But Tom said something that caught my attention. He thought that my earlier methodological work on Johannine and Thomasine traditions in my book *Voices of the Mystics* was quite close to what he understood about Social Memory studies. Could he send me a bibliography that Alan had put together?

Be it Fate or Providence, that day changed forever the way I look at 'historical' documents. I found myself literally submerged for the next year in anthropological, psychological, social, and historical studies about memory and its formation. I came to understand how and why our texts formed as they did, and the fate of the traditions along the way. What I had been struggling to define in terms of a historian of religion had already been studied, defined and documented by social scientists! I pressed on with great enthusiasm, rethinking, refining, writing and rewriting chapters in this monograph, applying these fabulous insights to my previous thoughts and work. I cannot thank Tom and Alan enough for offering me the opportunity to collaborate with them on their book. Without their offer, I would have remained ignorant of Social Memory studies and my studies of the Gospel in this monograph would have been deficient. The paper that I wrote for them is called, 'Reading the *Gospel of Thomas* as a Repository of Early Christian Communal Memory.' It is a summary of material appearing in Chapters 1, 6, 7 and 9.

As I immersed myself in these studies of memory, I came across a whole body of literature on orality that I had not been exposed to previously. Aside from references to A. Lord's famous book, *The Singer of Tales*, and

W. Kelber's, *The Oral and Written Gospel*, I was not familiar with the explosion in studies of orality which has been happening over the last several decades. In graduate school, I had taken the Form and Redaction Critical methods as my standard tools, believing that R. Bultmann and his students had based their approach on folk literature and studies of orality. But as I began reading actual studies in orality, I found much to my dismay, that Form and Redaction Criticism have very little to do with oral consciousness and transmission. My previous understanding of the Gospel had been based on my literate imagination, not the oral registry of the ancient world! This insight brought with it further reflection, reading, and modification of my model for the composition of the Gospel and particularly impacted Chapters 1, 2 and 3.

When the manuscript was finally drafted and sent to my editor John Barclay, he suggested that the book be split into two independent volumes since I had included a commentary and translation of the Gospel as appendices. So the commentary and translation will be appearing as a sister volume under the title, *The Original* Gospel of Thomas *in Translation, with Commentary and New English Translation of the Complete Gospel*. The translations in *Recovering the Original* Gospel of Thomas are based on my reconstructions in the commentary. I rely heavily on the Greek fragments, attempting to bring them into the full translation of the Gospel. So my translation is not a straightforward translation of the fourth-century Coptic manuscript. I have used the following marks to indicate these decisions, but the companion commentary should be consulted for my reasoning.

( )	Parentheses are placed around words not in the manuscript but that the translation needs in order to capture the meaning of the Greek or Coptic.
(( ))	Double parentheses surround text where the translation is based on the Greek manuscript tradition rather than the Coptic.
[ ]	Square brackets indicate lacunae and their possible reconstructions.
[[ ]]	Double square brackets surround text where it has been emended. In these cases, the translation is based on a correction of an error perceived in the manuscript tradition.
<< >>	Double pointed brackets surround text where an alternative reading is presented based on a possible Aramaic text behind the Greek or Coptic.

My heartfelt gratitude goes to all who read pieces of this manuscript and provided me comments, especially Bart Ehrman, Birger Pearson, Gilles Quispel, Vernon Robbins, Alan Segal, Christopher Rowland, Kevin

Sullivan, Andrei Orlov, Andrea Lieber-Merwin, Jarl Fossum and Bill Arnal. To my secretary, Regina Linsalata, who worked as my research assistant, gathering articles, creating a system of storage and retrieval, and building biographies. To Illinois Wesleyan University, which awarded me Artistic and Scholarly Development grants (1999–2000 and 2001–2002) to prepare the two articles that became the basis for this monograph. To my husband, Wade Greiner, who gives me unconditional support and encouragement. To my son, Alexander DeGreiner, who was born last year in the midst of all of this.

Finally, a note about the dedication to my *Großdoktorvater*, Gilles Quispel. Years ago when I wrote my first book, *Seek to See Him*, Gilles asked me about the historical context of the Gospel which I had not addressed in that book but which he felt I should have. I remember responding honestly that I could not write about that which I did not know. Well, that was then and this is now. Now I know.

April DeConick

Christmas Eve, 2004

ABBREVIATIONS

AcadBib	Academia Biblica
AcOr	*Acta orientalia*
AGAJU	Arbeiten zur Geschichte des Antiken Judentums und des Urchristentums
AGJU	Arbeiten zur Geschichte des antiken Judentums und des Urchristentums
ANRW	Hildegard Temporini and Wolfgang Haase (eds.), *Aufstieg und Niedergang der römischen Welt: Geschichte und Kultur Roms im Spiegel der neueren Forschung* (Berlin: W. de Gruyter, 1972–)
ARW	*Archiv für Religionswissenschaft*
AsiaJT	*Asia Journal of Theology*
ASR	*American Sociological Review*
AUSS	*Andrews University Seminary Studies*
BCNH	Bibliothèque Copte de Nag Hammadi
BETL	Bibliotheca ephemeridum theologicarum lovaniensium
BIFAO	*Bulletin de l'Institut français d'archéologie orientale*
BJRL	*Bulletin of the John Rylands University Library of Manchester*
BLE	*Bulletin de littérature ecclésiastique*
BZ	*Biblische Zeitschrift*
BZNW	Beihefte zur *ZNW*
CBQ	*Catholic Biblical Quarterly*
CSCO	Corpus scriptorum christianorum orientalium
CSMC	*Critical Studies in Mass Communication*
EPRO	Etudes preliminaries aux religions orientales dans l'empire romain
ErJb	*Eranos-Jahrbuch*
EvT	*Evangelische Theologie*
ExpTim	*Expository Times*
FFF	*Foundations and Facets Forum*

FRLANT	Forschungen zur Religion und Literatur des Alten und Neuen Testaments
FZPhTh	*Freiburger Zeitschrift für Philosophie und Theologie*
HA	*History and Anthropology*
Hen	*Henoch*
HeyJ	*Heythrop Journal*
HNT	Handbuch zum Neuen Testament
HSCL	Harvard Studies in Comparative Literature
HSS	Harvard Semitic Studies
HTR	*Harvard Theological Review*
HUCA	*Hebrew Union College Annual*
HvTSt	*Hervormde Teologiese Studies*
Int	*Interpretation*
JA	*Journal asiatique*
JAAR	*Journal of the American Academy of Religion*
JAF	*Journal of American Folklore*
JAH	*Journal of American History*
JAOS	*Journal of the American Oriental Society*
JASP	*Journal of Abnormal and Social Psychology*
JBL	*Journal of Biblical Literature*
JECS	*Journal of Early Christian Studies*
JJS	*Journal of Jewish Studies*
JR	*Journal of Religion*
JSJ	*Journal for the Study of Judaism in the Persian, Hellenistic and Roman Period*
JSJSup	*Journal for the Study of Judaism in the Persian, Hellenistic and Roman Period*, Supplement Series
JSNT	*Journal for the Study of the New Testament*
JSNTSup	*Journal for the Study of the New Testament*, Supplement Series
JSQ	*Jewish Studies Quarterly*
JSPSup	*Journal for the Study of the Pseudepigrapha*, Supplement Series
JTS	*Journal of Theological Studies*
MH	*Museum helveticum*
Mus	*Muséon: Revue d'études orientales*
MTSR	*Method and Theory in the Study of Religion*
NHMS	Nag Hammadi and Manichaean Studies
NHS	Nag Hammadi Studies
NovT	*Novum Testamentum*
NovTSup	*Novum Testamentum*, Supplements
NTS	*New Testament Studies*
Numen	*Numen: International Review for the History of Religions*
NumenSup	*Numen: International Review for the History of Religions*, Supplement Series

OT	*Oral Tradition*
OTP	James Charlesworth (ed.), *Old Testament Pseudepigrapha*
QS	*Qualitative Sociology*
RB	*Revue biblique*
REG	*Revue de études grecques*
REJ	*Revue des études juives*
RGG	*Religion in Geschichte und Gegenwart*
Rhist	*Relexions Historiques*
RSR	*Recherches de science religieuse*
RTP	*Revue de théologie et de philosophie*
SA	Studia anselmiana
SAC	Studies in Antiquity and Christianity
SBLDS	*SBL Dissertation Series*
SF	*Social Forces*
SNTSMS	Society for New Testament Studies Monograph Series
SBLSBS	*SBL Sources for Biblical Study*
SBLSP	*SBL Seminar Papers*
SecCent	Second Century
SNT	Studien zum Neuen Testament
SNTSMS	*Society for New Testament Studies Monograph Series*
ST	Studia theologica
StBL	Studies in Biblical Literature
STDJ	*Studies on the Texts of the Desert of Judah*
STRev	*Sewanee Theological Review*
SUNT	Studien zur Umwelt des Neuen Testaments
SVTP	Studia in Veteris Testamenti pseudepigrapha
TBT	Theologische Bibliothek Töpelmann
TDNT	Gerhard Kittel and Gerhard Friedrich (eds.), *Theological Dictionary of the New Testament* (trans. Geoffrey W. Bromiley; 10 vols.; Grand Rapids: Eerdmans, 1964–)
TLZ	*Theologische Literaturzeitung*
TRu	*Theologische Rundschau*
TS	*Theological Studies*
TSAJ	Texte und Studien zum antiken Judentum
TTZ	*Trierer theologische Zeitschrift*
TU	Texte und Untersuchungen
TynBul	*Tyndale Bulletin*
VC	*Vigiliae christianae*
VCSup	*Vigiliae christianae*, Supplement Series
VTSup	*Vetus Testamentum*, Supplements
WMANT	Wissenschaftliche Monographien zum Alten und Neuen Testament
WUNT	Wissenschaftliche Untersuchungen zum Neuen Testament
WZKM	*Wiener Zeitschrift für die Kunde des Morgenlandes*

| ZKG | *Zeitschrift für Kirchengeschichte* |
| ZNW | *Zeitschrift für die neutestamentliche Wissenschaft* |

LIST OF ILLUSTRATIONS

PART ONE

MAPPING A METHODOLOGY

Chapter 1

THE 'NEW' *TRADITIONSGESCHICHTLICHE* APPROACH

Communication, like knowledge itself, flowers in speech. ~ *W.J. Ong*

The history of traditions approach has a long prestigious history originating in the decades surrounding J. Wellhausen's classic formulation of the Documentary Hypothesis.[1] Responding to Wellhausen in the late 1900s, H. Gunkel became interested in showing a way *behind* the written Pentateuchal sources to yet earlier sources of Israel's history. According to Gunkel, the authors of the Pentateuch are best characterized as collectors or 'redactors' of the oral traditions of the people of Israel. What these collectors received and recorded was the latest stage of a long process of the formulation of the traditions and their faithful oral transmission across the generations.

But Gunkel was not originally a scholar of the Tanakh. He began his career as a New Testament scholar. In his early book on the New Testament teaching *about* Jesus, he wrote, 'Early Christianity is like a river that is the confluence of two great streams: the one specifically Israelite, it originates in the Old Testament; the other, however, flows through Judaism from foreign oriental religions. Then added to this in the West is the Greek factor...It is not the Gospel of Jesus, as we know it predominately from the synoptics, but the early Christianity of Paul and John which is a syncretistic religion.'[2] Gunkel argued that the teaching *about* Jesus in the New Testament was heir to traditional 'oriental' savior myths that had worked their way into certain Jewish circles. Thus, the Christianity of Paul and John was a synthesis of religious traditions. It was

---

1. Cf. K. Koch, *The Growth of the Biblical Tradition* (trans. S.M. Cupitt; New York: Charles Scribner's Sons, 1969); W.E. Rast, *Tradition History and the Old Testament*, Guides to Biblical Scholarship (Philadelphia: Fortress Press, 1972); R.S. Barbour, *Tradition-Historical Criticism of the Gospels* (London: SPCK, 1972); D.A. Knight, *Rediscovering the Traditions of Israel*, SBLDS 9 (Missoula: Scholars Press, 1975); D.R. Catchpole, 'Tradition History,' in I.H. Marshall (ed.), *New Testament Interpretation: Essays on Principles and Methods* (Grand Rapids: Eerdmans Publishing Company, 1977) pp. 165–180.

2. H. Gunkel, *Zum religionsgeschichtlichen Verständnis des Neuen Testaments*, FRLANT 1 (Göttingen, 1903). This book was based on lectures given in the autumn of 1901.

a 'syncretistic religion,' as was Judaism upon which Christianity was founded.

Gunkel's words belong to a conversation among a group of scholars at Göttingen who came to be known as 'The History of Religions School,' the *Religionsgeschichtliche Schule*. The group of scholars who first developed this School is impressive: A. Eichhorn (1856–1926), W. Wrede (1859–1906), H. Gunkel (1862–1932); H. Hackmann (1865–1920), A. Rahlfs (1865–1935), J. Weiss (1863–1914), W. Bousset (1865–1920), and E. Troelsch (1865–1923). This group launched what would become a revolution in biblical criticism and theology. The School's main conviction was that religion is not static, rather it is subject to human history and develops over time. The traditions which are found in our biblical texts have an oral or written pre-history that one needs to trace in order to understand the ideas as they are presented in the texts themselves. The main project of the *Religionsgeschichtliche Schule* was to explain the rise of Christianity as the appropriation of pagan mythology and practices, as the assimilation of Hellenistic religious traditions with a brand of Judaism to which alien Iranian elements had already fused.

Even though the work that this School generated was extraordinary and in many ways unsurpassed even today, it was not without criticism. It eventually became clear that even though the School had demonstrated that early Christianity must be understood within the context of contemporaneous religious traditions, it had not always been sensitive enough to *how* the traditions were being used in the various texts. Were the authors using the tradition to say similar things? Or not? Did similar traditions across texts suggest derivations, one from the other? Or might both go back to a common source prior to their manifestation in our texts? For instance, it is true that some parallels can be seen in the terminology used by the Emperor Cult and the Christians. The emperor was called, '*Kyrios*' and '*Kosmokrator.*' He was understood to be the universal '*Soter.*' His birth, accession to the throne, and his decrees were '*evangelion.*' This terminological correspondence, however, does not mean that the Christians relied on the Emperor Cult for these terms. In fact, both applied the terms in very different senses. It is more likely that the Emperor Cult and Christianity adapted common ancient Near Eastern epithets more or less independently of each other. Thus critics objected that comparative parallels were not enough to warrant arguments of origination or dependence.

Out of the *Religionsgeschichtliche Schule* though developed the essential historical-critical tools: source criticism, form criticism, and later redaction criticism. These tools have become indispensable to tradition historians, helping us answer multitudes of questions about the traditional material in our texts. Unfortunately, however, the application of these tools has largely failed to move our analyses very far beyond the scope of individual texts to that of the history of traditions and their interrelationships.

In the last few decades, scholars who have become disenchanted with historical-critical tools because they have failed to provide adequate answers to these difficult historical questions, have explored alternative literary methods and have applied theories gleaned from other disciplines to our texts. On the one hand, the results of their studies have been restrictive because they have further suspended us inside individual texts so that we are left to garner meaning of the traditions in isolation from other ancient texts and their traditions. As a result, interpretations are now being imposed on the ancient texts that would not have made sense in the ancient world. The Academy is in the precarious position of supporting a reconstruction of the history of Jesus and early Christianity that is historically implausible if not impossible, a reconstruction that empties the texts of the Christians' strong feelings about and hopes for religious experience, a reconstruction that fails to recognize that the Christian texts came out of living communities of people with deep roots in streams of Jewish religious traditions. On the other hand, the results of their studies have been impressive because they have provided us with a whole body of new information and tools to use in our research.

For these reasons, in my own research, I find it critical to return to the tradition-historical method and weld into it the information and tools that have been developed by scholars who have been applying to our texts literary methods and theories from outside disciplines. When these are welded with our old historical methods, in my opinion, we finally have the necessary models and tools to examine the traditions within and across texts even in cases where we are not dealing with direct literary dependence or intertextuality. To do so successfully will require knowledge of the origins and ancient meanings of the traditions identified in our texts. Any traditional interrelationships across our texts, any changes that have taken place in the traditions, and any differences in their contemporary use must also be determined. In this way, the new *Traditionsgeschichtliche* approach will be sensitive to issues of false parallels while maintaining a heuristic of historical plausibility and integrity.

1.1 *The Historical Contexture of Traditions*

The new *Traditionsgeschichtliche* approach is founded on the old premise of the *Religionsgeschichtliche Schule*: the traditions in our texts are best understood in relation to contemporaneous religious traditions. In other words, every tradition has a historical contexture, an intimate relationship to traditions found in other texts. Traditions are not 'invented' *ex nihilo*. They have a pre-history *and* a contemporary history. Because ancient authors and readers alike brought to the text frameworks of traditional understanding as well as deep exegetical streams of interpretation, it is impossible to understand ideas found in our texts in isolation from ideas found in other contemporaneous texts or to interpret an ancient text isolated from others.

In order to map the traditional frameworks and relationships success-fully, the proximity of the traditions must be taken into consideration. In my judgment, this was the great flaw in the work of the *Religionsgeschich-tliche Schule*. Those of the *Religionsgeschichtliche Schule* often relied on comparisons with traditions farther removed from the first Christians than they needed to. Many of the Göttingen scholars looked to the Greco-Roman and Persian literature rather than the Second Temple Jewish materials for the origins of the traditional material. This, preference for Greco-Roman-Persian traditions is not as much a product of good scholarship as the politics of scholarship and prejudice at a time when Christianity was considered the jewel of Western civilization while Judaism was viewed as a degenerate religion. It took most of the nineteenth and twentieth centuries for the discipline of Jewish studies to emerge in its own right. In the words of Susannah Heschel, 'its scholarship was not simply a presentation of Jewish history but a counterhistory of prevailing Christian scholarship.' Scholars of Judaism argued that Judaism had not 'outlived its significance with the dawn of Christianity,' nor were Jews 'a fossil of history.' Rather Judaism stood 'at the center of Western civilization, having given birth to both Christianity and Islam.'[3]

Fortunately, today we are better equipped to look to Judaism because our knowledge of Judaism in the Hellenistic period has been so enriched in the last century not only with the constructive work of scholars of Judaism, but also because we possess texts that the *Religionsgeschichtliche Schule* did not, particularly the Dead Sea Scrolls, the Nag Hammadi collection and hordes of magical papyri. Our knowledge of the 'apocryphal,' 'pseudepigraphical,' hekhalot, and rabbinic literature has been substan-tially improved since the time of the *Religionsgeschichtliche Schule*. Thus, we have a much more precise picture of early Judaism, its varieties and manifestations in different geographical locations and in different eras.[4]

3. S. Heschel, 'Jewish Studies as Counterhistory,' in D. Biale, M. Galchinsky, and S. Heschel (eds.), *Insider/Outsider: American Jews & Multiculturalism* (Berkeley: University of California Press, 1998) p. 102.

4. Some studies that I have found to be particularly helpful include M. Hengel, *Judaism and Hellenism*, 2 vols. (trans. J. Bowden; Philadelphia: Fortress Press, 1974); J.D. Cohen, *From the Maccabees to the Mishnah* (Philadelphia: The Westminster Press, 1987); E.P. Sanders, *Jewish Law From Jesus to the Mishnah: Five Studies*, Philadelphia: Trinity Press International, 1990); L.H. Schiffman, *From Text to Tradition: A History of the Second Temple and Rabbinic Judaism* (Hoboken, KTAV, 1991); E.P. Sanders, *Judaism: Practice & Belief 63*

We know now that Jesus was Jewish and his first followers were Jewish, including the Pharisee Paul. Early Christianity, in fact, was a form of Judaism, 'Rebecca's child' so to speak.[5] Most of the New Testament literature, if not all of it, is Jewish literature of the first century.

Because of this knowledge, the terminology we use to describe early Christianity has shifted since the early 1900s. Instead of dividing formative Christianity into 'Jewish Christianity' and 'Gentile Christianity' as did the Göttingen scholars, our new knowledge of Second Temple Judaism has made it possible to talk more accurately about the origins of Christianity and Christianity's connection with other traditions.[6] In my judgment, Christianity is better characterized in this early period, 'Christian Judaism,' that is *a form of Judaism in which Jesus was believed to be the Messiah.* The first 'Christians' were actually 'Christian Jews.' Quite early in the movement, conservative and liberal factions developed within the

BCE–66CE (Philadelphia: Trinity Press International, 1992); E. Ferguson, *Backgrounds of Early Christianity* (Grand Rapids: Eerdman's Publishing Company, 2nd edn. 1993); S. Cohen, *The Beginnings of Jewishness: Boundaries, Varieties, Uncertainties* (Berkeley: University of California Press, 1999); S. Schwartz, *Imperialism and Jewish Society: 200 B.C.E. to 640 C.E.* (Princeton: Princeton University Press, 2001); F. Murphy, *Early Judaism:The Exile to the Time of Jesus* (Peabody: Hendrickson Publishers, 2002).

    5. A. Segal, *Rebecca's Children: Judaism and Christianity in the Roman World* (Cambridge: Harvard University Press, 1986); cf. J.T. Sanders, *Schismatics, Sectarians, Dissidents, Deviants: The First One Hundred Years of Jewish–Christian Relations* (Valley Forge: Trinity Press International, 1993).

    6. For highlights of this discussion, see M. Simon, *Verus Israel* (Paris: Boccard, 1948); H.-J. Schoeps, *Theologie und Geschichte des Judenchristentums* (Tübingen: Mohr, 1956); G. Strecker, *Das Judenchristentum in den Pseudoclementinen* (Berlin: Akademie, 1958); H.-J. Schoeps, *Jewish Christianity* (Philadelphia: Fortress Press, 1964); J. Danielou, *The Theology of Jewish Christianity* (London: Darton, Longman and Todd, 1964); G. Quispel, 'The Discussion of Judaic Christianity,' *VC* 22 (1968) pp. 81–93; R. Longenecker, *The Christology of Early Jewish Christianity: Studies in Biblical Theology* (Naperville: Allenson, 1970); G. Strecker, 'On the Problem of Jewish Christianity,' in W. Bauer, *Orthodoxy and Heresy in Earliest Christianity* (ed. R. Kraft and G. Krodel; Philadelphia: Fortress Press, 2nd edn. 1971) pp. 241–285; B. Bagatti, *Church from the Circumcision* (Jerusalem: Franciscan, 1971); R.A. Kraft, 'In Search of "Jewish Christianity" and its "Theology",' *RSR* 60 (1972) pp. 81–92; A.F.J. Klijn, 'The Study of Jewish Christianity,' *NTS* 20 (1974) pp. 419–431; R. Murray, 'Defining Judeo-Christianity,' *HeyJ* 13 (1972) pp. 303–310 and 'On Early Christianity and Judaism: Some Recent Studies,' pp. 441–451; M. Simon, 'Réflexions sur le Judeo-Christianisme,' in J. Neusner (ed.), *Christianity, Judaism and Other Greco-Roman Cults: Studies for Morton Smith at Sixty*, Part 2: *Early Christianity* (Leiden: E.J. Brill, 1975) pp. 53–76; F. Manns, *Bibliographie du Judeo-Christianisme* (Jerusalem: Franciscan, 1978); R. Murray, 'Jews, Hebrews and Christians: Some Needed Distinctions,' *NovT* 24 (1983) pp. 194–208; N. Pritz, *Nazarene Jewish Christianity: From the End of the New Testament Period until Its Disappearance in the Fourth Century* (Leiden: E.J. Brill, 1988); G. Luedemann, *Opposition to Paul in Jewish Christianity* (trans. M. Eugene Boring; Philadelphia: Fortress Press, 1989); A. Segal, 'Jewish Christianity,' in H. Attridge and G. Hata (eds.), *Eusebius, Christianity, and Judaism* (Leiden: E.J. Brill, 1992) pp. 326–351.

movement. The conservative faction was centered in Jerusalem, led by Jesus' brother James and some of the disciples. They were not as accommodating to the needs of their Gentile converts as were the liberal Christian Jews. The liberal faction operated out of Antioch and Paul became its primary missionary, theologian and leader before he broke away as a 'lone wolf.' It is not until the end of the first century and the beginning of the second century that the Christian Jews begin identifying themselves over and against Judaism rather than from within it. At this point, we find 'Christians' and 'Jewish Christians.' The latter term should be reserved to describe those groups in this later period that maintained the conservative attitude of Christian Judaism while, at the same time, identifying themselves as Christian rather than as Jews.

Therefore, *in order accurately to understand the historical contexture of the formative Christian traditions, it will be essential to examine them as living religious traditions within Second Temple Judaism, to see them as manifestations of Jewish religiosity in the Hellenistic period.* As the constituency of the movement shifted over the course of the first century and non-Jews came to dominate the movement's population and discourse, the contexture of traditions began to shift as well. Christianity began incorporating more and more attitudes and traditions from the non-Jewish horizon, even to the extent of fostering anti-Jewish sentiments within the movement. So appeal to broader Mediterranean traditions is warranted, especially in this period of Christian development.

1.2 *The Referential Horizon of Traditions*

Related to the broad historical contexture of traditions is the principle that *traditions belong to unspoken horizons of reference*, what J.M. Foley calls 'traditional referentiality.'[7] That is, traditions are embedded in larger story blocks which are left unspoken. The audiences would have related the fragments of the traditions they were hearing or reading to specific stories which were familiar to them. Drawing upon the receptionalist theory of modern literary criticism (especially those of H.R. Jauss and W. Iser) and contemporary ethnographic and linguistic studies (particularly those of R. Bauman, D. Hymes, and M.A.K. Halliday) Foley explains that these horizons represent 'a set of traditional ideas much larger and richer than any single performance or text,' providing an interpretative frame within which the oral performance or text was understood.[8] The traditional units

---

7.   J.M. Foley, *Immanent Art: From Structure to Meaning in Traditional Oral Epic* (Bloomington: Indiana University, 1991); J.M. Foley, *The Singer of Tales in Performance* (Bloomington: Indiana University, 1995).

8.   Foley, *Singer*, p. 6.

present in the performance or text would have evoked 'the fecund totality of the entire tradition,' bearing 'meanings as wide and deep as the tradition they encode.'[9] This referential horizon thus evokes the echo of a larger traditional story, 'a context that is enormously larger and more echoic than the text or work itself.'[10]

Deriving meaning this way is metonymic, 'a mode of signification wherein the part stands for the whole.'[11] Foley explains that a performance or text 'is enriched by an unspoken context that dwarfs the textual artifact.'[12] Audiences and readers would have been plugged into the appropriate referential horizon for the traditions that they were hearing or reading. This unconscious engagement with the horizon was what made it possible for them to respond to and decode the traditional signals in the text, to bridge the 'gaps of indeterminancy' between the textual signals, and to engage in 'constituency-building.'[13] In other words, the hearer or reader was responsible for filling the gaps between the traditions referred to in the performance or text with their shared knowledge of the traditions' horizons. So traditions within performances and texts resonated within a deeper extra-textual traditional complex or stream that was inherent to the audience. The performance of the traditions evoked a 'metonymic referencing' from deep within the traditions' horizon.[14] As Foley states, 'each metonymic integer functions as an index-point or node in a grand, untextualizable network of traditional associations. Activation of any single node brings into play an enormous wellspring of meaning that can be tapped in no other way...'[15]

This, of course, has enormous implications for modern interpreters of ancient texts. It suggests that a text does not relate the complete story. Rather *the story was completed by the audience with the story they already knew*. The specific traditions related in the text represent only fragments of the fuller story, fragments which trigger the fuller complex of traditions in the mind of the ancient hearer or reader. Because the traditions in our texts are presented as fragments, it may be the case that 'silences' in a text with respect to some elements of the story probably do *not* represent a lack of knowledge or a conscious omission of that element. Thus one of the biggest challenges for the modern scholar is to reconstruct and supply the referential horizon that the ancient interpreter would have known if we are

9. Foley, *Immanent Art*, p. 7.
10. Foley, *Immanent Art*, p. 7.
11. Foley, *Immanent Art*, p. 7.
12. Foley, *Immanent Art*, pp. 40–41.
13. Foley, *Immanent Art*, pp. 44, 47–48.
14. Foley, *Singer*, p. 16.
15. Foley, *Singer*, p. 16.

going to be at all successful with our attempts to understand what these old texts have to tell us about early Christianity.

1.3 *The Communal Nature of Traditions*

Traditions are passed down through language from generation to generation in the form of stories, sayings, myths, creeds, liturgies, and so on. At certain moments in the history of a given community, its oral traditions enter written texts, crystallizing the community's traditions at a particular stage in particular language. Because rhetorical critics study the language in a text as a means of communicating among people, rhetorical analyses can help us to reconstruct the self-understanding of a community of people from its texts: their sense of the past, their systems of religious belief, and their manner of conduct. This communication among people can occur not only within a particular text – a matter of intratraditions – but also can be heard between different texts – a matter of intertraditions. By examining the topics rhetorically within and across the texts we can better understand their thoughts, speeches, stories, and arguments. A rhetorical focus helps us to see how language is being used by people in the texts to establish bonds, to identify opponents, to negotiate shared interests, to pursue self-interests, and to offer a new perspective.[16]

Thus rhetorical analyses have confirmed and enriched our understanding of the communal nature of traditions. *The traditions – the ideas, stories, sayings, and so on – found in the ancient texts do not represent the imagination and opinions of an isolated author as much as they do those of living religious communities of people.* They are attached to specific groups, locations, and regions. Rhetorical critics insist that 'a person's ideology concerns her or his conscious or unconscious enactment of presuppositions, dispositions, and values held in common with other people.' It is not very satisfactory to speak about one person's ideology since this is not so much the subject of ideology as of psychology.[17] According to J. Elliot, 'Ideologies are shaped by specific world views of reality shared by groups – specific perspectives on the world, society and human beings, and on limitations and potentialities of human existence.'[18] At the heart of the matter is V. Robbin's statement that ideology 'concern's people's

16. V.K. Robbins, *Exploring the Texture of Texts: A Guide to Socio-rhetorical Interpretation* (Valley Forge: Trinity Press International, 1996) p. 1.

17. Robbins, *Texture*, p. 1.

18. J. Elliot, *A Home for the Homeless: A Social-Scientific Criticism of 1 Peter: Its Situation and Strategy* (Philadelphia: Fortress Press, 1990) p. 268.

relationship to other people. But, ideology does not just concern people; it concerns the discourse of people.'[19]

C. Afzal in his work on social imagination in early Christianity has emphasized the communal nature of traditions by going so far as to describe them as 'communal icons.' They are 'patterns of the imagination that participants in communal conversation can assume they have in common.'[20] The communal icons are 'configurations of symbols' that can be 'manipulated by individuals and groups in order to change how a community perceives aspects of reality embodied in the constituent symbols.'[21] Afzal correctly notes that the use of images in a text 'depends on the prior knowledge of these images by his audience.'[22] Thus, the communal icon represents 'a pattern of thought that an author inherits by virtue of participation in society.'[23] This means that such icons are a 'repository' at the disposal of authors. While writing, the author assumes that his intended audience also has knowledge of these patterns of thought. His text, therefore, does not simply 'reproduce' the communal icons, the text may in fact be written to modify or destroy them. In this way, the reality of the reader is subtly manipulated.[24] For Afzal, the interpretative process means that we must try to understand the communal icons which the author had assumed on the part of his audience or the text will remain impenetrable to later readers.[25] Moreover, if we focus on the relationship between texts with reference to their use of communal icons, we do not need to establish direct literary dependence of one Christian text upon another in order to draw meaningful conclusions.[26]

Afzal's work borders on the theories of social memory that have been informing the research of scholars in the social sciences, especially in the last decade. Understanding the shape of communal memory is essential when studying cultures that possess some literacy but experience a heavy oral residue. In such cultures, the dominant power of the mind is memory.[27] Social memory, or communal memory as I prefer to call it, is

---

19. Robbins, *Texture*, p. 110.

20. C. Afzal, 'The Communal Icon: Complex Cultural Schemas, Elements of the Social Imagination (Matthew 10:32//Luke 12:8 and Revelation 3:5, A Case Study,' in V. Wiles, A. Brown, and G. Synder (eds.), *Putting Body and Soul Together: Essays in Honor of Robin Scroggs* (Valley Forge: Trinity Press International, 1997) p. 58.

21. Afzal, 'Communal Icon,' pp. 58–59.

22. Afzal, 'Communal Icon,' p. 63.

23. Afzal, 'Communal Icon,' p. 65.

24. Afzal, 'Communal Icon,' p. 68.

25. Afzal, 'Communal Icon,' p. 79.

26. Afzal, 'Communal Icon,' p. 64.

27. W.J. Ong, *Orality and Literacy: The Technologizing of the Word* (New York, 1982) p. 36.

'the shared dimension of remembering.'[28] It is particularly important to understand its nature because it literally is the 'repository of tradition.'[29] It is a group's 'remembered history,'[30] the 'recollections of the past that are determined and shaped by a group' in the present.[31] As such, it transcends the individual, consisting of traditions and properties larger than the personal sphere: literature, art, sanctuaries, ruins, place names, holidays, relics, rituals, and so on.[32]

Further, it depends on shared frames of reference within a culture and thrives on remaking the past into material with contemporaneous meaning.[33] It is filled with traditions, with 'reused and reusable material' that become resources for giving meaning to and making sense of the past.[34] It is not a matter of 'vegetating under the weight of the past' but of continually correlating the past with the present and the anticipated future of the community.[35] So the formation of communal memory is not a retrieval of past traditions and history. Rather it is the 'reconfiguration' of the past, making it conform to the present experiences and future expectations of the group.[36] 'Remembering' is not a matter of recall, but a selection and reorganization of traditions so that the present can be better understood in light of its past and a sense of continuity between the present and the past is achieved. In this sense, it is best characterized as retrospective. These retrospective reconstructions of the past are largely achieved by adapting traditions and historical facts to the beliefs and spiritual needs of the contemporary group.[37]

28. B. Zelizer, 'Reading the Past Against the Grain: The Shape of Memory Studies,' *CSMC* 12 (1995) p. 214.

29. M. Halbwachs, *The Collective Memory* (trans. F. Ditter and V. Ditter; New York: Harper and Row, 1980 [1950]) p. 78.

30. B. Lewis, *History: Remembered, Recovered, Invented* (Princeton: Princeton University Press, 1975) pp. 11–12.

31. Zelizer, 'Reading the Past Against the Grain,' p. 214.

32. B. Swartz, *Abraham Lincoln and the Forge of National Memory* (Chicago: University of Chicago Press, 2000) p. 9.

33. Zelizer, 'Reading the Past Against the Grain,' p. 228.

34. M. Halbwachs, *On Collective Memory* (trans. L.A. Coser; Chicago: University of Chicago Press, 1992 [1925]) p. 40; J. Bodnar, *Remaking America: Public Memory, Commemoration, and Patriotism in the Twentieth Century* (Princeton: Princeton University Press, 1992) p. 75; I. Irwin-Zarecka, *Frames of Remembrance: The Dynamics of Collective Memory* (New Brunswick: Transaction Publishers, 1994) p. 7.

35. F. Zonabend, *The Enduring Memory: Time and History in a French Village* (trans. A. Forster; Manchester: Manchester University Press, 1984) p. 203.

36. P. Hutton, 'Collective Memory and Collective Mentalities: The Halbwachs-Aries Connection,' *RHist* 15 (1988) p. 314.

37. M. Halbwachs, *The Legendary Topography of the Gospels in the Holy Land* (trans. L. Coser; Chicago: Chicago University Press, 1992 [1941]) p. 7.

The process of constructing memory is fragmentary, connecting remembrances to certain reference points or existing collective frameworks.[38] Communal memory is 'pieced together like a mosaic.'[39] It is not the sum total of what actually happened. Rather it retains only those traditions from the past that it needs to keep the contemporary group memory alive.[40] This construction involves discourse and recitation that weave together the otherwise fragmented and disconnected remembrances into a shared memory that is coherent. In this way, meaning is imposed upon the fragments. R. Rosenzweig and D. Thelen found in their study of memory that people assemble 'isolated experiences into patterns.' These larger narratives allow them to make sense of their personal histories. From them, they set priorities, project what might happen next, and try to shape their futures.[41] According to their study, respondents 'probed experiences and constructed traditions that they wanted to sustain' with people 'they trusted or at least knew.' Through dialogue with these people, 'they discovered what they shared and did not share with others, shaped and reshaped memories into trajectories, made and changed commitments to sustain and change heritages and generally created the perceptual world that they wanted to inhabit.'[42]

A group attributes constitutive significance to certain traditions from its past. The group's identity and survival depends upon its continual renewal or revival of the memories of the community's origins and other landmark events in its history.[43] These particular traditions are woven into what Y. Zerubavel calls a community's 'master commemorative narrative.' With each new generation, the community will align its contemporary experiences with this master narrative as well as realign the master narrative with their present experiences.[44] 'By focusing attention on some aspects of the past,' Zerubavel notes, 'it necessarily covers up others that are deemed irrelevant or disruptive to the flow of the narrative and its ideological message.'[45]

---

38. Halbwachs, *The Collective Memory*, pp. 59–60.

39. Zelizer, 'Reading the Past Against the Grain,' p. 224.

40. Halbwachs, *The Collective Memory*, pp. 80–81.

41. R. Rosenzweig and D. Thelen, *The Presence of the Past: Popular Uses of History in American Life* (New York: Columbia University Press, 1988) p. 68.

42. Rosenzweig and Thelen, *Presence of the Past*, p. 196.

43. Y. Zerubavel, *Recovered Roots: Collective Memory and the Making of Israeli National Tradition* (Chicago: University of Chicago Press, 1997) pp. 4, 7; J. Assman, *Das kulturelle Gedächtnis: Schrift, Erinnerung und politische Identität in frühen Hochkulturen* (München: D.H. Beck, 1992) pp. 30, 132–133; B. Schwartz, 'Postmodernity and Historical Reputation: Abraham Lincoln in Late Twentieth-Century American Memory,' *SF* 77 (1998) p. 67.

44. Zerubavel, *Recovered Roots*, p. 7.

45. Zerubavel, *Recovered Roots*, pp. 8, 216.

This does not mean that the past is fabricated *ex nihilo* or is some 'limitless and plastic symbolic resource, infinitely susceptible to the whims of contemporary interest and the distortions of contemporary ideology.'[46] It is always emerging from its own past. But it does mean that issues of historical accuracy or authenticity accommodate other issues like social identity, political authority, religious orthodoxy and so forth.[47] The important issue for the historian is not how accurately a recollection depicts what actually happened, but why a particular group constructed their memories in a particular way at a particular time.[48]

Just as the construction of communal memory depends on group activity, so does the retention of that memory.[49] D. Lowenthal notes that we, in fact, 'need other people's memories both to confirm our own and to give them endurance.'[50] To retain memory, it is necessary for us to knit 'our own discontinuous recollections into narratives' and 'revise personal components to fit the collectively remembered past' so that we 'gradually cease to distinguish between them.'[51] This process invites communal sharing and validating activities.[52] This helps to explain why communities 'constantly tell and retell their constitutive memories' and engage in other commemorative activities.[53] In these communal activities, groups particularly make use of ritual and recital of both oral and written linguistic artifacts.[54]

1.4 *The Responsive Nature of Traditions*

Since people create versions of a harmonious past in response to various developments that make them feel uncomfortable in the present, the growth of traditions is responsive to societal, political, cultural and religious

46.   A. Appadurai, 'The Past as a Scarce Resource,' *Man* 16 (1981) p. 20; see also Casey, *Remembering*, p. 275; Schwartz, *Abraham Lincoln*, pp. 6, 297.

47.   Zelizer, 'Against the Grain,' p. 217.

48.   D. Thelen, 'Memory and American History,' *JAH* 75 (1989) p. 1125.

49.   Halbwachs, *On Collective Memory*, pp. 38–42.

50.   D. Lowenthal, *The Past is a Foreign Country* (Cambridge: Cambridge University Press, 1985) p. 196.

51.   Lowenthal, *Past is Foreign Country*, p. 196.

52.   Lowenthal, *Past is Foreign Country*, p. 196.

53.   J. Olick, 'Genre Memories and Memory Genres: A Dialogical Analysis of May 8, 1945 Commemorations in the Federal Republic of Germany,' *ASR* 64 (1999) p. 344; cf. E. Zerubavel, 'Social Memories: Steps to a Sociology of the Past,' *QS* 19 (1996) p. 289; Halbwachs, *On Collective Memory*, p. 54; L. Coser, 'Introduction to Maurice Halbwachs,' in Halbwachs, *On Collective Memory*, p. 22; Schwartz, 'Postmodernity,' p. 67.

54.   Y. Yerushalmi, *Zakhor: Jewish History and Jewish Memory* (Seattle: University of Washington Press, 1982) p. 11.

pressures exerted on a group.[55] The community's experience of the pressure causes memories of the traditions to 'confront each other, intermingle, fuse, or erase each other.'[56] This means that a 'memory crisis' can ensue in which the present's connection with the past is threatened and revised.[57] The community will ultimately transform its traditions.

In order to explain this aspect of communal behavior, social psychologists have pointed to the theory of cognitive dissonance.[58] Cognitive dissonance is the gap between one's expectation or belief and the reality of the situation. Where there are specific expectations that either remain unfulfilled or are refuted by one's experience, dissonance is said to occur.[59] In L. Festinger's famous application of the theory in his book *When Prophecy Fails: A Social and Psychological Study of a Modern Group That Predicted the Destruction of the World*, he demonstrates that under certain conditions, if the fundamental beliefs of a religious group are disconfirmed by events in the world, the group will not necessarily collapse.[60] Instead, the community will respond to the disconfirmation by proselytizing to build up community support, by creating explanatory schemes that rationalize the source of dissonance, or by avoiding the thing that produced the dissonance in the first place.

Not all groups whose beliefs or expectations are disconfirmed will respond in this manner. Festinger determines that five conditions must be present for a group to increase its fervor following the disconfirmation of a belief rather than collapse.[61]

1. The belief must be one of deep conviction and have consequences for the believer's behavior.

---

55. J. Bodnar, 'Power and Memory in Oral History: Workers and Managers at Studebaker,' *JAH* 74 (1989) pp. 1201–1221.

56. N. Wachtel, 'Memory and History: Introduction,' *HA* 12 (1986) pp. 216–217.

57. R. Terdiman, *Present Past: Modernity and the Memory Crisis* (Ithaca: Cornell University Press, 1993) p. 3.

58. L. Festinger, *A Theory of Cognitive Dissonance* (Stanford: Stanford University Press, 1957). Cf. R.P. Ableson, *et. al.* (eds.), *Theories of Cognitive Consistency: A Sourcebook* (Chicago: Rand McNally, 1968); E. Aronson, *The Social Animal* (San Francisco: W.H. Freeman, 1976) pp. 85–139; J.W. Brehm and A.R. Cohen, *Explorations in Cognitive Dissonance* (New York: Wiley, 1962); R. Brown, *Social Psychology* (New York: Free Press, 1965) pp. 584–609; A.R. Cohen, *Attitude Change and Social Influence* (New York: Basic Books, 1964); M. Deutsch and R.M. Krauss, *Theories in Social Psychology* (New York: Basic Books, 1965) pp. 62–76.

59. R. Carroll, *When Prophecy Failed: Cognitive Dissonance in the Prophetic Traditions of the Old Testament* (New York: The Seabury Press, 1979) p. 109.

60. L. Festinger, H.W. Riecken, and S. Schachter, *When Prophecy Fails* (Minneapolis: University of Minnesota Press, 1956).

61. Festinger, *Prophecy Fails*, pp. 3–4.

2. The believer must have committed him/herself to the belief and have taken actions on the basis of the belief, actions which are difficult to undo.
3. The belief must be concerned with the real world in a specific way so that events may disconfirm the belief unequivocally.
4. The undeniable disconfirming evidence must be experienced and recognized by the believer.
5. The believer must have social support, that is, the believer must be a member of a group of convinced people who can support each other.

Groups that meet these conditions, in the face of disconfirming evidence, will increase public activity in an attempt to gain converts and thereby provide social validation for their belief system.[62] Research since Festinger has shown that proselytization is most likely to follow disconfirmation within groups that have minimal social support from outside the group or have experienced hostility from outsiders.[63]

Disconfirmation under these conditions also leads groups to new hermeneutical levels since they develop explanatory schemes to rationalize the disconfirmation. The hermeneutic consists of demonstrating that 'the disconfirming event was not disconfirmation but actually confirmation of their expectations.'[64] The dissonance had only arisen in the first place because the group did not interpret the traditions or scriptures properly. In fact, it is a normative move for the community to say that the group did not correctly understand the original text, tradition, or prediction. In so doing, the group can maintain that, indeed, the expectation has not actually been disconfirmed.[65] Explanatory schemes may also give rise to a hermeneutic that is designed to change the original cognitive holdings of the community. The dissonant experience can cause the group to reinterpret their baseline traditions or, conversely, their understanding of the contemporary events.[66] Modifications in the offending cognitions are made, resulting in interpretive shifts in the original traditions.[67]

The hermeneutic for properly reading the text or understanding the tradition is provided and supported by the religious community. This is referred to as 'the resultant system.' It is the second level of reading a text or understanding a tradition, the first being the text or tradition itself. The

62. Festinger, *Prophecy Fails*, pp. 212–214.
63. J.A. Hardyck and M. Braden, 'Prophecy Fails Again: A Report of a Failure to Replicate,' *JASP* 65 (1962) pp. 136–141.
64. Carroll, *Prophecy Failed*, p. 126.
65. Carroll, *Prophecy Failed*, p. 105.
66. Carroll, *Prophecy Failed*, p. 110.
67. Carroll, *Prophecy Failed*, p. 96.

resultant system is imposed on the text or tradition out of which the interpretation unfolds. Thus it determines how the text will be read properly by the community or how the tradition will be understood.[68] Different systems can provide different interpretations for the same texts and tradition. It is quite possible that a particular community might not see any problems with a text or tradition if its hermeneutic focuses on other aspects of the text or tradition. In this way, problematic elements of the text or tradition might be disregarded or become irrelevant.[69]

Whatever the event or opinion that caused the dissonance, the community will try to avoid references to it in the future, especially when the belief impinges on reality in a severe way. The community may attempt to create an environment or ideology that avoids the subject completely.[70] Or the community may identify current events with past predictions or traditions, collapsing the expectations as it demonstrates their fulfillment in the present. This not only works to avoid the dissonance, but also keeps unfulfilled expectations from arising in the first place.[71] Another avoidance technique is the 'forgetting' of the original cognitions or attitudes altogether.[72]

J. Gager is to be credited with the initial attempt to apply this theory to early Christianity.[73] He demonstrated in the 1970s that the communities of the first Christians fit all of the conditions necessary for this type of responsive behavior. He located textual evidence for at least two important early Christian beliefs that were specific enough to be disconfirmed by events in the world and cause dissonance responses: the death of Jesus and the failure of their end-of-the-world expectations to be fulfilled.[74] Whether or not cognitive dissonance was the cause of specific responses to the disconfirmation of eschatological expectations will probably be difficult to resolve.[75] For this reason, I prefer to talk concretely about mitigative responses, responses intended to relieve disconfirmation whether they be caused by cognitive dissonance or something else.

Gager's arguments, however, that the early Christians did, in fact, respond to the disconfirmation of their expectations following Jesus' death

---

68. J. Barr, *Old and New in Interpretation: A Study of the Two Testaments* (London: SCM Press, 1966) p. 108.

69. Carroll, *Prophecy Failed*, pp. 126–127.

70. Carroll, *Prophecy Failed*, pp. 93–94.

71. Carroll, *Prophecy Failed*, p. 114.

72. Carroll, *Prophecy Failed*, p. 108.

73. J. Gager, *Kingdom and Community: The Social World of Early Christianity* (Englewood Cliffs: Prentice-Hall, 1975) pp. 37–49; J. Jackson, 'The Resurrection Belief of the Earliest Church: A Response to the Failure of Prophecy?' *JR* 55 (1975) pp. 414–425; U. Wernik, 'Frustrated Beliefs and Early Christianity,' *Numen* 22 (1975) pp. 96–130.

74. Gager, 'Earliest Christianity,' pp. 37–49.

75. Cf. Carroll, *Prophecy Failed*, p. 103.

and the eschatological delay by prosyletizing, developing explanatory schemes, and creating ways to avoid the disconfirmation makes very concrete for me the conclusions of other scholars who have argued for a long time that the delay of the *parousia* is one of the most significant problems that faced early Christian communities and impacted deeply the development of their theology.[76] Even though we do not have much overt evidence of the delay in the early Christian literature, studies like Gager's have shown that we do have an enormous amount of implicit evidence in materials that reemphasize the hope of the *parousia* or play down the imminence of the expectation by omitting mention of the hope or subtly shifting the parameters of the expectation.[77] We should add to this the possibility of another mitigative response, that some Christians may have shifted their discussions to the mystical dimension, partially or entirely, collapsing the eschatological expectations into their present experience of God.

Communities' responses to external pressures like these will result in dialogue, in 'sharing, discussing, negotiation, and often, contestation.' As a result, groups will try to legitimate their traditions, often at the expense of the perceived counter-positions, by appropriating the past and mobilizing people to act according to that past.[78] In this way, in addition to the rationalization of specific beliefs, the development of traditions can be the direct result of polemic or crisis management, growing out of the need to justify particular positions or offer practical strategies for relieving crises.[79] It is not unusual for this process of dialogue to result in 'subuniverses' of meaning forming out of the group's common stock of knowledge, the summation of 'what everybody [in the group] knows'

---

76.   Cf. M. Werner, *The Formation of Christian Dogma* (London: Harper, 1957); E. Grässer, *Das Problem der Parusieverzögerung in den synoptischen Evangelien und in der Apostelgeschichte* (Berlin: A. Töpelmann, 1960); A. Strobel, *Untersuchungen zum eschatologischen Verzögerungsproblem*, SNT 2 (Leiden: E.J. Brill, 1961); A. Schweitzer, *The Mysticism of Paul the Apostle* (trans W. Montgomery, Baltimore: The Johns Hopkins University Press, 1931, reprinted 1998); A.L. Moore, *The Parousia in the New Testament* (Leiden: E.J. Brill, 1966); R.H. Hiers, 'The Delay of the Parousia in Luke-Acts,' *NTS* 20 (1973–1974) pp. 145–155; R.J. Bauckman, 'The Delay of the Parousia,' *TynBul* 31 (1980) pp. 3–36.; C. Rowland, *Christian Origins: An Account of the Setting and Character of the Most Important Messianic Sect of Judaism* (London: SPCK, 2nd edn., 2002) pp. 287–296.

77.   For the most recent study, see J.T. Carroll, *The Return of Jesus in Early Christianity* (Peabody: Hendrickson Publishers, 2000).

78.   Zelizer, 'Reading the Past Against the Grain,' p. 214; Zerubavel, *Recovered Roots*, p. 8.

79.   Cf. J.H. Elliot, *Social-Scientific Criticism of the New Testament and its Social World*, *Semeia* 35 (1986); C. Osiek, 'The New Handmaid: The Bible and the Social Sciences,' *TS* 50 (1989) pp. 260–278.

about their world.[80] This stock is the group's traditions, an integration of rules of conduct, maxims, morals, values, beliefs, and myths.[81] If the forming subuniverses of knowledge are perceived by the group as radical departures from the common stock of knowledge, conflict and competition can arise within the group.[82] Contestation between subuniverses or alternative memories results in one rendition of the traditions wiping out the alternative versions.[83] In studies of repression, the dominant subuniverse of memory is known to silence the voices of those who seek to interpret the past in ways contradictory to the larger group.[84] Memories perceived to be deviant or no longer useful are erased, forgotten, willed absent, or exchanged so that the group can put them aside and find resolution.[85] Often the dominant group will explain the deviance as mental instability, immorality, or ignorance and measures will be taken to reaffirm or reinterpret the communal memory so that the dominant position is consolidated.[86]

How is communal conflict and discourse captured in our ancient sources? The work of R. Wuthnow outlines the characteristics of the textualization of social conflict and discourse. He published his theory in 1989 in his voluminous work, *Communities of Discourse*, where he analyzes the interaction between ideology and social structure in the Reformation, the Enlightenment, and European Socialism.[87] Wuthnow understands ideology to be something that exists within a dynamic social context. According to Wuthnow, one must first identify the 'social horizon,' the actual social experience which produced the ideology embedded in our texts. For religious texts, I would modify this horizon to a dynamic religio-historical one, the actual religious environment in which the author participated. According to Wuthnow, the development or transformation of ideology subsumes discourse between actual parties of people. Wuthnow cautions us not to forget that the process of textualization of ideology is selective and transformative so that the actual social horizon and the social world represented in the text may only resemble each other partially. Struggles between different social classes or political parties in

---

80. P. Berger and T. Luckmann, *The Social Construction of Reality: A Treatise in the Sociology of Knowledge* (New York: Doubleday, 1966) pp. 53–85.

81. Berger and Luckmann, *Social Construction*, p. 65.

82. Berger and Luckmann, *Social Construction*, p. 85.

83. Zelizer, 'Reading the Past Against the Grain,' p. 217.

84. Zelizer, 'Reading the Past Against the Grain,' p. 228.

85. Halbwachs, *On Collective Memory*, p. 172; N. Davis and R. Starn, 'Memory and Counter-memory,' *Representations* 26 (1989) p. 2; Zelizer, 'Reading the Past Against the Grain,' p. 220.

86. Berger and Luckmann, *Social Construction*, p. 66.

87. See especially his 'Introduction: The Problem of Articulation', *Communities of Discourse* (Cambridge, Massachusetts: Harvard University Press,1989), pp. 1–22.

the real world may differ in part from those found in the narrative or in the theoretical representation of these conflicts. Wuthnow calls the range of the problem between the two factions, the 'discursive field.' Descriptions of the discursive field are most often made on a symbolic level where actual features of the social horizon are incorporated into the text as symbolic acts, events, and characters. Thus, the real opposition and conflict between the factions is usually dramatized in our ancient texts.

In order to clarify the literary dimensions of conflict in our ancient texts, M. Hirshman distinguishes between 'open' and 'hidden' controversy. In open controversy, 'the source explicitly mentions its ideological rival, either by name or appellation, and ascribes to him a particular stance.'[88] The hidden controversy is more difficult to demonstrate explicitly because it does not provide the above information directly. According to Hirshman, the author might ignore it altogether, insist on the status quo, or conceal any material that might be helpful to his opponents.[89] We might add to this list the possibilities that the author might modify the disagreeable ideology, condemn it outright, or provide an alternative model. To recover 'hidden' conflict will require that we read our texts against the grain.

Do we see such controversy embedded in our Christian texts? Gager's socio-historical work again reinforces the work of other scholars who have written from different perspectives on this subject for many years. Basing his work on the sociological research of L. Coser, *The Functions of Social Conflict*, Gager argued that within early Christian texts was embedded conflict of the most intense level involving competing ideologies or competing views of the same ideology. He determined three critical moments in early Christian history when traditions were transformed as a consequence of conflict: (1) conflict with Judaism over the claim to be the *true* Israel; (2) conflict with paganism over the claim to have *true* wisdom; and (3) conflict among different Christian communities over the claim to possess the *true* faith of Jesus and the apostles.[90] I would add to this a fourth critical moment when traditions were modified as a consequence of conflict: conflict within early Christian communities as they began to define themselves over and against Judaism rather than from within it.

---

88.   M. Hirshman, *Jewish and Christian Biblical Intepretation in Late Antiquity* (trans. B. Stein; Albany: State University of New York Press, 1996) p. 126.

89.   Hirshman, *Biblical Interpretation*, pp. 129–130.

90.   Gager, *Kingdom and Community*, p. 82; cf. L. Coser, *The Functions of Social Conflict* (New York: Free Press, 1956).

1.5 *The Shift of Traditions*

As traditions stand frozen in our texts, they can be perceived as essentially stable and fixed in meaning. This is a false perception. *Traditions belong to living communities and therefore contain the potentiality of being changed by people.*[91] Such a shift can occur within the process of composition and transmission, whether oral or written. The shift in meaning also can occur in the interpretative process when a text is recited or read and a particular community imposes a hermeneutic on it.[92] The tradition is only understood within the interpreter's complex world, a fore-structure including the person's 'preunderstanding' or presuppositions as well as his purpose for making the interpretation in the first place. The person's world would have intruded into the 'process of actualizing meaning.'[93] In the poetic words of M. Heidegger, 'If, when one is engaged in a particular concrete kind of interpretation, one likes to appeal to what "stands there," then one finds that what "stands there" in the first instance is nothing other than the obvious undiscussed assumption of the person who does the interpreting.'[94] S. Fish, a major proponent of the Reader-Response approach to exegesis, has gone as far as stating that 'it is the reader who "makes" the literature.' He notes, however, that readers belong to interpretative communities which determine the kind of literature 'made' by the reader and the attention the reader gives to certain aspects of the text.[95]

Shifts in traditions can be endogenous, originating within the community, or exogenous, resulting from influences outside the group. Endogenous changes might result from the desire of a community to improve upon the tradition, repair imperfections in the tradition, or exercise imagination within the tradition.[96] The latter is particularly true of traditions that develop within communities associated with charismatic individuals where innovations in the tradition are most likely to occur.[97] As time passes, 'the charismatic message becomes rationalized, elaborated, clarified, and fortified to withstand criticisms from rival traditions.'[98] Exogenous change begins to occur in these traditions when 'the adherence of the traditions expands,' gaining converts whose prior beliefs and current circumstances

91. E. Shils, *Tradition* (Chicago: University of Chicago Press, 1981) p. 213.

92. Barr, *Old and New*, p. 108.

93. W. Randolph Tate, *Biblical Interpretation: An Integrated Approach* (Peabody: Hendrickson Publishers, 1997, revised edition) p. 158.

94. M. Heidegger, *Being and Time* (trans. J. Macquarrie and E. Robinson; New York: Harper & Row, 1962) p. 192.

95. S. Fish, *Is There a Text in this Class? The Authority of Interpretative Communities* (Cambridge, MA: Harvard University Press, 1980) p. 67.

96. Shils, *Tradition*, pp. 214–215, 228.

97. Shils, *Tradition*, p. 229.

98. Shils, *Tradition*, p. 230.

are different from those of the first proponents of the message.[99] This means that the traditions change when a constituency shift occurs within the group and adherents are brought into the presence of other traditions.[100] These changes are the consequence of alien traditions colliding with the original community's traditions as well as alien hermeneutics merging with or supplanting the group's older interpretative foils. Such is the case as well when traditions migrate across time or across groups.[101] They change because the circumstances to which they refer change.[102]

Certain patterns of change can be identified within traditions. New material can be added to old traditions.[103] Amalgamation of traditions can occur where an element integral to the old tradition is replaced with a corresponding element from the new tradition. The incorporation of the new element 'automatically brings with it the past history of that element.'[104] An old tradition can be completely absorbed into a newer one so that the old tradition is actually replaced by the new.[105] Or a fusion of traditions can occur where there emerges a 'unitary pattern with a new and distinctive central, pervasive theme.' In this synthesis of traditions, the new theme embraces elements from previously independent traditions.[106]

The shifting nature of traditions may be the consequence of the fact that communal memory is grounded in both the past and the present. Memory formations are not static but unceasingly dynamic and tied into the ever-changing present. The formation and survival of memory is an ongoing process of negotiation whereby the group will relate its situatedness in the shifting present in meaningful ways to its formative past.[107] To remember is not to re-collect, but to reconstruct, to constantly conform a group's presentation of its past to shifts in its social morphology, situation, and membership.[108] As internal and external factors change, the

---

99. Shils, *Tradition*, p. 231.

100. Shils, *Tradition*, p. 240.

101. Shils, *Tradition*, p. 244.

102. Shils, *Tradition*, p. 258.

103. Shils, *Tradition*, p. 275.

104. Shils, *Tradition*, pp. 276–278.

105. Shils, *Tradition*, p. 278.

106. Shils, *Tradition*, p. 279.

107. E. Casey, *Remembering: A Phenomemological Study* (Bloomington: Indiana University Press, 1987) p. 292; R. Handler and J. Linnekin, 'Tradition, Genuine or Spurious,' *JAF* 97 (1984) p. 30; Lowenthal, *Past is Foreign Country*, p. 206; R. Gillis, 'Memory and Identity: The History of a Relationship,' in J.R. Gillis (ed.), *Commemorations: The Politics of National Identity* (Princeton: Princeton University Press, 1994) p. 3; Zelizer, 'Reading the Past Against the Grain,' p. 218.

108. G. Namer, *Mémoire et société* (Méridiens Lincksieck, 1987) p. 53; Halbwachs, *On Collective Memory*, p. 40.

group's memory is continually subjected to renovation in both gradual and sudden ways.[109]

1.6 *Streams of Traditions*

Traditions and their interpretations accumulate and cluster, forming into complexes which became part of particular streams of traditions.[110] In other words, they come together and form 'families of traditions' which then circulate as units.[111] Some scholars have gone as far as arguing for the possible existence of *Elementargedanken* or 'unit-ideas' in which the distinguishability of the component traditions is even questioned.[112]

Traditions become part of particular streams because they are perceived to somehow 'fit' with each other, to be connected logically in some way.[113] When certain traditions are regarded by a community as 'belonging together,' they form a distinguishable 'cluster of elements' connected with each other by 'ties of logical derivation, identity of moral and aesthetic tone, and traditionally long association.'[114] In cultures dominated by an oral consciousness, the material in these growing streams of traditions is often organized mnemonically. Material will accumulate that share motifs, themes, structures, principal characters, keywords, or historical subject matter.

This growth process is not simply the addition of more and more material to the stream. Rather it is a selective process whereby traditions will be altered.[115] They fade or are forgotten due to the waning of the stream. They resurge or shift due to the confluence of merging traditions. Since traditions most frequently develop through ramification, splitting into branches, a stream of traditions might fork and continue on its course as two or more independent streams.[116] Because the traditions in the multiple streams may have moved at different rates and in different directions, we can expect to see some differences in them. But the separate branches will also contain similar material originating from the parental stream. Thus, comparing branches can be very useful when we wish to understand the 'origins' of the traditional material in the parental stream

---

109. J. Assmann, *Das kulturelle Gedächtnis* (München: C.H. Beck, 1992) pp. 41–42.
110. Lord, *Singer of Tales*, p. 58.
111. Shils, *Tradition*, p. 272.
112. A. Bastian, *Ethnische Elementargedanken in der Lehre vom Menschen* (Berlin: Weidmannsche Buchhandlung, 1895); A.O. Lovejoy, *The Great Chain of Being* (Cambridge, MA: Harvard University Press, 1954) pp. 3–7.
113. Shils, *Tradition*, p. 271.
114. Shils, *Tradition*, p. 269.
115. Shils, *Tradition*, pp. 285–286.
116. Shils, *Tradition*, pp. 280–281.

and its development in the derivative branches. Chronologically later texts can be used to elucidate chronologically earlier texts when the texts contain comparable streams of tradition because the streams of tradition in the texts are ramifications either from an 'original' stream or from an earlier ramification of that stream.

The formation of streams of tradition may, in fact, be the result of the way that communal memory operates. In order to provide coherence and meaning to fragmented memories, communal memory 'acts to organize what might otherwise be a mere assemblage of contingently connected events. It does this by selecting, emphasizing, collocating – sometimes condensing and sometimes expanding – and in general regrouping and reconfigurating' experiences.[117] Memory is an 'in-gathering' of emotions, perceptions, traditions and discourse – 'all the parts of our life history' – into a unity that 'we retain, keep, and guard.'[118] In order to accomplish this it has the proclivity to arrange all the parts in 'ordered groupings.'[119]

1.7 *Transmission of Traditions*

For the last two hundred years, we have thought of the 'authors' of the Gospels as men who collected materials from sources and edited them together, preserving much of the original source material. We have perceived modifications to the sources to be minimal, for editorial or specific theological purposes. We have located most of these modifications in the editorial bridges that linked the source materials or characteristic clauses appended to the source materials. Oral tradition was perceived to be *behind* or *beneath* these written sources, preserving the material's 'authentic' or 'original' form. It was understood that oral transmission in some way preceded the advent of literacy and, in fact, supplanted it. As long ago as J.G. Herder it was argued that the pre-Gospel traditions existed as a 'free, oral narrative,' a 'common gospel' behind the Synoptics. According to Herder, this oral tradition served as the source for the Synoptics in contrast to Lessing's proposal of a written Aramaic Gospel of the Nazarenes.[120]

Although this idea was proposed by Herder in the late 1700s, it was not until the 1900s that it became the mainstay of Form Criticism as developed by R. Bultmann and his students. Bultmann, in fact, defined the purpose of Form Criticism as the study of 'the history of the oral tradition behind the

---

117. Casey, *Remembering*, p. 291.
118. Casey, *Remembering*, p. 292.
119. Casey, *Remembering*, p. 294.
120. J.G. Herder, in B. Suphan (ed.), *Herders sämmtliche Werke*, volume 19 (Berlin: Weidmann, 1877–1913).

gospels.'[121] Even though he spoke of recovering 'oral tradition' and claims to have been aquainted with the transmission of forms from his familiarity with folklore studies, he still seems to have envisioned the process in *literary terms rather than oral mentalities.*[122] Thus he imagined the gospel compositional process in terms of literary 'layering' and 'editing' where each additional layer is an edited version of an earlier layer. He thought it possible to remove the later 'Hellenistic' layers to reveal the earlier 'Palestinian' layer. He then retrojected his observations about literary composition onto the pre-Gospel sources, assuming that it was 'a matter of indifference whether the traditions were oral or written.'[123] In so doing, he failed to appreciate orality and the transmission of traditions within this mentality as an organic process with distinct tendencies. Even his greatest detractors, H. Riesenfeld and B. Gerhardsson, who argued that Bultmann had ignored the Rabbinic precedent for the Palestinian transmission of traditions, believed that *behind* the written Gospels were the direct oral teachings of Jesus, though they thought the transmission of the traditions was made in a rigid and fixed form because they had been memorized by the apostles.[124] Unfortunately, Riesenfeld's and Gerhardsson's understanding of oral transmission in terms of memorization was no more sensitive to oral mentalities in a rhetorical culture than the Form Critics, as the recent studies about orality and Rabbinic materials are revealing.[125]

121. R. Bultmann and K. Kundsin, *Form Criticism: Two Essays on New Testament Research* (trans. F.C. Grant; New York: Harper Torchbook, 1962) p. 1.

122. R. Bultmann, *History of the Synoptic Tradition* (trans. J. Marsh; New York: Harper and Row, revised edition, 1963) pp. 6–7. E.P. Sanders criticized Bultmann on this point, arguing that Bultmann did not derive his 'laws of transmission' from an analysis of folk literature. See his critique in *The Tendencies of the Synoptic Tradition*, SNTSMS 9 (Cambridge: Cambridge University Press, 1969) p. 18, n. 4.

123. Bultmann, *Synoptic Tradition*, pp. 6, 92–93.

124. H. Riesenfeld, 'The Gospel Tradition and Its Beginning,' in *The Gospel Tradition* (Philadelphia: Fortress Press, 1970) p. 24 (1–29); B. Gerhardsson, *Memory and Manuscript: Oral Tradition and Written Transmission in Rabbinic Judaism and Early Christianity* (Lund: Gleerup, 1961).

125. J. Neusner, *Oral Tradition in Judaism: The Case of the Mishnah* (New York: Garland, 1987); M. Fraade, *From Tradition to Commentary: Torah and Its Interpretation in the Midrash Sifre to Deuteronomy* (Albany: State University of New York Press, 1991) pp. 69–121; S. Fraade, 'Literary Composition and Oral Performance in Early Midrashim,' *OT* 14 (1999) pp. 33–51; M. Jaffee, 'How Much Orality in Oral Torah? New Perspectives on the Composition and Transmission of Early Rabbinic Tradition,' *Shofar* 10 (1992) pp. 53–72; M. Jaffee, 'A Rabbinic Ontology of the Written and Spoken Word: On Discipleship, Transformative Knowledge, and the Living Texts of Oral Torah,' *JAAR* 65 (1997) pp. 525–549; M. Jaffee, 'Oral Tradition in the Writings of Rabbinic Oral Torah: On Theorizing Rabbinic Orality,' *OT* 14 (1999) pp. 3–32; Y. Elman, 'Orality and the Redaction of the Babylonian Talmud,' *OT* 14 (1999) pp. 52–99.

It was not until the work of W. Kelber, *The Oral and Written Gospel*, that New Testament scholarship finally took seriously the distinctive features of oral mentality and began to incorporate into the discussion the long overlooked studies of folklorists, anthropologists, and classicists.[126] Kelber's work, though, placed too much distinction on the transition from oral to written gospel, as the rhetorical critics of the past decade have shown us. They have argued that the scribal culture that began to dominate the transmission of ancient Christian literature in the late second century when some of the texts began gaining scriptural status has been imposed by most scholars upon the earlier compositional period.[127] This earlier period, it is argued, is better understood as a 'rhetorical culture' enlivened by a creative *interaction between oral and written composition*. It is a culture that uses both oral and written language interactively *and* rhetorically in the compositional process, a culture in which oral performance and literary composition interface each other in a very dynamic way.[128] As Steven Fraade has put it, texts are composed to be orally enacted 'with the enactments in turn suffusing the process of their literary textualization, and so on.'[129] What emerges is a more 'circulatory' understanding of oral performance of the ancient texts, 'an orality that is grounded in a textuality that remains orally fluid.'[130]

What do we know about the oral compositional process and the transmission of traditions within the oral register? From the archives of anthropologists who have studied modern oral cultures and literary analyses of scholars who have studied ancient texts, we can begin to piece together how traditional material is affected by this process of transmis-

---

126.   W.H. Kelber, *The Oral and the Written Gospel* (Philadelphia: Fortress Press, 1983).

127.   V. Robbins, 'Progymnastic Rhetorical Composition and Pre-Gospel Traditions: A New Approach,' in C. Focant (ed.), *The Synoptic Gospels: Source Criticism and the New Literary Criticism*, BETL 110 (Leuven: University Press, 1993) pp. 111–147; cf. H. Koester, *Ancient Christian Gospels: Their History and Development* (Philadelphia: Trinity Press International, 1990) pp. 31–43.

128.   T.M. Lentz, *Orality and Literacy in Hellenic Greece* (Carbondale: Southern Illinois University Press, 1989); W. McKane, *Proverbs: A New Approach*, The Old Testament Library (Philadelphia: The Westminster Press, 1977); W. McKane, *A Critical and Exegetical Commentary on Jeremiah*, The International Critical Commentary, volume 1 (Edinburgh: T&T Clark, 1986); Robbins, 'Progymnastic Rhetorical Composition,' pp. 116–121; V. Robbins, 'The Chreia,' in D.E. Aune (ed.), *Greco-Roman Literature and the New Testament: Selected Forms and Genres*, SBLSBS 21 (Atlanta: Scholars Press, 1988) pp. 13–16; Robbins, 'Writing as a Rhetorical Act in Plutarch and the Gospels,' in D.F. Watson (ed.), *Persuasive Artistry: Studies in New Testament Rhetoric in Honor of George A. Kennedy* (Sheffield: JSOT, 1991) pp. 142–168.

129.   Fraade, 'Literary Composition,' p. 35.

130.   Fraade, 'Literary Composition,' p. 36.

sion.[131] To begin, it is essential for us to recognize that an oral world is characterized by markedly different presuppositions and thought patterns from our own.[132] The primary features of oral thought are described by W. Ong as additive, aggregative, redundant, conservative, agonistic, empathetic, homeostatic, and situational.[133] We should add to this list the fact that in such cultures there is reliance on memory with little to no dependence on external sources of information.[134]

Frequently information is spread by singers who perform stories with the accompaniment of simple instruments. So the information dispersed is largely subject to established rhythmic rules which sometimes are captured in our texts. Popular also was oration in which speeches of heros and the like were reperformed without music. In both cases, the moment of the performance is the moment of composition, when the singer or orator provides his audience with *his* understanding of the traditional material he has learned from his teacher. He never reproduces the story or speech since he has not memorized it 'word for word' in the sense that we understand the 'word.'[135] Ong explains, 'The way verbal memory works in oral art forms is quite different from what literates in the past commonly have imagined. In a literate culture verbatim memorization is commonly done from a text, to which the memorizer returns as often as necessary to perfect and test verbatim mastery. In the past, literates have commonly assumed that oral memorization in an oral culture normally achieved the same goal of absolutely verbatim repetition.'[136]

A. Lord's research has demonstrated that composition in oral cultures is accomplished by performing the story or song anew from memory of certain formulaic structures, themes, and larger story or speech structures.[137] Lord summarizes:

> To the singer of the song, which cannot be changed (since to change it would, in his mind, be to tell an untrue story or to falsify history), is the

---

131. Cf. M. Parry, *The Making of Homeric Verse: The Collected Papers of Milman Perry*, ed. A. Parry (Oxford, 1971); A. Lord, *Singer of Tales*, HSCL 24 (Cambridge: Harvard University Press, 2nd edn, 2000); E.A. Havelock, *Preface to Plato* (New York: Grosset and Dunlap, 1967); Ong, *Orality and Literacy;* W.J. Ong, *The Presence of the Word* (New Haven: Yale University Press, 1967); Ong, *Rhetoric, Romance, and Technology*; E.A. Havelock, *Origins of Western Literacy*, The Ontario Institute for Studies in Education, Monograph Series 14 (Toronto, 1976); K. O'Brien O'Keeffe, *Visible Song: Transitional Literacy in Old English Verse*, Cambridge Studies in Anglo-Saxon England 4 (Cambridge: Cambridge University Press, 1990).
132. Ong, *Orality and Literacy*, p. 36.
133. Ong, *Orality and Literacy*, pp. 31–57.
134. O'Brien O'Keeffe, *Visible Song*, p. 9.
135. Lord, *Singer of Tales*, pp. 13–29.
136. Ong, *Orality and Literary*, pp. 57–58.
137. Lord, *Singer of Tales*, pp. 54, 70.

essence of the story itself. His idea of stability, to which he is deeply devoted, does not include the wording, which to him has never been fixed, nor the unessential parts of the story. He builds his performance, or song in our sense, on the stable skeleton of narrative, which is the song in his sense.[138]

Thus the performer's memory of materials is conditioned by rhythm, meter, acoustics, syntax and structure rather than verbatim verbal remembrances. What he 'remembers' is the 'essence' of the story along with key phrases and their relative relationship to each other. He would naturally link materials in his composition by using mnemonic devices: stock phrases as transitions between segments, parallelisms to keep the desired balance of words, and alliteration of catchwords to acoustically join segments.[139]

The details, he provides himself, shaping, embellishing, and interpreting the traditions as he sang or orated.[140] He alters sequences in the traditional material. He adjusts the beginning and endings of his song or oration. He is quite aware of the need to remodel the traditional material in order to provide his audience with the most up-to-date version of the story or oration. So he injects new words and ideas into old patterns. He embellishes the traditional material with contemporary details and interpretations. He substitutes one incident or theme for another. He introduces new themes into the versions of the songs or orations he learned from his teacher. He is sensitive to his audience, changing themes or outcomes that he believes might be offensive to his audience. He omits themes that do not interest or are unfamiliar to his audience. He shortens his presentations if he is interrupted or if time restraints are placed on him. Sometimes under the pressure of performance, inconsistencies and contradictions develop in the traditional material and are retained in future performances.[141] Thus the same song or oration differed from performer to performer as well as from performance to performance within the career of a single performer.[142] Consistently, he assumes that the story he tells is part of a larger story familiar to his audience. The audience's familiarity with this meta-narrative helps complete his performance since his telling is fragmented.[143]

138. Lord, *Singer of Tales*, p. 99.
139. Lord, *Singer of Tales*, p. 54.
140. Lord, *Singer of Tales*, pp. 19, 99–123.
141. Lord, *Singer of Tales*, pp. 28, 94–98.
142. Lord, *Singer of Tales*, p. 100.
143. J.M. Foley, *Immanent Art: From Structure to Meaning in Traditional Oral Epic* (Bloomington: Indiana University, 1991); J.M. Foley, *The Singer of Tales in Performance* (Bloomington: Indiana University, 1995).

The audience also acts as a 'control' for the orator so that the traditions do not become unpredictable or disconnected from the community's memory and experience. The observations of oral culture in contemporary Middle Eastern villages by K. Bailey reinforce this point. He found that there was less flexibility with poems and proverbs than with parables and narratives about community memories. The most flexible was material that the community judged irrelevant to its identity like casual news and jokes.[144] Bailey writes:

> In the *haflat samar* the *community* exercises control over the recitation.
> These poems, proverbs, and stories form their identity. The right telling
> of these stories is critical for that identity. If someone tells the story
> 'wrong,' the reciter is corrected by a chorus of voices.[145]

Bailey, like Lord, observed that when orators pass on stories, they do *not* do so by editing a previous performance. Instead, orators carry on the same subject and theme which they garner from the common memories of the community, but retell the stories with their own details, patterns, and contexts. The most fixed element in the story is its core, its meaning. Thus, traditions in oral culture are flexible as long as the orator does not reshape the stories – especially those which are considered valuable to maintaining the community's identity – in directions that heuristically make no sense to the community or invalidate its memories. So the community will exercise control over how the traditions are passed on and reshaped in this process.[146]

The rhetorical culture of the ancient Christians represented the beginning of a transition from orality to literacy so it was dominated by an oral consciousness and a lively interaction between oral compositional processes and writing.[147] In such cultures, written materials 'remained associated with the oral to a degree seldom appreciated today.' Reading, in fact, was performed aloud even when it was to oneself. Even the educational institutions did not foster writing to the extent that we imagine today. Testing and performance was largely oral. When writing was used it was in connection with oral expression. Ong explains that teaching 'consisted of no more than dictating to students who copied down

---

144. K. Bailey, 'Informal Controlled Oral Tradition and the Synoptic Gospels,' *AsiaJT* 5 (1991) pp. 42–45.

145. K. Bailey, 'Middle Eastern Oral Tradition and the Synoptic Gospels,' *ExpTim* 106 (1995) p. 365.

146. See also the ethno-historical studies by J. Vansina, *Oral Tradition: A Study in Historical Methodology* (London: Routledge and Kegan Paul, 1965); *Oral Tradition as History* (Madison: University of Wisconsin, 1985).

147. For a good description of rhetorical thought processes and their connection to oral consciousness in transitional cultures, see Ong, *Orality and Literacy*, pp. 108–112.

what their masters had copied down before them and were now droning out, if they were better teachers, in improved form.' Teachers 'committed to writing what they said in lecture halls' but the writing was 'subordinated to the oral.'[148]

Evidence of this process of transmission of traditions is preserved in the rhetorical handbooks from the ancient world.[149] Aelius Theon of Alexandria reveals in the earliest manuscript of *Progymnasmata*, that a composition, whether verbal or written, will have its own inner rhetorical nature even when the topic of the composition is focused on the *chreia*, the speech or action of a specific personage. This inner rhetorical nature was argumentative, the composition was meant to persuade the hearer or reader to a particular action or point of view. The *chreia* could be presented as a maxim, an explanation, a witty remark, a syllogism, an enthymene, an example, a wish, a symbol, an ambiguous statement, a change of subject, or a combination of these. In fact, Theon tells us that a *chreia* could be elaborated into a fuller speech or essay in order to create a more complete argument by adding rationales, statements from the opposite, examples, amplifications, and more. This type of elaboration will often develop an argument that would give a meaning to the *chreia* that a hearer or reader might not be able to gain for him or herself.[150]

Part of this compositional process, Theon reveals, is that it involved an oral dimension. Theon's first exercise with the *chreia* is 'the recitation.' The teacher would present a speech or action gleamed from oral or written sources, and his students would write it down 'clearly in the same words or in others as well.'[151] The students were encouraged to write down as much or as little verbatim from the speech as they saw fit. The point of the exercise was for the students to develop clarity of argument, not verbatim repetition. Certainly their arguments would contain a significant repetition of the teacher's speech, but this would appear in varied contexts in order to make the old traditions meet the needs of a new day or persuade a different audience. Examples from the *Progymnasmata* show that the students'

---

148. Ong, *Presence*, pp. 58–59.

149. R.F. Hock, E.N. O'Neil, *The Chreia in Ancient Rhetoric: The Progymnasmata*, volume 1 (Atlanta: Scholars Press, 1986); J. Butts, *The 'Progymnasmata' of Theon: A New Text with Translation and Commentary* (Ann Arbor: University Microfilms International, 1987); G.A. Kennedy, *New Testament Interpretation through Rhetorical Criticism* (Chapel Hill: University of North Carolina Press, 1984); B.L. Mack, *A Myth of Innocence: Mark and Christian Origins* (Philadelphia: Fortress Press, 1988) pp. 161–165, 186–192, 198–204; B.L. Mack and V.K. Robbins, *Patterns of Persuasion in the Gospels* (Sonoma: Polebridge Press, 1989); B.L. Mack, *Rhetoric and the New Testament* (Minneapolis: Fortress Press, 1990).

150. I am indebted to Vernon Robbins for this understanding of the compositional process which he lays out so eloquently in 'Progymnastic Rhetorical Composition,' pp. 119–121.

151. Hock and O'Neil, *The Progymnasmata*, p. 95.

compositions featured different inflections, expansions, and abbreviations. The beginnings and endings of the recitations were frequently modified to link subjects, provide commentary, or extend the argument. The body of the recitations could be abbreviated as well as lengthened by adding questions, responses, acts, and much more.[152]

Understanding the oral register of ancient composition certainly explains well what we have long observed in early Christian texts: the extensive variation of words in the gospels alongside extensive verbatim repetition.[153] It also gives us insight into the combining of older traditions with newer traditions in our gospels as well. Our early Christian gospel texts are about the 'reperformance' of Jesus' words and deeds within the context and control of the Christian community. In the process of the reperformance, the old oral and written traditions are given new life by juxtaposing them with newer oral and written traditions, interpretations and contexts. In this way, the relevance of the older material is maintained in the face of changing times and situations. The reperformance, of course, would have varied depending upon the audience, the purpose of the speaker or author, and the occasion. This illuminates the passing remarks made by Papias when he writes that Peter used to 'adapt his teachings to the occasion' and that Mark, 'his interpreter, wrote down carefully, but not in order' the traditions of the Lord. Papias sees his own work, *The Sayings of the Lord Explained*, in much the same manner: he is furnishing his reader with the traditions he has heard and remembered from the presbyters 'along with the interpretations' of the traditions (Eus., *Eccl. Hist.* 39).

The writing down of traditions in cultures dominated by orality is of enormous significance because it marks either the point of loss of the 'communicative memory,' the 'eyewitness' or 'living' memory, through the death of the actual people involved in the formation and emergence of the group, or a moment of historical crisis or upheaval.[154] Under these conditions, communities relying heavily on oral consciousness are confronted with the potential loss of their memories. So they will turn to writing as a way to ensure the survival of the traditions and to provide meaning to their past, reconnecting with it amidst drastically changing historical circumstances.[155] 'For it is true that whatever is written, and more generally is inscribed, demonstrates, by the fact of being inscribed, a

152. Robbins, '*The Chreia*,' pp. 13–16; Robbins, 'Progymnastic Rhetorical Composition,' pp. 119–121.

153. Robbins, 'Writing as a Rhetorical Act,' pp. 142–168.

154. Assmann, *kulturelle Gedächtnis*, pp. 30, 50–56; J. Assmann, *Religion und kulturelles Gedächtnis: zehn Studien* (München: Beck, 2000) p. 88.

155. Assmann, *Religion*, p. 54, 87–88; Assmann, *kulturelle Gedächtnis*, p. 165.

will to be remembered...'[156] Written texts have a physical state that enables the diffusion and storage of the traditions, if not their permanency.[157] They served as aids for memory as Plato so aptly suggests in this regard when he says that written words are nothing more than 'a reminder to the man who knows the subjects to which the things written relate' (*Phaedrus* 275 c–d).

We should keep in mind that access to manuscripts in cultures dominated by oral modes of transmission is limited to a few tragents who are responsible for maintaining the written traditions and providing the non-literate audience with orations and explanations of the actual texts. Alongside them are other tragents who are not literate and who pass on the traditions completely from memory. This means, of course, that in the formative years of early Christianity there was great fluidity between oral performances and texts so that traditions moved in and out of these contexts while always being subject to the effects of oral consciousness. We must dissociate ourselves from what W. Kelber has called 'the great divide thesis,'[158] the belief that when an oral story was written down, it was totally removed from orality and its trappings, becoming a text preserved and transmitted accurately by scribes. The model we should be operating from is that of an oral-literate continuum where there is a great interaction between orality and literacy.[159]

According to the few references we have to the compositional process in early Christian literature, it began with either the transcription of an oral performance or oration (cf. *Ps.-Clem. Rec.* 1.17, 21, 23; *Hom. Epistle of Peter to James* 2), or the remembrance of a performance or oration (cf. *Apoc. Jas.* 2.7–16). Papias describes the compositional process in these words:

> I shall not hesitate to set down for you, along with my interpretations, everything that I learned well from the elders and have remembered well, for I can guarantee its truth. Unlike most people, I felt at home

156. P. Connerton, *How Societies Remember* (Cambridge: Cambridge University Press, 1989) p. 102.

157. Casey, *Remembering*, p. 227; Shils, *Tradition*, p. 91.

158. W. Kelber, 'Scripture and Logos: The Hermeneutics of Communication,' (paper presented at the annual meeting of the Society of Biblical Literature, Kansas City, November 1991).

159. For discussions of this model, see M.T. Clanchy, *From Memory to Written Record: England, 1066–1307* (Cambridge, MA: Harvard University Press, 1979); B. Stock, *The Implications of Literacy: Written Language and Models of Interpretation in the Eleventh and Twelfth Centuries* (Princeton: Princeton University Press, 1983); B. Stock, *Listening for the Text: On the Uses of the Past* (Baltimore: Johns Hopkins University Press, 1990); R. Thomas, *Oral Tradition and Written Records in Classical Athens* (Cambridge: Cambridge University Press, 1989); Nidtich, *Oral World*.

with those who taught the truth rather than with those who had a lot to say. [I felt at home] with those who [remember] the commandments given to the faith by the Lord, deriving from truth itself, rather than with those who remember the commandments of others. And whenever anyone came who had gone around with the elders, I inquired into the words of the elders, what Andrew or Peter had said, or Philip or Thomas or James or John or Matthew, or any other disciple of the Lord, and what Aristion and the elder John, disciples of the Lord, were still saying. For I did not imagine that what came out of books would help me as much as what came from a living and abiding voice (Eus., *Eccl. Hist.* 39).

Even though Papias is literate and is aware of traditional material set down in books, he *scribes down his remembrances*. Papias is more confident in the 'truth' of his remembrances than 'what came out of books' because he can guarantee the 'truth' of his memories and interpretations. The author of Luke-Acts operates from a similar perspective. He is literate and aware of written accounts which, in his opinion, had tried to capture the traditions handed down from the eyewitnesses. But he questions their accuracy and instead launches his own investigation into the matter. He then reshapes the story in his own composition so that his reader may finally 'know the truth' about the traditions (Luke 1.1–4). The gospel of John was written from the perspective of eyewitness accounts which provide verification of the truth of their written account. These testimonies reflect an oral consciousness common in societies where literacy is limited. Ong's research has shown that this perspective is common to transitional cultures: 'A present-day literate usually assumes that written records have more force than spoken words as evidence of a long-past state of affairs... Earlier cultures that knew literacy but had not so fully interiorized it, have often assumed quite the opposite.'[160]

'Literacy' in the ancient world appears to have been very different from what we understand as 'literacy' in our own society.[161] Ong notes that our literate minds have 'no way of conceiving of oral compositions except as a variety of writing – nonwritten writing.' He warns that 'this kind of cultural squint shows how the communications media of our own culture impose themselves on us surreptitiously as absolutes, with crippling effect.' For centuries, Ong concludes, our understanding of ancient epic, ballad, and rhetorical traditions have been 'blocked' because of this.[162] So we must be very cautious about applying our own assumptions about the nature of

---

160. Ong, *Orality and Literacy*, p. 96; cf. Ong, *Presence*, p. 57.
161. O'Brien O'Keeffe, *Visible Song*, pp. 5–8.
162. Ong, *Presence*, pp. 20–21.

literacy to the circumstances of earlier cultures. It appears that, in cultures dominated by oral techniques of transmission, once a written text of the performance is established, it does not become for another performer or author the fixed 'original' that has to be transmitted verbatim. Rather the future performance or composition continues to develop the traditions in order to transmit their 'truth' to new audiences.[163] If a performer or author comes in contact with a text – whether he hears the text read, reads it himself, or hears it orally performed by someone else – it is perceived by him as a version which he may recompose in his own future (and true!) performance or composition of the story or speech.[164] In the words of Lord, 'For though it is written, it is oral.'[165]

This type of transmission is very clearly described by Clement in the *Pseudo-Clementine* corpus. The process of composition is characterized here in very interactive terms, having both oral and written dimensions of remembrance and interpretation, beginning with a teacher delivering a speech to his pupils. The pupils were commissioned to transmit these teachings and their interpretations in both verbal and written formats. Thus, in the *Recognitions*, Peter tells us that the charge to Jesus' disciples was an oral one, to go out and 'expound the sayings and affirm the judgments' of the Prophet Jesus. 'We are not commissioned to say anything of our own, but to unfold the truth of his words' (*Rec.* 2.34). After Clement is instructed about the teachings of the True Prophet by Peter, he makes some fascinating comments about the sequencing of Peter's speeches:

> I shall now call to mind the things which were spoken, in which the order of your discussion greatly helps me; for the way in which the things that you said followed by consequence upon one another, and were arranged in a balanced manner, makes them easily recalled to memory by the lines of their order. For the order of sayings is useful for remembering them: for when you begin to follow them point by point in succession, when anything is wanting, immediately the sense seeks for it; and when it has found it, retains it, or at all events, if it cannot discover it, there will be no reluctance to ask it of the master (*Rec.* 1.23).

The *Pseudo-Clementines* seem to be preserving a very old memory from the early movement about the process of transmission of the traditions associated with Jesus. It appears that the sayings of Jesus first began to be collected into speeches in which the sayings were arranged rhetorically to provide a memorable interpretation or present an argument to the audience. If the sense of the rhetoric was unclear, it was expected that the

163. Lord, *Singer of Tales*, p. 125; see also W. Kelber, *The Oral and Written Gospel* (Philadelpia: Fortress Press, 1983) p. 30.

164. Lord, *Singer of Tales*, p. 19.

165. Lord, *Singer of Tales*, p. 124.

pupil would inquire after it by asking the teacher. The teacher would expound or justify the sayings accordingly.

Clement goes on to tell us that he himself has been commissioned to write down the words and instructions of the True Prophet which had been spoken by his own teacher, Peter. This record was to be sent to James for use in proselytizing (*Rec.* 1.17; *Hom. Epistle of Peter to James* 2). When the pupil wrote down the speech of his teacher, it appears that another layer of interpretation was imposed upon the sayings since Clement says that after he heard the teachings of the True Prophet from Peter, he '*reduced into order what he had spoken to me* and compiled a book concerning the True Prophet' (*Rec.* 1.17). This seems to have further complicated the matter since Peter tells us that the words which Jesus himself said were 'plainly spoken' by him but 'not plainly written' afterwards. This meant that 'when they were read' to proselytites, they could not be understood 'without an expounder' (*Rec.* 1.21).

Thus, the first Christians did not just preserve traditions of Jesus in haphazard collections or lists that were later organized and used as 'sources' for the Gospel authors. Rather, when they first began to orally collect the sayings of Jesus, they apparently did so rhetorically in speeches with the knowledge or intent that these speeches would be taught to the missionaries who would reperform and interpret them for the proselytites. At some early point, these oral speeches were written down in speech collections which were then used by the early Jerusalem church in its continued mission. These written speech gospels were *aids for memory*, helping the missionaries and preachers recall the catechism. In fact, we are told by Clement that James himself commissioned these compositions to be used for proselytizing. Thus, the first written speech gospels must predate James' death and probably reflect Christian traditions prior to 50 CE. In this writing process, the sayings were once again rearranged and reinterpreted. When these written speeches were then read to audiences or reperformed from memory, they too had to be expounded in order to continue to make sense of them or perhaps to provide alternative interpretations for them. But, all in all, in them the hearers encountered the voice of Jesus and his revelation from God. Thus they appear to have functioned in ways comparable to the enactments of Oral Torah by the rabbis whose performances were viewed as reenactments and extensions of the 'original' revelation at Sinai. 'Just as that revelation is midrashically represented as an oral and aural encounter with the divine utterance prior to its textual inscription,' writes Steven Fraade, 'so too its reenactment is a reversion of the written text of Scripture to a more initimate, interactive, and interpretative engagment with the polyphony of "words of Torah."' [166]

---

166. Fraade, 'Literary Composition,' p. 45.

Thus, the gospel texts we possess are the result of a multifaceted dynamic process of composition and transmission. The traditions began to be collected in oral compositions. As such, they were subject to the rules of oral performance and governed by the processes of communal memory. There may have been an 'original,' or better 'initial,' scribing of these traditions by dictation or the recording of a memory of a previously heard performance. Such texts were scribed at critical moments, when the eyewitnesses were dying, when historical situations threatened the retention of the traditions or required a reinterpretation of them. At such junctures, the traditions entered a period of oral-literate recomposition. When they were reperformed orally as catechism or liturgy, they were freed from the constraints of the text. Some traditions, especially when they were *rescribed*, might have experienced recomposition through 'literate redaction,' although this 'redaction' reflected the register of orality, not literacy as we know it. Through oral-literate recomposition, the old traditions were refreshed and the ideas were kept current. They continued to be subject to the processes of communal memory which functioned in such a way that the traditions were reinterpreted to reflect contemporary concerns and situations. When the traditions finally reached the stage that they were considered the 'ancient' or 'authoritative' record of the community, one of the scribings began to stabilize and the community became less flexible as to its adaptation and interpretation. Then it became the property of scribes who transmitted the text by translating it and copying it. But even this process to some extent seems to have been subject to oral consciousness.

This means that the 'final' form of the traditions preserved in our Gospels is thus the result of their reperformance over a lengthy period of time. Our texts are accumulations of traditions that have been spoken and respoken, collected and recollected, arranged and rearranged, written and rewritten to promote various theologies by multiple agents during the formative years of early Christianity. They represent a creative and theologically-motivated composition *process* with a continual interplay between the oral and written dimensions at the communal level. This has resulted in not only the reformulation of the inherited traditions but also the reformulation of the earlier forms of the gospels themselves.

Is it possible to recover any of these first speech gospels? I think so. A study of the *Gospel of Thomas* affords us the optimal opportunity to restore one of these first gospels because it was not rewritten into a narrative or theological discourse as was the case with the Synoptics and John. Nor is it a reconstructed text developed out of a source hypothesis like Quelle. In the process of this reconstruction, it will become necessary for us to develop a new compositional model for the *Gospel of Thomas* as well as develop a method to identify the later accretions, a method that is consistent with the new *traditionsgeschichtliche* approach. Through this process, we will finally be able to reconstruct the history of the community whose memories the *Gospel of Thomas* preserves. Even more significant is the fact that the restored Kernel will provide us with our earliest picture of Christianity, a picture that most likely pre-dates Paul's letters.

Chapter 2

THE ENIGMATIC *GOSPEL OF THOMAS*

Keeping is the fundamental nature and essence of memory. ~ *M. Heidegger*

Interpreters of the *Gospel of Thomas,* for decades now, have been confronted with an enigmatic set of loosely organized sayings which contain a wide diversity of religious traditions including Christian-Jewish, encratic, hermetic wisdom, and Jewish apocalyptic oracles with both eschatological and mystical emphases.[1] Particularly curious aporiae appear in the text, aporiae that hint at the origin and growth of the gospel. Such difficulties include the variant readings of Jesus' sayings found in this gospel and the perplexing presence of doublets (L. 3 and 113; L. 38 and 92; L. 48 and 106; 55 and 101; 56 and 80; L. 87 and 112). Several sayings contradict themselves. For instance, the gospel lauds the authority and legitimacy of James (L. 12), the first bishop of Jerusalem and leader of conservative Christian-Judaism, while at the same time applauding the 'true circumcision in spirit' and rejecting physical circumcision: 'If it were advantageous, the father (of the children) would conceive them in their mother already circumcised' (L. 53.2). Sabbath observation is preserved (L. 27) while other Jewish observances like dietary regulations, fasting practices, almsgiving, and even praying are viewed as 'harmful' (L. 14). References to a present spiritualized 'Kingdom' abound (cf. L. 3.1–4, 113). But, what about those allusions to an imminent Eschaton, predictions like, 'The heavens and earth will roll up in your presence' (111.1; cf. L. 11.1, 16.1–3)?

How is the multivalency of the text explained? The diversity of religious traditions? The presence of contradictory materials? The doublets? How is the loose structure, seemingly based on rhetorical phrases like 'Jesus said' and simple catchwords, understood? Given the enigmatic nature of *Thomas* and its peculiar aporiae, is it possible to recover its provenance?

---

1. For a complete discussion of the traditions which make up this gospel, see A.D. DeConick, *Seek to See Him: Ascent and Vision Mysticism in the Gospel of Thomas*, VCSupp 33 (1996).

To reconstruct an adequate history of composition? To offer historically-sensible interpretations of its sayings?

2.1 *Previously Proposed Compositional Models*

Over the decades, scholars have recognized that in order to solve the mystery of the origin and development of *Thomas*, it is essential to explicate its multivalency. In light of the gospel's complexities, several theoretical models have been developed that attempt to place the *Gospel of Thomas* within early Christian history. The first hypothesis to emerge was the Literate model.

2.1.1 *Literate Model (Diagram 1)*
The earliest formulation of the Literate model proposed that the author largely used written gospels as sources when composing his own gospel. Gilles Quispel was the first to advocate three non-canonical written sources for *Thomas*:[2] a Jewish-Christian gospel (possibly the *Gospel of the Nazorees*),[3] an encratic gospel (probably the *Gospel of the Egyptians*), and a Hermetic gnomology.[4] An encratic author from Edessa edited this material along with his own occasional comments into the present collection. His religious ideal was 'the androgynous man or woman,' the holy people of Syria. Thus: 'He did not intend his document to be esoteric, but an exoteric, accessible writing containing divine Sayings whose saving sense could be grasped by spiritual men.'[5] In his most recent comment on the *Gospel of Thomas*, he states that the 'Judaic Christian' sayings were written down in 50 CE in Jerusalem and that the encratitic source was combined with them by the Edessian author of the gospel around 140 CE.[6]

While Quispel's call for an independent source for *Thomas* became the call of many scholars, his attempt to recover the actual written sources for

---

2. Refer to his articles: 'The Gospel of Thomas and the New Testament,' *VC* 11 (1957) pp. 189–207; 'Some Remarks on the Gospel of Thomas,' *NTS* 5 (1958/1959) pp. 276–290; 'L'Évangile selon Thomas et les Clémentines,' *VC* 12 (1958) pp. 181–196; 'L'Évangile selon Thomas et le Diatesssaron,' *VC* 13 (1959) pp. 87–117; 'The "Gospel of Thomas" and the "Gospel of the Hebrews",' *NTS* 12 (1966) pp. 371–382; 'The *Gospel of Thomas* Revisited,' *Colloque International sur les Textes de Nag Hammadi. Québec, 22–25 août 1978*, BCNH 1 (ed. B. Barc; Québec, 1981) pp. 218–266.

3. Early in his career, G. Quispel identified the source with the *Gospel of the Hebrews*.

4. The Hermetic gnomology source was an idea developed later by G. Quispel and represents a modification of his original two-source theory.

5. Quispel, 'Revisited,' p. 234.

6. G. Quispel, 'Reincarnation and Magic in the Ascelpius,' in R. van den Broek (ed.), *From Poimandres to Jacob Böhme: Gnosis, Hermetism and the Christian Tradition* (Amsterdam: Bibliotheca Philosophica Hermetica with E.J. Brill, 2000) pp. 214–215.

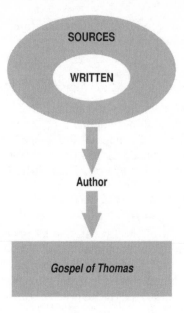

Diagram 1:   Literate Model

Thomas drew criticism on methodological grounds because it developed out of a circular argument.[7] That is, once the sayings that contain Jewish-Christian, encratic, or Hermetic elements were identified, the sources are determined to be Jewish-Christian, encratic, or Hermetic because some of the identified sayings reflect versions of the sayings in the Jewish-Christian and encratic gospel fragments or in Hermetic gnomologies.

The reason Quispel's theory looks to be circular is due to the fact that we do not possess a complete Jewish-Christian or encratic gospel to use comparatively against *Thomas*. So critics contemporaneous with Quispel argued instead for the dependence of the gospel on one or more of the canonical Gospels or even the *Diatessaron*.[8] These theorists, however,

---

7.   Early supporters of his thesis included H.-Ch. Puech, 'Das Thomasevangelium,' in E. Hennecke (ed.), *Neutestamentliche Apokryphen*, volume 1 (Tübingen: J.C.B. Mohr, 1958) pp. 214–216; G.W. MacRae, 'The Gospel of Thomas – LOGIA IESOU?' *CBQ* 22 (1960) pp. 63–64; J. Doresse, *Les livres secrets des gnostiques d'Égypt* (Paris: Libraire Plon, 1965) p. 73; H. Montefiore, 'A Comparison of the Parables of the Gospel According to Thomas and the Synoptic Gospels,' *NTS* 7 (1960/61) pp. 223–224, 248. But following E. Haenchen's rebuttal against his position, support for Quispel's thesis failed to gain strength: 'Literatur zum Thomasevangelium,' *TRu* 27 (1961/1962) pp. 164–169.

8.   R.M. Grant with D.N. Freedman, *The Secret Sayings of Jesus* (New York: Doubleday, 1960); H.K. McArthur, 'The Gospel According to Thomas,' in *New Testament Sidelights: Essays in Honor of Alexander Converse Purdy, Hosner Professor of New Testament,*

faced what has become an insurmountable problem: the difficulty in providing an adequate explanation for the presence of variant readings and variant combinations of sayings and parts of sayings in *Thomas*.

Immediately this problem was recognized, so some scholars suggested that the additions, deletions, transpositions and conflations were due to the author's freedom with his sources. R. Grant and D.N. Freedman thought that this freedom was typical of the second-century Gnostics, the Naaseenes in particular. But they also admitted that it was a freedom typical of the early Church Fathers too.[9] Along these same lines, E. Haenchen argued that the author drew on the canonical Gospels and a gnostic exegetical tradition with its own memories and used a scheme of verbal association in order to structure his gospel. This explained for him the ways in which the sayings diverged from their canonical versions, although this explanation has not become a scholarly consensus.[10]

It soon became clear that the problem of variant readings and combinations of sayings was not the only puzzle that the Literate model did not solve. Because the model assumed that one author brought together a variety of sayings from written sources at some historical moment, creating the *Gospel of Thomas*, it struggled to explain *why* a single author would choose to include in his composition conflicting sayings and doublets from his written sources. The model was vexed to demonstrate

Dean of the Hartford Theological Seminary, the Hartford Seminary Foundation (Hartford: Hartford Seminary Foundation, 1960) pp. 43–77; J. Munck, 'Bemerkungen zum koptischen Thomasevangelium,' *ST* 14 (1960) pp. 130–147; W.R. Schoedel, 'Naassene Themes in the Coptic Gospel of Thomas,' *VC* 14 (1960) pp. 225–234; B. Gärtner, *The Theology of the Gospel of Thomas* (London: Collins, 1961); E. Haenchen, *Die Botschaft des Thomas-Evangeliums*, TBT 6 (Berlin: Töpelmann, 1961); R. Kasser, *L'Évangile selon Thomas*, Bibliothèque théologique (Neuchâtel: Delachaux et Niestlé, 1961); H. Schürmann, 'Das Thomasevangelium und das lukanische Sondergut,' *BZ* 7 (1963) pp. 236–260; W. Schrage, *Das Verhältnis des Thomas-Evangeliums zur synoptischen Tradition und zu den koptischen Evangelienübersetzungen*, BZNW 29 (Berlin: Töpelmann, 1964); J. Leipoldt, *Das Evangelium nach Thomas*, TU 101 (Berlin: Akademie-Verlag, 1967); J.-E. Ménard, *L'Évangile selon Thomas*, NHS 5 (Leiden: E.J. Brill, 1975); A. Lindemann, 'Zur Gleichnisinterpretation im Thomas-Evangelium,' ZNW 71 (1980) pp. 214–243; T. Baarda, 'Thomas and Tatian,' in J. Helderman and S. Noorda (eds.), *Early Transmission of Words of Jesus: Thomas, Tatian and the Text of the New Testament* (Amsterdam: Uitgeverij, 1983) pp. 37–49; ' "Chose" or "Collected": Concerning an Aramaism in Logion 8 of the Gospel of Thomas and the Question of Independence,' *HTR* 84 (1991) pp. 373–397; N. Perrin, *Thomas and Tatian: The Relationship between the Gospel of Thomas and the Diatessaron*, AcadBib 5 (Atlanta: Society of Biblical Literature, 2002).

For a summary of the dependence question, see S.J. Patterson, 'The Gospel of Thomas and the Synoptic Tradition: A Forschungsbericht and Critique,' *FFF* 8 (1992) pp. 45–97; F.T. Fallon and R. Cameron, 'The Gospel of Thomas: A Forschungsbericht and Analysis,' *ANRW* 2:25.6 (New York, 1988) pp. 4195–4251.

9.   Grant and Freedman, *Secret Sayings*, p. 141.

10.   E. Haenchen, 'Literatur zum Thomasevangelium,' *TRu* 27 (1961/1962) pp. 147–178, 306–338.

why an author would select from his sources the sayings that he did, while neglecting others. Moreover, the unification of extremely diverse religious traditions in the *Gospel of Thomas* was very difficult to perceive as the intended product of one mind. Finally, there was the problem of structure. Formulations of the Literate model were not able to explain *why* one author would choose to structure the gospel so loosely, although there continues to be a proliferation of unconvincing attempts to explain *how* this structure really is not so loose.[11]

A fascinating variation of the Literate model was proposed by Hans Martin Schenke in the mid-90s.[12] Schenke's keen observations demonstrate an awareness of these fundamental aporiae and a desire to solve them. He proposes a hypothesis that particularly addresses what he calls the 'rough edges' of *Thomas:* the doublets, the stereotypical formula 'Jesus said,' artificial and sometimes inappropriate framing devices, the 'frameless' sayings, the secondary incipit, the separation and dislocation of complexes that obviously belong together, and echoes of multi-voices. As one reads his article, one expects Schenke to opt for a multi-staged, multi-authored solution to the aporiae. But he firmly denies this, stating that the starting point for the solution is not the aporiae themselves, but how 'it is possible to explain all of these various aporiae as coming from one and the same root.'[13] Although he does not explain why, he says further, 'I am of the conviction that in the case of the Gospel of Thomas a single-stage hypothesis should be preferred to any pluralistic one.'[14] The hypothesis he proposes is that an 'author' had in hand a copy of a commentary of Jesus' sayings like that of Papias. He selected various sayings from this written source, freeing them from the restricting

---

11. Structured by forms: H. Puech, 'The Gospel of Thomas,' in E. Hennecke and W. Schneemelcher (eds.) and R. McL. Wilson (trans.), *New Testament Apocrypha*, volume 1 (Philadelphia: Westminster, 1963) pp. 288–305. Structured by catchwords: Grant with Freedman, *Secret Sayings*, p. 104; Gärtner, *Thomas*, 28–29; Haenchen, *Botschaft*, 12–13; K. Rudolph, 'Gnosis und Gnostizismus, ein Forschungsbericht,' *TRu* 34 (1969) pp. 185–187; H. Koester, 'One Jesus and Four Primitive Gospels,' in J. Robinson and H. Koester, *Trajectories through Early Christianity* (Philadelphia: Fortress Press, 1971) pp. 166–187. Structured by themes: Y. Janssens, 'L'Évangile selon Thomas et son caractère gnostique,' *Mus* 75 (1962) pp. 301–302; S.L. Davies, *The Gospel of Thomas and Christian Wisdom* (New York: Seabury, 1983) pp. 149–155; Structured by the disciples' questions: D.H. Tripp, 'The Aim of the Gospel of Thomas,' *ExpTim* 92 (1980/1981) pp. 41–44. Structured by modifying another source: B. de Solages, 'L'Évangile de Thomas et les Évangiles Canoniques: L'order des Péricopes,' *BLE* 80 (1979) pp. 102–108.

12. H.-M. Schenke, 'On the Compositional History of the Gospel of Thomas,' FFF 10 (1994) pp. 9–30.

13. Schenke, 'Compositional History,' p. 26.

14. Schenke, 'Compositional History,' p. 26.

framework of the commentary, sometimes failing to eliminate the original voice of the commentator.[15]

Schenke realizes that the hypothesis' biggest weakness is that it is difficult to imagine why the author would make the selections he did, not only the particular sayings, but also their interpretations. Why select this saying and not that one? Why omit the commentator's interpretation in some cases and not others?[16] In order to answer these questions adequately, there would need to be a thorough discussion about the ideological position of the author as reflected in his choice of particular sayings and interpretations, since we must assume that the author's ideology was dictating his selection and reorganization. Schenke does not attempt to do this. So we are left with a possible model for composition but no firm reason why someone would want to do this or what it meant once it was done. Although this is no small matter, what overshadows the discussion for me, however, is Schenke's problematic starting point: the assumption that a single-stage hypothesis is better than a pluralistic one. His assumption determines the outcome because it forces Schenke to consider only some of the possibilities at the expense of others. Rather the starting point should be the text itself and its aporiae, out of which grows the simplest but no simpler solution.

2.1.2 *Oral-Literate Model (Diagram 2)*
Scholars who recognized the fundamental problems of the Literate model began critiquing it immediately. In one of R. McL. Wilson's early works on *Thomas*, he noted:

> In some cases we can indeed speak of intentional or unintentional harmonization, words or phrases occurring to the mind of the author by association with what he is writing, but in others it is difficult to imagine him selecting a word here, a saying there, and keeping part of another saying for use at a later stage. Explanations which are to be valid must take account of what we can learn of the writer's methods, and free citation from memory would appear nearer the mark than an extensive use of scissors and paste.[17]

This line of reasoning opened the door for another early approach which proposed that the author of the gospel used one or more pre-gospel

---

15. Schenke, 'Compositional History,' pp. 26–27.
16. Schenke, 'Compositional History,' p. 27.
17. R. McL. Wilson, *Studies in the Gospel of Thomas* (London: A.R. Mowbray & Co., 1960) p. 100.

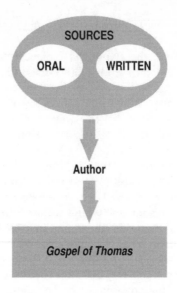

Diagram 2:   Oral-Literate Model

collections of Jesus' sayings. The variations were due to their oral pre-history.[18]

According to the major proponent of this position, H. Koester, the author was 'a collector and compiler who used a number of smaller units of collected sayings, some perhaps available in written form, and composed them randomly.' He was not an author 'who deliberately composed his book according to a general master plan.' The point of his collection, rather, was hermeneutical: it was supposed to provide the reader with sayings which could be interpreted by the individual.[19] Even though here Koester offers a plausible solution to the persistent problem of conflicting and diverse traditions coming together under the pen of one

18.   J. Doresse, *The Secret Books of the Egyptian Gnostics* (New York: Viking, 1960) p. 347; K. Grobel, 'How Gnostic is the Gospel of Thomas?' *NTS* 8 (1961/1962) pp. 367–373; O. Cullmann, 'The Gospel of Thomas and the Problem of the Age of the Traditions Contained Therein: A Survey,' *Int* 16 (1962) pp. 418–438; A. Strobel, 'Textgeschichtliches zum Thomas-Logion 86 (Mt 8,20/Luk 9,58),' *VC* 17 (1963) pp. 211–224; W.H.C. Frend, 'Is Rehabilitation Possible?' *JTS* 18 (1967) pp. 13–26; H. Koester, 'GNOMAI DIAPHOROI: The Origin and Nature of Diversification in the History of Early Christianity,' *HTR* 58 (1965) pp. 297–318; H. Koester, 'One Jesus and Four Primitive Gospels,' *HTR* 61 (1968) pp. 203–247; H. Koester, 'Three Thomas Parables,' in A.H.B. Logan and A.J.M. Wedderburn, *The New Testatment and Gnosis, Essays in Honour of Robert McLachlan Wilson* (Edinburgh: T.&T. Clark, 1983) pp. 195–203.

19.   H. Koester, *Ancient Christian Gospels: Their History and Development* (Philadelphia: Trinity Press International, 1990) pp. 81–82.

author, his solution is not without its own difficulties. Certainly sayings of *Thomas* were meant to be interpreted by the hearer or reader, and this interpretation was believed to be somehow redemptive. But nothing in the text indicates that an author was deliberately setting up conflicting sayings or diverse traditions so that the reader was provided with hermeneutical puzzles to solve. Koester's solution seems to me to be more of an imposition on the text than a deduction from it.

As Koester attempted to solve the problem of the variant readings and combinations of sayings in *Thomas*, he argued that the author not only used a very old collection of sayings of Jesus, but also that *Thomas* drew from them the emphasis on 'the presence of the kingdom for the believer, rather than its future coming.'[20] He understood this to be 'an interpretation and elaboration of Jesus' most original proclamation.'[21] This position has become the fundamental operating premise for many scholars over the years and continues to be favored.[22] It developed alongside Koester's interest in the genre of the 'sayings gospel.' *Thomas* provided Koester with an actual illustration of the sayings gospel genre, representing for him the parallel to Q's original genre.[23] Because the *Gospel of Thomas* lacks the traditional passion kergyma, Koester concluded that the purpose of the sayings gospel genre was to promote 'belief in Jesus' words, a belief which makes what Jesus proclaimed present and real for the believer.'[24]

Since *Thomas* lacked apocalyptic Son of Man sayings so prevalent in Q, Koester argued that 'Thomas presupposes a stage and form of the tradition of eschatological sayings which did not yet contain an apocalyptic expectation of the Son of man.'[25] This early stage of sayings appeared to be 'a direct continuation of the eschatological sayings of Jesus' in which 'his message demands that the mysterious presence of the kingdom in his words be recognized.'[26] Koester seems here to be using the term 'eschatological' in the Bultmannian existential sense so that it becomes juxtaposed with the word 'apocalyptic.' By 'apocalyptic,' he seems to be referring to traditional mythological thinking about the world actually coming to an end through a series of events initiated by God.

According to Koester, the oldest sayings gospels were therefore 'wisdom gospels' which Christologically identified Jesus with the 'teacher' and

---

20. Koester, 'One Jesus,' p. 172.
21. Koester, 'One Jesus,' p. 172.
22. Cf. T. Zoeckler, *Jesu Lehren im Thomasevangelium*, NHMS 47 (Leiden: E.J. Brill, 1999).
23. Koester, 'One Jesus,' pp. 158–204.
24. Koester, 'One Jesus,' p. 186.
25. Koester, 'One Jesus,' p. 171.
26. Koester, 'One Jesus,' p. 175.

'presence' of heavenly Wisdom whose words revealed some kind of existential eschatology, some decisive moment of encounter with the power of God's Kingdom. This Christology was understood to be older than that of the apocalyptic Son of Man. From this Koester drew the conclusion that the Son of Man sayings entered the older wisdom book Q secondarily.[27]

This assessment of Q and *Thomas* has certainly worried more than a few scholars. One of the most poignant, perhaps, has been James Dunn who wrote in response to Koester's position: 'I do not think that the apocalyptic elements of Jesus' teachings can be sloughed off quite so readily.'[28] He thinks that 'Q is almost certainly earlier and nearer to Jesus' emphasis than any non-apocalyptic version of the Jesus-tradition.'[29] More to the point, he argues that 'the Thomas material in these logia just mentioned (1, 3, 8, 11, 19, 21, 35, 37, 51, 59, 76, 103, 109, 111, 113) looks much more like *de-eschatologized* tradition rather than pre-apocalyptic tradition.'[30]

Like Dunn, I am reluctant to concede an early 'sapiential' *Thomas*. I find it impossible to work from the premise that the *Gospel of Thomas* represents a collection of early sapiential non-apocalyptic sayings and that the earliest stratification of Q must have been similar in content to it. As both Margaretha Lelyveld's monograph and my own previous book have shown, the traditions in *Thomas* are much more complex than this.[31] Our works have independently suggested that we must be open to the possibility that the *Gospel of Thomas* was steeped in Jewish apocalyptic traditions. We cannot assume that the *Gospel of Thomas* was *originally* or *entirely* a sapiential gospel. This also means that we cannot assume that Q was sapiential because *Thomas* was sapiential.

Moreover, I think it is safe to say that, *even if* Q existed as a written document, because we are working with a minimal reconstruction, we cannot really know much about Q's genre or content. Was it comparable to the genre and content of the *Gospel of Thomas*? Q certainly seems to have been more than a sayings gospel since, unlike *Thomas*, it does contain some substantial narrative material *even in its minimal reconstruction*. Did it lack a passion narrative or a traditional kerygma? Who knows. It is very possible that these were part of Q and that they were incorporated into either Matthew or Luke. Based on my current research, I even venture to suggest that the Q we have reconstructed was a speech gospel of which

27. H. Koester, 'Apocryphal and Canonical Gospels,' *HTR* 73 (1980) p. 113.

28. J.D.G. Dunn, *Unity and Diversity in the New Testament: An Inquiry Into the Character of Earliest Christianity* (Philadelphia: Westminster Press, 1977) p. 286.

29. Dunn, *Unity*, p. 286.

30. Dunn, *Unity*, p. 286.

31. See especially, M. Lelyveld, *Les Logia de la Vie dans L'Évangile selon Thomas*, NHS 34 (Leiden: E. J. Brill, 1987); DeConick, *Seek to See Him*.

Matthew and Luke had very different versions.[32] So, although, at the moment, I think that Q and the two-source hypothesis is our best tested explanation for the literary history of the synoptic gospels, I am very reluctant to theorize about the nature of particular stratifications of Q and their alleged ramifications for understanding the composition of the *Gospel of Thomas* as Koester has done.

His argument, however, that *Thomas* was indebted in some way to oral tradition was a fundamental breakthrough in our understanding of *Thomas'* complex compositional history. Since Koester's original formulation, there has been an enormous amount of research conducted on orality, research that gives even more cause for us to see the variant sayings in *Thomas* as reflections of residual orality.[33] However, in spite of these studies in orality and the heroic efforts of a few biblical scholars to align their research with it, scholars of early Christianity in general remain unfamiliar with the compositional process common to cultures dominated by orality or have ignored it.[34] Most continue to impose upon the ancient authors a 'literate imagination,' suggesting that composition occurred by

32.   H.D. Betz, 'The Sermon on the Mount and Q: Some Aspects of the Problem,' in J. Goehring, C. Hedrick, J. Sanders and H.D. Betz (eds.), *Gospel Origins and Christian Beginnings in Honor of James M. Robinson* (Sonoma: Polebridge Press, 1990) pp. 19–34.

33.   Cf. A. Lord, *The Singer of Tales*, HSCL 24 (Cambridge: Harvard University Press, 1960, 2nd edn. 2000); W. Ong, *The Presence of the Word* (New Haven: Yale University Press, 1967); W. Ong, *Rhetoric, Romance, and Technology: Studies in the Interaction of Expression and Culture* (Ithaca: Cornell University Press, 1971; W. Ong, *Interfaces of the Word* (Ithaca: Cornell University Press, 1977); W. Ong, *Orality and Literacy: The Technologizing of the Word* (London: Methuen, 1982); J. Goody, *The Interface between the Written and the Oral* (Cambridge: Cambridge University Press, 1987); R. Finnegan, *Literacy and Orality: Studies in the Technology of Communication* (Oxford: Blackwell, 1988); J.M. Foley, *The Theory of Oral Composition: History and Methodology* (Bloomington: Indiana University Press, 1988); J.M. Foley, *Immanent Art: From Structure to Meaning in Traditional Oral Epic* (Bloomington: Indiana University Press, 1991); J.M. Foley, *The Singer of Tales in Performance*, Voices in Performance and Text (Bloomington: Indiana University Press, 1995).

34.   Cf. W.H. Kelber, *The Oral and the Written Gospel* (Philadephia: Fortress Press, 1983); R.C. Culley, 'Oral Tradition and Biblical Studies,' *OT* 1 (1986) pp. 30–65; J. Dewey, 'Oral Methods of Structuring Narrative in Mark,' *Int* 53 (1989) pp. 32–44; R.B. Coote, *The Bible's First History* (Philadephia: Fortress Press, 1989); P. Botha, 'Mark's Story as Oral Traditional Literature: Rethinking the Transmission of Some Traditions About Jesus,' *HvTSt* 47 (1991) pp. 304–331; J. Dewey, 'Mark as Interwoven Tapestry: Forecasts and Echoes for a Listening Audience,' *CBQ* 53 (1991) pp. 221–236; J. Dewey, 'Mark as Aural Narrative: Structures as Clues to Understanding,' *STRev* 36 (1992) pp. 45–56; V. Robbins, 'Oral, Rhetorical, and Literary Cultures,' *Semeia* 65 (1994); S. Niditch, *Oral World and Written Word: Ancient Israelite Literature* (Louisville: Westminster/John Knox Press, 1996); R.A. Horsley and J.A. Draper, *Whoever Hears You Hears Me: Prophets, Performance, and Tradition in Q* (Harrisburg: Trinity Press International, 1999); R. Horsley, *Hearing the Whole Story: The Politics of Plot in Mark's Gospel* (Louisville: Westminster/John Knox Press, 2001).

cutting and pasting information from written sources into their new text by editors or redactors.

For instance, recently Nick Perrin has attempted to revive the old cut-and-paste model. He tries to renew the position that the author of the *Gospel of Thomas*, an 'active and sometimes intrusive editor,' was dependent on the *Diatessaron*.[35] He comes to this conclusion because he thinks that *Thomas* was originally written in Syriac. Since the *Diatessaron* was the only Syriac version of the gospels in existence in the second century, 'history appears to have left us with no other option . . . Thomas had Tatian's work in hand.'[36]

But his theory has done no better in providing adequate solutions to the problems that have plagued past theorists of the Literate model. For instance, Perrin's thesis offers no compelling reason why an author in the late second century would select a few sayings from Tatian's harmony while avoiding others, and then rearrange them into a new text in the way he did. Moreover, there is a large amount of material in *Thomas* that has no direct parallel in the *Diatessaron*. This material largely remains unexplained in his monograph. Most troubling is his argument that the text is the result of one author using Syriac catchwords and puns to connect sayings and give structure to his text, sayings that he has lifted from written sources, mainly the *Diatessaron*. Over the last fifty years, studies in orality and transitional cultures have demonstrated the opposite, that texts exhibiting catchword structures are reflecting a long history of oral composition, not the cut-and-paste editorial policy such as we are familiar with from our own literate world. What Perrin's Syriac reconstruction points to is exactly the kind of text that we would expect to be produced in a culture dominated by oral modes of transmission, not the scribal mentality Perrin assumes. It is an accumulation of sayings based on commonly used mnemonic principles like alliteration, catchwords, and even puns.

Since Perrin argues for such a late written source for *Thomas*, there is the additional problem of the physical manuscript evidence. The Greek fragment P. Oxy. 1 is dated by B. Grenfell and A. Hunt to a date *no later than 200 CE*. This date has been accepted by scholars as the *terminus ad quem* for the manuscript copy because the paleographic analysis of the manuscript places it at 200 CE. Perrin's date of composition would make P. Oxy. 1 virtually an autograph, an implausibility especially if the text was composed originally in Syriac as Perrin contends. Furthermore, Perrin's cursory dismissal of the dating of the autograph of P. Oxy. 1 is not satisfactory. The 140 CE date has been generally accepted not because

35. Perrin, *Thomas and Tatian*, p. 183.
36. Perrin, *Thomas and Tatian*, p. 184.

'most scholars have not bothered to probe the issue'[37] but because the autograph of Thomas must be prior to 200 CE and the internal evidence suggests a compositional date no later than the beginning of the second century.[38] Even though Perrin makes a very convincing argument that *Thomas* was composed in some dialect of Aramaic, a position which supports the work of previous scholars and makes sense with regard to *Thomas'* provenance, this does not necessitate dependence on the *Diatessaron* as he concludes.

2.1.3 *Redaction Model (Diagram 3)*

Some scholars have favored the possibility of a later literary redaction. The redaction is understood to be very minimal and late by most supporting this position. Although these suggestions are not very developed in scholarly works, they all seem to be some variation of the process sketched in Diagram 3. For instance, in Tai Akagi's 1965 doctoral dissertation, one of the only analyses of the literary development of the *Gospel of Thomas*, he saw very little change from an original gospel to the Coptic text; but he does suggest that five logia might be later additions along with some minor alterations (L. 16, 49, 61, 75, and 114).[39] Some scholars have mentioned the possibility of redaction, making an occasional reference to *Thomas'* alleged 'gnostic' character. The first references to this are actually very early in *Thomas* scholarship. In 1959, R. Kasser wrote about the possibility that *Thomas* once existed as a gnostic hymn which he identified as the core gospel.[40] But he does not develop his theory even in his succeeding commentary.[41] It became much more common to see the opposite postulation in scholars' works: that the original version of *Thomas* was at the very least less gnostic than our extant Coptic version.[42] H.-Ch. Puech went so far as to postulate two

---

37. Perrin, *Thomas and Tatian*, pp. 5–6.

38. This was first argued by B.P. Grenfell and A.S. Hunt ΛΟΓΙΑ ΙΗΣΟΥ. *Sayings of Our Lord from an Early Greek Papyrus* (London: Henry Frowde, 1897) p. 16.

39. T. Akagi, *The Literary Development of the Coptic Gospel of Thomas* (Ph.D. dissertation; Western Reserve University, 1965) pp. 328, 361–363.

40. R. Kasser, 'Les manuscripts de Nag Hammâdi: faits, documents, problèmes,' *RTP* 9 (1959) pp. 365–367.

41. R. Kasser, *L'Évangile selon Thomas*, Bibliotèque Théologique (Neuchâtel: Delachaux et Niestlé, 1961) pp. 18–19.

42. Cf. O. Cullmann, 'Das Thomasevangelium und die Frage nach dem Alter der in ihm enthaltenen Tradition,' *Theologische Literaturzeitung* 85 (1960) pp. 330–331; Grant and Freedman, *Secret Sayings*, p. 68; A.J.B. Higgins, 'Non-Gnostic Sayings in the Gospel of Thomas,' *NovT* 4 (1960) p. 306; R. Schippers, *Het Evangelie van Thomas* (Kampen: J.H. Kok, 1960) p. 133; Doresse, *Secret Books*, pp. 343–344.

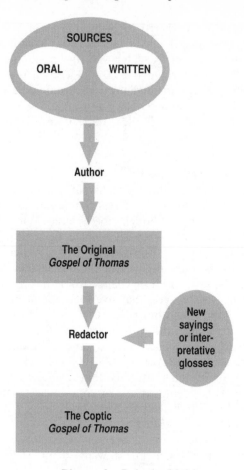

Diagram 3: Redaction Model

recensions of the gospel, one an 'orthodox' version and another a late gnostic or Manichean version.[43]

The work of R. McL. Wilson stands out in this period because he considered the redaction of *Thomas* to have happened several times. He based this index on H. Chadwick's observations about the nature of the *Sentences of Sextus*, a collection of sayings that Chadwick argued had taken on 'the character of a snowball.'[44] He identifies four types of material in *Thomas* based on their provenance:

43.   H.-Ch. Puech, 'The Gospel of Thomas,' *New Testament Apocrypha* 1 (ed. E. Hennecke and W. Schneemelcher; Eng. trans. R. McL. Wilson; Philadelphia, 1963) pp. 305–306.

44.   R. McL. Wilson, ' "Thomas" and the Growth of the Gospels,' *HTR* 53 (1960) p. 231; R. McL., Wilson, *Studies in the Gospel of Thomas* (London: Mowbray, 1960), pp. 9, 145.

> In the most general terms, we may perhaps speak of an element of genuine early tradition, possibly embodying a few authentic sayings; of an element parallel to but perhaps independent of our Gospels, but apparently from a later stage in the development of the tradition; of the influence of the canonical Gospels on the form and working of these two types of sayings, and of an element derived from the Synoptics; and finally of Gnostic redaction of the material as a whole, and Gnostic construction of further sayings.[45]

Although Wilson's study added some depth to the problem as he sought to explain *Thomas*' compositional history, he never presented a complete or clear source theory for the gospel nor was his critical analysis methodologically firm, because Wilson assumed that it was possible to identify authentic Jesus material based solely on its *Sitz im Leben*. His work was dependent on Form Criticism which he used to distinguish traditions that were originally independent and genuinely early from those which were secondary and borrowed from other sources. For him this meant that those sayings in *Thomas* which 'fit' into 'the context of Jesus' life' – they were words that Jesus could have uttered authentically – could be isolated as 'genuine early tradition' while those sayings which were 'no more than Gnostic composition based upon our Gospels' were secondary.[46]

An important step in the development of the Redaction model was made in 1991 by John Dominic Crossan who suggested that there might be two substantial 'layers' or strata of material in the *Gospel of Thomas*. The first layer, he thinks, was composed by the fifties CE, possibly in Jerusalem. The second layer was added to this in Edessa 'possibly as early as the sixties or seventies.' Crossan says that the early layer is discernable in 'those units with independent attestation elsewhere' while the later layer is made up of 'that which is unique to this collection.' This layering seems to be based on the assumption that multiply-attested sayings across independent sources are earlier than singly-attested sayings. This assumption, of course, may be the case, but is not certain by any means. It cannot be used, as Crossan has done, to successfully reconstruct the oldest layer of the text since it is quite probable that some of the singly-attested sayings are also early but just not preserved in other extant sources. I have to agree with Crossan's own confession that his stratification is 'rather crude' and 'underlines the need for a better one'![47]

Following John Kloppenberg's stratification of Q, Stephen Patterson

---

45. Wilson, *Studies*, pp. 147–148.

46. Wilson, *Studies*, p. 47.

47. J.D. Crossan, *The Historical Jesus: The Life of a Mediterranean Jewish Peasant* (New York: HarperSanFrancisco, 1991) pp. 427–428.

has put forward a compositional model for *Thomas* with two phases.[48] The first phase was a common oral source from which both the authors of *Thomas* and Q drew. This common tradition was redacted by the author of Q1 into a regime about seeking the reign of God, while it was redacted by the later author of Q2 into an apocalyptic scenario. In *Thomas*, the common tradition was redacted in order to privatize and adapt it to the 'gnosticizing' theology of the author. The common tradition shared by Q and *Thomas* is divided by Patterson into four classes.[49] The first includes logia that neither the author of Q nor *Thomas* recast as apocalyptic or gnostic (L. 6.3; 14.4; 20.2–4; 26.1–2; 32; 33.1; 33.2–3; 34; 36; 45.1; 45.2–3; 47.2; 54; 55; 58; 63; 68.1–2: 69.2: 72.1–2; 73; 76.3; 86.1–2; 94; 96.1–2; 107; 113.2). The second class includes Thomasine parallels with Q2 that are not apocalyptic in *Thomas* (L. 10; 16.1–4; 24; 35.1–2; 39.1–2; 41.1–2; 44.1–3; 46.1, 2b; 64.1–12; 78.1–3; 89.1–2; 91; 103.3). The third includes sayings which the author has gnosticized but which *Thomas* also knows in a non-gnostic format (L. 2 and 92 [cf. 94]; 3 [cf. 113]; 5.2 [cf. 6.3]; 69.1 [cf. 68.1–2]; 101 [cf. 55]). The fourth class includes logia that are apocalyptic in Q and gnostic in *Thomas* (L. 4.2; 21.3; 61.1; 61.3).

Similarly William Arnal makes his starting point the research that has been done on Q and its stratification by his mentor and doctoral advisor, John Kloppenborg, although he does not make his stratification of *Thomas* by classifying the layers according to Q's layers as Patterson has done.[50] Due to common features he sees between Q and *Thomas*, Arnal argues that *Thomas* must be a 'stratified' document with a 'historical complexity' and 'social setting' very similar to Q.[51] 'Both documents,' he writes, 'are products of a social history rather than a static social context.'[52] But Arnal identifies two main strands of material in *Thomas*, strands which he believes 'can be separated from each other on formal and thematic

---

48. Q1: 6.20b–23b, 27–35, 36–45, 46–49; 9.57–60 (61–62); 10.2–11, 16; 11.2–4, 9–13; 12.2–7, 11–12; 12.22b–31, 33–34; probably also 13:24, 14.26–27, 34–35; 17:33. Q2: 3.7–9, 16b–17; 6:23c; 7.1–10, 18–23, 31–35; 10:12, 13–15; 11.14–15, 16, 17–26 (27–28), 29–32, 33–36, 39b–44, 46–52; 12.39–40, 42b–46, 49, 50–53, 54–59; 17.23–24, 37b, 26–30, 34–35; 19.12–27; 22.28–30. On this see, J.S. Kloppenberg, *The Formation of Q: Trajectories in Ancient Wisdom Collections*, SAC (Philadelphia: Fortress Press, 1987) pp. 171–245.

49. S. Patterson, 'Wisdom in Q and Thomas,' in L.G. Perdue, B.B. Scott, and W.J. Wiseman (eds.), *In Search of Wisdom: Essays in Memory of John G. Gammie* (Louiseville: Westminster John Knox, 1993) pp. 194–196.

50. W. Arnal, 'The Rhetoric of Marginality: Apocalypticism, Gnosticism, and Sayings Gospels,' *HTR* 88 (1995) 471–494. H. Koester seems to have been influenced by Arnal's position since it is now reflected in his most current discussion of the *Gospel of Thomas* in the second edition of his *Introduction to the New Testament*, volume 2 (New York: Walter de Gruyter, 2000) pp. 154–158.

51. Arnal, 'Rhetoric of Marginality,' pp. 472–473.

52. Arnal, 'Rhetoric of Marginality,' p. 474.

grounds.' Each one of these strands forms 'a coherent unity.' The formal and thematic consistency of each of these suggests for Arnal that the gospel has been stratified.[53] The earliest of these strands includes wisdom sayings, similar in content and form to Q1 (3, 5, 6, 9, 14, 16, 20, 26, 31, 32, 34, 35, 36, 42, 45, 47, 54, 55, 57, 58, 63, 64, 65, 67, 68, 69, 74, 76, 86?, 89, 95, 96, 97, 98, 107, 109, 110).[54] The content of this material according to Arnal 'appears to react to a situation in which the intensification of the rural poor's exploitation and dispossession through heavy taxation and consequent indebtedness to the urban rich is a primary concern.'[55] Arnal concludes that this early *Thomas* very much like Q1 adopts a 'counter-cultural position in response to the increasing exploitation of the countryside by the urban wealthy' which he sees reflected in Antipas' establishment of Tiberias and Sepphoris as administrative centers.[56]

In contradistinction to this sapiential strand is another body of sayings which Arnal characterizes as 'gnostic' in orientation because of their 'invocation of gnostic mythological motifs' (11, 13, 15, 18, 21, 22, 27, 28, 48, 49, 50, 51, 60, 61, 83, 84, 101, 105, 108, 111, 114). Arnal thinks that some of the secondary glosses interpret the wisdom materials in a gnostic manner.[57] He suggests that Q, unlike *Thomas*, followed a remarkably different route in the later states of its development. Instead of becoming a gnostic gospel, it grew into an apocalyptic document by the time Q2 came into existence.[58] He concludes that this gnostic strand is secondary to *Thomas* because of the natural tendency of wisdom sayings to progress in this manner, a tendency mapped previously by James Robinson. Robinson had suggested that Q represented a genre of 'sayings of the sages' which could be located at the beginning of a 'trajectory' which developed in its treatment of the speaker of the sayings. The speaker, over time, became increasingly associated with the voice of Sophia herself, finally becoming identified with the voice of a gnostic revealer figure. Robinson believes that this trajectory extended from Proverbs through Q and the *Gospel of Thomas* ending in the *Pistis Sophia*. He finds proof of this in the popularity of sayings and dialogue genres in gnostic circles and their disappearance in orthodox circles.[59] Although Robinson's proposal represents a possible progression of traditions, in my opinion many scholars after Robinson,

---

53. Arnal, 'Rhetoric of Marginality,' p. 476.
54. Arnal, 'Rhetoric of Marginality,' pp. 476–477.
55. Arnal, 'Rhetoric of Marginality,' p. 491.
56. Arnal, 'Rhetoric of Marginality,' p. 491.
57. Arnal, 'Rhetoric of Marginality,' pp. 478–479.
58. Arnal, 'Rhetoric of Marginality,' p. 492.
59. J. Robinson, 'LOGOI SOPHON: On the Gattung of Q,' in J. Robinson and H. Koester, *Trajectories through Early Christianity* (Philadelphia: Fortress Press, 1971) pp. 71–113.

including Patterson and Arnal, have been too eager to assume that it is the only or natural one, at least when applied to the *Gospel of Thomas*.[60]

Patterson's and Arnal's theories, although attractive, do not adequately explain the interpretative problems we encounter in *Thomas*. For instance, their assumption that this text has affinities with Gnosticism certainly has had its share of press, but is by no means the best interpretative foil for this gospel as I have argued at great length in a previous monograph.[61] In my view, this interpretative position of scholars has only created a gridlock, hindering our exegetical progress with the *Gospel of Thomas* due to the fact that we have mistaken early Jewish esotericism for so-called 'Gnosticism' and have forced gnostic readings on the text. It is time for scholarship to mature in its previously indiscriminate and easy understanding and application of 'Gnosticism' and its corollaries.[62]

Equally questionable is the reliance on Kloppenberg's hypothetical model of stratification for Q, especially by Patterson. Although I agree that the Two-Source Hypothesis is our best explanation for the literary history of the Synoptic gospels, I am very reluctant to theorize about the nature of particular stratifications of a minimally reconstructed hypothetical document and then to further theorize about their alleged ramifications for understanding the composition of the *Gospel of Thomas*. In my opinion, it is not only better methodologically, but also necessary if we are to develop a compositional history *for the Gospel of Thomas out of the Gospel of Thomas*, to listen to its own voice first.

The Redaction model has moved the discussion about the compositional history of *Thomas* a step forward by providing us with a way to understand the presence of older and newer materials in the text – the earlier traditional material was overlaid with later material from different traditions. For this to work, however, with the diversity and age of the traditions in *Thomas*, the redaction cannot have been minimal as most have argued nor is one redaction enough. In my opinion, a *single* redaction still does not explain sufficiently how and why the traditions, widely diverse in type and age, became part of this single text. Moreover, the Redaction model as it has been formulated reflects too much the modern literate imagination and not enough the ancient oral consciousness. I think

---

60. See, for instance, the work of S. Patterson who summarizes this position in his *The Gospel of Thomas and Jesus* (Sonoma: Polebridge Press, 1993) pp. 17–110; cf. J.S. Kloppenborg, M. Meyer, *et al.*, *Q Thomas Reader* (Sonoma: Polebridge Press, 1990) pp. 93–99.

61. DeConick, *Seek to See Him*, especially pp. 3–39.

62. See my own detailed comments in *Seek to See Him*, especially pp. 3–27. See also, M. William's most recent discussion of the problem of 'Gnosticism' in his *Rethinking 'Gnosticism': An Argument for Dismantling a Dubious Category* (Princeton: Princeton University Press, 1996).

the moment has arrived to set aside our literate imaginations and develop a model that echoes the voices of antiquity.

2.2 *The Rolling Corpus Model (Diagram 4)*

What should this new compositional model look like? I am convinced that first and foremost, this new model must be informed by recent studies in orality and literacy so that it is sensitive to the oral consciousness of antiquity.

2.2.1 *Oral Consciousness*

We must suspend the processes of composition familiar to our own literate minds and try to enter into a process that makes sense within the ancient world where orality was not only the dominant form of transmission and preservation, but also the dominant form of consciousness. Thus, even though Koester's insight into the possible orality behind the text was groundbreaking for its time, it will now become necessary for us to suspend the concept of oral 'background' and replace it with oral consciousness and culture. There was no orality *behind Thomas*. *Thomas* was *orally-derived*. That is, it emerged *as an oral 'text.'*

To date, unlike Q studies,[63] Thomasine studies as far as I am aware have not examined the gospel as an orally-derived 'text' with the exception of an article by V. Robbins which explores the 'oral texture' of the Thomasine question and answer units and their relationship to similar traditions in Q and John.[64] Robbins concludes that the *Gospel of Thomas* 'reveals a status of "orally transmitted resources."' He notes in closing that this gospel 'maintains a focus on speech and hearing rather than writing and written testimony.'[65] He states that, in contrast to the Johannine tradition, the *Gospel of Thomas*

---

63. An excellent collection of articles by Horsley and Draper, *Whoever Hears You Hears Me*, recently has been published investigating the oral derivation of Q. See especially chapters 6, 7, and 8.

64. V. Robbins, 'Rhetorical Composition and Source in the Gospel of Thomas,' *SBL 1997 Seminar Papers*, SBLSP 36 (Atlanta: Scholars Press, 1997) pp. 86–114. R. Uro has published two pieces which discuss orality and *Thomas*. Neither piece attempts to create a hypothesis about *Thomas* as an orally-derived gospel although Uro appears to favor this position with the understanding that this oral culture was 'rhetorical' having scribal aspects too. See his '*Thomas* and Oral Gospel Tradition,' in R. Uro (ed.), *Thomas at the Crossroads: Essays on the Gospel of Thomas* (Edinburgh: T&T Clark, 1998) pp. 8–32; 'Orality and Texuality,' in his book, *Thomas: Seeking the Historical Context of the Gospel of Thomas* (Edinburgh: T&T Clark, 2003) pp. 106–133.

65. Robbins, 'Rhetorical Composition,' p. 102.

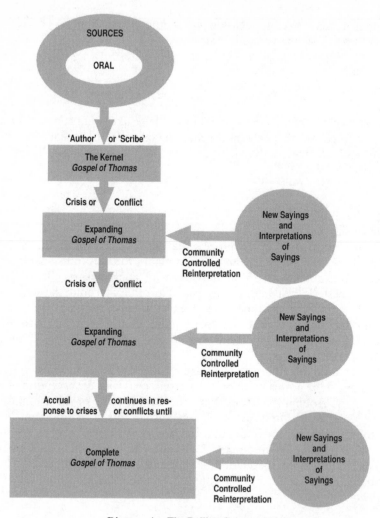

Diagram 4:   The Rolling Corpus Model

exhibits an environment in first century Christianity where followers of Jesus continued to generate questions through a process of oral transmission, rather than turning toward the process of 'scribalizing' the tradition that focused on ancient written testimony...The *Gos. Thom.* maintains a persistent focus on that which was spoken by Jesus, that which disciples spoke to Jesus and to one another, and that which disciples are supposed to speak to others and to themselves.[66]

66.   Robbins, 'Rhetorical Composition,' p. 103.

Robbin's study demonstrates that at least the question and answer pericopes perpetuate 'in an oral manner portions of first-century traditions that were "scribalized" in the Q Sayings Gospel, Mark, Matthew, Luke, and John.'[67]

What does it mean to understand *Thomas* as an orally-derived text? What this means to me is that the 'text' not only mainly developed in the process of oral reperformance, but also that, even when written versions of it may have been scribed, an oral consciousness dominated the process. Saying this, however, does not exclude the possiblity that a new written source may have become available to the community and that elements from it may have accrued in the Kernel, updating this 'original,' or better 'initial,' scribing of the traditions. But I have come to recognize that this accrual more likely took place during a reperformance or a scribing of that reperformance than as a conscious literary redaction.

As I discussed in Chapter 1, the gospel texts we possess were not authored by one person but represent traditions that have developed within the memory of the community. The few references that we do have to the compositional process in early Christian literature tell us that it began with either the transcription of an oral performance or oration, or the remembrance of a performance or oration. Furthermore, we know from these references that the Christians were more confident scribing down their own remembrances than copying written sources because they could guarantee the 'truth' of their memories. Traditions that were scribed down into texts continued to develop as the texts were remembered, read aloud, recited, expounded, exegeted, translated, reinterpreted, and rescribed for various audiences over long periods of time. They moved freely in and out of oral and written formats. Texts that were reperformed by recitation or rewriting were subject to the demands of oral consciousness and display the residue of these mentalities. So it is difficult, if not impossible, to identify the 'original,'[68] although we might recover an 'initial' scribing. In the case of *Thomas*, this is what I call the Kernel *Thomas*.

Let me be clear. I am not saying that ancient people did not rely on written sources in the composition process. Certainly they did. But the ancients did so as much from their memory of having heard or read those sources previously as from having written copies in hand. Also we must remember that they felt a certain skepticism about the accuracy of texts and preferred to rely on oral sources whenever possible. Moreover, when

---

67. Robbins, 'Rhetorical Composition,' p. 103.

68. M. Parry, 'A Comparative Study of Diction as One of the Elements of Style in Early Greek Epic Poetry,' in A. Parry (ed.), *The Making of Homeric Verse: The Collected Papers of Milman Parry* (Oxford: Oxford University Press, 1971) p. 421.

they were referring to, incorporating, or updating written sources, they subjected them to the mental habits and thought processes reflective of a society with an oral consciousness, not a literate one. They privileged 'voice over page.'[69] This brings to mind the words of an Asclepius' devotee who tells us that 'in writing the present book' about Asclepius' miracles, he 'throughout filled in the missing, deleted the superfluous and, though engaged in a rather lengthy narrative,' 'spoke succinctly and told a complicated story in straightforward fashion' (*P. Ent.* 60). Recently, it has been proposed that this oral consciousness influenced even more than the compositional process. To some extent, this oral consciousness even influenced the scribal copying and translation of 'authoritative' texts.[70]

While reading about contemporary theories regarding Rabbinic compilations and their interaction with the oral and aural world, I was struck by the paradigm offered by Martin Jaffee. Although there are striking differences between *Thomas* and the Rabbinic materials, the process that Jaffee described regarding their use and compilation is very similar to that which I am suggesting for *Thomas*. Jaffee regards each Rabbinic compilation as an 'anthological tradition' emerging out of 'related but distinct communal groups in the early Rabbinic world.' These groups draw upon a 'free-text' pool of material known widely from 'the oral-performance tradition' and reshape it in distinctive ways to serve as 'organized curricula.' The resulting tractates become 'fixed' or 'canonized' for the specific community of 'masters and disciples.' They are 'thematically guided anthologies' organized mnemonically to preserve the materials and to serve as 'a point of departure for a return to orality, as the preserved text triggers other literary and conceptual associations drawn from previous experiences in the aural/oral world of Rabbinic instruction.' This means that the 'editorial looseness' of such texts points to their function as a 'text-storage site.' The anthological compilation 'points attention away from itself to a world of speech in which there are no documents, but much discourse.'[71]

In my estimation, the Kernel represents the first attempt to capture in writing materials from the free-text oral pool known to the early Jerusalem-based preachers as part of their oral-performance tradition. As these materials were performed and then recorded, they were organized mnemonically and thematically into speeches of Jesus. When

69. M. Jaffee, 'A Rabbinic Ontology of the Written and Spoken Word: On Discipleship, Transformative Knowledge, and the Living Texts of Oral Torah,' *JAAR* 65 (1997) p. 528.

70. The earliest evidence we have to study this phenonemon is the Qumran material. On this, see R. Person, Jr., *The Deuteronomic School: History, Social Setting, and Literature*, StBL 2 (Atlanta: Society of Biblical Literature, 2002) pp. 77–78.

71. M. Jaffee, 'Oral Tradition in the Writings of Rabbinic Oral Torah: On Theorizing Rabbinic Orality,' *OT* 14 (1999) pp. 25–26.

this was done, they were also reshaped in ways distinctive to the community's memory. Over the next four decades, this Kernel served as the 'storage site' for the materials and was used as the point of departure for the return to orality when the community received instruction from its leaders. The preserved gospel as it was reperformed regularly served as a trigger for additional materials to accrue from other literary texts and from traditions drawn from the oral world when the preacher instructed the community. These accretive materials represent the community's discourse over its shared text. Eventually, the updated gospel was rescribed and became the new 'fixed' text for the community. As a text shaped in this way, it allowed the user of the gospel to encounter what was already familiar in his or her memory, and to anchor the traditions and their interpretations even more fully every time it was performed.

The manuscript remains of the *Gospel of Thomas* certainly show signs of this oral mentality. When we compare the extant manuscripts of *Thomas* (P.Oxy. 1, P.Oxy. 654, P.Oxy. 655, and NHC II,2), we discover that the text exhibits signs of instability on several levels. As in all biblical manuscripts, the Greek and Coptic of *Thomas* exhibit differences in wording in some sayings, differences due to loose translations and scribal error (L. 2, 3, 6, 24, 26, 30, 31, 32, 37, and 39). On another level, we find different combinations of elements, particularly in P.Oxy. 1 (L. 30.1 and 77.2–3).[72] In this case, it is possible that either 30.2–77.1 was deleted from the Greek fragment when it was copied, or that the Coptic text represents a version of *Thomas* which has been expanded with the additions of verses 30.2–77.1 or that the sequence of logia was not stable but shifted during recitations of the text. In my opinion, given the nature of oral performance, the latter is the best option.

The Greek fragments also contain significant elements that are not found in the Coptic text. Of particular interest for our study is P.Oxy. 654 which has several sayings or parts of sayings not present in the Coptic text: '[whoever] knows [himself] will discover this' (lines 16–17); '[and] the last will be first' (lines 25–26); and 'nor buried that [will not be raised]' (line 31). Equally important is the fact that the Coptic contains several sayings or parts of sayings not found in the Greek fragments: 'he will be astonished, and' (L. 2 but not P.Oxy. 654.7–8); 'then you will become known' (L. 3 but not P.Oxy. 654.18); 'and nothing covered will remain without being uncovered' (L. 6 but not P.Oxy. 654.40).

We should also mention the textual problems within the Coptic version itself. For instance, it is clear from the content of L. 6.1 and 14.1–3 that 6.1 (the disciples' questions about certain Jewish practices) originally was

---

72. Cf. K.H. Kuhn, 'Some Observations on the Coptic Gospel According to Thomas,' *Mus* 73 (1960) pp. 317–318.

succeeded by 14.1–3 at one time (Jesus' poignant answer to their questions). At a certain point in *Thomas'* history, L. 6.2 to 13 could have been inserted between the question and answer, breaking up the original unit, or the question could have been separated from the answer during the process of reciting, scribing down or copying the text. It is also possible that the question and answer unit became separated through the process of transmission, perhaps as the result of a flipped leaf of the manuscript being copied out of sequence. Or, given the oral texture of *Thomas*, it is equally likely that the question and answer unit was split by an orator who wished to make a 'new' point about the material.

There is also a *testimonia* from Hippolytus about *Thomas* that suggests that the text was continually being adapted as it fell into the hands of different Christian groups. The Naasenes seem to have transmited a saying similiar to L. 4 which they attributed to 'the Gospel entitled According to Thomas': 'The one who seeks me will find me in children from seven years of age and onwards. For there, hiding in the fourteenth aeon, I am revealed' (Hippolytus, *Ref.* 5.7.20). Clearly, this is a very different version of the Logion we find in the Coptic manuscript (L. 4): 'The old man will not hesitate to ask a little child seven days old about the place of life, and he will live. For many who are first will be last, and they will become single people.'

2.2.2 *Multivalency*

The new compositional model for the *Gospel of Thomas* must not only reflect the fact that the Christians shaped and reshaped their traditions and texts due to the oral consciousness that dominated their world, but must also explain adequately the multivalency of the text: the diverse traditions both in age and content, the variant readings, the doublets, the contradictory content, and the interpretative patina glossing older traditions. Could the wide variety and age of traditions have accumulated in *Thomas* over a period of time in response to shifting constituencies within the community and crises? Could a variant reading be the result of oral reperformance, a predictable consequence of oral transmission? Could a contradictory saying or doublet be an 'updated' version of a saying already present in *Thomas*, perhaps originating from a new source of Jesus' sayings that came into the community's possession or from the oral reperformance of the traditions within the community? Could the interpretative clauses have entered the text at various stages in the life of the community in order to shift the hermeneutic?

A long history of oral-literate composition and performance seems even more likely when we become aware of the fact that the existence of inconsistencies and contradictions in *Thomas* actually is evidence of oral residue as is the stitching together, the supplementation, of newer material to the older. J. Goody notes that literate minds make 'backward scanning' possible so that inconsistencies in a writing can be eliminated.[73] 'With writing,' Ong notes, 'words once "uttered," outered, put down on the surface, can be eliminated, erased, changed. There is no equivalent for this in an oral performance, no way to erase a spoken word: *corrections do not remove an infelicity or an error, they merely supplement it with denial or patchwork'* (italics mine).[74]

2.2.3 *Structure*

A compositional process involving oral performance also helps to explain the rhetorical stacking of some of *Thomas'* sayings to make arguments or *chreia*[75] as well as the patchwork structure of the sayings tied together by catchwords and repetitive formulaic phrases such as 'Jesus said,' 'the Living One,' 'shall not taste death,' and 'the world does not deserve.' Such structures are common for texts that display a large amount of oral residue since characteristics of orally-based thought and expression are addictive, aggregative, and redundant.[76]

There has been some discussion in recent years about accumulative catchword texts that began with oral recitations of the words of a prophet. William McKane, in his commentary on Jeremiah, explains this type of compositional history of Jeremiah in terms of a 'rolling *corpus*.'[77] According to his study, a rolling corpus is a book that begins with the *ipsissima verba* of a prophet. Over time, additional material becomes aggregated and organized in relation to the core. These new materials often serve to interpret, explain, or update the Kernel. In the case of prophetic words, old and new words of the prophet are strung together by a reservoir of vocabulary that has 'triggered' or 'generated' the new material. Thus the Kernel can function as a 'reservoir' for the additional material.

Furthermore, McKane argues that in Jeremiah we are dealing with 'a complicated, untidy accumulation of material, extending over a very long

---

73. J. Goody, *The Domestication of the Savage Mind* (Cambridge: Cambridge University Press, 1977) pp. 49–50, and 128.

74. Ong, *Orality and Literacy*, p. 104.

75. V.K. Robbins, 'Enthumemic Texture in the Gospel of Thomas,' *SBL Seminar Papers 1998*, SBLSP 37 (Atlanta: Scholars Press, 1998) pp. 343–366; see also J.A. Asgeirsson, 'Arguments and Audience(s) in the Gospel of Thomas (Part One),' *SBL Seminar Papers 1997*, SBLSP 36 (Atlanta: Scholar's Press, 1997) pp. 47–85; J.A. Asgeirsson, 'Arguments and Audience(s) in the Gospel of Thomas (Part II),' *SBL Seminar Papers 1998*, SBLSP 37 (Atlanta: Scholars Press, 1998) pp. 325–342.

76. Ong, *Orality and Literacy*, pp. 36–41.

77. W. McKane, *A Critical and Exegetical Commentary on Jeremiah*, The International Critical Commentary, volume 1 (Edinburgh: T&T Clark, 1986) pp. xlix–xcix.

period and to which many people have contributed.'[78] He warns that scholars too often invest the so-called editor with an editorial policy that is thoughtful and systematic, wanting to determine 'the contours of his mind.'[79] When they do this, they only force their own interpretations of the prose to be amenable to their hypothesis.[80] I might add that McKane in his earlier commentary on Proverbs (a text that he understands to be 'a reinterpretation of the vocabulary of old wisdom') concludes that collections of sentence literature do not show a 'coherence of theme or consistency of artistic intention' because of the manner in which sentence literature is compiled over time.[81] He notes that in Proverbs bribery is both recommended (17.8; 18.16; 21.14) and condemned (15.27; 17.23) in different sentences. 'If this is not evidence of reinterpretation,' he states, 'it is at least irreconcilable with the view that all of the material in Proverbs can be accommodated within a single theological structure or unitary ethos.'[82]

So what if the compositional history of the *Gospel of Thomas* was that of a rolling corpus rather than a statically-authored or singly-redacted document? What if this gospel is not a book of sayings written down at one moment in history and does not represent a consistent theology from the authored moment? What if the *Gospel of Thomas* is a collection of sayings that grew over time, 'beginning' as a simple written gospel containing oracles of the prophet Jesus? Could this initial gospel have 'originated' when a Christian transcribed some of the 'speeches' of Jesus from memory or during recitation such as the stories about Peter and Clement relate? Is it likely that as new needs arose in the community, additional sayings would have accrued in this collection in order to address these needs? Is it not reasonable to assume that as new converts joined the community, they would have brought with them new ideas, interpretations, traditions and even Jesus sayings which they might have heard from Christians in other communities or from wandering prophets?

Such a new paradigm of reading *Thomas* would mean that the sayings in the *Gospel of Thomas* represent different moments in its history and might be read as memoirs of practices and conflicts which arose over time *within* the community. Such an aggregate text likely was the result of the recitation and exposition of the traditions during community gatherings when the written speeches of Jesus were orally reperformed. We can imagine that the developing traditions were rescribed at crucial moments in

---

78. McKane, *Jeremiah*, p. xlvii.
79. McKane, *Jeremiah*, p. xlix.
80. McKane, *Jeremiah*, p. xlix.
81. W. McKane, *Proverbs, A New Approach*, The Old Testament Library (Philadelphia: The Westminster Press, 1977) pp. 19 and 10 respectively.
82. McKane, *Proverbs*, p. 18.

the history of the community when members feared the loss of their traditions or when pressure within the group demanded significant reinterpretation. The 'version' that we know as the extant *Gospel of Thomas* would represent a late scribing of one of these recitations or a memory of it, a version which then was transmitted and translated by scribal hands into the Greek and Coptic copies we possess.

How is it possible to read the *Gospel of Thomas* in this manner? How are we able to distinguish between earlier and later sayings? How do we determine the various conflicts that this community endured and the responses that it might have made to these conflicts? How can we map its theological developments or interpretative shifts? All of these are tough questions, but not impossible to answer, I would wager, if we are willing to reapproach this gospel from the new *traditionsgeschichtliche* perspective.

Chapter 3

THE ROLLING *GOSPEL OF THOMAS*

Memory is the gathering of thought. ~ *M. Heidegger*

Since I understand *Thomas* to be an aggregate text, an accumulation of traditions and their interpretations, I understand it to contain old core traditions to which additional material accrued over time. The newer materials were organized in relation to old core sayings, serving to interpret, explain, and update the core. The agglutinative process through which the *Gospel of Thomas* evolved was a process within the oral registry. The traditions were not *mainly* developed by a redactor with a pen in hand. Rather, the oral *and* written traditions which they collected were gathered and adapted *mainly* in the process of the oral reperformance and recreation of the words of Jesus over the entire life of the community – a community that experienced shifts in its membership, memories, and ideologies, a community in dialogue with and connected to the memories of other communities. In other words, the text appears to have started as a small written gospel of oracles of the prophet Jesus, the Kernel *Thomas*. This 'original' or initial scribing of the traditions was reperformed and recreated over time by different constituencies for different presents. It was a text that was always subject to oral consciousness, even when it moved in and out of written formats. Our extant *Gospel of Thomas* is the *end result* of this lengthy process.

3.1 *Principle of Development*

What was the nature of the earliest traditions collected in the first speech gospels? The Form Critics have argued for simple sayings of Jesus and short narratives.[1] On this point, the Form Critics had insight, since ancient writers like Clement tell us that he listened to Peter's exposition of Jesus' teachings – that is, Jesus' words and his instructions – and afterwards compiled them in writing so that they would be 'read' to proselytites and

---

1. R. Bultmann, *Form Criticism: Two Essays on New Testament Research* (trans. by F.C. Grant; New York: Harper and Row, 1934, 1962) p. 25.

interpreted orally by the preacher (*Rec.* 1.17–23). The contents of *Thomas*, our only extant speech gospel, affirm this, consisting of simple sentences and brief discourses. *Thomas'* sentence types include proverbs, parables, apocalyptic logia, and nomistic sayings. Its brief discourses have a narrative quality in that they are short speech blocks in which Jesus responds directly to a question or situation with sage advice.

So how is it possible in *Thomas* to distinguish earlier sayings and discourses from later sayings and discourses? How are the later accretions identified and separated from the older Kernel sayings? The elementary starting point for the task seems to me the identification and examination of the materials in *Thomas* considered revisions or expansions by identifying those areas in the *Gospel of Thomas* where we see obvious development of the traditions. Such accretive developments are noted because they represent reflective changes to the older traditional material: when interpretative clauses are appended to older sentences; when sentences of Jesus have been reshaped into *rhetorical* question and answer units; and when sayings have been reperformed as *retrospective* dialogues. The accretive discourses can be differentiated from the older Thomasine discourses in which the question posed to Jesus or the situation recounted appear integral to Jesus' response rather than rhetorical, and in which they do *not* reflect interests common to later Christianity. Once these accretive clauses and discourses are identified, they can be examined in order to further identify vocabulary and themes characteristic of the accretive material. Only after the characteristic vocabulary and themes have been demarcated, can they be used to expose additional accretions by searching the remaining logia for coherence to the cited vocabulary and themes. Finally, the logia that remain must be examined for references that are anachronistic to the first Christians and are representative of later Christian thought and practices. Such references are more likely accretions than not, so they are delineated as such. The remaining logia are the oldest sayings, the sayings which likely were contained in the Kernel.

3.1.1 *Development of Discourses*

What happens to traditions as they are transmitted in a culture dominated by oral consciousness and modes of transmission which rely almost exclusively on memory but are controlled by the community? We learned in Chapter 1.7 that traditions are developed during their performance by the orator who remodels the material in light of contemporary details and interpretations, even to the point of introducing new material into the older version he learned from his teacher. In the history of the Thomasine traditions, we can see this remodeling most succinctly in the discourse material where, posed to Jesus, are questions quite anachronistic to the first years of Christianity but quite contemporary to the later years of early

Christianity. When intense study is made of these discourse units, it appears that someone familiar with older sentences of Jesus has secondarily developed them into dialogues and elaborate question and answer units between Jesus and his disciples. The purpose of these rhetorical flourishes appears to have been to enrich the meaning of the traditions for the present community, aligning them with the contemporary memory of the community by providing sayings with new contexts and interpretations. In this way, perplexing questions posed within the community could be answered by Jesus himself. Polemic for opposing views could be supported by Jesus' words. Instruction about emerging ideas and practices could be addressed with Jesus' voice. The old traditions were made contemporary and, in the process, were sanctioned by Jesus.

So the questions that the disciples pose are invariably the questions that the community has raised and seeks to resolve. The dialogues between Jesus and his disciples are constructed to force new meaning or significance on the traditional material and highlight communal concerns. In the *Gospel of Thomas*, these developments are found in L. 6.1/14.1–3, 12, 13, 18, 20, 21.1–4, 37, 43, 51, 52, 53, 60, 61.2–5, 91, 113, and 114. It is possible that an earlier version of one of these logia may have been original to the Kernel gospel and that it was significantly modified at a later date so that the earlier saying cannot be recovered. For instance, some early form of a parable about a Samaritan sacrificing a lamb in Judea might have been in the Kernel gospel, but it has been so altered in the process of constructing the later dialogue that it is unrecoverable if, indeed, it was original to the gospel in the first place (L. 60).

In most cases, the identified unit in its entirety should be considered *secondary*, especially when it functions as a tight unit of explanatory material and when the saying itself is anachronistic or mirrors the interests and ideologies of later Christians (L. 6.1/14.1–3, 12, 13, 18, 21.1–4, 37, 43, 51, 52, 53, 60, 61.2–5, 113, 114). In three cases, however, a *secondary introductory clause* seems to have been added to the old Kernel saying since the saying itself does not appear to reflect later Christian interests. This rhetorical decision would have preserved the general integrity of the Kernel saying (L. 20.2–4, 24.2–3, 91.2) while emphasizing a particular concern of the community with the leading question or clause (L. 20.1, 24.1, 91.1). In the case of L. 24, the question that the disciples pose causes the following saying to be read in a way that goes beyond the scope of the original saying entirely. In other words, the disjuncture between the introductory clause and the successive saying in L. 24 is so great that it is best to conclude that the introductory clause entered the text or was moved into that sequence sometime after the saying itself.

3.1.1.1 *Question and Answer Units*

(Kernel text in regular type; *accretions in italics*)

(6) [1]*((His disciples questioned him and said, 'How should we fast? How should we pray? How should we give alms? What diet should we observe?))'*

(14) [1]*Jesus said to them, 'If you fast, you will generate sin for yourselves.* [2]*And if you pray, you will be condemned.* [3]*And if you give alms, you will harm <<yourselves>>.'*

(12) [1]*The disciples said to Jesus, 'We know that you are going to leave us. Who will be our leader?'*
[2]*Jesus said to them, 'No matter where you came from, you should go to James the Righteous One, for whose sake heaven and earth exist.'*

(18) [1]*The disciples said to Jesus, 'Tell us, how will our end come about?'*
[2]*Jesus said, 'Have you discovered the beginning that you seek the end? Because where the beginning is, the end will be also.* [3]*Whoever will stand in the beginning is blessed. This person will know the end, yet will not die.'*

(20) [1]*The disciples said to Jesus, 'Tell us, what is the Kingdom of Heaven like?'*
[2]He said to them, 'It is like a mustard seed, [2]smaller than all seeds. [4]But when it falls on cultivated soil, it puts forth a large branch and becomes a shelter for birds of the sky.'

(21) [1]*Mary said to Jesus, 'Whom are your disciples like?'*
He said, 'They are like little children sojourning in a field that is not theirs. When the owners of the field come, they will say, "Leave our field!" In front of them, they strip naked in order to abandon it, returning their field to them.'

(24) [1]*His disciples said, 'Teach us about the place where you are, because we must seek it.'*
[2]He said to them, 'Whoever has ears should listen! [3]There is light inside a person of light. And it lights up the whole world. If it does not shine, it is dark.'

(37) [1]*His disciples said, 'When will you appear to us? When will we see you?'*
[2]*Jesus said, 'When you strip naked without shame, take your garments, put them under your feet like little children, and trample on them.* [3]*Then [you will see] the Son of the Living One and you will not be afraid.'*

(43) [1]*His disciples said to him, 'Who are you to say these things to us?'*
[2]*'From what I say to you, you do not know who I am.* [3]*Rather, you are like the Jews, for they love the tree (but) hate its fruit, or they love the fruit (but) hate the tree.'*

(51) [1]*His disciples said to him, 'When will the dead rest, and when will the new world come?'*

[2]He said to them, 'What you look for has come, but you have not perceived it.'

(52)   *[1]His disciples said to him, 'Twenty-four prophets have spoken in Israel, and all of them have spoken about you.'*

[2]He said to them, 'You have left out the Living One who is in your presence and you have spoken about the dead.'

(53)   *[1]His disciples said to him, 'Is circumcision advantageous or not?'*

[2]He said to them, 'If it were advantageous, the father (of the children) would conceive them in their mother already circumcised. [3]Rather circumcision in the spirit is true (circumcision). This person has procured all of the advantage.'

(91)   *[1]They said to him, 'Tell us so that we may believe in you! Who are you?'*

[2]He said to them, 'You examine the appearance of the sky and the earth, but, he who is in your midst, you do not understand. Nor this critical time! you do not understand how to examine it.'

(113)   *[1]His disciples said to him, 'When will the Kingdom come?'*

[2]'It will not come by waiting. [3]It will not be said, "Look! Here it is!" or "Look! There it is!" [4]Rather, the Kingdom of the Father is spread out over the earth, but people do not see it.'

3.1.1.2 *Dialogues*

(Kernel text in regular type; *accretions in italics*)

(13)   *[1]Jesus said to his disciples, 'Speculate about me. Tell me, who am I like?'*

[2]Simon Peter said to him, 'You are like a righteous angel.'

[3]Matthew said to him, 'You are like a sage, a temperate person.'

[4]Thomas said to him, 'Master, my mouth cannot attempt at all to say whom you are like.'

[5]Jesus said, 'I am not your master. After you drank, you became intoxicated from the bubbling fount which I had measured out.'

[6]And he took him and retreated. He told him three words.

[7]Then, when Thomas returned to his friends, they asked him, 'What did Jesus say to you?'

[8]Thomas said to them, 'If I tell you one of the words which he told me, you will pick up stones and throw them at me. Then fire will come out of the stones and burn you up.'

(22)   *[1]Jesus saw little babies nursing. [2]He said to his disciples, 'These little ones nursing are like those who enter the Kingdom.'*

[3]They said to him, 'Will we enter the Kingdom as little babies?'

[4]Jesus said to them, 'When you make the two one, and when you make the inside like the outside, and the outside like the inside, and the above like the below. [5]And when you make the male and the female into a single being, with the result that the male is not male nor the female female. [6]When you make eyes in place of an eye, and

a hand in place of a hand, and a foot in place of a foot, and an image in place of an image, ⁷then you will enter the Kingdom.'

(60)   *¹A Samaritan <<was carrying>> a lamb as he traveled to Judea. ²He said to his disciples, 'That man is holding the lamb.'*

³They said to him, '(He is holding the lamb) so that he may slaughter it and eat it.'

⁴He said to them, 'While it is alive, he will not eat it. Rather, (he will eat the lamb) after he has slaughtered it and it is carcass.'

⁵They said, 'He is not permitted to do it any other way.'

⁶He said to them, 'Moreover, so that you will not become a carcass and be eaten, seek for yourselves a place within rest!'

(61)   *²Salome said, 'Who are you, sir? That is, from [[whom]]? You have reclined on my couch and eaten at my table.'*

³Jesus said to her, 'I am he who comes from the one who is an equal. I was given some who belong to my Father.'

⁴'I am your disciple.'

⁵'Therefore I say, when a person becomes [[equal]] (with me), he will be filled with light. But if he becomes separated (from me), he will be filled with darkness.'

(114)   *¹Simon Peter said to them, 'Mary should leave us because women do not deserve life.'*

²Jesus said, 'Look, I myself will <<guide>> her in order to make her male, so that she too may become a living spirit – male, resembling you. For every woman who will make herself male will enter the Kingdom of Heaven.'

3.1.2 *Formation of Interpretative Clauses*

Another signal of secondary development in the sayings tradition are phrases that the community has added to the old sayings as interpretative clauses. These clauses are identified in the text by observing abrupt changes in the structure of the saying or subject. Most often, the subject change will reflect interests, theological or otherwise, developed and promoted by later Christians. Where possible, comparative analysis with parallels in the sayings tradition aids the identification of these secondary clauses. The clauses most frequently occur as introductions to the old sayings or conclusions.

As Christianity developed, a saying often was updated in this way when its 'original' meaning began losing favor or was in need of clarification. Developing theologies and interests could be accommodated to the tradition of sayings quite easily with these additional clauses. By embellishing a traditional saying with an interpretative clause, the community's most recent position on the subject could be taken into account. At the same time, this new position would be given Jesus' personal stamp of approval. Not surprisingly, in all the cases where this occurs in *Thomas* (4.3, 16.4, 21.6–8, 23.2, 38.2, 44.1, 46.2b, 64.2, 68.2,

100.4, and 111.2–3), the *interpretative clause* represents Christian traditions that developed post-50 CE while the 'original' saying necessarily does not.

3.1.2.1 *Sayings with Interpretative Clauses*

(Kernel text in regular type; *accretions in italics*)

(4)   ²'For many who are first will be last, ³((and the last will be first,)) *⁴and they will become single people.*'

(16)   ¹Jesus said, 'Perhaps people think it is peace that I have come to cast upon the world. ²And they do not know it is division that I have come to cast upon the earth – fire, sword, war! ³For there will be five people in a house. There will be three people against two, and two against three, father against son, and son against father. *⁴And they will stand as celibate people.*'

(21)   ⁵'*For this reason I say,* 'If the owner of a house knows that a thief is coming, he will keep watch before he arrives. He will not allow him to break into his house, part of his estate, to steal his furnishings. ⁶*You, then, keep watch against the world.* ⁷*Arm yourselves with great strength so that the robbers do not find a way to come to you,* ⁸*because the possessions you are looking after, they will find.* ⁹*There ought to be a wise person among you!*'

(23)   ¹Jesus said, 'I will select you, one from a thousand, and two from ten thousand. ² *And they will stand as single people.*'

(38)   ¹Jesus said, 'The words that I am speaking to you, often you have longed to hear them. And you have no other person from whom to hear them. ²*There will be days when you will seek me, (but) will not find me.*'

(44)   ¹Jesus said, '*Whoever blasphemes against the Father will be forgiven,* ²*and* whoever blasphemes against the Son will be forgiven. ³But whoever blasphemes against the Holy Spirit will not be forgiven, neither on earth nor in heaven.'

(46)   ¹Jesus said, 'From Adam to John the Baptist, no one among those born of women is more exalted than John the Baptist that the person's gaze should not be deferent. ² Yet I have said, "Whoever from among you will become a child, *this person will know the Kingdom* and he will be more exalted than John."'

(64)   ¹Jesus said, 'A man had guests. When he had prepared the dinner, he sent his servant to invite the guests.
²He went to the first person. He said to him, "My master invites you."
³He said, "I have some payments for some merchants. They are coming to me this evening. I must go and give them instructions. I decline the dinner."
⁴He went to another person. He said to him, "My master has invited you."

[5]He said to him, "I have purchased a house and they have requested me for the day. I will not have time."

[6]He went to another person. He said to him, "My master invites you."

[7]He said to him, "My friend is going to be wed and I am the person who will be preparing the meal. I will not be able to come. I decline the dinner."

[8]He went to another person. He said to him, "My master invites you."

[9]He said to him, "I have purchased a villa. Since I am going to collect the rent, I will not be able to come. I decline."

[10]The servant left. He said to his master, "The people whom you invited to the dinner have declined."

[11]The master said to his servant, "Go outside on the streets. The people you find, bring them to dine."

[12]*Buyers and merchants [will] not enter the places of my Father.'*

(68) [1]Jesus said, 'Blessed are you when you are hated and persecuted.' [2]*[[A place will be found, where you will not be persecuted]].'*

(100) [1]They showed Jesus a gold coin and said to him, 'Caesar's men extort taxes from us.'

[2]He said to them, 'Give to Caesar, what is Caesar's. [3]Give to God what is God's. [4]*And what is mine, give me.'*

(111) [1]Jesus said, 'The heavens and the earth will roll up in your presence. [2]*And whoever is alive because of the Living One will not see death. [3]Does not Jesus say, "The world does not deserve the person who has found himself"?'*

3.1.3 *Coherence to Characteristic Vocabulary*

Once the secondary accretions are identified on the basis of the development of discourse material and the formation of interpretative clauses, it is possible to examine these accretions for characteristic vocabulary. Across these accretions, several characteristic words and phrases emerge.

3.1.3.1 *Characteristic Vocabulary*

1.   ⲉⲧⲟⲛϩ: The title, 'Living One' (ⲡⲉⲧⲟⲛϩ), used as a name of God or used as a cognate designation for the believer, 'the one who is alive' (ⲡⲉⲧⲟⲛϩ) (L. 37, 52, 111.2, 114.2).

2.   ⲙⲟⲛⲁⲭⲟⲥ, ⲟⲩⲁ ⲟⲩⲱⲧ: The expressions ⲙⲟⲛⲁⲭⲟⲥ and ⲟⲩⲁ ⲟⲩⲱⲧ applied to the ideal follower of Jesus (L. 4.4, 16.4, 22.5, 23.2).

3.   ⲱϩⲉ ⲉⲣⲁⲧ: The description of the ideal follower of Jesus as 'standing' (ⲱϩⲉ ⲉⲣⲁⲧ) (L. 16.4, 18.3, 23.2).

4.   ⲱⲏⲣⲉ ⲱⲏⲙ, ⲕⲟⲩⲉⲓ, ⲕⲟⲩⲉⲓ ⲛ̄ⲱⲏⲣⲉ ⲱⲏⲙ: The description of the ideal follower of Jesus as a 'little child' in sayings with encratic tendencies

(ϢΗΡЄ ϢΗΜ or ΚΟΥЄΙ or ΚΟΥЄΙ ÑϢΗΡЄ ϢΗΜ) (L. 21.2, 22.1–3, 37.2).

5.   ΝΑΧΙ †ΠЄ ΑΝ Ñ̄ΜΟΥ: The soteriological expression, 'will not taste death' (ΝΑΧΙ †ΠЄ ΑΝ Ñ̄ΜΟΥ) or 'will not see death' (ΝΑΝΑΥ ΑΝ ЄΜΟΥ) (L. 18.3, 111.2).

6.   ΠΚΟΣΜΟΣ ΜΠϢΑ Ñ̄ΜΟϤ ΑΝ: The expression 'the world does not deserve' (L. 111.3).

7.   ΣΟΥϢΝ: The expression, 'to know,' used as a soteriological category (L. 18.3, 46.2b).

3.1.3.2 *Sayings that Cohere to Characteristic Vocabulary*

Any of the sayings in *Thomas* that were not determined secondary on the grounds of development of discourses or formation of interpretative clauses but that also employ the *characteristic vocabulary* just outlined become very suspect. It is more reasonable than not to conclude that they are also secondary accretions, reflecting theology that developed later in the community, accruing in the gospel with its sister material. Therefore, the following sayings are considered to be *late accretions* too: Incipit, L. 1, 3.4, 3.5, 4.1, 11.2–4, 19, 49, 50, 56, 59, 67, 69.1, 75, 80, 85, 111.2. In many cases, the saying exhibits signs of belonging to more than one category (L. 3.5 [3 categories]; 4.1 [2 categories]; 19 [2 categories]; 56 [2 categories]; 80 [2 categories]; 85 [2 categories]).

> 1. ЄΤΟΝ𝟤
> (Incipit) *((These are the secret words that the Living Jesus spoke and that Judas Thomas wrote down))*.
>
> (3.5)   [5]*((And when you know yourselves, you will understand that you are the children of the Living Father. But if you will not know yourselves, you live in poverty and you are poverty))*.
>
> (4.1)   [1]*Jesus said, 'The old man will not hesitate to ask a little child seven days old about the place of life, and he will live.'*
>
> (11.2–4)   [2]*'And the dead are not alive, and the living will not die.* [3]*In the days when you ate what is dead, you made it something living. When you are in the light, what will you become?* [4]*On the day when you were one, you became two. When you are two, what will you become?'*
>
> (50)   [1]*Jesus said, 'If they say to you, "Where did you come from?", say to them, "We came from the light" – the place where the light came into being on its own accord and established [itself] and became manifest through their image.* [2]*If they say to you, "Is it you?", say "We are its children, and we are the chosen people of the living Father."* [3]*If they ask you, "What is the sign of your Father in you?", say to them, "It is movement and rest."'*
>
> (59)   *Jesus said, 'Gaze upon the Living One while you are alive, in case you die and (then) seek to see him, and you will not be able to see (him).'*

2. ΜΟΝΑΧΟΣ, ΟΥΑ ΟΥѠΤ

(49) [1]*Jesus said, 'Blessed are the celibate people, the chosen ones, because you will find the Kingdom.* [2]*For you are from it. You will return there again.'*

(75) *Jesus said, 'Many people are standing at the door, but those who are celibate are the people who will enter the bridal chamber.'*

3. ѠϨЄ ЄΡΑΤ

No additional accretions identified.

4. ѰΗΡЄ ѰΗΜ, ΚΟΥЄΙ, ΚΟΥЄΙ Ν̄ѰΗΡЄ ѰΗΜ

(3.5) [5]*((And when you know yourselves, you will understand that you are the children of the Living Father. But if you will not know yourselves, you live in poverty and you are poverty)).*

(4.1) [1]*Jesus said, 'The old man will not hesitate to ask a little child seven days old about the place of life, and he will live.'*

5. ΝΑϪΙ †ΠЄ ΑΝ Μ̄ΜΟΥ

(1) *And he said, 'Whoever finds the meaning of these words will not die.'*

(19) [1]*Jesus said, 'Whoever existed before being born is blessed.* [2]*If you become my disciples and listen to my teachings, these stones will support you.* [3]*For you, there are five trees in Paradise. They do not change, summer and winter, and their leaves do not fall. Whoever knows them will not die.'*

(85) [1]*Jesus said, 'Adam came into being out of a great power and great wealth. But he was not deserving of you.* [2]*For, had he been deserving, [he would] not [have] died.'*

6. ΠΚΟΣΜΟΣ ΜΠѰΑ Μ̄ΜΟϤ ΑΝ

(56) [1]*Jesus said, 'Whoever has come to know the world has found a corpse.* [2]*The world does not deserve the person who has found (that the world is) a corpse.'*

(80) [1]*Jesus said, 'Whoever has come to know the world has found the corpse.* [2]*The world does not deserve the person who has found (that the world is) the corpse.'*

(85) [1]*Jesus said, 'Adam came into being out of a great power and great wealth. But he was not deserving of you.* [2]*For, had he been deserving, [he would] not [have] died.'*

7. ΣΟΥѠΝ

(3.4–5) [4]*'((Whoever knows himself will find it.* [5]*And when you know yourselves, you will understand that you are the children of the Living Father. But if you will not know yourselves, you live in poverty and you are poverty)).'*

(19) [1]*Jesus said, 'Whoever existed before being born is blessed.* [2]*If you become my disciples and listen to my teachings, these stones will*

support you. [3]*For you, there are five trees in Paradise. They do not change, summer and winter, and their leaves do not fall. Whoever knows them will not die.'*

(56)   [1]*Jesus said, 'Whoever has come to know the world has found a corpse.* [2]*The world does not deserve the person who has found (that the world is) a corpse.'*

(67)   *Jesus said, 'Whoever knows everything, but needs (to know) himself, is in need of everything.'*

(69.1) [1]*'Blessed are those who have been persecuted in their hearts. They are the people who truly have known the Father.'*

(80)   [1]*Jesus said, 'Whoever has come to know the world has found the corpse.* [2]*The world does not deserve the person who has found (that the world is) the corpse.'*

3.1.4 *Coherence to Characteristic Themes*
Similarly, the material that has been developed into discourses and interpretative clauses can be studied in order to identify themes characteristic to the accretions. Three obvious themes present themselves.

3.1.4.1 *Characteristic Themes*
1. ***Speculation about the primordial Adam:*** An exegetical tradition of the Genesis story in which salvation is understood to be the return to Paradise and Adam's primordial condition before the division of the sexes (L. 16.4, 18, 22, 23.2, 37, 114). Words and phrases that characterize this exegetical tradition include some already identified (ⲙⲟⲛⲁⲭⲟⲥ and ⲟⲩⲁ ⲟⲩⲱⲧ, ϣⲏⲣⲉ ϣⲏⲙ or ⲕⲟⲩⲉⲓ or ⲕⲟⲩⲉⲓ ⲛ̄ϣⲏⲣⲉ ϣⲏⲙ). Also 'standing in the beginning' (ⲱϩⲉ ⲉⲣⲁⲧϥ ϩⲛ̄ ⲧⲁⲣⲭⲏ) (L. 18), 'undressing' (ⲕⲁⲕ or ⲕⲉⲕ) (L. 21, 37), 'making the two one' (ⲣ̄-ⲡⲥⲛⲁⲩ ⲟⲩⲁ) (L. 22), 'making the male and female one and the same' (ⲉⲓⲣⲉ ⲙ̄ⲫⲟⲟⲩⲧ ⲙⲛ̄ ⲧⲥϩⲓⲙⲉ ⲙ̄ⲡⲓⲟⲩⲁ ⲟⲩⲱⲧ) (L. 22), 'fashioning an image in place of an image' (ⲟⲩϩⲓⲕⲱⲛ ⲉⲡⲙⲁ ⲛ̄ⲟⲩϩⲓⲕⲱⲛ) (L. 22), 'making male' (ⲉⲓⲣⲉ ⲛ̄ϩⲟⲟⲩⲧ) (L. 114).

2. ***Disdain for the world and admiration for the divine Self:*** A disdain for this world over and against an admiration of the internalized divine Self and its discovery. The world must be guarded against (ⲣⲟⲉⲓⲥ ϩⲁ ⲧⲉϩⲏ ⲙ̄ⲡⲕⲟⲥⲙⲟⲥ) (L. 21.6) and 'is not worthy of the one who has found his Self' (ⲡⲉⲧⲁϩⲉ ⲉⲣⲟϥ ⲟⲩⲁⲁϥ ⲡⲕⲟⲥⲙⲟⲥ ⲙ̄ⲡϣⲁ ⲙ̄ⲙⲟϥ ⲁⲛ) (L. 111.3).

3. ***Belief that the Kingdom is fully established on earth:*** Expressed in L. 113 as 'spread out upon the earth' (ⲡⲟⲣϣ ⲉⲃⲟⲗ ϩⲓⲭⲙ̄ ⲡⲕⲁϩ).

3.1.4.2 *Sayings that Cohere to Characteristic Themes*
Additional sayings that reference one of these three characteristic themes are viewed with considerable skepticism. It is more plausible to consider

them secondary accretions, reflecting themes that were developed by the later community and accruing in the gospel with its sister material. Based on thematic coherence, the following sayings are considered to be *late accretions* too: L. 3.1–3, 3.4–5, 4.1, 7, 11.2–4, 19, 27, 29, 56, 67, 69.1, 70, 80, 83, 84, 85, 87, 106, 110, and 112. In many cases, the accretion exhibits signs of belonging to more than one vocabulary or thematic category (L. 3.4 [2 categories]; 3.5 [4 categories]; 4.1 [3 categories]; 11.2–4 [2 categories]; 19 [3 categories]; 56 [3 categories]; 67 [2 categories]; 69.1 [2 categories]; 80 [3 categories]; 83 [2 categories]; 84 [2 categories]; 85 [3 categories]).

1. *Speculation about the primordial Adam*

(4.1) [1]*Jesus said, 'The old man will not hesitate to ask a little child seven days old about the place of life, and he will live.'*

(11.2–4) [2]*'But the dead are not alive, and the living will not die.* [3]*In the days when you ate what is dead, you made it something living. When you are in the light, what will you become?* [4]*On the day when you were one, you became two. When you are two, what will you become?'*

(19) [1]*Jesus said, 'Whoever existed before being born is blessed.* [2]*If you become my disciples and listen to my teachings, these stones will support you.* [3]*For you, there are five trees in Paradise. They do not change, summer and winter, and their leaves do not fall. Whoever knows them will not die.'*

(83) [1]*Jesus said, 'The images are visible to people, but the light in them is concealed in the image of the Father's light.* [2]*The light will be revealed, but his image is concealed by his light.'*

(84) [1]*Jesus said, 'When you see the likeness of yourselves, you are delighted.* [2]*But when you see the images of yourselves which came into being before you – they neither die nor are visible – how much you will suffer!'*

(85) [1]*Jesus said, 'Adam came into being out of a great power and great wealth. But he was not deserving of you.* [2]*For, had he been deserving, [he would] not [have] died.'*

(106) [1]*Jesus said, 'When you make the two one, you will become children of Man.* [2]*And when you say, "Mountain, go forth!" it will move.'*

2. *Disdain for the world and admiration for the divine Self*

(3.4–5) [4]*((Whoever knows himself will find it.* [5]*And when you know yourselves, you will understand that you are the children of the Living Father. But if you will not know yourselves, you live in poverty and you are poverty)).'*

(7) [1]*Jesus said, 'Blessed is the lion that the human will eat, and the lion becomes human.* [2]*And cursed is the human who the lion eats, [[and the human becomes a lion]].'*

(27) [1]*((Jesus said)), 'If you do not fast from the world, you will not find the Kingdom.'*

(29) [1]*Jesus said, 'It would be a miracle if the flesh existed for the sake of*

the Spirit. [2]*It would be a miracle of miracles if the Spirit (existed) for the sake of the body!* [3]*Nevertheless, I marvel at how this great wealth settled in this poverty.'*

(56)   [1]*Jesus said, 'Whoever has come to know the world has found a corpse.* [2]*The world does not deserve the person who has found (that the world is) a corpse.'*

(67)   *Jesus said, 'Whoever knows everything, but needs (to know) himself, is in need of everything.'*

(69.1)   [1]*'Blessed are those who have been persecuted in their hearts. They are the people who truly have known the Father.'*

(70)   [1]*Jesus said, 'When you become what is within you, what is within you will save you.* [2]*If you do not have it within you, what you do not have within you will kill you.'*

(80)   [1]*Jesus said, 'Whoever has come to know the world has found the corpse.* [2]*The world does not deserve the person who has found (that the world is) the corpse.'*

(83)   [1]*Jesus said, 'The images are visible to people, but the light in them is concealed in the image of the Father's light.* [2]*The light will be revealed, but his image is concealed by his light.'*

(84)   [1]*Jesus said, 'When you see the likeness of yourselves, you are delighted.* [2]*But when you see the images of yourselves which came into being before you – they neither die nor are visible – how much you will suffer!'*

(87)   [1]*Jesus said, 'Miserable is the body, which is crucified by a body.* [2]*Miserable is the soul, which is crucified by these together.'*

(110)   *Jesus said, 'Whoever has found the world and become wealthy, he should disown the world.'*

(112)   [1]*Jesus said, 'Woe to the flesh, which is crucified by the soul.* [2]*Woe to the soul, which is crucified by the flesh.'*

3. *Belief that the Kingdom is fully established on earth*

(3.1–3)   [1]*(((Jesus said, 'If your <<leaders>> say to you, "Look! the Kingdom is in heaven," then the birds of heaven will arrive first before you.* [2]*If they say, "It is under the earth," then the fish of the sea will enter it, arriving first before you.* [3]*But the Kingdom of Heaven is inside of you and outside.'*

3.1.5 Anachronisms

Sayings which show signs of secondary development in the interest of explaining or promoting ideologies or activities that reflect post-50 CE Christianity, but do not appear to have been reworked into discourses, nor look to be interpretative clauses, nor cohere to the characteristic vocabulary or themes of the identified accretions, are still considered with skepticism. Because of their late content, they are considered more likely accretions than Kernel sayings, particularly those logia which refer to developments of christologies and soteriologies common to later

Christian texts (L. 28, 77, 101, 108). The same is true of L. 88 which reflects a sociological discussion that developed in later communities, a discussion about the continued teaching and revelation that the community can expect from itinerant prophets with instructions about how the community should receive the prophet and what the community should give the prophet. Also L. 14.5, an accretion that presupposes a Christian decision to use Jesus' words to nullify the Jewish dietary regulations for missionaries staying in Gentile households. L. 105 appears to be a late Christian polemic against marriage.

3.1.5.1 *Anachronistic Sayings*

(Kernel text in regular type; *accretions in italics*)

(14.5) [5]*'For what goes into your mouth will not make you unclean, rather what comes out of your mouth. It is this which will make you unclean!'*

(28) [1]*Jesus said, 'I stood in the midst of the world and I appeared to them in flesh.* [2]*I found all of them drunk. I found none of them thirsty.* [3]*And my soul suffered in pain for human beings because they are blind in their hearts and they do not see. For they, empty, came into the world. And they, empty, seek to leave the world.* [4]*For the moment, they are drunk. When they shake off their wine, then they will repent.'*

(77) [1]*Jesus said, 'I am the light which is above all things. I am everything. From me, everything came forth, and up to me, everything reached.* [2]*Split a piece of wood. I am there.* [3]*Lift the stone, and you will find me there.'*

(88) [1]*Jesus said, 'The angels and the prophets will come to you. They will give to you what is yours,* [2]*and, in turn, what is yours, you will give to them. You will say to yourselves, "When will they come and receive what is theirs?"'*

(101) [1]*'Whoever does not hate his [father] and his mother in the same manner as I do, he cannot be a [disciple] of mine.* [2]*Also whoever does [not] love his [father and] his mother in the same manner as I do, he cannot be a [disciple] of mine.* [3]*For my [birth] mother [gave death], while my true [mother] gave life to me.'*

(105) *Jesus said, 'Whoever is aquainted with (one's) father and mother will be called, "the child of a prostitute."'*

(108) [1]*Jesus said, 'Whoever drinks from my mouth will become as I am.* [2]*I myself will become that person,* [3]*and what is hidden will be revealed to him.'*

3.2 *Principle of Responsiveness*

The secondary units identified above fall into several thematic categories, themes which reflect the concerns that the community faced. Their questions and dialogues very specifically address topics about leadership, discipleship, Jewish law, Christology, soteriology, or eschatology, and reflect the problems associated with shifting constituencies within their community. These concerns are not unique to the *Gospel of Thomas* but are standard across the early Christian literature, reflecting retrospective and responsive thought common to early Christian experience and theology.

Since early Christian ideology is fundamentally dialectical in nature, it is responsive to other ideological positions and to community crises. For instance, it can be the consequence of discourse or polemics, it can be the attempt to resolve the disconfirmation of unfulfilled expectations, and it can be the result of crisis management. Certain sayings accrued in the speech book as responses to particular historical experiences, answering the community's questions about ideology or responding to crises it faced. As we shall see, it appears that these accretions accrued in the Kernel over a period of several decades, 50 to 120 CE, when the community was faced with particular historical circumstances and shifts in its memory, circumstances and shifts which can be recovered by examining the content of the accretions.

3.2.1 *Sayings that are Responsive to Christian Experiences* (Kernel in regular type; *accretions in italics*)

1. **Leadership**
(Incipit) *((These are the secret words that the Living Jesus spoke and that Judas Thomas wrote down))*.

(12) [1]*The disciples said to Jesus, 'We know that you are going to leave us. Who will be our leader?'*
[2]*Jesus said to them, 'No matter where you came from, you should go to James the Righteous One, for whose sake heaven and earth exist.'*

(13) [1]Jesus said to his disciples, 'Speculate about me. Tell me, who am I like?'
[2]Simon Peter said to him, 'You are like a righteous angel.'
[3]Matthew said to him, 'You are like a sage, a temperate person.'
[4]Thomas said to him, 'Master, my mouth cannot attempt at all to say whom you are like.'
[5]Jesus said, 'I am not your master. After you drank, you became intoxicated from the bubbling fount which I had measured out.'
[6]And he took him and retreated. He told him three words.
[7]Then, when Thomas returned to his friends, they asked him, 'What did Jesus say to you?'
[8]Thomas said to them, 'If I tell you one of the words which he told me, you will pick up stones and throw them at me. Then fire will come out of the stones and burn you up.'

2. *Discipleship*

(21) *¹Mary said to Jesus, 'Whom are your disciples like?'*
He said, 'They are like little children sojourning in a field that is not theirs. When the owners of the field come, they will say, "Leave our field!" In front of them, they strip naked in order to abandon it, returning their field to them.'

(22) *¹Jesus saw little babies nursing. ²He said to his disciples, 'These little ones nursing are like those who enter the Kingdom.'*
³They said to him, 'Will we enter the Kingdom as little babies?'
⁴Jesus said to them, 'When you make the two one, and when you make the inside like the outside, and the outside like the inside, and the above like the below. ⁵And when you make the male and the female into a single being, with the result that the male is not male nor the female female. ⁶When you make eyes in place of an eye, and a hand in place of a hand, and a foot in place of a foot, and an image in place of an image, ⁷then you will enter the Kingdom.'

(49) *¹Jesus said, 'Blessed are the celibate people, the chosen ones, because you will find the Kingdom. ²For you are from it. You will return there again.'*

(61) *²Salome said, 'Who are you, sir? That is, from [[whom]]? You have reclined on my couch and eaten at my table.'*
³Jesus said to her, 'I am he who comes from the one who is an equal. I was given some who belong to my Father.'
⁴'I am your disciple.'
⁵'Therefore I say, when a person becomes [[equal]] (with me), he will be filled with light. But if he becomes separated (from me), he will be filled with darkness.'

(75) *Jesus said, 'Many people are standing at the door, but those who are celibate are the people who will enter the bridal chamber.'*

3. **Jewish Law**

(6) *¹((His disciples questioned him and said, 'How should we fast? How should we pray? How should we give alms? What diet should we observe?))'*

(14) *¹Jesus said to them, 'If you fast, you will generate sin for yourselves. ²And if you pray, you will be condemned. ³And if you give alms, you will harm ⟨yourselves⟩.* ⁴When you enter any district and walk around the countryside, if they take you in, whatever they serve you, eat! The people among them who are sick, heal! *⁵For what goes into your mouth will not make you unclean, rather what is sent forth from your mouth. It is this which will make you unclean!'*

(27) *²'If you do not observe the Sabbath day as a Sabbath, you will not see the Father.'*

(44) ¹Jesus said, *'Whoever blasphemes against the Father will be forgiven, ²and* whoever blasphemes against the Son will be

forgiven. [3]But whoever blasphemes against the Holy Spirit will not be forgiven, neither on earth nor in heaven.'

(53)   [1]*His disciples said to him, 'Is circumcision advantageous or not?'*
[2]*He said to them, 'If it were advantageous, the father (of the children) would conceive them in their mother already circumcised.*
[3]*Rather circumcision in the spirit is true (circumcision). This person has procured all of the advantage.'*

4. *Christology*

(Incipit) *((These are the secret words that the Living Jesus spoke and that Judas Thomas wrote down)).*

(13)   [1]*Jesus said to his disciples, 'Speculate about me. Tell me, who am I like?'*
[2]*Simon Peter said to him, 'You are like a righteous angel.'*
[3]*Matthew said to him, 'You are like a sage, a temperate person.'*
[4]*Thomas said to him, 'Master, my mouth cannot attempt at all to say whom you are like.'*
[5]*Jesus said, 'I am not your master. After you drank, you became intoxicated from the bubbling fount which I had measured out.'*
[6]*And he took him and retreated. He told him three words.*
[7]*Then, when Thomas returned to his friends, they asked him, 'What did Jesus say to you?'*
[8]*Thomas said to them, 'If I tell you one of the words which he told me, you will pick up stones and throw them at me. Then fire will come out of the stones and burn you up.'*

(28)   [1]*Jesus said, 'I stood in the midst of the world and I appeared to them in flesh.* [2]*I found all of them drunk. I found none of them thirsty.* [3]*And my soul suffered in pain for human beings because they are blind in their hearts and they do not see. For they, empty, came into the world. And they, empty, seek to leave the world.* [4]*For the moment, they are drunk. When they shake off their wine, then they will repent.'*

(37)   [1]*His disciples said, 'When will you appear to us? When will we see you?'*
[2]*Jesus said, 'When you strip naked without shame, take your garments, put them under your feet like little children, and trample on them.* [3]*Then [you will see] the Son of the Living One and you will not be afraid.'*

(43)   [1]*His disciples said to him, 'Who are you to say these things to us?'*
[2]*'From what I say to you, you do not know who I am.* [3]*Rather, you are like the Jews, for they love the tree (but) hate its fruit, or they love the fruit (but) hate the tree.'*

(52)   [1]*His disciples said to him, 'Twenty-four prophets have spoken in Israel, and all of them have spoken about you.'*
[2]*He said to them, 'You have left out the Living One who is in your presence and you have spoken about the dead.'*

(61) *²Salome said, 'Who are you, sir? That is, from [[whom]]? You have reclined on my couch and eaten at my table.'*
³Jesus said to her, 'I am he who comes from the one who is an equal. I was given some who belong to my Father.'
⁴'I am your disciple.'
⁵'Therefore I say, when a person becomes [[equal]] (with me), he will be filled with light. But if he becomes separated (from me), he will be filled with darkness.'

(77) *¹Jesus said, 'I am the light which is above all things. I am everything. From me, everything came forth, and up to me, everything reached. ²Split a piece of wood. I am there. ³Lift the stone, and you will find me there.'*

(91) *¹They said to him, 'Tell us so that we may believe in you! Who are you?'*
²He said to them, 'You examine the appearance of the sky and the earth, but, he who is in your midst, you do not understand. Nor this critical time! you do not understand how to examine it.'

(100) ¹They showed Jesus a gold coin and said to him, 'Caesar's men extort taxes from us.'
²He said to them, 'Give to Caesar, what is Caesar's. ³Give to God what is God's. *⁴And what is mine, give me.'*

(101) *¹'Whoever does not hate his [father] and his mother in the same manner as I do, he cannot be a [disciple] of mine. ²Also whoever does [not] love his [father and] his mother in the same manner as I do, he cannot be a [disciple] of mine. ³For my [birth] mother [gave death], while my true [mother] gave life to me.'*

5. *Soteriology*

(1) *And he said, 'Whoever finds the meaning of these words will not die.'*

(3) *¹((Jesus said, 'If your ⟨leaders⟩ say to you, "Look! the Kingdom is in heaven," then the birds of heaven will arrive first before you. ²If they say, "It is under the earth," then the fish of the sea will enter it, arriving first before you. ³But the Kingdom of Heaven is inside of you and outside. ⁴Whoever knows himself will find it. ⁵And when you know yourselves, you will understand that you are the children of the Living Father. But if you will not know yourselves, you live in poverty and you are poverty)).'*

(4) *¹Jesus said, 'The old man will not hesitate to ask a little child seven days old about the place of life, and he will live. ²For many who are first will be last, ³((and the last will be first,)) ⁴and they will become single people.'*

(7) *¹Jesus said, 'Blessed is the lion that the human will eat, and the lion becomes human. ²And cursed is the human who the lion eats, [[and the human becomes a lion]].'*

(11) *²'But the dead are not alive, and the living will not die. ³In the days when you ate what is dead, you made it something living. When you*

are in the light, what will you become? *[4]On the day when you were
one, you became two. When you are two, what will you become?'*

(16) *[4]'And they will stand as celibate people.'*

(18) *[1]The disciples said to Jesus, 'Tell us, how will our end come about?'
[2]Jesus said, 'Have you discovered the beginning that you seek the
end? Because where the beginning is, the end will be also. [3]Whoever
will stand in the beginning is blessed. This person will know the end,
yet will not die.'*

(19) *[1]Jesus said, 'Whoever existed before being born is blessed. [2]If you
become my disciples and listen to my teachings, these stones will
support you. [3]For you, there are five trees in Paradise. They do not
change, summer and winter, and their leaves do not fall. Whoever
knows them will not die.'*

(21) *[1]Mary said to Jesus, 'Whom are your disciples like?'
He said, 'They are like little children sojourning in a field that is not
theirs. When the owners of the field come, they will say, "Leave our
field!" In front of them, they strip naked in order to abandon it,
returning their field to them.'*

(22) *[1]Jesus saw little babies nursing. [2]He said to his disciples, 'These
little ones nursing are like those who enter the Kingdom.'
[3]They said to him, 'Will we enter the Kingdom as little babies?'
[4]Jesus said to them, 'When you make the two one, and when you
make the inside like the outside, and the outside like the inside, and
the above like the below. [5]And when you make the male and the
female into a single being, with the result that the male is not male
nor the female female. [6]When you make eyes in place of an eye, and
a hand in place of a hand, and a foot in place of a foot, and an image
in place of an image, [7]then you will enter the Kingdom.'*

(24) *[1]His disciples said, 'Teach us about the place where you are, because
we must seek it.'*
[2]He said to them, 'Whoever has ears should listen! [3]There is light
inside a person of light. And it lights up the whole world. If it does
not shine, it is dark.'

(27) *[1]((Jesus said)), 'If you do not fast from the world, you will not find
the Kingdom. [2]If you do not observe the Sabbath day as a Sabbath,
you will not see the Father.'*

(37) *[1]His disciples said, 'When will you appear to us? When will we see
you?'
[2]Jesus said, 'When you strip naked without shame, take your
garments, put them under your feet like little children, and trample
on them. [3]Then [you will see] the Son of the Living One and you
will not be afraid.'*

(38) [1]Jesus said, 'The words that I am speaking to you, often you have
longed to hear them. And you have no other person from whom
to hear them. *[2]There will be days when you will seek me, (but) will
not find me.'*

(49)   [1]*Jesus said, 'Blessed are the celibate people, the chosen ones, because you will find the Kingdom.* [2]*For you are from it. You will return there again.'*

(50)   [1]*Jesus said, 'If they say to you, "Where did you come from?", say to them, "We came from the light" – the place where the light came into being on its own accord and established [itself] and became manifest through their image.* [2]*If they say to you, "Is it you?", say "We are its children, and we are the chosen people of the living Father."* [3]*If they ask you, "What is the sign of your Father in you?", say to them, "It is movement and rest."'*

(56)   [1]*Jesus said, 'Whoever has come to know the world has found a corpse.* [2]*The world does not deserve the person who has found (that the world is) a corpse.'*

(59)   *Jesus said, 'Gaze upon the Living One while you are alive, in case you die and (then) seek to see him, and you will not be able to see (him).'*

(60)   [1]*A Samaritan was carrying a lamb as he traveled to Judea.* [2]*He said to his disciples, 'That man is holding the lamb.'*
[3]*They said to him, '(He is holding the lamb) so that he may slaughter it and eat it.'*
[4]*He said to them, 'While it is alive, he will not eat it. Rather, (he will eat the lamb) after he has slaughtered it and it is carcass.'*
[5]*They said, 'He is not permitted to do it any other way.'*
[6]*He said to them, 'Moreover, so that you will not become a carcass and be eaten, seek for yourselves a place within rest!'*

(64)   [12]*'Buyers and merchants [will] not enter the places of my Father.'*

(67)   *Jesus said, 'Whoever knows everything, but needs (to know) himself, is in need of everything.'*

(69)   [1]*'Blessed are those who have been persecuted in their hearts. They are the people who truly have known the Father.'*

(70)   [1]*Jesus said, 'When you become what is within you, what is within you will save you.* [2]*If you do not have it within you, what you do not have within you will kill you.'*

(75)   *Jesus said, 'Many people are standing at the door, but those who are celibate are the people who will enter the bridal chamber.'*

(80)   [1]*Jesus said, 'Whoever has come to know the world has found the corpse.* [2]*The world does not deserve the person who has found (that the world is) the corpse.'*

(83)   [1]*Jesus said, 'The images are visible to people, but the light in them is concealed in the image of the Father's light.* [2]*The light will be revealed, but his image is concealed by his light.'*

(84)   [1]*Jesus said, 'When you see the likeness of yourselves, you are delighted.* [2]*But when you see the images of yourselves which came into being before you – they neither die nor are visible – how much you will suffer!'*

(85)   *¹Jesus said, 'Adam came into being out of a great power and great wealth. But he was not deserving of you. ²For, had he been deserving, [he would] not [have] died.'*

(87)   *¹Jesus said, 'Miserable is the body, which is crucified by a body. ²Miserable is the soul, which is crucified by these together.'*

(106) *¹Jesus said, 'When you make the two one, you will become children of Man. ²And when you say, "Mountain, go forth!" it will move.'*

(108) *¹Jesus said, 'Whoever drinks from my mouth will become as I am. ²I myself will become that person, ³and what is hidden will be revealed to him.'*

(110) *Jesus said, 'Whoever has found the world and become wealthy, he should disown the world.'*

(111) ¹Jesus said, 'The heavens and the earth will roll up in your presence. *²And whoever is alive because of the Living One will not see death. ³Does not Jesus say, "The world does not deserve the person who has found himself"?'*

(112) *¹Jesus said, 'Woe to the flesh, which is crucified by the soul. ²Woe to the soul, which is crucified by the flesh.'*

(114) *¹Simon Peter said to them, 'Mary should leave us because women do not deserve life.'*

²Jesus said, 'Look, I myself will <<guide>> her in order to make her male, so that she too may become a living spirit – male, resembling you. For every woman who will make herself male will enter the Kingdom of Heaven.'

6. *Eschatology*

(3)   *¹((Jesus said, 'If your ⟨leaders⟩ say to you, "Look! the Kingdom is in heaven," then the birds of heaven will arrive first before you. ²If they say, "It is under the earth," then the fish of the sea will enter it, arriving first before you. ³But the Kingdom of Heaven is inside of you and outside. ⁴Whoever knows himself will find it. ⁵And when you know yourselves, you will understand that you are the children of the Living Father. But if you will not know yourselves, you live in poverty and you are poverty)).'*

(18)   *¹The disciples said to Jesus, 'Tell us, how will our end come about?' ²Jesus said, 'Have you discovered the beginning that you seek the end? Because where the beginning is, the end will be also. ³Whoever will stand in the beginning is blessed. This person will know the end, yet will not die.'*

(20)   *¹The disciples said to Jesus, 'Tell us, what is the Kingdom of Heaven like?'*

²He said to them, 'It is like a mustard seed, ²smaller than all seeds. ⁴But when it falls on cultivated soil, it puts forth a large branch and becomes a shelter for birds of the sky.'

(22)   *¹Jesus saw little babies nursing. ²He said to his disciples, 'These little ones nursing are like those who enter the Kingdom.' ³They said to him, 'Will we enter the Kingdom as little babies?'*

^{4}*Jesus said to them, 'When you make the two one, and when you make the inside like the outside, and the outside like the inside, and the above like the below. ^{5}And when you make the male and the female into a single being, with the result that the male is not male nor the female female. ^{6}When you make eyes in place of an eye, and a hand in place of a hand, and a foot in place of a foot, and an image in place of an image, ^{7}then you will enter the Kingdom.'*

(27) ^{1}*((Jesus said)), 'If you do not fast from the world, you will not find the Kingdom.'*

(37) ^{1}*His disciples said, 'When will you appear to us? When will we see you?'*
^{2}*Jesus said, 'When you strip naked without shame, take your garments, put them under your feet like little children, and trample on them. ^{3}Then [you will see] the Son of the Living One and you will not be afraid.'*

(38) ^{2}*'There will be days when you will seek me, (but) will not find me.'*

(49) ^{1}*Jesus said, 'Blessed are the celibate people, the chosen ones, because you will find the Kingdom. ^{2}For you are from it. You will return there again.'*

(51) ^{1}*His disciples said to him, 'When will the dead rest, and when will the new world come?'*
^{2}*He said to them, 'What you look for has come, but you have not perceived it.'*

(59) *Jesus said, 'Gaze upon the Living One while you are alive, in case you die and (then) seek to see him, and you will not be able to see (him).'*

(111) ^{1}*Jesus said, 'The heavens and the earth will roll up in your presence. ^{2}And whoever is alive because of the Living One will not see death. ^{3}Does not Jesus say, "The world does not deserve the person who has found himself"?'*

(113) ^{1}*His disciples said to him, 'When will the Kingdom come?'*
^{2}*'It will not come by waiting. ^{3}It will not be said, "Look! Here it is!" or "Look! There it is!" ^{4}Rather, the Kingdom of the Father is spread out over the earth, but people do not see it.'*

3.2.2 *Responses Reflecting General Christian Experiences*

Some of the crises experienced by the Thomasine Christians were experienced by other Christian communities as well. In this case, at least three such crises can be detected upon examination of the accretions: the death of the eyewitnesses, the delay of the Eschaton, and the accommodation of Gentile converts to the community. It is assumed that sayings in *Thomas* which reflect the crises within the broader Christian community probably entered the collection contemporaneous to the time when other communities were experiencing similar crises. This assumption is based on the recognition that certain discussions or problems seemed to have occurred at particular times in the broader early Christian experience.

The Principle of Responsiveness is concerned with understanding the gospel as a text that makes sense *within* the broader Christian experience of its time, within its historical contexture of traditions. Any reconstruction should be historically probable and coherent with what we know about early Judaism and early Christianity from other contemporaneous texts. This means that it is vital to compare the sayings in *Thomas* with other ancient Jewish and Christian documents even in those cases where we are not dealing with direct literary dependence or intertextuality. The sayings in *Thomas* ultimately reflect the traditions and conflicts familiar to us from Jewish sources and Christian gospel and epistolary literature even though the community of *Thomas* may have responded to conflicts and shifted the meaning of the traditions in ways distinct from these other Jews or Christians.

3.2.2.1 *Death of the Eyewitnesses*

Allusions to the death of the eyewitnesses are prominent in the accretions which stand to secure the testimony of the community's apostolic hero, Judas Thomas (incipit; L. 13). The community wished to secure its memory of Judas Thomas' witness and involvement in its history at a time when he was no longer alive to recite and teach about Jesus' words. Whether he was the founding apostle from Jerusalem or a prominent teacher at some time is open to debate. I have become convinced, however, that the tradition connecting the mission of Judas Thomas with the establishment of the Church in eastern Syria alluded to in the *Gospel of Thomas* is earlier and more reliable than the presentation of the 'founding' story in the *Doctrine of Addai*, where Addai is the named missionary. H.J.W. Drijvers has shown that this legend was created in the second half of the third century as an anti-Manichean treatise with little factual information about the formative period of Edessian Christianity.[2] In my opinion, the only traditions of historical value in this legend are the prominence given to Judas Thomas as the disciple responsible for initiating the mission in the Edessian area, and the remembrance that the mission began in Jewish households.[3]

The impact of the death of the eyewitnesses cannot be overrated since, because of this, all Christian communities faced the reality of losing their memories. In oral cultures, the death of the eyewitnesses, along with war which the Christians also faced during this same time period when the mother Church in Jerusalem was destroyed, are two of the main reasons

---

2. H.J.W. Drijvers, 'Facts and Problems in Early Syriac-Speaking Christianity,' *SecCent* 2 (1982) pp. 157–175.

3. G. Howard, *The Teaching of Addai*, Texts and Translations 16, Early Christian Literature 4 (Chico: Scholars Press, 1981) p. 11.

why people set down their memories in writing. Since they were confronted with the loss of their traditions, it is not without reason that the Christian communities, the Thomasine included, became much more interested in scribing down their traditions and retrospective reflections on them between 50 and 120 CE, the time to which I attribute the accrual of the accretions and the 'final' scribing of the full *Gospel of Thomas*.

3.2.2.2 *The Delay of the Eschaton*

The delay of the Eschaton, reflected in L. 3, 18, 20.1, 22, 27.1, 37, 38.2, 49, 51, 59, 111.2, 113, caused a critical rethinking and severe overhaul of the theology of the Thomasine community, pushing its members to return to the Jewish scripture, in particular Genesis 1–3, and develop a specific exegetical tradition.[4] The result of this exegesis is reflected in many of their accretions which focus on the salvific model of the primordial androgynous Adam, the luminous Image of God (L.4.1, 11.2–4, 16.4, 18, 19, 21.1–4, 22, 23.2, 37, 61.5, 83, 84, 85, 106, and 114). According to this exegetical tradition, in order achieve salvation, the person had to return to the 'beginning' and the sinless state of the prelapsarian Man. This process would involve encounter with one's heavenly Image, the Image that had been altered when Adam sinned. A host of these sayings belong to an encratic tradition honoring celibacy and the unmarried life of 'singlehood' and virginity (L. L. 4.1, 4.3, 11.2–4, 16.4, 21.1–4, 21.6–9, 22, 23.2, 27.1, 37, 49, 64.12, 75, 85, 101, 105, 106, 110, 111.2, 114). This encounter was equivocated with the Hermetic process of seeking and finding knowledge of one's divine Self whose origin was the Light (L. 3.4–5, 67, 111.3). The delay of the Eschaton forced the community to develop a soteriology centered around Jewish mystical traditions and the Hermetic search for the Self rather than hopes of an imminent End (L. 3.4–5, 7, 19, 24.1, 37, 38.2, 50, 56, 59, 67, 80, 83, 84, 108, 111.3).

The recasting of apocalyptic expectations found in the accretions is in tandem with post-50 CE Christianity when the delay of the Eschaton seems to have been most acute. Questions and concerns similar to those found in the *Gospel of Thomas* reverberate throughout early Christian literature.[5] In this literature, it can be shown that the early eschatological traditions have been subjected to interpretative shifts. From the pragmatism of Paul to the prolongation of apocalyptic expectation in the Synoptics to the collapse of eschatology in John, early Christian

---

4. For detailed analysis of this exegetical tradition, see AD DeConick, *Seek to See Him: Ascent and Vision Mysticism in the Gospel of Thomas*, VCSupp 33 (Leiden: E.J. Brill, 1996).

5. For recent discussions about this, refer to J.T. Carroll, *The Return of Jesus in Early Christianity* (Peabody: Hendrickson Publishers, 2000); C. Rowland, *Christian Origins: The Setting and Character of the Most Important Messianic Sect of Judaism* (London: SPCK, 2nd edn 2002) pp. 287–296.

traditions underwent profound shifts as historical time lengthened. The response in the accretions of *Thomas*, in some ways, is similar to the response recorded in the Gospel of John: apocalyptic expectations were collapsed, the End, including the Resurrection and Judgment, were perceived to have already taken place, and God's presence had become immediately and fully available to the communities. Both the Thomasine and the Johannine communities had shifted to the mystical dimension of apocalyptic, although, as I've argued elsewhere, there were significant differences in the mystical systems developed and promoted by these communities.[6] At any rate, it appears that this shift in Thomasine theology took place in at least two phases. At first the community began to emphasize its mystical heritage at the expense of the eschatological (60–100 CE). But as time continued to lengthen and the crisis became more acute, the community began welding into this mystical ideology, encratic and then hermetic traditions (80–120 CE).

The delay also fostered a stationary lifestyle (L. 88). It was a time when the Thomasine community favored a stationary lifestyle for its converts and addressed the concerns of itinerant preachers who expected support from the Thomasine community. While the Kernel gospel sayings contain references to the reversal of normal society values and practices, including familial ones, the accretions witness to settled community members who expected to support financially the wandering prophets who continued to visit their community and teach (L. 88). The concern over how properly to receive wandering prophets by settled communities of Christians can also be found in James 3.1–12, 2 and 3 John, and *Didache* 11–13, texts written near the end of the first century.

3.2.2.3 *Accommodation of Gentile Converts*
The accretions also tell us that the Thomasine community eventually experienced an influx of Gentiles, resulting in their accommodation, especially in regard to Torah prescriptions (L. 6.1/14.1–3, 14.5, 27.2, 53, 60).[7] These sayings accrued in the Kernel in the second half of the first century, at the same time that other Christian communities were experiencing major growth in their Gentile population and were adjusting their own Jesus traditions to deal with this phenomenon. Questions about the continued relevancy of Torah observation was foremost in the minds of many of these Christians. So they were responding to questions similar to

---

6.   A.D. DeConick, *Voices of the Mystics: Early Christian Discourse in the Gospels of John and Thomas and Other Ancient Christian Literature*, JSNTSup 157 (Sheffield: Sheffield Academic Press, 2001).

7.   For a balanced overview of ritual practices in *Thomas*, see A. Marjanen, '*Thomas* and Jewish Religious Practices,' in U. Risto (ed.), *Thomas At the Crossroads* (Edinburgh: T&T Clark, 1998) pp. 163–182.

those that the disciples ask in *Thomas*, questions in which we hear the voices of the Gentile converts: '((How should we fast? How should we pray? How should we give alms? What diet should we observe?))' (L. 6.1) and 'Is circumcision advantageous or not?' (L. 53).[8]

The later Thomasine attitude toward fasting, prayer, almsgiving, and diet can be found in Jesus' response in L. 6.2–4, '[2]Do not tell lies [3]and what you hate, do not do. [4]((For everything, when faced with truth, is brought to light. [5]For there is nothing hidden that will not be manifested))' and later, '[1]If you fast, you will generate sin for yourselves. [2]And if you pray, you will be condemned. [3]And if you give alms, you will harm your spirits' (L. 14.1–3). Does the attitude expressed in L. 14.1–3 mean that these particular Jewish ritual practices were abandoned altogether by the Thomasine community because they were considered spiritually harmful?

Before assuming this, it should be remembered that Kernel saying 104 reflects a more favorable attitude toward prayer and fasting for the purposes of atonement and self-control. This saying remained in the gospel *even after* L. 14.1–3 accrued in *Thomas*. This suggests that the language in L. 14.1–3 was understood to be rhetorical rather than literal, perhaps criticizing *obligatory* practices once customary to the community. It may be that the Thomasine community had in mind something akin to the Matthean position: that obligatory ritual observance for the sake of observance is of no value. So they questioned the earlier Thomasine community's dietary and fasting regulations, prayer rituals, and rules regarding almsgiving. According to L. 6.2, they wished to make central to their religious life ethical practices, including the 'golden rule,' 'Do not do what you hate' (cf. Tob 4.15; Mt 7.12; Lk 6.31) and a second ethic, 'Do not lie' (cf. Sirach 7.12). It is worthwhile to note that the Antiochean tradition found in the Western Text of Acts similarly redacts the Jerusalem ruling on the Noahide Laws. It replaces καὶ πνικτῶν with the Golden Rule![9] In any case, the later Thomasine community appears to have replaced its earlier obligatory fasting practices with a renunciatory lifestyle, fasting from the world (L. 27.1). This position seems to me to be more rigorous, not more lenient!

Why did the later Thomasine community experience this shift in its practices, especially moving away from the observance of the kosher diet?

---

8. Cf. Matt 6.1–18; 9.14–17; 15.10–20; 22; Mark 2.18–22; 7.14–19; Luke 5.33–39; Acts 10.9–16; 11.3; 15.1, 5, 9; 19–29; Romans 2.25–29; 4.1–12; 12.8; 14; 15.20–29; 1 Cor 8; 10; 2 Cor 6.5; 8.13–14; 11.27; Gal 2.3–12; 5.2–12; Phil 3.2–3; Rev 2.14, 20; *2 Clem* 16.4; *Did.* 8.1–3; 15.4; *Ps.-Clem. Hom.* 13.4.

9. G. Quispel, 'African Christianity Before Minucius Felix and Tertullian,' in J. den Boeft and A.H.M. Kessels, *Studies in Honour of H.L.W. Nelson* (Utrecht: Instituut voor Kassieke Talen, 1982) p. 286.

The accrual of sayings around Kernel saying 14.4 suggests that the members of the community found that the dietary laws were too difficult to maintain in the course of actively missionizing the Gentiles. Thus we find that L. 14.4, a Kernel saying, is sandwiched between *two accretions* which serve this hermeneutical purpose:

> *¹Jesus said to them, 'If you fast, you will generate sin for yourselves. ²And if you pray, you will be condemned. ³And if you give alms, you will harm your spirits.* ⁴When you enter any district and walk around the countryside, if they take you in, whatever they serve you, eat! The people among them who are sick, heal! *⁵For what goes into your mouth will not make you unclean, rather what comes out of your mouth. It is this which will make you unclean!'*

For the later Thomasine community, the Temple cult also was obsolete. This fact is signaled in L. 60. My scholarly instinct leads me to think that the Kernel contained an early version of L. 60 before it was fashioned into a dialogue, although, because the creation of the dialogue has so distorted the earlier saying, the Kernel version is impossible to retrieve. So what we have extant in L. 60 is almost entirely late development. Why do I think this? Because in L. 60 the community is reworking older material it considers authoritative, trying to make it conform to its present opinion on the subject. The older material was probably a parable about a Samaritan taking a lamb to Jerusalem to sacrifice at the Temple. Because the community did not participate in sacrificial rites, it updated the parable by turning it into the present dialogue. Jesus is no longer telling a story about a Samaritan slaughtering an animal at the Temple, but admonishing the hearers to seek a place of rest in themselves so that they do not become a carcass like the lamb, and be eaten by worms!

Another problem for the Thomasine community as its population shifted in the latter half of the first century and became dominated by Gentiles was circumcision. Because of this situation, we again hear their voice behind the disciples' question to Jesus: 'Is circumcision advantageous or not?' (L. 53.1). Paul asks a similar question in Romans 3.1: 'What is the value of circumcision?' He responds, 'He is a Jew who is one inwardly, and real circumcision is a matter of the heart, spiritual and not literal' (Rom 2.29). What is most fascinating, however, is that Thomas' response (L. 53.2) – *'if it were advantageous, the father (of the children) would conceive them in their mother already circumcised'* – relies on an argument comparable to other Jewish and Christian stories containing anti-Jewish polemic. 'If God is so pleased with circumcision, why does the child not come out of the womb circumcised?' King Rufus asks Rabbi Akiba (*Tanchuma* B 7 [18a]). 'For if circumcision were necessary, God would not have made Adam uncircumcised,' Justin Martyr reasoned (*Dial.* 19.3). Thus, while this accretion clearly resonates with the early Christian tradition that the convert had to be circumcised by the Holy Spirit in order to be quickened to the faith (Rom 2.25–29; Phil 3.3; Col 2.11; *Barn.* 9.1–5; *Odes Sol.* 11.1–3; Justin Martyr, *Dial.* 113.7; Epiph., *Pan.* 33.5.11, quoting the *Letter to Flora* by Ptolemy), a position likely developed by the Christians with reference to Deuteronomy 10.16 and Jeremiah 4.4, it also reflects an anti-Jewish argument that is found developed in texts much later than Paul. This suggests that this accretion, like the other accretions regarding Jewish practices, belongs more to late first-century Christianity than earlier.

Thomas also contains a saying that encourages the readers to continue observing the Sabbath for the sake of salvation (L.27.2). We can conceive of a scenario in which the new Gentile converts tried to convince the community that they should be worshiping on the Lord's Day rather than on the Sabbath. The Thomasine community did not abandon Sabbath worship, however. Rather the community insisted that Sabbath observation was necessary if one wanted to 'see the Father.'[10] The Thomasine community was not unique in its decision to continue Sabbath worship (cf. Col 2.16).[11] In fact, still at the time of Epiphanius, worship was held on Saturday in several churches (*De fide* 24.7). Socrates states that the Egyptians in the environs of Alexandria and Thebais were especially known to have assembled on the Sabbath (*HE* 5.22; cf. Sozomen, *HE* 7.19.8). And according to the Council of Laodicea (*Can.* 16), 'the Gospels and other parts of scripture shall be read aloud' on the Sabbath (cf. Cassian, *Inst. Coenob.* 2.6 and 3.2). Some churches held services on both Sabbath and Sunday (cf. *Apos. Const.* 2.36.2; 7.23.3; 7.36.1; Ign., *Magn.* 9.1).

Thus, one of the responses of the Thomasine Christians was to accommodate the Gentile converts in their community by reinterpreting the sayings of Jesus. In the process of responding to these emerging concerns, they modified their records of Jesus' words, bringing them in line with their shifting communal memories and providing the contemporary community with formal addresses of Jesus on these difficult subjects. It is essential, however, to recognize that early Christianity developed not only out of Judaism, but also in tension and conflict with Judaism. This spiral of tension tended to become more intense as the second half of the first century progressed and a largely Gentile population converted to Christianity. Thus, at first, the Thomasine Christians tried to maintain their connection with their Jewish heritage, as can be seen especially by

10. DeConick, *Seek to See Him*, pp. 126–143.
11. W. Rordorf, *Sunday. The History of the Day of Rest and Worship in the Earliest Centuries of the Christian Church* (trans. A.A.K. Graham; Philadelphia: Westminster Press, 1968) pp. 118–153.

their decision to continue to honor the holiness of the Sabbath. But the continued pressure from the domination of the Gentiles and the eventual expulsion from the Jewish community altogether became too intense, resulting in a gradual separation of the Thomasine community from Judaism (43, 52, 53).

This separation affected their self-definition as a community so much that, by the last decade of the first century, they saw the 'Jews' as 'the Other' in much the same way as the Johannine community. So, in accretion 43, Jesus characterizes the Jews as Other-Than- Himself and uses them as a negative foil for some community members who were holding onto an older christology:

> [1]His disciples said to him, 'Who are you to say these things to us?'
> [2]'From what I say to you, you do not know who I am. [3]Rather, you are like the Jews, for they love the tree (but) hate its fruit, or they love the fruit (but) hate the tree.'

This Logion in *Thomas* must represent a late stage in the development of the community when the Thomasine Christians, like the Johannine Christians, had begun to identify themselves as Christians rather than Christian Jews.

It appears that the Thomasine community ran into christological problems when this separation from Christian Judaism became permanent because its old prophet christology was undermined (L. 31, 52). How could Jesus be a Jewish Prophet in a community that perceived the Jews to be Other-Than-Themselves? This, of course, was a problem across Christian communities in general and was responsible for continued speculation about and development of christological traditions in early Christian writings. The Thomasine community's resolution can be found in L. 52 where his disciples present to Jesus the opinion of the old Thomasine community, that Jesus was the culmination of the prophets of Israel, the fulfillment of the prophecies in the twenty-four books of the Jewish testament (*f. 2 Esdras* 14.45):

> [1]His disciples said to him, 'Twenty-four prophets have spoken in Israel, and all of them have spoken about you.'

This old christology which is 'dead' is modified with the inclusion of the community's more contemporary view of Jesus as the 'Living Jesus' (Incipit), the 'Son of the Living One' (L. 37):

> [2]He said to them, 'You have left out the Living One who is in your presence and you have spoken about the dead.'

Does this saying suggest that the Thomasine Christians, like Marcion, had come to the conclusion that the Hebrew Scriptures were irrelevant or obselete? Not necessarily. There is an Ebionite tradition that presents an alternative. As the Ebionites faced a similar situation in the second century when they began defining themselves over and against the Jews and other Christians, they recorded the tradition that Jesus was not to be heralded Messiah because the Jewish prophets foretold his advent and mission. Rather, it was the 'presence and coming of Christ' that showed that the prophets were truly prophets 'for testimony must be borne by the superior to his inferiors, not by the inferiors to their superior' (*Pseudo-Clementines, Rec.* 1.59). John 5.36–40 expresses this tradition in its nascent form. Given the provenance of this tradition, it may represent the best interpretative foil for L. 52. In this case, the disciples are rebuked for believing that the prophets bore witness to Jesus, when, in fact, Jesus, the Living God, is the one whose testimony must be heard and heeded.

The attribution 'Living' has its origins in Jewish traditions where it refers to God as a divine being who acts in history, giving the Decalogue, indwelling the Temple, and prophesying through his chosen servants (Hos 2.1; Deut 4.33; 5.26; 1 Sam 17.26, 36; Josh 3.10–11; 2 Kgs 19.4, 16; Ps 41.3; 84.2).[12] In the Hellenistic period, it is used as idol polemic especially when dealing with proselytes (Dan 5.23; 6.27 LXX; *Jos. Asen.* 8.5; *Sib. Or.* 3.762–766; Bel and the Dragon 5–6)[13] or to characterize Yahweh who restores an unfaithful idolatrous Israel to the covenant (*Jub.* 1.25: *3 Macc.* 6.28; *Jos. Asen.* 19.8). The Christians were heir to this tradition, applying the title to God the Father as well as Jesus (Mt 16.16; 26.63; Acts 14.15; 1 Thess 1.9–10; 2 Cor 3.3; 6.16; Rom 9.25–26; 1 Tim 3.10; 4.10; Heb 3.12; 9.14; 10.31; 12.22; Rev 1.18; 4.9–10; 15.7; *Acts of Paul* 7.2; *Dial. Sav.* 44; 46; *Acts Thom.* 60; 136; cf. 1 Pet 1.23). In Christian texts, the epithet is associated with Gentile conversion since Gentiles who become Christian are converting to the 'Living' God, abandoning the worship of their 'dead' idols. In this way, the Christians proclaimed their one true God in contrast to the polytheism of the Gentiles.[14] In one case at least, Paul uses

---

12.   Scholarly discussion of this epipthet is scanty. For all of the occurences of this title in Greek versions of the Old Testament and Pseudepigrapha, refer to W. Boussett, *Die Religion des Judentums im späthellenistischen Zeitalter,* HNT 21 (3rd edn. H. Gressmann; Tübingen: J.C.B. Mohr, 1966) p. 311, n. 4. H.J. Kraus focuses exclusively on Old Testament usage of the phrase in his article, 'Der lebendige Gott,' *EvT* 27 (1967) pp. 169–201. W. Stenger appeals to Jewish background to explain the New Testament usage of the title in his article, 'Die Gottesbezeichnung "lebendiger Gott" im Neuen Testament,' *TTZ* 87 (1978) pp. 61–69. R. Bultmann comments on parallels in, 'zavw,' *TDNT* 2, pp. 855, 858. The best overview of the Jewish use of the term is an unpublished dissertation by H. Everding, *The Living God: A Study in the Function and Meaning of Biblical Terminology* (PhD dissertation, Harvard, 1968). As far as Paul's usage of the phrase in relation to his Jewish heritage, see M.J. Goodwin, *Paul, Apostle of the Living God* (Harrisburg: Trinity Press International, 2001).

13.   Goodwin, *Paul, Apostle of the Living God,* pp. 86–108.

14.   Goodwin, *Paul, Apostle of the Living God,* pp. 109–160.

the title to teach that the 'Living' God, through his Spirit, brings new life to converts (2 Cor 3.3).[15]

The application of the title to Jesus and the Father in the accretions of *Thomas* provides more evidence that the community at some point in its history was actively missionizing Gentiles, teaching them that their God was the 'Living' God in contrast to 'dead' idols, as well as the God responsible for giving life to his converts (incipit; L. 37; 111.2). In fact, the converted are even called 'children' and 'elect of the Living Father' (L. 3.5; 50). This theme is developed along mystical lines in a couple of logia where it is taught that visions of the Living Father and his Son are to be sought by believers, lest they 'die' and then are unable to see God (L. 59; cf. 37). These traditions have been further modified in an even later accretion, L. 52, where the contrast between the Living God and dead idols is now punned back onto Israel. The Jews are characterized here as people who rely on dead prophets for their religious 'life' while the Thomasine Christians have discovered the true God, the Living Father and his Son, through direct mystical experience. As so often happens in religious movements, the Thomasine Christians eventually spurned and objectified what they once were.

3.2.3 *Reponses Reflecting Particular Community Experiences*
Some responses embedded in the Christian literature reflect crises or dialogues within a *particular* community. These may be uniquely experienced and not reflected by the majority of other Christian communities. They may be intra-community conflicts rather than inter-community crises. The community responsible for the *Gospel of Thomas* seems to have experienced at least one of these crises, and it elicited the addition of new material to their speech gospel. The initial Thomasine community looked to Jerusalem and the leadership of James. It was under the authority of the Jerusalem Church. This connection with Jerusalem is explicitly delineated in L. 12. This is one more piece of evidence that the origin of the Thomasine community is to be traced back to the mission activity of early itinerants from Jerusalem.

Having said this, however, it must be recognized that L. 12 was not part of the Kernel since the presence of the disciples' question, 'Who will be our leader?' is indicative of development of discourse material. This saying may, in fact, be one of the first accretions to the original *corpus*. Based on the content of the logion, this addition to the original collection must have occurred before 62 CE when James died but not necessarily during the initial formation of the Thomasine community. In fact, I am convinced that this saying actually accrued in the collection as the result of the

15. Goodwin, *Paul, Apostle of the Living God*, pp. 161–189.

community's first crisis – a significant threat to James' authority must have occurred within the community. What that threat was, is difficult to tell from the accretion. What we can say confidently, however, is that at an early point in their history, the Thomasine Christians questioned the legitimacy and authority of the Jerusalem Church. They opted, at this juncture at least, to maintain their connection with Jerusalem and the leadership of James.

Because this saying assumes that James is still alive and the leader of the Jerusalem Church, the Thomasine Church must have been established in Syria sometime before James' death in 62 CE. There is, of course, the famous tradition that the Jerusalem community moved east across the Jordan to Pella sometime before the onset of the Jewish war after the death of James (Eusebius, *Hist. Eccl.* 3.5.3). This tradition, however, if historical, cannot refer to the beginnings of the Thomasine community since L. 12 suggests that the community was well established before James' death in 62 CE. The Pella tradition must refer to an event entirely separate from the one we are investigating. Having said this, however, the early community does appear to have relocated to Syria as the result of persecution (L. 68.2).

3.3 *Principle of Constituency*

Early gospel texts developed within the context of more than one *interpretative* community. We might talk about the Thomasine community or the Johannine community, for instance, but we cannot assume that over its lifetime the community associated with a particular gospel consisted of the same *interpretative* community. This shift in the constituency of the community would have resulted in shifts in the traditions transmitted in the gospel as well as hermeneutics imposed upon the traditions when they were heard or read.

3.3.1 *Shifts in Composition*
As new groups of people joined the community, new types of sayings would have been incorporated into the text, sayings which would have reflected the needs, desires, beliefs, and interpretations of the shifting constituency. The accretions in the *Gospel of Thomas* reflect a couple of major constituency shifts. The first was a shift from a Christian-Jewish population to a population dominated by Gentiles and their interests, a shift which we can recover and date with some accuracy because it occurred across Christian communities generally. This shift began to exert pressure on the community in the mid-first century and by 100 CE the domination of the Gentiles was enough to question the legitimacy of maintaining Jewish practices (L. 6.1/14.1–3, 14.5, 27.2, 53, and 60) and

prophet christology (L. 52). By 100 CE, the Thomasine community's shift to a Gentile memory was complete (L. 43).

The second constituency shift was from a Christian-Jewish community, which understood sexuality in terms similar to other Second Temple Jews, to an encratic community which took the value of self-control to the extreme and heralded the need for the mind to rule over the passions of the body. As we will see in Chapter 7, this shift took place as the result of eschatology gone awry. As history lengthened rather than ended, some Christian communities began to conclude that the events of the Eschaton like the resurrection from the dead and the Judgment had already happened (1 Cor 4.8; 15.12–28; 2 Thess 2.2; Mt 27.52–53; Jn 3.18–21; 3.36; 5.26–27; 8.14–16; 9.39; 11.25–26; 12:17; 12.31–32). Because of this, some even went so far as to conclude that the angelic life should be taken up, permanent abstinence adopted, and marriage suspected of being a state of sin (Lk 20.34–36; 1 Tim 4.3; cf. Col 2.18; Clement of Alexandria, *Strom.* 3).

The encratic accretions heralding singlehood and renunciation and championing the 'child' (L. 4.1; 4.3; 11.2–4; 16.4; 21.1–4; 21.6–9; 22; 23.2; 27.1; 37; 49; 64.12; 75; 85; 101; 105; 106; 110; 111.2; 114) belong to a time from 80–120 CE when the Thomasine community was responding theologically to the delay of the Eschaton, developing a call to celibacy and mystical experience based on a particular exegetical tradition concerning Genesis 1–3 as I have already outlined above. As we will see in a later chapter, this explanation was steeped in a story built from both Jewish and Hermetic traditions. The fusion of Hermetic elements included the attribution of classic Hermetic sayings to Jesus, sayings which portray him as the new voice of Hermes in which he promotes Self-knowledge as the avenue to overcome the world and death (L. 3.4–5, 7, 28, 56, 67, 80, 111.3).

3.3.2 *Shifts in Hermeneutics*

Not only would changes in the membership of the community have resulted in new material entering the gospel but also it would have resulted in shifts within the hermeneutic through which the text was understood. As the interpretative community changed, so did the interpretation of the sayings because different readers would have brought to the text different worldviews and different conceptions of reality. Gentile converts, for instance, would have very different interpretative foils than Christian Jews, encratite Christians than married Christians, mystical Christians than eschatological Christians, and so forth. So it is likely that static historical interpretations do not exist for most sayings in the gospel. Instead, the accepted meaning of most sayings would have varied over time as the interpretative community changed. This suggests, of course, that over the course of history, most sayings in the *Gospel of Thomas* had numerous meanings depending upon the identity of the community responsible for reading and interpreting the text.

3.4 *A Rolling Corpus*

The application of the principles described in this chapter has made it possible to distinguish the older Kernel sayings from later accretions and explain, on a general level, why the gospel was adapted in these particular ways. The following charts of the sayings in the *Gospel of Thomas* yield in shorthand these results. The first outlines the approximate dates for the accrual of the accretions in the gospel between the years 50 and 120 CE. The chart should not be read as representing three stages of 'redaction' (literary or oral) of *Thomas*. Such a reading would represent a complete misunderstanding of my argument. *The accrual occurred mainly within the field of oral performance and was gradual.* The second chart distinguishes Kernel sayings from accretions and provides in a convenient checklist fashion the reasons for these decisions. In my quest to understand the beginnings of the Thomasine community and its 'original' gospel, we are now able to press on in the next chapter and separate out the Kernel sayings from the rest of the sayings of *Thomas,* recovering as far as we can the oldest form of the *Gospel of Thomas.*

3.4.1 *Chart: Gradual Accrual of Logia*

		Kernel Gospel, 30–50 CE	
2	30	61.1	86
4.2–3	31	62.1	89
5	32	62.2	90
6.2–3	33	63.1–3	91.2
8	34	63.4	92
9	35	64.1–11	93
10	36	65.1–7	94
11.1	38.1	65.8	95
14.4	39	66	96.1–2
15	40	68.1	96.3
16.1–3	41	69.2	97
17	42	71	98
20.2–4	45	72	99
21.5	46.1–2a, c	73	100.1–3
21.10	47	74	102
21.11	48	76	103

23.1	54	78	104
24.3	55	79	107
25	57	81	109
26	58	82	111.1

Accretions, 50–60 CE
Relocation and leadership crisis

12
68.2

Accretions, 60–100 CE
Accommodation to Gentiles and early eschatological crisis (with shift to mystical dimension of apocalyptic thought)

3.1–3	24.1	51	69.1
6.1	27.2	52	70
14.1–3	37	53	88
14.5	38.2	59	91.1
18	43	60	113
20.1	50	64.12	

Accretions, 80–120 CE
Death of eyewitnesses, christological developments and continued eschatological crisis (with incorporation of encratic and hermetic traditions)

Incipit	21.1–4	61.2–5	105
1	21.6–9	67	106
3.4–5	22	75	108
4.1	23.2	77	110
4.4	27.1	80	111.2
6.4–5	28	83	111.3
7	29	84	112
11.2–4	44.1	85	114
13	46.2b	87	
16.4	49	100.4	
19	56	101	

3.4.2 *Chart: Sayings by Attribution (Kernel sayings are shaded)*

Principle	Incipit	1	2	3.1-3	3.4-5	4.1	4.2-3	4.4	5	6.1	6.2-3	6.4-5	7	8
Development of Discourses										X				
Formation of Interpret. Clauses								X						
Characteristic Vocab. 'Living'	X				X	X								
Characteristic Vocab. 'Single' or 'Celibate'								X						
Characteristic Vocab. 'Standing One'														
Characteristic Vocab. 'Child'					X	X								
Characteristic Vocab. 'will not taste death'		X												
Characteristic Vocab. 'world does not deserve'														
Characteristic Vocab. 'to know' as a salvific category					X									
Characteristic Theme Speculation about Adam						X								
Characteristic Theme Disdain for world & admiration for Self					X								X	
Characteristic Theme Kingdom fully estab.				X										
Anachronism														
Responsiveness Death of Eyewitnesses	X													
Responsiveness Delay of the Eschaton				X	X	X		X						
Responsiveness Accomodation of Gentiles										X		X		
Responsiveness Development of Christology	X													
Responsiveness Leadership Crisis														
Constituency From Christian Jew to Gentile										X				
Constituency Encratic sayings					X			X						
Constituency Hermetic saying					X								X	

Principle	9	10	11.1	11.2-4	12	13	14.1-3	14.4	14.5	15	16.1-3	16.4	17
Development of Discourses					X	X	X						
Formation of Interpret. Clauses												X	
Characteristic Vocab. 'Living'				X									
Characteristic Vocab. 'Single' or 'Celibate'												X	
Characteristic Vocab. 'Standing One'												X	
Characteristic Vocab. 'Child'													
Characteristic Vocab. 'will not taste death'													
Characteristic Vocab. 'world does not deserve'													
Characteristic Vocab. 'to know' as a salvific category													
Characteristic Theme Speculation about Adam				X								X	
Characteristic Theme Disdain for world & admiration for Self													
Characteristic Theme Kingdom fully estab.													
Anachronism									X				
Responsiveness Death of Eyewitnesses						X							
Responsiveness Delay of the Eschaton				X								X	
Responsiveness Accommodation of Gentiles							X		X				
Responsiveness Development of Christology						X							
Responsiveness Leadership Crisis					X								
Constituency From Christian Jew to Gentile					X		X		X				
Constituency Encratic sayings					X							X	
Constituency Hermetic sayings													

Principle	18	19	20.1	20.2-4	21.1-4	21.5	21.6-9	21.10	21.11	22	23.1	23.2	24.1
Development of Discourses	X		X		X					X			X
Formation of Interpret. Clauses							X					X	
Characteristic Vocab. 'Living'													
Characteristic Vocab. 'Single' or 'Celibate'										X		X	
Characteristic Vocab. 'Standing One'	X											X	
Characteristic Vocab. 'Child'					X					X			
Characteristic Vocab. 'will not taste death'	X	X											
Characteristic Vocab. 'world does not deserve'													
Characteristic Vocab. 'to know' as a salvific category	X	X											
Characteristic Theme Speculation about Adam	X	X			X					X		X	
Characteristic Theme Disdain for world & admiration for Self							X						
Characteristic Theme Kingdom fully estab.													
Anachronism													
Responsiveness Death of Eyewitnesses													
Responsiveness Delay of the Eschaton	X	X	X		X		X			X		X	X
Responsiveness Accommodation of Gentiles													
Responsiveness Development of Christology													
Responsiveness Leadership Crisis													
Constituency From Christian Jew to Gentile													
Constituency Encratic sayings					X		X			X		X	
Constituency Hermetic sayings/ Thomas		X											

Principle	24.2	24.3	25	26	27.1	27.2	28	29	30	31	32	33	34
Development of Discourses													
Formation of Interpret. Clauses													
Characteristic Vocab. 'Living'													
Characteristic Vocab. 'Single' or 'Celibate'													
Characteristic Vocab. 'Standing One'													
Characteristic Vocab. 'Child'													
Characteristic Vocab. 'will not taste death'													
Characteristic Vocab. 'world does not deserve'													
Characteristic Vocab. 'to know' as a salvific category													
Characteristic Theme Speculation about Adam													
Characteristic Theme Disdain for world & admiration for Self					X			X					
Characteristic Theme Kingdom fully estab.													
Anachronism							X						
Responsiveness Death of Eyewitnesses													
Responsiveness Delay of the Eschaton					X								
Responsiveness Accomodation of Gentiles						X							
Responsiveness Development of Christology							X						
Responsiveness Leadership Crisis						X							
Constituency From Christian Jew to Gentile													
Constituency Encratic sayings					X								
Constituency Hermetic sayings							X						

Principle	35	36	37	38.1	38.2	39	40	41	42	43	44.1	44.2-3
Development of Discourses			X							X		
Formation of Interpret. Clauses					X						X	
Characteristic Vocab. 'Living'			X									
Characteristic Vocab. 'Single' or 'Celibate'												
Characteristic Vocab. 'Standing One'												
Characteristic Vocab. 'Child'			X									
Characteristic Vocab. 'will not taste death'												
Characteristic Vocab. 'world does not deserve'												
Characteristic Vocab. 'to know' as a salvific category												
Characteristic Theme Speculation about Adam			X									
Characteristic Theme Disdain for world & admiration for Self												
Characteristic Theme Kingdom fully estab.												
Anachronism												
Responsiveness Death of Eyewitnesses												
Responsiveness Delay of the Eschaton			X		X							
Responsiveness Accomodation of Gentiles										X		
Responsiveness Development of Christology			X							X		
Responsiveness Leadership Crisis												
Constituency From Christian Jew to Gentile										X		
Constituency Encratic sayings			X									
Constituency Hermetic sayings												

Principle	45	46.1-2a,c	46.2b	47	48	49	50	51	52	53	54	55
Development of Discourses								X	X	X		
Formation of Interpret. Clauses			X									
Characteristic Vocab. 'Living'							X		X			
Characteristic Vocab. 'Single' or 'Celibate'						X						
Characteristic Vocab. 'Standing One'												
Characteristic Vocab. 'Child'												
Characteristic Vocab. 'will not taste death'												
Characteristic Vocab. 'world does not deserve'												
Characteristic Vocab. 'to know' as a salvific category			X									
Characteristic Theme Speculation about Adam												
Characteristic Theme Disdain for world & admiration for Self												
Characteristic Theme Kingdom fully estab.												
Anachronism												
Responsiveness Death of Eyewitnesses												
Responsiveness Delay of the Eschaton						X	X	X				
Responsiveness Accomodation of Gentiles									X	X		
Responsiveness Development of Christology									X			
Responsiveness Leadership Crisis												
Constituency From Christian Jew to Gentile									X	X		
Constituency Encratic sayings						X						
Constituency Hermetic sayings							X					

Principle	56	57	58	59	60	61.1	61.2-5	62.1	62.2	63.1-3	63.4	64.1-11
Development of Discourses					X		X					
Formation of Interpret. Clauses												
Characteristic Vocab. 'Living'				X								
Characteristic Vocab. 'Single' or 'Celibate'												
Characteristic Vocab. 'Standing One'												
Characteristic Vocab. 'Child'												
Characteristic Vocab. 'will not taste death'												
Characteristic Vocab. 'world does not deserve'	X											
Characteristic Vocab. 'to know' as a salvific category	X											
Characteristic Theme Speculation about Adam												
Characteristic Theme Disdain for world & admiration for Self	X											
Characteristic Theme Kingdom fully estab.												
Anachronism												
Responsiveness Death of Eyewitnesses												
Responsiveness Delay of the Eschaton				X			X					
Responsiveness Accomodation of Gentiles					X							
Responsiveness Development of Christology							X					
Responsiveness Leadership Crisis												
Constituency From Christian Jew to Gentile												
Constituency Encratic sayings												
Constituency Hermetic sayings	X				X							

Principle	64.12	65.1-7	65.8	66	67	68.1	68.2	69.1	69.2	70	71	72
Development of Discourses												
Formation of Interpret. Clauses	X						X					
Characteristic Vocab. 'Living'												
Characteristic Vocab. 'Single' or 'Celibate'												
Characteristic Vocab. 'Standing One'												
Characteristic Vocab. 'Child'												
Characteristic Vocab. 'will not taste death'												
Characteristic Vocab. 'world does not deserve'												
Characteristic Vocab. 'to know' as a salvific category					X			X				
Characteristic Theme Speculation about Adam												
Characteristic Theme Disdain for world & admiration for Self					X			X		X		
Characteristic Theme Kingdom fully estab.												
Anachronism												
Responsiveness Death of Eyewitnesses												
Responsiveness Delay of the Eschaton	X				X					X		
Responsiveness Accomodation of Gentiles												
Responsiveness Development of Christology												
Responsiveness Leadership Crisis												
Constituency From Christian Jew to Gentile												
Constituency Encratic sayings	X											
Constituency Hermetic sayings					X							

Principle	73	74	75	76	77	78	79	80	81	82	83	84
Development of Discourses												
Formation of Interpret. Clauses												
Characteristic Vocab. 'Living'												
Characteristic Vocab. 'Single' or 'Celibate'			X									
Characteristic Vocab. 'Standing One'												
Characteristic Vocab. 'Child'												
Characteristic Vocab. 'will not taste death'												
Characteristic Vocab. 'world does not deserve'								X				
Characteristic Vocab. 'to know' as a salvific category								X				
Characteristic Theme Speculation about Adam											X	X
Characteristic Theme Disdain for world & admiration for Self								X			X	X
Characteristic Theme Kingdom fully estab.												
Anachronism					X							
Responsiveness Death of Eyewitnesses												
Responsiveness Delay of the Eschaton			X								X	X
Responsiveness Accomodation of Gentiles												
Responsiveness Development of Christology					X							
Responsiveness Leadership Crisis												
Constituency From Christian Jew to Gentile												
Constituency Encratic sayings			X									
Constituency Hermetic sayings								X				

Principle	85	86	87	88	89	90	91.1	91.2	92	93	94
Development of Discourses							X				
Formation of Interpret. Clauses											
Characteristic Vocab. 'Living'											
Characteristic Vocab. 'Single' or 'Celibate'											
Characteristic Vocab. 'Standing One'											
Characteristic Vocab. 'Child'											
Characteristic Vocab. 'will not taste death'	X										
Characteristic Vocab. 'world does not deserve'	X										
Characteristic Vocab. 'to know' as a salvific category											
Characteristic Theme Speculation about Adam	X										
Characteristic Theme Disdain for world & admiration for Self			X								
Characteristic Theme Kingdom fully estab.											
Anachronism				X							
Responsiveness Death of Eyewitnesses											
Responsiveness Delay of the Eschaton	X			X							
Responsiveness Accomodation of Gentiles							X				
Responsiveness Development of Christology											
Responsiveness Leadership Crisis											
Constituency From Christian Jew to Gentile											
Constituency Encratic sayings	X										
Constituency Hermetic sayings											

Principle	95	96.1-2	96.3	97	98	99	100.1-3	100.4	101	102	103	104
Development of Discourses												
Formation of Interpret. Clauses								X				
Characteristic Vocab. 'Living'												
Characteristic Vocab. 'Single' or 'Celibate'												
Characteristic Vocab. 'Standing One'												
Characteristic Vocab. 'Child'												
Characteristic Vocab. 'will not taste death'												
Characteristic Vocab. 'world does not deserve'												
Characteristic Vocab. 'to know' as a salvific category												
Characteristic Theme Speculation about Adam												
Characteristic Theme Disdain for world & admiration for Self												
Characteristic Theme Kingdom fully estab.												
Anachronism									X			
Responsiveness Death of Eyewitnesses												
Responsiveness Delay of the Eschaton									X			
Responsiveness Accomodation of Gentiles												
Responsiveness Development of Christology								X	X			
Responsiveness Leadership Crisis												
Constituency From Christian Jew to Gentile												
Constituency Encratic sayings									X			
Constituency Hermetic sayings												

Principle	105	106	107	108	109	110	111.1	111.2	111.3	112	113	114
Development of Discourses											X	X
Formation of Interpret. Clauses								X	X			
Characteristic Vocab. 'Living'								X				X
Characteristic Vocab. 'Single' or 'Celibate'												
Characteristic Vocab. 'Standing One'												
Characteristic Vocab. 'Child'												
Characteristic Vocab. 'will not taste death'								X				
Characteristic Vocab. 'world does not deserve'									X			
Characteristic Vocab. 'to know' as a salvific category												
Characteristic Theme Speculation about Adam		X										X
Characteristic Theme Disdain for world & admiration for Self						X			X	X		
Characteristic Theme Kingdom fully estab.											X	
Anachronism	X			X								
Responsiveness Death of Eyewitnesses												
Responsiveness Delay of the Eschaton	X	X		X		X		X	X		X	X
Responsiveness Accomodation of Gentiles												
Responsiveness Development of Christology												
Responsiveness Leadership Crisis												
Constituency From Christian Jew to Gentile												
Constituency Encratic sayings	X	X				X			X			X
Constituency Hermetic sayings									X			

PART TWO

RECOVERING THE KERNEL

Chapter 4

AN EARLY CHRISTIAN SPEECH GOSPEL

Words are always primarily spoken things. ~ *W.J. Ong*

Because it is impossible for us to know the extent to which various Kernel sayings may have been moved around or deleted entirely at the levels of revision and manuscript transmission, any attempt to discuss the original structure or sequence of sayings in Kernel *Thomas* must, to some extent, be speculative. Therefore, the reconstruction of the 'original' gospel must be understood to be a minimal and tentative reconstruction of the initial scribing. My translation and analysis, in this monograph and in the companion volume *The Original* Gospel of Thomas *In Translation*, should not be mistaken to suggest that I understand the Kernel sayings I have isolated to be a complete coherent document.

Having said this, however, it is intriguing that once the later sayings have been removed, upon examination of the remaining sayings in their present order, a striking structure for the Kernel gospel and rhetorical arrangement of sayings emerges. Buried beneath layers of later interpretation there emerges an early gospel that, even in its minimal form, seems to have consisted of five speeches of Jesus: speeches which were intended to 'reperform' and 'compose anew' selections of Jesus' sayings.

4.1 *Five Kernel Speeches*

Each of the five speeches begin with admonitions calling the person to seek the truth or promises offering the hearer revelation of the truth (L. 2, 17, 38.1, 62.1, 92).

(2) [1]((Jesus said, 'Whoever seeks should not cease seeking until he finds. [2]And when he finds, he will be amazed. [3]And when he is amazed, he will be a king. [4]And once he is a king, he will rest)).'

(17) Jesus said, 'I will give you what no eye has seen, what no ear has heard, what no hand has touched, and (what) has not arisen in the human mind.'

(38) [1]Jesus said, 'The words that I am speaking to you, often you have longed to hear them. And you have no other person from whom to hear them.'

(62) [1]Jesus said, 'I tell my mysteries to [those people who are worthy of my] mysteries.'

(92) [1]Jesus said, 'Seek and you will find. [2]However, the questions you asked me previously but which I did not address then, now I want to address, yet you do not seek (answers).'

The sayings that follow each of these opening 'calls' seem to have been strung together mnemonically in order to elaborate the meanings and meaning-effects of a particular theme, a theme which is more often than not left unexpressed with the presumption that it will be obvious from the overall content of the sayings within each discourse. The speech is centered around certain admonitions and promises which are then elaborated upon in order to convict the reader to consent to the admonition or believe the promise. These speeches appear to have concluded with a saying about the Eschaton or its demands, serving to underscore the gravity of the discourse and urgency of the message, thusly bringing each speech to a close (L. 16.1–3, L. 36, 61.1, 91.2, 111.1).

(16) [1]Jesus said, 'Perhaps people think it is peace that I have come to cast upon the world. [2]And they do not know it is division that I have come to cast upon the earth – fire, sword, war! [3]For there will be five people in a house. There will be three people against two, and two against three, father against son, and son against father.'

(36) [1](([Jesus said, 'Do not be anxious] from morning [until evening and] from evening [until] morning, neither [about] your [food] and what [you will] eat, [nor] about [your clothing] and what you [will] wear. [2][You are far] better than the [lilies] which [neither] card nor [spin]. [3]As for you, when you have no garment, what [will you put on]? Who might add to your stature? The same one will give you your garment)).'

(61) [1]Jesus said, 'Two people will rest on a couch. One will die. One will live.'

(91) [2]'You examine the appearance of the sky and the earth, but, he who is in your midst, you do not understand. Nor this critical time! you do not understand how to examine it.'

(111) [1]Jesus said, 'The heavens and the earth will roll up in your presence.'

So it appears that the speech themes were developed by a rhetorical process of elaboration consisting of a compilation of rhetorical questions, maxims, examples, analogies, promises and even warnings.

This structure suggests to me that *Thomas* began as a gospel of speech-acts of Jesus in which select themes were elaborated through a rhetorical arrangement of sayings of the Lord. Is this type of rhetorical composition and gospel speech-structure a salient plausibility in early Christianity, especially since we have understood the compositional process of the ancient Jewish and Christian texts to be very scribal?[1] Traditionally, we have thought of an ancient 'author' as someone who collects materials from oral and written sources and edits them together, preserving much of the original source material. Modifications are perceived to be minimal, for editorial or specific theological purposes. Most of these modifications are to be located in the editorial bridges that link together the source materials or characteristic clauses appended to the source materials.

As I discussed in Chapter 1, recently rhetorical critics have challenged this understanding of the ancient compositional process, arguing that the scribal culture that began to dominate the transmission of ancient Christian literature in the late second century has been imposed upon the earlier compositional period.[2] This earlier period, it is argued, is better understood as a 'rhetorical culture' enlivened by a creative interaction between oral and written composition. It is a culture that uses both oral and written language interactively *and* rhetorically in the compositional process.[3] The type of elaboration evidenced in the Kernel reflects the *progymnastic* patterns of recitation and composition such as those referred to by Aelius Theon of Alexandria in his *Progymnasmata* and other pre-Gospel sources like Luke's Sermon on the Plain.[4]

We might add that these patterns of rhetoric form the basis for much of the writings of the Church Fathers. For instance, Clement of Alexandria in *Stromateis* 1.1 tells us that he is recording the speeches of his teacher Pantaenus in order to preserve the oral traditions which were fading and being forgotten. He states that the divine mysteries are communicated to the select 'few', not the 'many,' through the power of speech, not writing. For 'there is nothing secret which shall not be revealed, nor hidden which shall not be disclosed.' The mysteries are 'delivered mystically' from the 'mouth of the speaker.' He goes on to relate, as we might expect from this man with an oral consciousness, that 'the writing of these memoranda of mine, I well know, is weak when compared with that spirit, full of grace, which I was privileged to hear.'

---

1. V. Robbins, 'Progymnastic Rhetorical Composition and Pre-Gospel Traditions: A New Approach,' in C. Focant (ed.), *The Synoptic Gospels: Source Criticism and the New Literary Criticism*, BETL 110 (Leuven: University Press, 1993) pp. 116–121.

2. Robbins, 'Progymnastic Rhetorical Composition,' pp. 111–147; cf. H. Koester, *Ancient Christian Gospels: Their History and Development* (Philadelphia: Trinity Press International, 1990) pp. 31–43.

3. T.M. Lentz, *Orality and Literacy in Hellenic Greece* (Carbondale: Southern Illinois University Press, 1989).

4. Robbins, 'Progymnastic Rhetorical Composition,' pp. 111–147.

So he professes 'not to explain secret things sufficiently – far from it – but only to recall them to memory' in order that the traditions not be forgotten or lost completely. He expresses concern over the fact that 'many things . . . have escaped us, through length of time, that have dropped away unwritten.' In order 'to aid the weakness of my memory,' Clement explains, he decides to write down these oral teachings in a 'systematic arrangement of chapters.' He wishes to revive in his commentaries the oral teachings that have for too long been 'unnoted' or 'effaced' because they have begun to fade from memory. He also says that he will 'purposefully omit' what he guards even in speaking because he fears these teachings will be misinterpreted by readers who do not have a teacher to explain the meaning of the traditions orally to them. He worries that writing and reading will set up a situation of 'wrong sense' because the traditions 'require of necessity the aid of someone, either the one who wrote, or of someone else who walked in his footsteps'!

Clement then proceeds to record from memory the traditions that had been handed down to him through the oral teachings of Pantaneus. The form that they take is that of *progymnastic* speeches – strings of sayings and prooftexts listed out and flowing directly from one to the next. The reader with the aid of *Clement's interjections and written interpretations* is supposed to supply the progressive argument just as the orator would have. The *written interpretation* of the list of sayings and prooftexts usually is appended to the beginning and end of the lists, just as the oral interpretation would have been whenever these lists were reperformed before an audience. This is quite vivid in *Stromateis* 1.11 where the theme of the speech is that most, but not all of the world's wisdom is folly to God:

> *This, then,* 'the wisdom of the world is foolishness with God,'
> and of those who are 'the wise the Lord knows their thoughts that they are vain.'
> *Let no man therefore glory on account of pre-eminence in human thought. For it is written well in Jeremiah,* 'Let not the wise man glory in his wisdom, and let not the mighty man glory in his might, and let not the rich man glory in his riches. But let him who glories glory in this, that he understands and knows that I am Yahweh, who executes mercy and judgment and righteousness upon the earth. For in these things is my delight, says Yahweh.'
> 'That we should trust not in ourselves, but in God who raises the dead,' says the apostle, 'who delivered us from so great a death, that our faith should not stand in the wisdom of men, but in the power of God.'
> 'For the spiritual man judges all things, but he himself is judged of no man.'
> *I hear also those words of his,* 'And these things I say, lest any man should beguile you with enticing words, or one should enter in to spoil you.'

And again, 'Beware lest any man spoil you through philosophy and vain deceit, after the tradition of men, after the rudiments of the world, and not after Christ.'
[This] branding not all philosophy, but the Epicurean, which Paul mentions in the Acts of the Apostles, which abolishes providence and deifies pleasure, and whatever other philosophy honors the elements, but places not over them the efficient cause, nor apprehends the Creator.

Page after page of Clement's writings embed this *progymnastic* oral speech form within Clement's written reinterpretation (cf. *Inst.* 3.12; *Strom.* 2.14; *Rich Man* 31). His records provide us with ample examples of how the reperformance of the lists proceeded – how the orator interjected elements to aid the flow of the argument and framed the list with his own interpretation or explanation. Clement tells us that these lists were written so that the traditions would not be forgotten and as an aid for the weakness of the memory of the orator.

Clement's remarks and records help us to understand the purpose of the Kernel gospel. It must have been an orator's handbook written to preserve Jesus' teachings and aid the memory of the leader of the community who would regularly reperform, in Jesus' stead, these speeches, providing his interpretation or explanation orally as the oration progressed. What were the themes of these five Kernel speeches? How might the rhetoric have flowed and been interpreted by the orator? I offer here a possible reading of the speeches based on my reconstruction of their *progymnastic* rhetorical patterns.

4.1.1 *Speech One: Eschatological Urgency*
Jesus introduces the collected speeches by leading off his first speech with two admonitions that the hearer seek the truth (L. 2.1, 5.1: opening admonitions). The person who seeks the truth is promised an amazing journey that will ultimately lead to 'rest' (L. 2.2–4: rationale). Counter the wisdom of the world, those hearers who think they already know the truth are told that they do not, while those who think themselves to be ignorant will be the ones to gain knowledge. Thus '[2]for many who are first will be last, [3]((and the last will be first,))' (L. 4.2–3: contrawisdom rule). Jesus promises to reveal what has previously been hidden because [2]there is nothing hidden that will not be manifested' (L. 5.2: rationale).

The subsequent sayings in this first speech, through rhetorical elaboration, stress the critical nature of the times. Jesus tells his followers that they must behave correctly: they must not lie or do to others what they hate to have done to themselves (L. 6.2–3: admonitions). They should be exclusively committed to the truth which is about to be revealed to them just like the fisherman who casts his net into the sea keeping only the one fine large fish and casting all others back (L. 8: analogy). The hearers are

admonished to listen to Jesus (L. 8.4). They should be like the seed that fell
on good soil and produced good fruit rather than the seed that the birds
gathered, or fell on rock or among thorns and did not survive (L. 9:
analogy). Their decision is critical since Jesus is already casting God's
Judgment upon the world (L. 10: rationale). The universe is quickly
passing away (L. 11.1: rationale). They should take this message to others,
eating what is set before them and healing the sick (L. 14.4). So imminent
is the end, that they, even now, have direct access to God's throne where
they can bow down before God in worship (L. 15: admonition).
Unfortunately, people have not understood Jesus or this time of distress.
Although people think that Jesus came to cast peace on the earth, the truth
is that he came to cast God's Judgment: fire, sword and war (L. 16.1–3:
contrawisdom rule).

4.1.2 *Speech Two: Eschatological Challenges of Discipleship*

This type of *progymnastic* rhetorical discourse is visible in the second
speech as well which elaborates the theme of true discipleship in an
eschatological time. In this speech the truth about discipleship is revealed
to the hearer, truth that Jesus claims has been hidden until now (L. 17:
promise). The time is ripe for this revelation since the Kingdom of God has
already broken into the world and soon will be fully manifested; like a
small mustard seed which has been sown in tilled soil, the Kingdom will
quickly mature into 'a large branch' (L. 20: rationale). Jesus tells the hearer
that his disciple must be ready for the coming of God's Kingdom and the
practical difficulties that are expected to come along with it (L. 21. 5:
analogy), to understand that the Judgment is as near as the sickle which is
in hand ready to reap the ripened grain (L. 21.9–10: analogy). The hearers
are admonished to listen to Jesus (L. 21.11). Jesus promises that he himself
will be the judge, choosing 'you, one from a thousand, and two from ten
thousand' (L. 23.1: promise). Again the hearer is told to pay attention to
these words (L. 24.2).

Jesus says that he expects the hearer will follow him as 'a person of
light,' lighting up 'the whole world' (L. 24.3: maxim). He admonishes the
hearer to 'love' and 'watch over' his brother like his own 'soul' and to
remove the 'beam' from his own eye before trying to do the same to his
brother's (L. 25 and 26: admonitions). Jesus both promises his hearer that
he will be with him (L. 30.2: promise) and warns him that his followers will
be persecuted like he was. Like all prophets, they can expect to be rejected,
like a physician, they cannot heal people they know (L. 31: examples).
Even so, they must be like a city built on a high mountain (L. 32: analogy),
preaching from the housetops (L. 33.1: admonition). They must be like a
lamp set out on a lampstand rather than hiding themselves under a bushel
basket (L. 33.2–3: analogy). They are not to be like blind men leading blind

men (L. 34: statement from the opposite). When faced with an opponent, they should bind him first and then take him on (L. 35: example). The situation that the disciples face is so urgent that they cannot be concerned about even the most essential daily matters like clothing or food. They must rely on God for all of their needs (L. 36: admonition).

4.1.3 *Speech Three: Exclusive Commitment to Jesus*

The focus of this speech is on the theme that *only* Jesus reveals the truth so the hearer must listen to him and serve him exclusively (L. 38.1: maxim). Particularly important to this section is Jesus' insistence that the Pharisees, even though they possess the keys of the Kingdom, should not be heeded by the hearer because they have hidden the truth from themselves and others (L. 39.1–2: example). Hearers are admonished to be as 'wise as serpents and as innocent as doves' when it comes to listening to the Pharisees (L. 39.3: admonition). The rationale for this is twofold: the Pharisees are compared to a grapevine that has been planted outside the Father and that will be yanked out by its roots (L. 40: rationale); the Pharisees have nothing and will be deprived even of that (L. 41: rationale). In this context, Jesus commands the hearer to 'pass by' the teaching of the Pharisees and others (L. 42: admonitions). The Pharisees are blasphemers who will not be forgiven (L. 44: maxim). The truth cannot be harvested from the Pharisees because they have evil in their hearts (L. 45: analogy). Even John the Baptist who is so highly regarded does not have the truth. In fact, the person to whom Jesus has revealed the truth is greater than John (L. 46: example).

Because of this, the hearer must choose to serve Jesus alone. Rationale is provided: 'it is impossible for a person to mount two horses and to bend two bows' or 'to serve two masters' (L. 47.1–2: rationale). Analogies are made to wine drinking, wine manufacturing, and mending a garment (47.3–5: analogies) and promises are given: serving Jesus means that the disciple is a peacemaker whose words will have tremendous power, even moving mountains (L. 48). By blessing the poor, Jesus is telling the hearer that serving him alone means that the disciple must divide his interests between Jesus and wealth (L. 54: example). Serving Jesus alone means that the disciple must even hate his own family (L. 55: example). The hearer is reminded that his decision to follow Jesus exclusively is critical because he will be held accountable for it. There will be a harvest. The hearer does not want to make the wrong decision and, like a weed, be pulled up on that day and burned (L. 57: rationale). Rather those disciples who suffer by serving Jesus now are blessed (L. 58: rule). At the End, only the few who make the right choices will receive the final reward (L. 61.1: promise): 'Two people will rest on a couch. One will die. One will live.'

4.1.4 *Speech Four: The Selection of the Worthy Few*

In the fourth speech, this type of *progymnastic* elaboration continues, emphasizing that only a select number of people are worthy to know the truth that Jesus reveals about himself (62.1: promise). The rationale that Jesus provides for this seems to come from some ancient adage that a person generally does not let his left hand know what his right hand is doing (L. 62.2: rationale). Jesus then discusses the characteristics of those who are not worthy to receive his teaching: the person who does things for personal gain (L. 63.1–3: statement of the opposite) and the person who has other obligations, obligations that keep him from the Messianic banquet table (L. 64.1: analogy). The hearers are admonished to listen to the speech (L. 63.4). They are told that most of the people that Jesus met were so unworthy that they were even responsible for his death (L. 65: example), a fact that is given authoritative testimony as support (L. 66: authoritative testimony).

The speech then appears to turn to elaborate on the characteristics of those who are worthy of his teaching. Those people who are hated and persecuted are the worthy ones (L. 68.1: contrawisdom rule) as well as those who are hungry (L. 69.2: contrawisdom rule). Counter to the wisdom of the majority, Jesus denies that the Temple provides the way to achieve worthiness by warning that the Temple will be destroyed and will not be rebuilt (L. 71: contrawisdom rule). Those who are worthy of Jesus' teaching are not to be like the silly man who came to Jesus concerned about his inheritance (L. 72: example from the opposite). Rather they are to be like a few hardworking field hands bringing in a large harvest (L. 73: analogy). The worthy are not to be counted among the many who are standing around a well but refuse to enter the well (L. 74: analogy from the opposite). Rather they are to be like the shrewd merchant who sold everything for a single pearl (L. 76: analogy).

This speech seems to have used a set of rhetorical questions to shift the discussion so that the sayings progressively begin to reveal to the worthy the truth about Jesus. The worthy disciple is unlike those people who journey to the desert to see great men because Jesus is not like a king or other men (L. 78: rhetorical questions). Jesus is not like these kings and great men because he alone is blessed from the womb and speaks God's word (L. 79: rationale). In fact, Jesus admonishes people other than himself to be kings (L. 81: admonition). In contrast, Jesus dwells in a heavenly Kingdom of fire and it is there that he will reveal himself to the worthy (L. 82: maxim) because the earth is not the permanent residence of the human being and 'rest' cannot be found here (L. 86: rationale). The hearer is asked in the two rhetorical questions that follow, why the hearer is concerned with observing Jewish rituals in the way that some Pharisees have demanded (L. 89: rhetorical questions). The hearer is admonished to choose Jesus' leadership instead because his yoke is 'easy' and his lordship is 'mild' and his future promise is 'rest' (L. 90: admonition). The speech concludes on the note that there are some who are not worthy since they have examined 'the face of heaven and earth' but do not understand who Jesus is or the urgency of this time (L. 91.2: contrawisdom rule).

4.1.5 *Speech Five: The Imminent Kingdom of God*

In the last speech, the truth about God's Kingdom is revealed. Hearers are admonished to seek the truth because Jesus wants to reveal it now even though Jesus has not always done so (L. 92: admonition). Jesus has not revealed the truth previously because a person must be careful not to give 'what is holy to the dogs' or throw 'the pearls to swine' (L. 93: rationale). But now if the hearer seeks the truth, Jesus will give it to him; if the hearer knocks on the door, Jesus will let him in (L. 94: promise). Jesus implies that because the hearer has received the truth freely, he must now freely give it to others by presenting an analogous situation in which a person is told to give money at no interest to the person who cannot pay it back (L. 95: admonition).

What follows is a series of parables and examples that reveal the truth of God's Kingdom. The inauguration of the Kingdom is like the amazing surprise of a pinch of leaven growing large loaves of bread (L. 96: analogy); although its beginnings look small and impossible now, the rule of God will soon be fully established. Its coming is astonishing like the reaction of a woman who returns home with a jar of meal, only to find it empty because the handle had broken off on the way (L. 97: analogy). It requires preparation like the man who prepared himself before murdering another man (L. 98: analogy). Those people who do the will of God will enter the Kingdom and they will form a family that will replace their human families (L. 99: example). Unlike earthly rulers such as Caesar and his earthly kingdom Rome, God does not demand money and taxes (L. 100.1–2: example). The Pharisees do not have the answers about God's Kingdom because they are like a dog sleeping in the cattle trough, 'For the dog neither eats nor [lets] the cattle eat' (L. 102: woe). The hearer is warned that he must be ready for God's Kingdom and any distress associated with its coming (L. 103: maxim): 'Blessed is the man who knows where the thieves are going to enter, so that [he] may arise, gather at his estate, and arm himself.' The time of God's Kingdom is compared to a wedding, a time of celebration rather than a time of fasting (L. 104: analogy). It is compared to the joyous story about recovering a sheep that had strayed from the flock (L. 107: analogy). The surprise and elation that the disciple experiences as the Kingdom is established is like finding a hidden treasure in a field and being able to loan money to other people (L. 109). The imminence of God's Kingdom is underscored with what appears to have been the closing words in the last speech in the collection: 'The heavens and the earth will roll up in your presence' (L. 111.1: promise).

4.2 *The Prophet-Orator*

Jesus appears to have a very specific role in the sayings found in the old Kernel gospel. The sayings are oracles collected into instructional speeches pronounced by the Prophet-Orator Jesus. Through their regular reperformance by a Christian leader, the community is reminded that Jesus' words are to be heeded because he alone is able to reveal the truth about God's Kingdom and instruct people how to prepare for the imminent Judgment. Like the faithful remnant that heeded the voices of the previous prophets of Israel, only a few people are worthy enough to hear and understand Jesus' message, a message that *only* Jesus can give. Because this message has been previously hidden and is only known to God, the person who wants to know the truth must receive it from Jesus who alone reveals God's word. We might recall that this is exactly the manner in which Clement of Alexandria opens his memoirs of Pantaneus' teachings in *Stromateis* 1.1!

> The Lord allowed us to communicate of those divine mysteries, and of that holy light, to those who are able to receive them. He did not certainly disclose to the many what did not belong to the many. But to the few to whom he knew that they belonged, who were capable of receiving and being molded according to them. But secret things are entrusted to speech, not to writing, as is the case with God. And if one say that it is written, 'There is nothing secret which shall not be revealed, nor hidden which shall not be disclosed,' let him also hear from us, that to him who hears secretly, even what is secret shall be manifested. This is what was predicted by this oracle. And to him who is able to observe secretly what is delivered to him, that which is veiled shall be disclosed as truth, and what is hidden to the many, shall appear manifest to the few.

Jesus introduces the collected speeches with two admonitions that the hearer seek the truth (L. 2.1, 5.1). The person who seeks the truth is promised an amazing journey that will ultimately lead to 'rest' (L. 2.4). Jesus promises to reveal what has previously been hidden because 'there is nothing hidden which will not become manifest' (L. 5.1–2). Hearers are admonished repeatedly to seek the truth because Jesus wants to reveal it now even though Jesus has not always done so (L. 92). Jesus has not revealed the truth previously because a person must be careful not to give 'what is holy to the dogs' or throw 'the pearls [to] pigs' (L. 93). But now if the hearer seeks the truth, Jesus will give it to him; if the hearer knocks on the door, Jesus will let him in (L. 94).

Like previous Jewish prophets, Jesus is portrayed in the Kernel sayings as the prophet who is rejected even in his own village (L. 31). In fact, he is characterized as a prophet in the long line of prophets who have been killed over the course of Jewish history. Comparable to the tenant farmers who seized and murdered the landlord's servants and son, the Israelites have killed all of God's prophets including Jesus (L. 65). This was understood to be the fulfillment of the prophecy in Psalm 118.22: 'Show me the stone which the builders have rejected. That one is the cornerstone' (L. 66). Jesus is a prophet whose message is superior even to the message of the revered John the Baptist (L. 46).

4.2.1 *The Prophet in Conservative Christian Judaism*
This depiction of Jesus in the Kernel gospel as a great Jewish 'prophet' is similar to the depiction of Jesus in the traditions of the early Christianity from Jerusalem, a tradition I call conservative Christian Judaism.[5] The Jerusalem tradition presented Jesus' earthly role in connection with a line of Jewish prophets who came as models of righteousness and interpreters of the Law. This Christology was grounded in Jewish expectations that during the Last days, God would send his Messianic Prophet who would restore God's Law to its original intent, preparing believers for the Final Judgment.[6]

In conservative Christian Judaism, Jesus most often was identified with the Prophet-like-Moses promised in Deuteronomy (Acts 3.18–26; 7.37; cf. Mark 6.4; 6.15; 8.28; Luke 4.24; 7.16; 9.8; 13.33; 24.19; John 1.19–27; 4.19; 4.25; 6.14; Hebrews 3.5). But he was understood to be greater than Moses or any other prophet, even his predecessor, John the Baptist (Acts 3.17–26; 7.37). Ultimately though, he was rejected, starting with his own village (Acts 2.23; 3.17–18; 7.51–53; cf. Mark 6.4–5; Matthew 13.57–58; Luke 4.23–24; John 4.44): he was the rejected cornerstone mentioned in the ancient prophecies referencing Psalm 118.22, the 'rejected stone which has become the head of the corner' (Acts 4.11; Mark 12.10–11; Matthew 21.42; Luke 20.17; 1 Peter 2.4–8); Isaiah 28.16, the 'foundational cornerstone' (1 Cor 3.11; Eph 2.20; 1 Peter 2.5–6); and Isaiah 8.14, the 'stone of stumbling and rock of offense' (Luke 20.18; Rom 9.33; 1 Peter 2.8).

---

5. See 1.1.

6. H.M. Teeple, *The Mosaic Eschatological Prophet* (Philadelphia: Society of Biblical Literature, 1957); R.N. Longenecker, *The Christology of Early Jewish Christianity*, Studies in Biblical Theology, Second Series 17 (Naperville: Alec R. Allenson, 1970) pp. 32–38.

4.2.2 *The Prophet in Ebionism*

This understanding of Jesus was not replaced in all forms of later Christianity. It survived and was further developed in communities of Ebionite Christians in eastern Syria, Christians responsible for the traditions recorded in the *Pseudo-Clementine* corpus. Although the Ebionite traditions display some later second-century Christological developments such as the description of Jesus as God's 'True Prophet' who came to abolish sacrificial commandments, and to require vegetarianism, poverty and water purification,[7] the core elements from the Jerusalem tradition remain embedded in the later Ebionite materials. These elements are remarkably similar to those features that characterize the Prophet Jesus so prominently in the Kernel *Thomas*.

The Ebionites state over and over again that Jesus is the only one who reveals the truth. He is the only one who could 'enlighten the soul' (*Hom.* 1.19) because 'it is impossible for a person to know anything, unless he learn from the True Prophet' (*Rec.* 9.1). Truth can be found nowhere but from him (*Hom.* 3.11). Jesus' revelation of the truth is so exclusive that it is even compared to the natural process of gaining knowledge through our human senses: 'no one can see without eyes, nor hear without ears, nor smell without nostrils, nor taste without a tongue, nor handle anything without hands, so it is impossible without the True Prophet to know what is pleasing to God' (*Rec.* 1.44). This 'knowledge' is the truth about the Kingdom of God (*Rec.* 5.10), righteous living, and promised Judgment (cf. *Rec.* 1.33; 2.20; 3.20).

The 'knowledge of truth' given to us by Jesus the Prophet must be 'eagerly sought after' because 'no one can confer it except the True Prophet' himself (*Rec.* 4.5). If anyone desires to learn 'all things, let him seek after the True Prophet' (*Rec.* 8.60; cf. 8.62). In one passage, people are admonished to 'seek the True Prophet' because

> it is he alone who knows all things and who knows what and how every person is seeking...he works in those who seek after that which is profitable to their souls, and kindles in them the light of knowledge. Wherefore, seek him first of all; and if you do not find him, expect not that you shall learn anything from any other. But he is soon found by those who diligently seek him through love of truth...(*Rec.* 8.59).

Thus believers are admonished consistently to seek the truth from Jesus solely because 'from none but himself alone can it be known what is true' (*Rec.* 1.16; cf. *Hom.* 1.19; 2.4; 2.5; 2.6; 2.7; 3.54).

---

7. H.-J. Schoeps, *Jewish Christianity: Factional Disputes in the Early Church* (trans. D.R.A. Hare; Philadelphia: Fortress Press, 1969) pp. 65–117.

There is also a very developed rhetoric in this corpus against the Pharisees who are said to possess the truth because they are the receivers of the tradition of Moses, the keeper of the keys of knowledge. It has already been recognized by Gilles Quispel that the *Pseudo-Clementines* preserve a variant of L. 39 that shows more affinity with the *Thomas* variant than its Synoptic counterparts (Mt 23.13; Lk 11.52). It has been suggested that the reason for this is a common Jewish-Christian source.[8] But the similarities may indicate something even more remarkable than this since it appears that several *Pseudo-Clementine* passages show knowledge of sayings that appear in clusters in the Kernel gospel and apply them hermeneutically in comparable ways. Are we possibly witnessing in the Kernel gospel a particular interpretation of some of Jesus' sayings that became standard in some forms of later eastern Christianity? Or is it possible that at least one of the sources of the *Pseudo-Clementine* corpus was some version of the Kernel gospel?

In the case of L. 39, many of the same rhetorical clusters that we find in the beginning of the third speech of the Kernel gospel, are also applied to the Pharisees in the *Clementine* literature. The focus of the third speech is on the theme that Jesus exclusively reveals the truth so the hearer must listen to him and serve him alone (L. 38.1). Just as Jesus insists in the Kernel speech that the Pharisees have the keys of knowledge, but they have 'hidden' them, not allowing themselves or others to enter (L. 39), so the *Pseudo-Clementines* state that the Pharisees have 'hidden the key of the Kingdom of Heaven' (*Rec.* 1.54; cf. *Rec.* 2.46; *Hom.* 3.18).[9] In the Kernel the Pharisees are immediately compared to a grapevine that is 'unsound' (L. 40) who bring forth 'evil' things from their hearts (L. 45). They are to be associated with John the Baptist who is great, but not greater than the followers of Jesus (L. 46). This understanding of the Pharisees is very similar to the description of them in *Clementines* as men with 'unsound doctrine' and 'evil deeds' who have hidden the key of knowledge (*Rec.* 2.30). The Pharisees elevate John the Baptist to the level of Moses and do not understand that Jesus, because he is the Christ, is greater than both; they have received the truth from Moses as 'the key of the Kingdom of Heaven' but have hidden it from the people (*Rec.* 1.54, 59–60).

Furthermore, in the Kernel, the worthy disciple is supposed to 'pass by (ⲣ̄-ⲡⲁⲣⲁⲅⲉ)' the teachings of the Pharisees and all others (L. 42).[10] So also,

---

8. G. Quispel, 'The Gospel of Thomas and the New Testament,' in *Gnostic Studies 2* (Leiden: Nederlands Historisch-Archaeologisch Instituut te Istanbul, 1975) pp. 13–14; G. Quispel, 'L'Evangile selon Thomas et les Clementines,' in *Gnostic Studies 2* (Leiden: Nederlands Historisch-Archaeologisch Instituut te Istanbul, 1975) pp. 24–25.

9. The Synoptics state that they have 'taken away' the key (Luke 11.52) or they have 'shut the kingdom' (Matthew 23.13).

10. B. Layton, *Nag Hammadi Codex II,2-7*, NHS 20 (Leiden: E.J. Brill, 1989) p. 70.

according to the *Pseudo-Clementines*, a person ought to 'pass by (παρέρχομαι)' all teachings other than those of Jesus and 'commit himself to the Prophet of the truth alone' (*Hom.* 2.9).[11] We should note that the Coptic translation ⲣ-ⲡⲁⲣⲁⲅⲉ probably was rendering the Greek phrase, ἔστε παρερχόμενοι.[12] This reconstruction is collaborated by this passage from the Greek *Homilies*. It is quite possible that this expression translated the Hebrew עבר as several scholars have suggested.[13] But it did not originally evoke the image of a traveller or wanderer, but the notion to pass by or turn away from someone or something such as we find in Psalm 119.37: 'Turn my eyes away from looking at vanities: and give me life in your ways' (cf. 2 Sam 12.13; 1 Kgs 15.12; Eccl 11.10). In this particular case, Jesus was instructing them to pass by the teachings of the Pharisees and other teachers, to listen exclusively to his words.

In the Kernel speech, another saying belonging to this rhetorical cluster implies that the Pharisees possess nothing to give, so they will be deprived even of that (L. 41). In *Homily* 18.16, also in the context of a discussion of the Pharisees' possession of the key of the Kingdom of Heaven, the point is made that the Pharisees will not be allowed to keep the key indefinitely: 'but from him who is not worthy, even should he seem to have anything, it is taken away, even if he be wise in other matters.' It is striking that the rhetorical use of this saying in the *Homilies* mirrors its use in the Kernel gospel which is so different from its Lukan context (Lk 8.19).

Like L. 5, in the Ebionite tradition we are told that the truth which people should seek is hidden and that Jesus alone can reveal it. As we have seen already, in the Kernel it is argued that the truth has not always been revealed to everyone who seeks for it (L. 92) because Jesus does not give 'what is holy to the dogs' or toss 'the pearls [to] pigs' (L. 93). Only if the worthy person seeks the truth, will Jesus give it to him (L. 94). Again we find that the *Pseudo-Clementine* literature seems to be familiar with this interpretative cluster of sayings, applying the 'Dogs and Pigs' saying to this precise situation, something that the Synoptic variant does not do (Mt 7.6).

---

11. B. Rehm, *Die Pseudoklementinen I. Homilien* (Berlin: Akademie Verlag, 1953) p. 39.

12. The first to propose this was R. Kasser, *L' Évangile selon Thomas*, Bibliotèque Théologique (Neuchâtel, 1961) p. 71. In fact, we find similar translations of παρέρχομαι in Matthew 5.18, 24.35, Mark 6.48, 13.13, and Luke 16.17. For further use of this verb in texts, refer to E. Peterson, *Frühkirche, Judentum und Gnosis* (Rome: Herder, 1959) pp. 297, 301 and n. 64. For other translation suggestions, see T. Baarda, 'Jesus said: Be Passersby. On the Meaning and Origin of Logion 42 of the Gospel of Thomas,' in *Early Transmission of Words of Jesus* (Amsterdam: Uitgeverij, 1983) pp. 179–206.

13. J. Jeremias, *Unbekannte Jesusworte* (Zurich: Zwingli-Verlag, 1948) pp. 107–110, esp. nn. 240 and 251; G. Quispel, *Makarius, Das Thomasevangelium, und das Lied von der Perle* (Leiden: E.J. Brill, 1967) pp. 20–22; G. Quispel, 'Gnosticism and the New Testament,' in *Gnostic Studies 1* (Leiden: Nederlands Historisch-Archaeologisch Instituut te Istanbul, 1974) p. 197.

In one passage we learn that 'we ought to be careful, yea, extremely careful, that we cast not our pearls before pigs' when we preach the words of truth to an audience filled with worthy and unworthy people alike (*Rec.* 2.3). The teacher of the truth must be very cautious when setting forth the truth in a mixed crowd because 'if he set forth pure truth to those who do not desire to obtain salvation, he does injury to him by whom he has been sent, and from whom he received the commandment not to throw the pearls of his words before pigs and dogs' (*Rec.* 3.1).

According to the *Pseudo-Clementines*, Jesus 'knows hidden things' (*Hom.* 3.13), and reveals 'that which lies secretly veiled in all human hearts' (*Hom.* 18.6). He 'enables some to find easily what they seek, while to others he renders even that obscure which is before their eyes.' This preserves the truth for the righteous, the worthy people whose minds 'will fill up secretly' with understanding (*Rec.* 2.25; cf. *Hom.* 18.8). Jesus explains the 'mysteries' to the disciples because the truth has had to be hidden from the impious (*Hom.* 19.20). In the Kernel gospel, Jesus similarly states that only a select number of people are worthy to know the truth that Jesus reveals (L. 62.1). The reason? Because a person does not normally let his left hand know what his right hand is doing (L. 62.2). We discover a comparable application of this saying in *Homily* 18.7–10, an application that is not made by its Synoptic variant (Mt 6.3). Embedded in a discussion about preaching to an audience that potentially contains both worthy and unworthy company is the explanatory note: 'Since God, who is just, judges the mind of each one, he would not have wished this [truth] to be given through the left hand to those on the right hand.' Thus, those present and listening must all be known to the Son and worthy of the revelation. The Son is 'alone appointed to give the revelation to those to whom he wishes to give it' (*Hom.* 18.13).

The theme emphasized in both the Kernel and the *Pseudo-Clementines*, that the Prophet Jesus has esoteric revelation for the worthy, is actually a development of a Jewish tradition about God's prophets which we find embedded, for instance, in *4 Ezra*. In chapter 14, the Lord reveals to the Prophet Moses 'many wondrous things, and showed him the secrets of the times and declared to him the end of times' (14.5). He tells Moses that some things he can make public while others he must only tell 'in secret to the wise' (14.26; cf. 14.45–46). In fact, the Qumranites appear to have developed this tradition in their own way, acknowledging the Mosaic Torah as the manifest (*nigleh*) teaching while at the same time regarding their own laws as the hidden (*nistar*) teaching.[14]

According to the Ebionites, part of the special revelation that Jesus is

---

14. S. Fraade, 'Literary Composition and Oral Performance in Early Midrashim,' *OT* 14 (1999) p. 40.

responsible for delivering is the teaching that 'God desires mercy and not sacrifice.' People were to learn from Jesus that the 'place' that God chooses for purification is baptism when one's sins are forgiven through 'his wisdom.' They are to hear from the Prophet Jesus that the Temple, although instrumental for a time, is the 'place' that has often been harassed by 'hostile invasions and plunderings' and 'at last' will be 'wholly destroyed' (*Rec.* 1.37–38; cf. 1.64). Similarly, the Kernel L. 71 implies that the Temple will be utterly destroyed. But an even more interesting parallel is the fact that the Kernel saying is embedded in a cluster of logia which are addressing the question, 'What makes a person worthy or blessed?' We are told that the hated, persecuted, and hungry are the blessed ones (L. 68.1, 69.2). The Temple will be destroyed. The worthy are not to be like the fool who came to Jesus seeking his portion of his father's inheritance (L. 72). The blessed are the hard workers laboring in the fields (L. 73). They are unlike the majority who are standing around a well but refuse to enter the well to draw water (L. 74). They are compared to the shrewd merchant who sold everything he had to buy a single pearl (L. 76). It appears that, in this rhetorical context, L. 71 was understood to imply what the *Pseudo-Clementines* make explicit: worship at the Temple does not make a person worthy before God or blessed by him as many mistakenly think.

A very striking cluster of sayings found in the Kernel (L. 9, 10, 11, 14.4, 15) is also embedded and interpreted in *Homily* 11. The speech of Peter begins in 11.2 with a reference to the Sower Parable, stating that a person must purify his or her mind from evil and sin, hastening to pluck out the 'many thorns' of the heart. The eschatological urgency driven home in L. 11 is referenced too. Peter tells the person that the time remaining is short and should be used for purposes of purification. In 11.3 (cf. *Rec.* 6.4.2–4), the saying in L. 10 is alluded to, admonishing the audience to let into the mind the fire of righteous indignation kindled by the teaching of Jesus so that evil lust can be consumed. L. 14.4 and Matthew 25.35–36 are referenced in 11.4 where Peter tells the hearers that they are the 'image of the invisible God' when their minds are pure, transforming the soul. To honor this Image, they should take care of the sick, feed the hungry, give drink to the thirsty, clothe the naked, shelter the stranger, and visit the prisoner. This appears to me to be a developed interpretation of L. 14.4 which commands the hearer to heal the sick. The following three chapters, 11.5–7, appear to be a discussion of the saying found in L. 15, explaining the importance of proper worship of the Father, the one True God, rather than the worship of false things which will only end in punishment.

In the *Recognitions* it is stated that although the seeker will find a difficult journey to the Kingdom, the 'labor' should not be considered 'hard' because 'at the end of it there shall be rest' (*Rec.* 2.22), a teaching not unlike that of L. 2 and 90. Why is it so essential for the person to seek the truth from Jesus? What 'rest' is being promised? As was implied by the sayings in the Kernel gospel (L. 10, 16, 21.10, 40, 57, 61.1), the *Clementine* literature states consistently that the reason for this journey is because it will result in Judgment: 'Humans must inquire whether they have it in their power by seeking to find what is good, and to do it when they have found it; for this is that for which they are to be judged' (*Rec.* 3.37). The looming Judgment means that people must make the immediate choice to seek the truth or perish (*Hom.* 9.19; 15.6; 20.3). 'At the time of harvest,' the *Recognitions* say, 'the crops are gathered into the barn, but the chaff or the tares are burned in the fire.' This is the Day of Judgment, 'when the righteous shall be introduced into the Kingdom of Heaven, and the unrighteous shall be cast out, then the justice of God shall be known' (*Rec.* 3.38). At the Judgment, the worthy person will be the one whose mind has received 'the best seed' and has brought forth 'joyful fruits by good deeds.' If a person refuses to receive this seed, 'he shall have the cause of his perishing, not from us, but from himself' (*Rec.* 4.6–8; 5.8). 'Ignorance' will make a person 'the enemy of God,' and he can be certain that he will perish (*Rec.* 5.18, 28).

The rhetorical reading of the speeches presented earlier in this chapter confirm a picture of Christianity very comparable to that embedded in the *Pseudo-Clementines*. The first Thomasine Christians thought that the world was rapidly coming to a close. As this happened, they, the faithful, were to realize how essential it was for them to prepare for the inevitable chaos and the day of Judgment. How were they to prepare? They were to devote themselves exclusively to Jesus the Prophet and heed his instructions since he was the only person who revealed God's Truth (L. 2.1, 5.1, 8.4, 17, 21.11, 38.1, 39, 42, 62.1, 63.4, 65.8, 92–94, 96.3). He had even been blessed from the womb with the possession of God's word (L. 79).

The community members were encouraged in the Kernel speeches to keep their faith in Jesus' promises and protection, hoping in their election and believing in the inauguration of God's Kingdom. Relief from the failing world would only come to those who persevered, maintaining their commitment to Jesus and the steadily advancing Kingdom (L. 10, 15, 23.1, 40, 57, 61.1, 82, 107). In fact, they are told that they must be as shrewd and committed as the merchant who sells all his merchandise in order to buy a fine pearl which he came across in the marketplace (L. 76) and as wise as the fisherman who kept an excellent catch (L. 8). Jesus warns them that their commitment to him and the coming Kingdom would not make their lives easier in the meantime, but instead even more demanding. Thus the decision to follow him exclusively was not only urgent but also extremely difficult in these chaotic times.

The Kernel, then, has close affinities with the Christian traditions associated with Jerusalem in terms of its Christology and possibly in terms of a literary and hermeneutical connection since it appears that the *Pseudo-*

Clementines were familiar with the Kernel *Thomas* and provide meaningful interpretations of some clusters of sayings also located in the Kernel. Since the Kernel has close affinities with Christian traditions from Jerusalem, are we to trace its origin there? A more detailed study of the Kernel's apocalyptic message should provide us with some answers.

Chapter 5

The Imminent Apocalypse

An unspoken context dwarfs the textual artifact ~ *J.M. Foley*

Many of the Kernel sayings are striking because they are most comparable to material that belongs to the apocalyptic tradition and appear to be fragments of a larger apocalyptic story, a referential horizon echoing the eschatological myth common to many first-century Jews and Christians. The Thomasine expectations found in the Kernel sayings are expressions of a complex of first-century Jewish apocalyptic ideas that had been developing, at the very latest, since the Maccabean period.

5.1 *Apocalyptic Expectations in the Kernel Sayings*

Many Kernel sayings appear to be eschatological warnings about the impending cosmic destruction, and advice from Jesus about preparing for the final day and God's Judgment. The times alluded to in these sayings are the end times, chaotic and abnormal (L. 11.1, 16.1–3, 35, 58, 64, 65, 68.1, 69.2, 71, 74, 79, 81, 82, 98, 103, 111.1). Only the faithful few who are able to persevere, maintaining their exclusive commitment to God and Jesus, will find relief in the hope of their election while the unfaithful will be judged accordingly (L. 10, 15, 23.1, 40, 57, 61.1, 82, 107). The day of Judgment and the coming Kingdom are imminent, an apocalyptic idea expressed vividly in the Kernel's Kingdom parables. The Kingdom is like a mustard seed which will soon become a big shrub tree or a pinch of yeast which will soon leaven fine loaves: although its beginnings appear tiny and mysterious, the Kingdom of God will be quickly established in its fullness (L. 20, 96). The arrival of the Kingdom is so near it will be a surprise to many, like the woman who did not notice the crack in her jar until she got home and found it empty or the man who unexpectedly found a buried treasure in his field (L. 97, 109). It is likely that the people of the audience would have heard the Kernel speeches as echoes within the deeper apocalyptic story of their time.

5.1.1 *Eschatological and Mystical Dimensions of Apocalyptic*

The Jewish apocalypticists believed that their own generation was among the last to live on earth because this world was rapidly coming to an end. This sense of immediacy is a fundamental idea running through apocalyptic literature, as we can see even in a few lines from *2 Baruch*:

> For the youth of this world has passed away, and the power of creation is already exhausted, and the coming of the times is very near and has passed by. And the pitcher is near the well, and the ship to the harbor, and the journey to the city, and life to its end. Further, prepare yourselves so that, when you sail and ascend from the ship, you may have rest and not be condemned when you have gone away. For behold, the Most High will cause all these things to come. There will not be opportunity to repent anymore, nor a limit to the times, nor a duration of the periods, nor a change to rest, nor an opportunity to prayer, nor sending up petition, nor supplicating offenses, nor prayers of the father, nor intercessions of the prophets, nor help of the righteous. There is the proclamation of judgment to corruption, regarding the way to the fire and the path that leads to the glowing coals. Therefore, there is one law by One, one world and an end for all those who exist. Then he will make alive those whom he has found, and he will purge them from sins, and at the same time he will destroy those who are polluted with sins (85.10–15).

The evil powers who ruled this world would soon be overcome by God and his armies of angels. As this heavenly battle ensued, the earth mirrored its conflict, experiencing wild war, complete chaos, and utter destruction. As the world collapsed under the weight of the cosmic siege and died, a new world was in the process of being born, a Kingdom which God ruled. As any mother can attest, it is not without significance that the apocalypticists described the end of history in terms of the birth pangs of a mother in labor!

Before the new world could fully replace the old, however, retribution must be paid. To this end, the Jewish apocalypticists expected the few living pious servants of Yahweh to be preserved from the final destruction of the world. Also to this end, they believed that at least some of the dead would be raised to receive punishment for their sins or eternal reward for their righteousness. God or his angelic viceroy would come into the heavenly court and preside over this Judgment. Sometimes it is the righteous themselves who carry out the sentence of destruction by sword and war. This complex of ideas about destruction, retribution, and salvation make up the *horizonal dimension* of apocalyptic thought, the *eschatological dimension* concerned with the progress of time and human history, a history that is brought to a rapid end with God's Judgment. Only after the old world and the sinners had been destroyed could God's Kingdom fully replace the kingdoms of the old world.

Because the apocalyptists were so convinced of the imminent end of history, they understood that they lived in a time when the traditional boundary between earth and heaven was starting to collapse. This idea is expressed variously in Jewish literature, sometimes imaged as the 'rolling up of the skies' (cf. Isa 34.4; *Sib. Or.* 3.81–82; Ps 102.25–26; Heb 1.12; Rev 6.14). Because the boundary was about to collapse, the heavens had become more permeable in the waning days of the world. As history marched toward its end and the Kingdom of God began replacing the kingdoms of this world, God was becoming immediately accessible to very pious humans who were crossing the threshold into his new world. The vision of the merkavah and Yahweh which previously had been reserved for the prophets and priests of Israel were now becoming available to the elect remnant.

This is what I call the *atemporal* aspect of apocalypticism, the vertical or mystical dimension.[1] Since the cosmology of the ancient Jews and Christians dictated that the presence of God dwelled in a heavenly sphere, crossing the threshold into his new world was framed in their literature as a glorious rapture event, a human invasion of the celestial realm where the heavenly Temple was situated, or the recreation of the heavenly Temple and world within their community. These rapture encounters, other-worldly journeys, and celestial recreations were featured in apocalyptic literature because they offered the believer a glimpse of or participation in the heavenly Temple and world to come, the world upon whose threshold he or she now stood. They provided the believer with the reassurance that God was available to him and could be worshiped, that God was enthroned and in control of life and nations' destinies at a time when the world was in shambles and passing away (cf. *Apoc. Abra.; Abr.; Life of Adam and Eve* 25–28; *Apoc. Mos.* 37–39; *3 Baruch; 1, 2, 3 Enoch; Asc. Isa.; Levi* 2.6–5.3; *Isaac; Ass. Mos.;* 4Q400–407; 11Q17; 4Q286–87; 4Q491; 1QH 14.13–14; 1QH 19.10–14, 20–23; 1QH 23.10; 1QS 11.5–10). These mystical experiences, then, were the means by which the ancients validated the promises of God in times of crisis or severe conditions, times they understood to be eschatological when God would become increasingly accessible to mystical gaze.

This tradition is connected to the ancient belief that, at the End of the world, the dead would be resurrected and transformed. They would live in the heavens like the angels, worshiping and looking upon the face of God continually. In fact, in several descriptions of these mystical journeys in

---

1. On this subject, see especially C. Rowland, *The Open Heaven* (London: SPCK, 1982).

apocalyptic literature, the visionary experiences a transformation quite similar to that which the ancients expected would occur on the day of the resurrection (cf. Dan 12.3, *2 Enoch* 66.7, *4 Ezra* 7.97, *2 Bar.* 51.3, *1 Enoch* 104.2–3, 108.11, Rev 7.9–17, *1QS* 4.23, *Ezek. Trag.* 73–81, *Apoc Zeph.* 3.3– 4, *Asc. Isa.* 7.25, 8.15, 9.1–2, 9.30–38, *1 Enoch* 71.10–14, *2 Enoch* 22.1–10, *3 Enoch* 15, *Apoc. Abr.* 13.15, *Levi* 8).[2] The apocalyptists appear to have believed that, because the Eschaton was in progress, it was possible for the very virtuous person to begin immediately undergoing bodily transformation and heavenly journeys culminating in brief celestial gazes, and that this would soon become a permanent situation. This, in fact, was probably the original understanding of the Gospel stories about Jesus' transfiguration and resurrection, as well as Paul's comments about the progressive transformation of the righteous faithful (2 Cor 3.18; cf. Gal 4.19; Rom 8.29; 12.2; Phil 2.5; 2 Cor 5.17; Col 3.9–10), a transformation that would be completed very soon on the pending Last Day (1 Cor 15.49–54; Phil 3.20–21).

The *Pseudo-Clementine* corpus provides a fine example of this line of reasoning. In this corpus, we find a tradition that directly correlates the eschatological collapse of the visible boundary between the highest heaven and earth with the availability of visions of God to Christians who are 'pure in heart.' In response to Simon's question, 'Why was the visible heaven made at first if it is to be dissolved?' Peter says:

> 'It was made for the sake of this present human life, that there might be some sort of interposition and separation, lest any unworthy one might see the habitation of the celestials and the abode of God himself, which are prepared in order to be seen by those only who are of pure heart' (*Rec.* 3.27; cf. *Rec.* 2.68).

According to Peter, the boundary had been created by God initially to keep unworthy people from ascending into heaven and gazing upon him in his celestial abode. He then makes the observation that the world in which he lives is experiencing a great 'time of conflict' as it comes to its end. The boundary between heaven and earth was about to collapse. The image of the scroll is used in Peter's description of this eschatological collapse: the 'visible heaven shall be folded up like a scroll and that which is higher shall appear' (*Rec.* 3.26). As this happens, he concludes, pious people will be able to ascend and gaze upon God in his divine abode. Simon responds, asking Peter how this can be when the Law teaches that none shall see God's face and live. Clearly Simon

---

2. W. Bousset suggested that pre-mortem ecstatic ascent to heaven was depicted in the apocalyptic texts as an 'anticipation' of the ascent of the soul after death. See his 'Die Himmelsreise der Seele,' *ARW* 4 (1901) p. 136.

understands Peter to be saying that the imminent End has made the boundary more permeable, permitting immediate mystical ascent and gaze.

In the continuation of the narrative, this tradition undergoes a redaction. The subsequent narrative seems to be responding in part to the failure of the End to precipitate and the vision to occur as well as providing polemic against Paul who based his authority on his own mystical *apocalypsis*. Peter tells Simon that he misunderstands the human condition itself is what makes it impossible for anyone to see God. 'But *after* the resurrection of the dead, when they shall be made like the angels, they shall be able to see God.' Angels are not made of flesh but are spirits that have the capacity to gaze upon God who is also spirit (*Rec.* 3.30). This tradition is quite developed in the *Homilies* where we find a thorough discussion of God's beautiful luminous body and face which even the angels of the 'least faithful' continually behold (*Hom.* 17.7). His beauty is said to be a reward for people who are 'pure in heart' who have suffered so much during their earthly lives (*Hom.* 17.7). The gaze of the pious on God is understood by Peter to be the *final* eschatological experience when the fleshly body will be 'changed into the nature of light' and will thus be able to behold God's own luminous body. 'The just people shall behold God. For in the resurrection of the dead, when they have been changed, as far as their bodies are concerned, into light, and become like the angels, they shall be able to see him' (*Hom.* 12.16).

Clearly, the time in which the Christians lived was perceived by them to be what anthropologists call a 'liminal' state.[3] They were caught 'betwixt and between,' in a period when the normal laws that governed the universe, society, and humans were suspended and changing.[4] In fact, they understood their Christian community to be the initial expression of the future Kingdom of God which was in the process of replacing the kingdoms of this world. The old world was passing away and the new world was on the way. They were, what I call, *apocalyptic threshold communities* (Diagram 5). In this regard, the first communities were both eschatological, anxiously awaiting the end of the old world, and mystical, participating already in the new world, a stance not unlike that found in

3. A. van Gennep, *The Rites of Passage* (trans. M.B. Vizedom and G.L. Caffe; London: Routledge & Kegan Paul, 1960); V.W. Turner, *The Ritual Process* (Chicago: Aldine Publishing Company, 1969).

4. K. Burridge, *New Heaven, New Earth: A Study of Millenarian Activities* (New York: Schocken Books, 1969; I.C. Jarvie, *The Revolution of Anthropology* (Chicago: Henry Regnery, 1967); V. Turner, *The Ritual Process*; J.G. Gager, 'Earliest Christianity as a Millenarian Movement,' in his *Kingdom and Community: The Social World of Early Christianity* (Prentice-Hall: Englewood Cliffs, 1975) pp. 19–65.

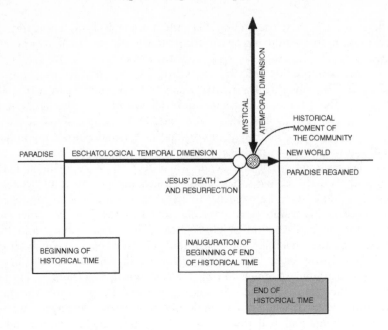

Diagram 5:   Threshold Community

the Qumran literature.[5] As they waited for the immediate destruction of the world and the emergence of God's Kingdom, they looked for the coming of Jesus as God's Judge. From their perspective, his resurrection to the right hand of God was the beginning of the general resurrection of the dead as well as his elevation to the angelic status of God's Judge. The Judgment would soon follow.

Both the horizontal and the vertical dimensions of apocalypticism are evident in the sayings preserved in the Kernel *Thomas*. A couple of sayings, in fact, actually invoke the image of the crumbling boundary between heaven and earth. In the Kernel *Thomas*, Jesus reveals that 'this heaven will pass away and the one above it will pass away' (L. 11.1). Comparable to the Synoptic version of the saying, in L. 111.1, Jesus describes this

5.   G. Jeremias, *Der Lehrer der Gerechtigkeit*, SUNT 2 (Göttingen, 1963) pp. 333–334; D.E. Aune, *The Cultic Setting of Realized Eschatology in Early Christianity* (E.J. Brill: Leiden, 1972) pp. 29–44. On Qumran, see now R. Elior, *The Three Temples: On the Emergence of Jewish Mysticism* (Oxford: The Littman Library of Jewish Civilization, 2004).

collapse by using the scroll image: 'The heavens and earth will roll up in your presence' (cf. Mk 13.31; Mt 24.35; Lk 21.33). Notice that this destruction was believed to be so imminent by the early Thomasine Christians that Jesus reveals to them in this saying that the heavens and earth will be rolled up *in their very presence*.

Since the barriers between earth and heaven had begun to crumble according to the 'original' *Gospel of Thomas*, it should not be surprising that the Kernel gospel would contain a saying which reveals the etiquette that Jesus' followers might need when they enter heaven to approach God's throne and worship him. Like the many heroes found in other apocalyptic traditions who had already ascended into heaven, when the faithful followers of Jesus come before the Father and see him enthroned, they are supposed to fall on their faces and worship him (L. 15; *1 En.* 14.24; *2 En.* 22.4).[6]

This atemporal or mystical dimension of apocalyptic is also the apparent context for L. 82. In apocalyptic literature, fire is frequently associated with theophanies. This association is rooted in the ancient Jewish traditions describing God's manifestation, his *kavod*, in fiery terms (Exod 16.10b; 24.16–17, 43–44; 40.34–35, 38; Num 17.7; 1 Kgs 8.10–11; Lev 9.23–24; 1 Sam 3.3; 4.21; Ezek 1.26–28). Speculations about the heavenly realm contain descriptions of its fiery nature (*1 En.* 14, 17.1–8; *3 En.* 18.19, 21; 19.4, 33.4–5; 36.1–2, 37.1; *Apoc. Abr.* 18–19; *Sib. Or.* 2.196–197, 2.252–253, 2.285–286; *Test. Issac.* 5.21–22), the fiery bodies of the angels who dwelled there (*2 En.* 1.5, 29.3; *3 En.* 22.3–10; *Test. Abr.* 19.1; *2 Baruch* 21.6; *4 Ezra* 8.22), and God enthroned above all, manifesting himself to his creatures and righteous seers in a fiery form (*1 En.* 14; *2 En.* 22; *3 En.* 42.3–7; *Quest. Ezra*, Rec. A, 26; *Vita. Mos.* 25.3). It is this theophantic understanding of fire that is referred to in L. 82:

> (82) ¹Jesus said, 'Whoever is near me, is near the fire. ²But whoever is
> far away from me, is far away from the Kingdom.'

The parallelism of this saying identifies Jesus with the fire of the heavenly realm, the Kingdom. Believers who draw near to him will experience a fiery theophany; those who remain far away from him will not be able to experience a theophany let alone enter the Kingdom. It is no surprise that L. 82, in fact, is embedded in the Kernel in the rhetorical argument of an eschatological speech about the requirements for worthiness, requirements which many prior to Jesus have mistaken. Why should people be concerned about their worthiness? L. 82 implies the rationale: only the

---

6. A.D. DeConick, *Seek to See Him: Ascent and Vision Mysticism in the Gospel of Thomas*, VCSupp 33 (Leiden: E.J. Brill, 1996) pp. 99–100.

worthy can enter the Kingdom, the heavenly realm of fire, where the transformed Jesus dwells and reveals himself. The rhetorical argument concludes this Kernel speech with the reminder that the world is not the permanent residence of human beings because 'rest' cannot be found on earth (L. 86). Rather the worthy people will only find their 'rest' with Jesus in his Kingdom (L. 90). Everyone else speculates about 'the face of heaven and earth' without knowing the truth about Jesus or the urgency of the times (L. 91).

5.1.2 *Unprecedented Chaos*

As a liminal state, eschatological time in Jewish and Christian apocalyptic literature was characterized by unprecedented chaos when the powers of good and evil would engage in battle for control of the world.[7] Sometimes this stage of chaos is described in general terms in the ancient literature as we find in Daniel 12.1. In other texts, however, more specific details are highlighted. For instance, according to *4 Ezra* 5.1–13, women will give birth to monsters, saltwater will be sweet, and 'all friends will conquer one another.' We read that fire will break out along with general chaos. Even wisdom will hide herself and many people will seek her in vain. People will hope and labor to no reward. According to chapter 6, the disorder and chaos will be so great that even 'friends will make war on friends like enemies' (6.24).

This theme is discussed in 1 Enoch 56.7. In this passage, Israel's enemies will begin 'to fight among themselves; and (by) their own right hands they will prevail against themselves. A man shall not recognize his brother, nor a son his mother, until there will be a number of corpses from among them' (cf. Mic 7.6; *Jub* 23.16, 19). *2 Baruch* describes this period of chaos as one of the 'twelve' events of the Eschaton: 'Disorder and a mixture of all that has been before' (27.13). People will hate each other and 'provoke one another to fight.' So contradictory and uncertain are these times that the author of *4 Ezra* tells the hearer, 'Prepare for battle! and in the midst of the calamities be like strangers on the earth' (16.40).

According to Paul, the end time chaos will be proceeded by a temporary moment of peace which will give people a mistaken sense of security: 'When some people say, "There is peace and security," then sudden destruction will come upon them as travail comes upon a woman with child, and there will be no escape' (1 Thess 5.3). This is also mentioned in *4 Ezra:* 'Provisions will be so cheap' that people 'will imagine that peace is assured for them' (16.21). Unexpectedly though, 'the calamities will spring up on the earth: sword, famine, and great confusion' (16.21). The

---

7.   For an overview of the primary literature, see D.S. Russell, *The Method and Message of Jewish Apocalyptic* (Philadelphia: Westminster Press, 1964) pp. 271–276.

destructive motifs 'fire,' 'famine,' 'calamities,' 'sword,' and 'war,' are so prevalent in the literature that they are considered characteristic features and stem out of exegetical speculations on texts like Ezekiel 13.11, 14.21, Jeremiah 14.12, 21.7, and Isaiah 13.10, 34.4.[8]

The members of the early Thomasine community seem to have been no different in their apocalyptic expectations. In fact, Jesus warns them in the Kernel gospel:

> (16)　[1]Jesus said, 'Perhaps people think it is peace that I have come to cast upon the world. [2]And they do not know it is division that I have come to cast upon the earth – fire, sword, war! [3]For there will be five people in a house. There will be three people against two, and two against three, father against son, and son against father.

In this saying, which we also find in the Synoptics (Lk 12.51–53//Mt 10.34–36), we find the common apocalyptic theme that people are mistaken about the times, believing that it is one of peace. Instead, Jesus is said to usher in the chaos of the Eschaton in language evoking the apocalyptic drama: 'fire, sword, and war.' So extreme is this chaos that families within their own homes can be expected to turn and fight against each other.

In fact, the advice to prepare oneself for the End is quite standard in the *Thomas* Kernel. In L. 98, Jesus tells the story about a man who trains himself for battle so that he will be prepared to defend himself as the chaos associated with the arrival of the Kingdom falls upon him. This advice is echoed in L. 103 where Jesus calls the man 'blessed' who 'knows where the thieves are going to enter, so that [he] may arise, gather at his estate, and arm himself.' Additionally, Jesus teaches that it is impossible for a person to break into a house and ransack it unless he first ties up the person in the house (L. 35). Jesus says that a person must keep watch before the thief tries to break in (L. 21.5). These sayings reflect the eschatological fears of chaos and war, and the very practical wisdom such as we noted in *4 Ezra* to 'prepare for battle!' rather than be caught off guard when the eschatological calamities ferociously hit.

5.1.3 *Reversal of World Order*
In Jewish apocalyptic literature, this liminal period of chaos is described further as a time when the world order and the status quo are reversed. In chapter 6 of *4 Ezra*, the reversal of normalcy is quite pronounced: infants will speak (6.21); premature babies will dance upon their birth (6.21);

8.　Cf. *1 Enoch* 90.13–20; 91.12–17; 93; *Jubilees* 23.13; *4 Ezra* 5.1; *2 Baruch* 25; Mk 13.13, 20 and parallels; Rev 6; 8–9; 16; 20.

seeded ground will appear unsown (6.22); full storehouses will be empty (6.22); flowing fountains will stand still (6.24). According to *2 Baruch*, the 'despised will rule over the honorable.' The powerless will rule over the 'strong.' The 'poor will be greater in number than the rich' (70.3–5). In this time of reversal, 'the earth will also yield fruits ten thousandfold ... And those who are hungry will enjoy themselves and they will, moreover, see marvels every day' (29.5–7).

Jesus in the Kernel *Gospel of Thomas* also is a strong advocate for the reversal of normalcy in a world rapidly coming to an End. Thus he blesses the maiden or barren woman, 'the womb that has not conceived and the breasts that have not given milk,' rather than blessing the mother (L. 79), an expectation quite pronounced in other apocalyptic texts including the Synoptics (Lk 23.29; Mk 13.17–19//Mt 24.19–21//Lk 21.20–24; *2 Baruch* 10.13b–16; *Apoc. Elijah* [C] 2.38).[9] Because the day of Judgment is so near, in the same logion Jesus also blesses those who have heard 'the word of the Father and have truly kept it' (L. 79). How much better it will be for them when they come before God on that day! The hungry are blessed because their bellies will be filled (L. 69.2), the suffering are blessed because they have found life (L. 58), and the hated and persecuted are blessed (L. 68.1) because they will have relief, apocalyptic themes also discussed in the Synoptics (Mt 5.6, 10–11//Lk 6.21–22; Mt 10.22–23).

In L. 46, as in the Synoptic parallels (Mt 11.11//Lk 7.28), we see a striking example of the reversal of power roles: in the Kingdom, even the child, the ultimate example of the powerless in the ancient world, will be superior to the great prophet John the Baptist himself. In fact, rulers are advised in the *Thomas* Kernel that it is in their best interest to renounce their power rather than retain it: 'Whoever has grown wealthy, that person should become a king. [2]But whoever possesses power, let that person disown (his power)' (L. 81). This is quite similar to the advice given in *1 Enoch* 62–63. Here we discover that the apocalyptists believed that the best course of action for kings was to renounce their power as God's Judgment drew near. In so doing, the kings demonstrated their loyalty to God, renouncing the forces of evil that have been controlling this world and supporting their kingdoms.

Voluntary poverty rather than wealth was valued by the first Thomasine Christians. So in the Kernel gospel, we find Jesus' blessing of the poor and those who hunger. In one of the Kernel parables, Jesus even focuses on the stupidity of the rich man whose intentions of gaining wealth are preposterous in face of death:

9. For more information on this apocalyptic theme, see B.J. Pitre, 'Blessing the Barren and Warning the Fecund: Jesus' Message for Women Concerning Pregnancy and Childbirth,' *JSNT* 81 (2001) pp. 59–80.

(63) [1]Jesus said, 'There was a wealthy man who had many assets. [2]He said, "I will use my assets to sow, harvest, plant and fill my granaries with produce, so that I will not need anything." [3]These were the things he was thinking in his heart. But that very night, he died.'

Jesus relates in the Kernel that those who dress in fine garments are 'unable to understand the truth' (L. 78). I imagine that many converts would have found voluntary poverty a very difficult experience. So it is not surprising that, as we have seen, they preserved a saying in which Jesus blesses those who suffer; it is they who have found life (L. 58).

The Kernel sayings call the believer to focus every intention, thought and activity on God, forsaking the conventions of society. Jesus commands them to forsake even their ordinary daily concerns, like considering how they are going to dress (L. 36). L. 72 reflects this radical ethic as well:

(72) [1]A man said to him, 'Tell my brothers that they must share with me my father's possessions.'
[2]He said to him, 'Mister, who has made me an executor?'
[3]He turned to his disciples and said to them, 'Surely I am not an executor, am I?'

The situation is one in which a man comes to Jesus for a judgment about the distribution of his deceased father's property, a situation which other rabbis encountered too (cf. *b. Shabbat* 116b). Since the man asks Jesus to command his brothers to divide his father's possessions with him, he had apparently not received his rightful inheritance, while his brothers had. He expected that Jesus would comply, righting the perceived wrong.

Jesus, however, provides a clever deflective response in which he indicates that the man has asked the wrong person to handle this situation. He asks the man, 'Mister, who has made me an executor?' Then he turns to his disciples and inquires, 'I am not an executor, am I?' In this way, Jesus indicates that his mission is to be distinguished from those of other rabbis. He is not the kind of rabbi who is concerned about civil matters like arbitrating inheritance disputes. Rather he is concerned with preaching about the urgency of the coming of the Kingdom, preparing people for the coming of God's Judgment.

5.1.4 *Destruction of the Temple*

Of course, the paramount image of God's Judgment was the destruction of the Jewish Temple. Thus, in apocalyptic literature, we find either that the Temple and its priesthood was believed to be corrupt and in need of purging or cleansing, or that it would be destroyed as the consequence of

God's Judgment; sometimes it would be rebuilt in the new world (*Jub.* 1.29, 23.21; *1 En.* 14.8–25, 71.5–6, 89.73, 91.13; *2 Bar.* 4.2–6, *T. Levi* 5.1, 18.1–14; *4Q266* 3.20–4.3), sometimes not (*T. Moses* 5–10). We find such musings already in the prophetic tradition, particularly in Ezekiel 40–48 where, following the destruction of the earthly Temple, the belief developed that the true Temple was in heaven (cf. Exod 25.9, 40; 26.30; 27.8), remaining there until the appointed time. Only then would the Temple descend to Jerusalem and God's *kavod* take up residence there permanently. The Zadokite priests would be in charge of this Temple, seemingly replacing the more general Levitical priests who had gone astray earlier (Ezekiel 44.15; 48.11).

In Third Isaiah, we find a condemnation of the Second Temple cultus and its priesthood (66.1–6) coupled with the promise of a glorious future Temple where all nations would gather to worship Yahweh (56.6–8; 60.10–14).

Given these types of speculations, I do not think it surprising that the early Christians believed that the Second Temple would be destroyed at the Eschaton and that Jesus would be instrumental in bringing about its collapse. Such musings are found in Mark 13.2; 14.58, 15.29–30, Matthew 24.2, 26.61, 27.40, Acts 6.14, John 2.19, and the *Gospel of Peter* 7.26. This eschatological expectation is also found in the Kernel *Thomas:*

> (71)   Jesus said, 'I will destroy [this] temple, and no one will build it
> [. . .].'

Unlike Mark, which is promoting the tradition that a divinely rebuilt Temple will take its place, a Temple 'not made with hands,' (14.58), this *Thomas* saying suggests that the Temple will not be raised again (cf. Revelation 21.22). It is likely that this tradition is older than the Synoptic variants, which tone down the harsh oracle by suggesting that there is hope, the Temple will be rebuilt. *Thomas* 71 looks to be an older variant and may provide some insight into the reason for Jesus' arrest and death. We must be cautious, however, not to put too much emphasis on this reading since the manuscript contains a laucanae of 8–9 letters following ⲚⲀϢⲔⲞⲦϤ. There is a mark suggesting the bottom of a letter immediately following the final ϥ.[10] This indicates that the saying probably did not end on this note. We can conclude minimally, however, that the early Thomasine Christians anticipated the destruction of the Temple through the intervention of Jesus at the Eschaton.

---

10.   B. Layton, *Nag Hammadi Codex II,2–7*, NHS 20 (Leiden: E.J. Brill, 1989), p. 80; *The Facsimile Edition of the Nag Hammadi Codices, Codex II* (Leiden: E.J. Brill, 1974), p. 55.

5.1.5 *Final Judgment*

In the apocalyptic Judgment tradition, God or his agent usually acts as the Judge, although sometimes it is the righteous themselves who carry out the sentence of destruction by sword and war (*1 Enoch* 90.19; *1QM*). In Zechariah 3.1–7, the angel of Yahweh represents Yahweh as the Judge of the heavenly court. In Jewish apocalyptic writings, the representative is either Michael (Dan 12.1; *1QM* 17.6–7; *As. Mos.; T. Dan.* 6.1–7), Melchizedek (11Q Melch), the Son of Man (Dan 7; *1 Enoch* 37–71; *4 Ezra* 13), the Messiah (*Ps. Sol.* 17; *4 Ezra* 11–12; *Sib. Or.* 5), or Abel (*Abr.*). In Christian apocalyptic traditions, this figure was identified with Jesus (i.e., Mk 8.38; Mk 14.62; Mt 25.31). So it is not surprising that the Kernel *Gospel of Thomas* also identifies Jesus with the role and functions of God's angelic Judge and applies to him many of the Judgment images common in Jewish apocalyptic thought.

5.1.5.1 *Selection of the Few*

A central feature of the Judgment tradition in Jewish apocalyptic texts is the separation of the few believers from the many unbelievers at the Judgment. For instance, in *4 Ezra* 7.45–61, Ezra is worried that 'the world to come will bring delight to few, but torments to many.' God tells him that at Judgment this will be the case unequivocally: 'I will rejoice over the few who shall be saved, because it is they who have made my glory to prevail now, and through them my name has now been honored. And I will not grieve over the multitude of those who perish; for it is they who are now like a mist, and are similar to flame and smoke – they are set on fire and burn hotly, and are extinguished.' The righteous people, according to *1 Enoch* 51, on that final day, 'shall be selected and saved.' The 'righteous elect' will be 'chosen' from among the many apostates (*1 Enoch* 93.10). God will 'preserve' them while the unrighteous will perish (*1 Enoch* 1.8).

Similar apocalyptic ideas are pronounced by Jesus in the Kernel gospel . He says that he, himself, will be the one who will select 'one from a thousand, and two from ten thousand' (L. 23.1). According to Logion 61.1, the odds of selection were slightly better: 'Two people will rest on a couch. One will die. One will live' (cf. Lk 17.34–35; Mt 24.40–41). The coming Kingdom is compared, in the Kernel, to the story of a shepherd who saved the one sheep among the hundred that made up his flock (L. 107; cf. Mt 18.12–13; Lk 15.3–6).

5.1.5.2 *Harvest Motif*

A common image used in Jewish apocalyptic tradition to describe the Judgment is that of the 'harvest,' having a long history in the Old Testament descriptions of the Judgment that God will cast upon Israel and the nations (Isa 17.5; 18.4–5; 24.13; 63.1–6; Jer 51.33; Hos 6.11; Mic

4.12–13; Joel 3.13). According to *4 Ezra* 4.28–32, this age is 'swiftly hastening to its end,' an age when evil is 'sown' before the 'harvest' comes. This 'evil seed' was sown in Adam's heart and it has produced a crop so great as to be immeasurable. 'When the heads of grain without number are sown, how great a threshing floor they will fill!' According to *2 Baruch* 70.2, at the end 'when the time of the world has ripened and the harvest of the seed of the evil ones and the good ones has come,' chaos will come over the world in the form of wars, fires, earthquakes and famine. In *Sib. Or.* 2.154–176, 'the [time of the] harvest of articulate men' is coming. Women will cease to bear children when this harvest, 'the gathering together,' draws near. The image of winnowing is used by the apocalyptic Baptist as a metaphor for the approaching Judgment (Mt 3.12; Lk 3.17). In Revelation 14.15, at the Judgment, an angel calls out to the Judge, 'Put in your sickle, and reap, for the hour to reap has come, for the harvest of the earth is fully ripe.'

In the Kernel, the harvest motif is employed by Jesus. He warns about the coming harvest and its consequences: [10]'When the grain ripened, he came quickly with his sickle in his hand. He harvested it. [11]Whoever has hears to hear should listen!' (L. 21.10–11; cf. Mk 4.29). Likewise, God's Kingdom is compared to the situation that faces the farmer who waits until the harvest to separate out the weeds from the crop so that the wheat stalks are not mistakenly destroyed along with the weeds:

(57)   [1]Jesus said, 'The Kingdom of the Father is like a man who had [good] seed. [2]His enemy came at night. He added darnel to the good seed. [3]The man did not let them pull out the darnel. He explained to them, "Lest you go to pull out the darnel, but pull out the wheat with it. [4]For on the day of the harvest, the darnel will be discernable, and will be pulled up and burned"' (cf. Mt 13.24–30, 36–43).

The underlying theme of Judgment is unmistakable in L. 40 where the unworthy Pharisees are compared to 'a grapevine' that 'has been planted apart from the Father's (planting).' It is 'not strong' and 'it will be plucked up by its roots, and it will perish' (cf. Mt 15.13). So great in number are those in need of redemption before the day of Judgment that Jesus admonishes his disciples to pray to God that more laborers be sent out to the harvest, since the 'harvest is plentiful' but the laborers 'few' (L. 73; cf. Mt 9.37–38; Lk 10.2).

Thus, the mission of the believer who faced the coming of the Eschaton, was to 'walk about in the districts,' healing the sick and preaching from the 'housetops' (L. 14.4, 33). Yet not everyone they encountered would respond positively to their preaching. Not everyone would convert. In fact, some might even hate the preachers and actually persecute them (L. 68.1). They could even expect to experience this animosity within their own familial units (L. 16.1–3). Since the Thomasine Christians were to devote themselves entirely to the mission of the imminent Kingdom and Judgment, they were told to sever ties with their nuclear family (L. 55; 99). Only when they 'hated' their parents and siblings could they 'take up the cross' and follow Jesus, imitating his suffering even to death (L. 55).

This demand for total commitment to the mission was the result of the urgency of their message and the fact that they believed that they were living in a liminal period when the normal rules and institutions of society were not only suspended, but were also being terminated. They were not preaching about the good society and how to maintain it. They were teaching about the end of the present social structure and the beginning of a new world. They believed that the new world could not be established with the old rules still in place. In Jesus' words: [3]'No one drinks aged wine and immediately wants to drink unaged wine. [4]Also, unaged wine is not put into old wineskins so that they may burst. Nor is aged wine put into a new wineskin so that it may spoil. [5]An old patch is not sewn onto a new garment because a tear would result.' (L. 47.3–5).

5.1.5.3 *Messianic Banquet*

The apocalyptic Judgment tradition similarly uses the 'banquet' motif to describe the selection of the faithful and the reward awaiting them in the world to come. The banquet motif is quite common in the Synoptic Gospels (Mt 8.11–12; 22.2–14; Lk 14.16–24) and in later Rabbinic tradition where it is used in metaphors and parables describing the age to come. Like the Synoptics, the Rabbis used this motif eschatologically. They specifically applied the images and expectations found in Isaiah 65.13 and Psalm 23.5 to the future age (*b. Shab.* 153a; *Qoh. Rab.* 9.8; *Shem. Rab.* 25.7; *Midr. Teh.* 23.7).

In L. 64, this banquet motif is set forth too. Jesus tells the story of a wealthy man who invites guests to a banquet. The guests refuse the rich man's invitation because they have other pressing obligations or commitments. These people are criticized for being busy with worldly concerns including attending a wedding, collecting rent, buying a villa, and following up on a claim against a merchant. Because they have these things to do, they do not have time to attend a special banquet. So the wealthy man has people from the street brought in to sit at his table. Significantly, this parable is embedded in a larger speech about the characteristics of the worthy disciple who must come to understand the truth about Jesus and his eschatological role. The saying suggests in this context that the worthy disciple is one who does not have any other obligations, but is exclusively committed to Jesus. Such a person will enjoy the delights of the banquet in the age to come.

5.1.5.4 *Fire of Retribution*

In apocalyptic texts, fire plays a dominant role in God's retributive and punitive actions of judgment in the last days. Images of fire being cast from heaven are so commonplace in the apocalyptic literature that they become redundant. Such images of a final destructive fire may have been influenced by the Stoics' or Persians' notion of the universal conflagration as well as biblical traditions of fiery retribution (Joel 2.1–3; Ps 50.3–6) destroying Israel (Isa 1.7; Jer 11.16; Amos 2.5; Lam 4.11) and other nations (Gen 19.24; Isa 30.27, 30; Amos 1.4, 7, 10, 12, 14). Thus in Jewish apocalyptic literature, fiery cataracts will fall from heaven (*Sib. Or.* 3.54), burning the earth and sea, and melting the heavens (*Sib. Or.* 3.84–86; cf. *1 Enoch* 52.6). A river of fire will blaze, flowing down from heaven and consuming the earth (*Sib. Or.* 2.196–197; cf. 7.120–121; 8.243). Swords of fire will fall from heaven to earth (*Sib. Or.* 3.672–3), destroying everything at once and leaving nothing but 'smoking dust' (*Sib. Or.* 4.176–178). According to *2 Baruch*, fire will fall as one of the twelve events of the Eschaton (27.11).

More specifically, in Jewish traditions, it was thought that God or his angel(s) would be responsible for pouring the fire of Judgment onto the earth. In the *Sibylline Oracles*, God himself will judge people 'by war and sword and fire and torrential rain' (*Sib. Or.* 3.689–690). God will hurl the fire (*Sib. Or.* 4.171–181). The author of *1 Enoch* agrees, 'In those days, when he hurls out against you terror of fire, where will you flee, and where will you find safety?' (102.1). In the *Apocalypse of Elijah*, the angels are responsible for pouring out the cosmic fires of judgment: 'It will come to pass on that day that the Lord will hear and command the heaven and the earth with great wrath. And they will send forth fire. And the fire will prevail over the earth seventy-two cubits. It will consume sinner and the devils like stubble. A true judgment will occur' (5.22–24). In *4 Ezra* 13.1–11, we find a fascinating passage, however, referring to a man-like angel who will appear on earth, judging with fire streaming from his mouth:

> As I kept looking the wind made something like the figure of a man come up out of the hearth of the sea. And I saw that this man flew with clouds of heaven; and everywhere he turned his face to look, everything under his gaze trembled... After this I looked and saw that an innumerable multitude of people were gathered together from the four winds of heaven to make war against the man who came up from the sea... When he saw the onrush of the approaching multitude, he neither lifted his hand nor held a spear, or any weapon of war; but I saw only how he sent forth from his mouth something like a stream of fire, and from his lips a flaming breath... [which] fell on the onrushing multitude that was prepared to fight, and burned up all of them, so that suddenly nothing was seen of the innumerable multitude but only dust of ashes and the smell of smoke.

Such speculations have their foundation in biblical texts like Isaiah 66, where the Lord 'will come in fire' in order to 'render his anger in fury, and his rebuke with flames of fire,' for 'by fire will the Lord execute judgment, and by his sword, upon all flesh.' In Malachi, we find the expectation that immediately preceding the day of Judgment, God would send a special angel, the prophet Elijah, who would purify the Temple and the priesthood. He would be like 'a refiner's fire' purifying the Levites and refining them 'like gold and silver' until they would be able to make holy offerings to God. Because Elijah was assumed into heaven in a chariot of fire (2 Kgs 2.1–11; cf. *Sir.* 48.1–11), he was given angelic status by many groups.[11]

This type of association may represent the broader tendency in Judaism to identify the prophets with angels (cf. 2 Chr 36.15–16; Isa 44.26; Hag 1.12–13; Jer 23.18–22; *Lev. Rab.* 1.1). Even the title assumed by the prophet 'Malachi' means simply 'my angel' (מלאכי). The prophet Malachi apparently was understood to be the Angel of Yahweh. The association of the category 'angel' with the prophets seems to have emerged after Moses and the establishment of the covenant when the prophets started to function as mediators between God and humans, a function which had previously been held by the Angel of Yahweh according to the earlier literature.[12] It is fascinating that the *Clementine* literature attributes to the True Prophet Jesus the role of Yahweh's angel who appears to the pious throughout the course of history (cf. *Rec.* 1.32; 1.52; 2.22; 2.47–48).[13]

In Christian literature, it is standard to find references to the fires of Judgment being released from heaven. Paul, for example, refers to it: 'each person's work will become manifest; for the Day will disclose it, because it will be revealed with fire, and the fire will test what sort of work each person has done' (1 Cor 3.13–15). In 2 Peter 3.7–14, the reader is warned that fire is being stored up in heaven to be released on the day of Judgment when the 'ungodly' will be destroyed. 'The heavens will pass away with a loud noise, and the elements will be dissolved with fire, and the earth and the works that are upon it will be burned up.' Revelation 8.5 even attests to the tradition that a great angel will be responsible for taking the fire from God's altar in a bowl and casting it upon the earth.

The Christology preserved in L. 10 and 16 connect Jesus with the apocalyptic expectations of God's coming Judgment by associating him

---

11. J. Jeremias, 'Ήλ(ε)ιας,' *TDNT* 2.928–941.

12. For this discussion, refer to C.A. Gieschen, *Angelomorphic Christology: Antecedents and Early Evidence*, AGAJU 42 (Leiden: E.J. Brill, 1998) esp. 161–169.

13. On this see Gieschen, pp. 211–213.

not only with fire, but also with the angelic role of casting it upon the earth:

> (10) Jesus said, 'I have cast fire upon the world. And Look! I am guarding it until it blazes.'
>
> (16) [1]Jesus said, 'Perhaps people think it is peace that I have come to cast upon the world. [2]And they do not know it is division that I have come to cast upon the earth – fire, sword, war! [3]For there will be five people in a house. There will be three people against two, and two against three, father against son, and son against father.'

L. 13 provides additional evidence that the original Thomas community understood Jesus in angelic terms. This particular saying very likely entered the collection in the latter part of the first century in order to develop the angelic Christology of the old Kernel gospel. The impetus for such a revision must have been a development in their ideas about Jesus and his role. By the end of the first century, the depiction of Jesus as God's eschatological angel bringing God's fire and sword of Judgment was adjusted to fit new Christological musings. Now he was understood to be the ineffable Divine Name, Yahweh manifest.[14] Of course, this development in Christology is a natural progression for the Thomasine Christians given the strong connection in Jewish literature with traditions about the Divine Name and traditions about the Angel of Yahweh.[15]

5.2 *The Son of Man Tradition*

The abundant presence of apocalyptic sayings and apocalyptic references in the Kernel gospel suggests that the people associated with this text believed that they were literally on the brink of the Eschaton. Because of this, they were eschatological thinkers, preparing themselves for the end of history and the establishment of God's Kingdom on earth. Since the old world was passing away before their eyes and the boundary between heaven and earth was collapsing, they also were mystics, believing that they were already enjoying the delights of the dawning new world. The imminence of their expectations suggests a date for the Kernel that precedes later concerns about the delay of the *parousia* as we already discover in Christian literature composed around 60 CE.

Is there more support in the Kernel for this *terminus ad quem*? The Christology of the Kernel may be the key since it represents an increment in the development of Christology when Jesus had been identified with the eschatological Judge, a great angel whose job it was to select God's worthy

---

14. DeConick, *Seek to See Him*, pp. 111–115.

15. J. Fossum, *The Name of God and the Angel of the Lord*, WUNT 36 (Tübingen: J.C.B. Mohr, 1985).

from the crowd of unworthy people and cast God's fire of Judgment upon the earth. But this identification had not yet been narrowed by the Christians to its titular use, Son of Man, evoking Daniel 7. What about L. 86 where the phrase 'son of man' does appear in the Kernel? Even though the phrase 'son of man' appears in L. 86, the saying itself does not invoke a Judgment theme. Rather the phrase functions easily as the Aramaic idiom for 'human being' and sensibly works well with the surrounding logia: humans cannot find 'rest' on earth (L. 86) but instead will attain 'rest' from Jesus (L. 90) who has been exalted to heaven (L. 82).

This interpretation of *Thomas'* Christology fits well within the parameters of the complexity of the Son of Man sayings and the development of early Christology. It suggests to me that the Son of Man Christology developed gradually and incrementally through four stages, with roots in the teachings of Jesus of Nazareth. Understanding the Son of Man sayings in this way clears up a morass of scholarly debates on the subject[16] and demonstrates fully the responsive and shifting nature of streams of traditions as they passed through communal memory.

First, a major dimension of Jesus of Nazareth's message was one of repentance in preparation for the imminent eschatological Judgment.[17] The scope of the material and its presence in our earliest layers of traditions is impressive and cannot be easily dismissed as a creation of the early Church, especially since this material does not necessarily contain references to the Son of Man.[18] The content and context of the materials are thoroughly Jewish and harken Jesus' continuity with expressions of Second Temple Judaism. This material also provides the foundation for the first interpretations of Jesus' person by other Christians, as well as their

16. For an overview of this morass, see D. Burkett, *The Son of Man Debate: A History and Evaluation*, SNTSMS 107 (Cambridge: Cambridge University Press, 1999).

17. The corrective that Marcus Reiser provides to the contemporary quest for the 'sapiential' Jesus is long overdue. I have appreciated its clarity and balanced method which seeks to contextualize Jesus within Second Temple Judaism. *Jesus and Judgment: The Eschatological Proclamation in Its Jewish Context* (trans. L. Maloney; Minneapolis: Fortress Press, 1997).

18. *Multiple witnesses*: Mt 9.37//Lk 10.2//*Thom* 73; Mt 10.34//Lk 12.51//*Thom* 16a; Mt 13.24–30//*Thom* 57; Mt 15.13//*Thom* 40; Mt 18.12–14//Lk 15.3–7//*Thom* 107; Mt 22.2–14//Lk 14.16–24//*Thom* 64; Mt 24.40–41//Lk 17.34–35// *Thom* 61a; Mk 4.29//*Thom* 21; Mk 10.31//Mt 19.30//Mt 20.16//Lk 13.30//*Thom* 4b; Lk 12.49//*Thom* 10.

Quelle: Mt 7.1–2//Lk 6.37–38; Mt 7.19//Lk 3.9; Mt 8.11–12//Lk 13.28–29; Mt 10.15//Lk 10.12; Mt 10.28//Lk 12.4–5; Mt 11.21–24//Lk 10.13–15; Mt 12.27//Lk 11.19; Mt 12.32//Lk 12.10; Mt 12.41–42//Lk 11.31–32; Mt 19.28 [has Son of Man]//Lk 22.28–30 [doesn't have Son of Man]; Mt 23.34–36//Lk 11.49–51; Mt 23.37–39//Lk 13.34–35; Mt 25.14–30//Lk 19.11–27.

Mk: Mk 4.24//Mt 7.2//Lk 6.38; Mk 4.25; Mk 4.29//Mt 9.37//Lk 10.2; Mk 9.43–48//Mt 5.29–30//Mt 18.6–9//Lk 17.1–2; Mk 9.49; Mk 10.39//Lk 17.33; Mk 12.40//Lk 20.47.

L: Lk 10.20; 12.48–49; Lk 13.1–5; Lk 13.6–9; Lk 14.11; Lk 16.1–9; Lk 16.19–31.

M: 5.22; 12.36–37; 18.21–35; 21.43; 23.33.

impressions about the advanced state of history and its delayed progress. It takes into account the fact that traditions do not change through discontinuous stages but through incremental shifts. This is the case even when an 'original' thinker emerges and 'breaks with the tradition' since the tradition still is the point of departure.[19]

As part of this eschatological program, did Jesus of Nazareth teach about a special eschatological angel, the 'Son of Man,' who would Judge the world or come in the clouds at the end of time? Probably not. Why? Because our earliest layer of Christian tradition, Paul's letters, do not apply this eschatological title to Jesus or anyone else, even though they identify Jesus as the eschatological Judge (Rom 2.16; 14.10; 1 Cor 4.5; 11.32). As we will see, this is evidence for an early stage in the development of the Son of Man Christology, a stage one increment removed from Jesus' teaching about the Judgment of God and one increment preceding the Christians' identification of Jesus with the Son of Man.

Did Jesus of Nazareth ever use the Aramaic idiom 'son of man (*bar enasha*)' to mean 'a human being' or 'humanity?'[20] Possibly. If he did so, I think that once the Aramaic phrase was translated into Greek, this provided part of the exegetical motivation for later Christians to overlay the Jesus traditions with speculations about the figure in Daniel 7, 'one like a son of man.' I would limit these 'authentic' usages to Matthew 12.32//Luke 12.10 (cf. *Thom* 44), Mark 2.28//Matthew 12.8//Luke 6.5, and Matthew 8.20//Luke 9.58//*Thom* 86, where the sense of the saying demands the understanding 'human being' or 'humanity': a person can blaspheme against another human being and be forgiven, but not against a person who is filled with the Holy Spirit (Matthew 12.32 and parallels); the human being is the lord of the Sabbath (Mark 2.28 and parallels); the human being will not find rest on earth but only in heaven (Matthew 8.20 and parallels). If Jesus used the Aramaic phrase as a circumlocution for 'I,' it is possible that Mark 2.10//Matthew 12.8//Luke 5.24 and Matthew 11.19//Luke 7.34 are 'authentic' as well and also provided fuel for Jesus' later identification with the angelic figure from Daniel, the 'Son of Man.'[21]

The first stage in the development of the Son of Man Christology occurred after Jesus' death when the Jerusalem Christian Jews began speculating about Jesus' resurrected and exalted state (cf. Acts 2.22–35; 3.14–15, 26; 4.2, 10, 33; 5.31), teaching that 'God raised him from the dead' after which God ordained him 'to be Judge of the living and the dead'

19.   E. Shils, *Tradition* (Chicago: University of Chicago Press, 1981) pp. 228–230.

20.   For a survey of the idiom in biblical literature, see G. Dalman, *The Words of Jesus Considered in the Light of Post-Biblical Jewish Writings and the Aramaic Language* (trans. D.M. Kay; Edinburgh: T&T Clark, 1902) pp. 234–235.

21.   For a discussion of this usage, see G. Vermes, *Jesus the Jew: A Historian's Reading of the Gospels* (Philadelphia: Fortress Press, 1973) pp. 160–191.

(Acts 10.40, 42). At this stage, they had not yet narrowed the identification of the exalted Jesus as Judge to the 'Son of Man' from Daniel 7. This first stage represents a period of time from Jesus' death to the mid-first century since Paul's writings agree that the exalted heavenly Jesus was characterized as the eschatological Judge, who is not yet called the 'Son of Man' (Romans 2.16; 14.10; 1 Corinthians 4.5; 11.32). This understanding of Jesus probably was based on a Christian *pesher* of images and expectations from Zechariah 3.1–7, Isaiah 66.15–16, and Malachi 3.1–5 that a great angel of Yahweh would judge the world with fire. Such images are found embedded in several early Christian texts (Lk 12.49//*Thom* 10; Mt 10.34//Lk 12.51//*Thom* 16.1–3; cf. Rev 8.5; 19.11–16; 2 Pet 3.7–14), including later Ebionite traditions which clearly identify Jesus with this angelic Judge.

Thus, in the *Pseudo-Clementines*, Jesus is appointed by God 'in the end of the world' to come and 'invite to his Kingdom all righteous people, and those who have been desirous to please him' (*Rec.* 1.60). Jesus will select those who will be saved: 'He saves adulterers and murders if they know him; but good, sober and merciful people, if they do not know him, in consequence of their having no information concerning him, he does not save' (*Rec.* 2.58). He is a righteous Judge (*Rec.* 2.36; 10.46; *Hom.* 2.46), an angel called 'God of Princes' (2.42). This title means that, in the Ebionite tradition, he was identified with Michael, the chief angel of the Most High (cf. Epiph. *Pan.* 30.16.2–5; Tert., *De carne Christi* 14).[22] He was 'humble in his first coming' but will be 'glorious in his second' when he 'shall come to judge, and condemn the wicked,' taking 'the pious into a share and association with himself in his Kingdom' (*Rec.* 1.49). His Judgment will not bring peace, but a sword, separating truth from error, destroying ignorance with knowledge, separating the believer from his unbelieving kinsfolk (*Hom.* 11.19). Thus Jesus sends fire, namely God's wrath, upon those who are sinners (*Hom.* 11.19). 'Those who do not repent shall be destroyed by the punishment of fire' (*Hom.* 3.6; cf. *Rec.* 6.9; *Hom.* 1.7; *Epistle of Clement to James* 11).

In the mid-first century, it appears that it became vogue in some Jewish and Christian circles to develop a *pesher* in which God's angel of Judgment was identified with 'the one like a son of man' from Daniel 7. Some Jews put forward the *pesher* that the blessed man Enoch had been exalted to heaven and enthroned as the 'Son of Man,' God's angelic Judge (*1 Enoch* 62). In the same period, in order to describe their eschatological

---

22. J. Daniélou, *The Development of Christian Doctrine before the Council of Nicaea, Volume I: The Theology of Jewish Christianity* (trans. J. Baker; Chicago: The Henry Regnery Company, 1964) pp. 126–127; Gieschen, pp. 126–131, 209–210. For discussion of the Son of Man's identification with Michael, see Rowland, *Open Heaven*, pp. 178–188.

expectations, another circle of Jews combined the imagery from Daniel 7 with the tradition of the angel of Yahweh who would judge the world with fire: a 'figure of a man' flew 'with clouds of heaven' and streams of fire poured out of his mouth, judging the wicked multitude below (4 Ezra 13.1–11). So the Christians are not unique in the development of their *pesher* when they began to identify the exalted Jesus, Yahweh's great angel of Judgment, with the Son of Man from Daniel 7. At this second stage, the Son of Man Christology was born, emerging most vividly in Quelle and the Synoptics around 60 CE.[23] It made its way into the Ebionite traditions as well, although the use of the title is sparse (i.e., *Rec.* 1.60). This suggests to me that the title was not original to their speculations, but rather represents a later development of the Angel of Judgment traditions inherited from Jerusalem. We might add that Luke appends the 'Son of Man' title to earlier Jerusalem traditions about Jesus' exaltation as an angel 'standing' at God's right hand. In Acts 7.55, we see the old Jerusalem tradition that Stephen saw 'the glory of God, and *Jesus* standing at the right hand of God' interpreted by Luke with the addition of 7.56, 'Behold, I see the heavens opened, and the *Son of Man* standing at the right hand of God.'

This Christian *pesher* took on its own uniqueness, however, in its third stage, once the lines between the earthly and exalted Jesus were crossed in Christological speculation. The Christians reasoned that, because the exalted Jesus was the Son of Man, the Son of Man must be a figure who was expected to suffer and die. In other words, the life and death experiences of Jesus were appropriated to the Son of Man figure. Thus, around 70 CE a number of Son of Man sayings and references were created by the Christians to express the profundity of this new revelation.[24] In a similar way, the gospel of John seems to be aware of the tradition that connected Jesus with the title 'Son of Man' so in the Johannine tradition the title is drawn back even further into Jesus' preexistent state (John 3.13; 6.62). In this way, by 100 CE, we see the fourth stage of development when it becomes connected to the Jewish traditions of the divine pre-cosmic Man, the Anthropos.

This analysis suggests that the Christology of the Kernel *Thomas* belongs to the first stage in the development of the Son of Man Christology. It is extremely early, predating even Quelle which represents

---

23.   Lk 11.29–30//Mt 12.38–40; Lk 12.39–40//Mt 24.43–44; Lk 17.24–30//Mt 24.27–39; Lk 22.28–30//Mt 19.29; Mk 14.62//Mt 26.64//Lk 22.69;Mk 13.24–27//Mt 24.29–31//Lk 21.25–28; Mt 10.23; Mt 13.36–43; Mt 16.28; Mt 25.31–46; Lk 17.22; Lk 18.1–8.

24.   Mk 9.9//Mt 17.9; Mk 9.12//Mt 17.12; Mk 14.41//Mt 26.45; Mk 9.30–32//Mt 17.22–23//Lk 9.43–45; Mk 10.32–34; Mt 20.17–19//Lk 18.31–34; Mk 10.45//Mt 20.28; Mark 8.31//Mt 16.21//Lk 9.22; Mk 14.21//Mt 26.24//Lk 22.22; Mt 26.1–2; Lk 6.22–23; Lk 17.25; Lk 19.10; Lk 22.48; Lk 24.7.

the Son of Man traditions at stage two. The Kernel represents a necessary incremental stage in the development of the Son of Man Christology immediately preceding the first attempt to identify Jesus specifically with the Son of Man figure from Daniel. It is a stage parallel to the earliest Jerusalem church and Paul's letters that recognizes Jesus as God's great angel of Judgment but has not yet narrowed his identification to that which is given to him in the later *pesher*. This would date the *terminus ad quem* for the Kernel to roughly 50 CE.

5.3 *The Origin of the Kernel*

The apocalyptic expectations and Christological ideas in the Kernel *Thomas* appear to be most similar to the traditions associated with conservative Christian Judaism from Jerusalem and those developed later by the Ebionites. It seems very likely that this collection of speeches was used by the Jerusalem mission between 30–50 CE as it labored to convert people to the faith, especially in Palestine and its environs (cf. Acts 10–11.18; 15.1, 22, 27, 32).[25] The earliest Christian Jews, the itinerant prophets from Jerusalem, in fact, were missionaries with a message, an eschatological message practically identical with the Kernel's. They took seriously the continuation of Jesus' own preaching that 'the time is fulfilled, the Kingdom of God has drawn near!' (Mark 1.15), insisting that people need to 'repent and believe in the gospel' (Mark 1.15). This stanza is taken up in Matthew's discourse on discipleship in chapter 10 of his Gospel. Jesus commissions the disciples to 'preach as you go, saying, "The Kingdom of Heaven has drawn near!" ' (Mt 10.5–7; cf. Lk 10.9, 11). So immediate was the coming of the Kingdom and the Judgment that they believed that the Judgment would occur even before they had finished preaching in all of the towns of Israel (Mt 10.23). So their message of repentance and piety was of the utmost urgency.[26] We should also note that the Jerusalem mission which came into conflict with Paul especially after the Antiochean Affair, promoted a religiosity grounded in heavenly visions and revelations (cf. 2 Cor 12.1; Col 2.18).[27]

---

25. For a detailed discussion of missionary activities among Jews and the first Christian-Jews, see D. Georgi, *The Opponents of Paul in Second Corinthians* (Philadelphia: Fortress Press, 1986) pp. 83–228.

26. For more discussion of the eschatological nature of the itinerants message and their connection to Jesus' proclamation, see D. Georgi, *The Opponents of Paul in Second Corinthians* (Philadelphia: Fortress Press, 1986) pp. 164–167.

27. See particularly the work of M. Goulder. Although I disagree strongly with his regard for an anti-mystical Paul, Goulder mounts a good argument for the centrality of visionary knowledge in the Jerusalem mission. M. Goulder, 'Vision and Knowledge,' *JSNT* 56 (1994) pp. 53–71; M. Goulder, 'The Visionaries of Laodicea,' *JSNT* 43 (1991) pp. 15–39.

It should not go unnoticed that the *Pseudo-Clementine* corpus claims to have the knowledge of the teachings of the True Prophet, teachings that had been collected into books of speeches in order to be used by Christian missionaries in their proselytizing efforts in and around Palestine. I think it is quite conceivable that the Kernel gospel is a representative example of one of these old speech books from Jerusalem. This association of the original Thomas Christians with the conservative Christian Jewish tradition certainly indicates that Gilles Quispel's intuition about the origin of the oldest source for the *Gospel of Thomas* was correct. But, based on the speech-structure of the Kernel that has emerged in my research, I am not convinced that such a source was an Aramaic narrative gospel.

It appears that the vogue hypothesis that the *Gospel of Thomas* is a collection of 'wisdom' sayings warrants substantial modification too. In its earliest form at least, it was not a collection of sayings of Jesus the Sage as some scholars have previously proposed. In fact, this early gospel of Jesus' sayings was not independent of the apocalyptic tradition. It did not represent the message of a non-eschatological proverbial Jesus. Rather it was a collection of oracles of the Prophet Jesus, the Prophet who taught the worthy how to live righteously in preparation for God's imminent Judgment. As God's Prophet, he embodied God's wisdom and passed on this wisdom to those who sought it.

Jesus' message at this early stage of interpretation had an apocalyptic character, featuring eschatological dimensions as well as mystical ones. He was the chosen one from birth, the one whose prophetic voice prepared the faithful for their glorious future and warned the unworthy of their future demise. He was God's Judge who was in the process of selecting the few from the many to receive fully the joys of God's Kingdom when its glorious establishment was complete. Jesus, according to the Kernel, taught that God's power and Judgment would soon bring this world to an end, that, in fact, this process was already underway. God's presence was directly accessible to the faithful now that the world was coming to an end and the boundary between heaven and earth was becoming more and more permeable. Members of the community believed that they were already participating in the Kingdom as it was gradually being inaugurated. They were already worshiping before God's throne. Jesus, in fact, instructs the faithful in the Kernel *Thomas* about the proper way to worship before God's throne in heaven, patterning the response after those of the heroes in apocalyptic lore (L. 15). He tells them to expect to experience a fiery theophany of him as they enter the Kingdom (L. 82).

These mystical ideas, however, took on a life of their own, after the Fall of the Jerusalem Temple, once the Thomasine Christians felt the impact of the 'delayed' Eschaton. With the collapse of their teleology came a reformation of their apocalyptic thought. This reformation resulted in a shift that served to isolate the mystical dimension from the temporal, making the mystical an end unto itself. The horizonal and vertical dimensions of the apocalyptic were collapsed leading to an interiorization of the apocalyptic where the present human body and world was made to conform to the perfected eschatological body and world. The End became the Now.

Part Three

Assessing the Accretions

Chapter 6

THE COLLAPSE OF THE APOCALYPSE

The past is not preserved but is reconstructed on the basis of the present.
~ *M. Halbwachs*

Many scholars questing after the historical Jesus have discovered in *Thomas* a Jesus who is a philosophical humanist, a Sage for all ages, a proverbial orator uninterested in issues of eschatology like cosmic destruction, God's Judgment, and the establishment of a new world.[1] Although some of these scholars have regarded a few of the more esoteric

1.   Proponents of this view rely heavily on the work of J. Robinson and H. Koester in their pioneering volume, *Trajectories through Early Christianity* (Philadelphia: Fortress Press, 1971). This view is most dominant in American scholarship, particularly among those scholars who belong to the Jesus Seminar. For examples of this position, see S.L. Davies, *The Gospel of Thomas and Christian Wisdom* (New York: Seabury Press, 1983) pp. 13–17; J.D. Crossan, *The Historical Jesus: The Life of a Mediterranean Jewish Peasant* (New York: HarperCollins, 1991) pp. 227–302; M. Meyer, *The Gospel of Thomas: The Hidden Sayings of Jesus* (San Francisco: HarperSanFrancisco, 1992); R. Cameron, 'The *Gospel of Thomas* and Christian Origins,' in B. Pearson (ed.), *The Future of Early Christianity: Essays in Honor of Helmut Koester* (Minneapolis: Fortress Press, 1991) pp. 381–392; S.J. Patterson, *The Gospel of Thomas and Jesus* (Sonoma: Polebridge Press, 1993) pp. 94–112; R.W. Funk, *Honest to Jesus* (New York: HarperCollins, 1996) pp. 121–139.

J.W. Marshall has provided a 'moderate' critique of this position in his article, 'The *Gospel of Thomas* and the Cynic Jesus,' in W.E. Arnal and M. Desjardins (eds.), *Whose Historical Jesus?* Studies in Christianity and Judaism 7 (Waterloo: Wilfrid Laurier University Press, 1997) pp. 37–60. From his form-critical analysis of the 'binary logia' and the Kingdom sayings, he concludes that, although 'the apocalyptic eschatology of Q2 and the Synoptics' is lacking in *Thomas*, some sayings reveal a redaction of 'a future orientation and the theme of reversal' in the interest of a theology of unification (p. 53). Although his analysis of *Thomas* reveals serious flaws in the picture that some scholars have painted of the Cynic Jesus, he offers no comprehensive explanation for how, when, or why this redactional shift was taken in *Thomas*, nor is he aware of the extent of this shift.

J.H. Sieber also has mentioned briefly in the concluding paragraphs of his article that Robinson's model requires more attention to be given to 'the eschatological nature of the early stage of the tradition' which Sieber sees gnosticized when the apocalyptic zeal could not be sustained in face of expectations unfulfilled: J.H. Sieber, 'The Gospel of Thomas and the New Testament,' in J.E. Goehring, C.W. Hedrick, J. Sanders, with H.D. Betz, *Gospel Origins*

sayings as later, perhaps representing proto-gnostic or gnostic traditions, they generally have viewed the *Gospel of Thomas* as an early Christian text which has not been tampered with by proponents of cross theology or apocalyptic destruction since, they argue, the *Gospel of Thomas* is silent when it comes to cross theology and apocalyptic Son of Man sayings. This has become evidence in their opinion for a very early form of non-apocalyptic Christianity perhaps going back to Jesus himself.[2]

If communal memory, however, operates as I have discussed in chapter 1, this perspective on *Thomas* is wholly flawed, a point also recognized in the voluminous work of J. Schröter.[3] It would *not* mean that the sayings in *Thomas* represent the words or perspective of the historical Jesus, sayings largely unadulterated by later Christian doctrines. To the contrary, it would mean that *they represent an accumulation and reinterpretation of remembrances of Jesus' words which have been accommodated to the present*

---

and Christian Beginnings. In Honor of James M. Robinson (Sonoma: Polebridge Press, 1990) pp. 64–73. Unfortunately, Sieber does not develop this idea at any length in this or any subsequent publication to date.

2. See especially R. Cameron's summary of this position in his articles, 'Alternate Beginnings, Different Ends: Eusebius, Thomas, and the Construction of Christian Origins,' in L. Bormann, K. Del Tredici, and A. Standhartinger (eds.), *Religious Propaganda and Missionary Competition in the New Testament World: Essays Honoring Dieter Georgi*, NTSup 74 (Leiden: E.J. Brill, 1994) pp. 507–521; 'Mythmaking and Intertextuality in Early Christianity,' in E. Castelli and H. Taussig (eds.), *Reimagining Christian Origins* (Valley Forge: Trinity Press International, 1996) pp. 37–50; 'Ancient Myths and Modern Theories of the Gospel of Thomas and Christian Origins,' *MTSR* 11 (1999) pp. 236–257. These ideas formed the basis of a SBL Seminar which has now produced its first volume of papers: R. Cameron and M.P. Miller, *Redescribing Christian Origins*, Symposium Series 28 (2004).

3. J. Schröter, in his monograph, *Erinnerung an Jesu Worte: Studien zur Rezeption der Logienüberlieferung in Markus, Q und Thomas*, WMANT 76 (Neukirchen-Vluyn: Neukirchener, 1997), is the only other scholar of whom I am aware that has applied Social Memory studies to the *Gospel of Thomas*. He limited his application to the foundational work of A. Assmann. Schröter proposed that Mark, Quelle, and *Thomas* should be understood as 'remembrance phenonemon.' The Jesus traditions within these texts, he says, represents early Christian reflection on the past rather than the transmission of authentic historical Jesus material. He argues that Mark, Quelle, and *Thomas* reflect three ways of remembering Jesus, ways that steered the process of selection and interpretation of the traditions. *Thomas*' 'remembrance' of Jesus is identified by Schröter as occurring in the post-Synoptic phase of early Christianity and as most similar to the remembrance of the Jesus tradition found in John, although much more ascetic and clearly on the path to Gnosticism. He thinks it essential methodologically to describe the place of the composition of *Thomas* through a comparative analysis with other early Christian texts while setting aside tradition-historical questions (pp. 462–481).

Because he has made this methodological move, separating comparative analysis from tradition-historical questions, he has not recognized either the lengthy evolution that this gospel underwent or the early Jesus traditions within it, early traditions that have been overlaid with newer traditions or reinterpreted in response to shifting communal experiences and reformulations of communal memory.

experiences of an early Christian community. In this case, *Thomas* would be read as a repository of communal memory containing not only early and later traditions but also the reformulations of these traditions based on the contemporary experience of the community. This would further suggest that *a reconstruction of the community and its memory can be distilled if we first examine the issues raised in Thomas' sayings and then reflect on their use and reuse of traditional ideas and materials*. This approach is markedly different from the common one which first assumes a community for *Thomas* – whether it be gnostic, encratite, Jewish-Christian, sapiential, or otherwise – and then works to interpret *Thomas* and reconstruct its tradition or traditions on this basis.

If *Thomas* is read as a repository of communal memory, what might this reading tell us about early Christianity, the Thomasine Christians in particular? Could we recover some of the pressures and experiences this community faced? Could we come to understand on some level how this community reconfigured its past, transformed the earlier traditions that it had inherited? Could we identify and explain some of the shifts that occurred in the thought-world of the Thomasine Christians? If so, what might this reveal to us about the development of their theology and practices, the morphology and membership of their group, their relationship with other Christian traditions, and their interaction with other Christian communities in the Mediterranean world?

6.1 *An Apocalyptic Memory Crisis*

An investigation into *Thomas'* connection with apocalypticism seems to me to be an excellent place to begin to seek answers to these questions because so many of the question and dialogue units in *Thomas* look to be concerned with apocalyptic issues. Why is this so significant? Because the voice of the community is most audible in the secondary questions and introductory clauses posed by the disciples to Jesus. Far from representing historical dialogues that Jesus held with his disciples, these units are reconfigurations of older traditional sayings. As I argued in chapter 3, by elaborating older sayings into question and answer units and dialogues, the Christians enriched the meaning of the traditions for their present communities, aligning them with their contemporary memory. They provided the old sayings with new contexts and interpretations. In this way, perplexing questions facing a community could be answered directly by Jesus in their gospel. Polemic for opposing views could be supported by Jesus' words. Instruction about emerging ideas and practices could be addressed with Jesus' voice. The old traditions were made contemporary and, in the process, sanctified by Jesus.

In the *Gospel of Thomas*, the community poses the following questions on the apocalyptic front, turning to Jesus for resolution:

(18)   [1]*The disciples said to Jesus, 'Tell us, how will our end come about?'*

(20)   [1]*The disciples said to Jesus, 'Tell us, what is the Kingdom of Heaven like?'*

(22)   [3]*They said to him, 'Will we enter the Kingdom as little babies?'*

(37)   [1]*His disciples said, 'When will you appear to us? When will we see you?'*

(51)   [1]*His disciples said to him, 'When will the dead rest, and when will the new world come?'*

(113) [1]*His disciples said to him, 'When will the Kingdom come?'*

These questions reveal substantial information about the Thomasine community. They are not simply rhetorical flourishes used to introduce some of Jesus' sayings in a collection, nor are they questions of curiosity on the part of the Thomasine Christians. They are serious mitigative questions raised by the community to confront some eschatological problem that faced the Thomasine Christians. In their gospel, they have posed a series of questions in order to bring forward the community's resolution through Jesus' responses. What will the End be like? When is the Kingdom going to come? What do we have to do to enter the Kingdom? When will we see Jesus? When will the dead achieve their final rest? When will the New World, the Kingdom of God, be established?

Why would a community of Christians pose these questions in their gospel and not others? What do their questions reveal to us about the problem facing their community? Undoubtedly, the eschatological expectations originally held by community members had been seriously challenged. From their questions, it appears that the contemporary community members were wondering when and how God would fulfil his eschatological promises, a problem not unfamiliar to other early Christian communities in the mid- to late first century.[4] The Thomasine Christians

---

4. For the impact of the delayed eschaton on the formation of early Christian theology, see M. Werner, *The Formation of Christian Dogma* (New York: Harper, 1957); E. Grässer, *Das Problem der Parusieverzögerung in den synoptischen Evangelien und in der Apostel-geschichte* (Berlin: A. Töpelmann, 1960); A. Strobel, *Untersuchungen zum eschatologischen Verzögerungsproblem*, SNT 2 (Leiden: E.J. Brill, 1961); A. Schweitzer, *The Mysticism of Paul the Apostle* (trans. W. Montgomery, Baltimore: Johns Hopkins University Press, 1931, repr. 1998); A.L. Moore, *The Parousia in the New Testament* (Leiden: E.J. Brill, 1966); R.H. Hiers, 'The Delay of the Parousia in Luke-Acts,' *NTS* 20 (1973–1974) pp. 145–155; R.J. Bauckman, 'The Delay of the Parousia,' *TynBul* 31 (1980) pp. 3–36; C. Rowland, *Christian Origins: An Account of the Setting and Character of the Most Important Messianic Sect of Judaism* (London: SPCK, 2nd edn., 2002) pp. 287–296. For the most recent study, see J.T. Carroll, *The Return of Jesus in Early Christianity* (Peabody: Hendrickson Publishers, 2000).

were concerned that the End of the World, the establishment of the Kingdom or the New World, the final rest of the dead, and the return of Jesus had not yet happened! They were a community in the middle of a memory crisis. Their traditional expectations were threatened by the reality of their present experience, the experience of the Non-Event, when the Kingdom did not come.

6.2 *A Reconfiguration of Apocalyptic Expectations*

The fact that these mitigative questions and their answers actually have accrued in its gospel, however, indicates that enough time had passed in the community's memory without the fulfillment of its original expectations for the older traditions to be reconfigured and aligned with the community's new expectations. Its members had weathered the crisis by shifting their apocalyptic expectations. What transformation did their traditions undergo in the process? The answers they provide to the very questions they posed in their gospel is a logical place to start this enquiry:

(18)   [2]Jesus said, 'Have you discovered the beginning that you seek the end? Because where the beginning is, the end will be also. [3]Whoever will stand in the beginning is blessed. This person will know the end, yet will not die.'

(20)   [2]He said to them, 'It is like a mustard seed, [2]smaller than all seeds. [4]But when it falls on cultivated soil, it puts forth a large branch and becomes a shelter for birds of the sky.'

(22)   [4]Jesus said to them, 'When you make the two one, and when you make the inside like the outside, and the outside like the inside, and the above like the below. [5]And when you make the male and the female into a single being, with the result that the male is not male nor the female female. [6]When you make eyes in place of an eye, and a hand in place of a hand, and a foot in place of a foot, and an image in place of an image, [7]then you will enter the Kingdom.'

(37)   [2]Jesus said, 'When you strip naked without shame, take your garments, put them under your feet like little children, and trample on them. [3]Then [you will see] the Son of the Living One and you will not be afraid.'

(51)   [2]He said to them, 'What you look for has come, but you have not perceived it.'

(113)   [2]'It will not come by waiting. [3]It will not be said, "Look! Here it is!" or "Look! There it is!" [4]Rather, the Kingdom of the Father is spread out over the earth, but people do not see it.'

It is clear from this handful of mitigative responses that the community appears to have reacted to the disconfirmation in the three typical ways predicted by social psychologists for close-knit groups holding certain

strong beliefs.[5] Disconfirmation will often lead groups to new hermeneutical levels since they develop explanatory schemes to rationalize the
disconfirmation. The hermeneutic consists of demonstrating that 'the
disconfirming event was not disconfirmation but actually confirmation of
their expectations.'[6] The disconfirmation had only arisen in the first place,
the group may conclude, because the group had not interpreted its
traditions or scripture properly. In fact, it is a normative move for a
community to say that the group did not correctly understand the original
tradition, text, or prediction.

This normative move is present in the Thomasine gospel where we can
see the development of explanatory schema to rationalize the disconfirmation along with arguments that the disconfirmation really was not
disconfirmation but misinterpretation on the part of the community. For
instance, they insist that the End of the World had not come as they had
expected. The members of the early community merely had misunderstood
Jesus by 'waiting' for the End to come or 'looking forward' to a future
event (L. 51, 113).

New explanatory schemes often give rise to new hermeneutics that the
community designs to change its original cognitive holdings. The
disconfirming experience can cause the group to reinterpret their baseline
traditions, or, conversely, its understanding of the contemporary events.[7]
This new hermeneutic determines how the tradition will be understood or
the text read from then on.

In the case of *Thomas,* we can see a new apocalyptic hermeneutic
replacing an older one. The community members maintained in their
responses to the questions they had posed that, indeed, their expectations
had not actually been disconfirmed but had been confirmed when the now
'correct' hermeneutic was applied to the old traditions. So, in their
responses to the questions, they posited that the Kingdom had already
been established on earth but no one had noticed its coming (L. 20, 51,
113). Did not their gospel tell them that Jesus in his lifetime had taught
that the Kingdom already had begun to break into the world? It was like a
tiny seed that had fallen unnoticed on tilled soil and now had grown into a
large plant (L. 20). They concluded that the Kingdom had continued to
grow since Jesus' death. Now, at the present time – just as Jesus had
predicted! – it had fully arrived on earth. The anticipated 'rest' of the dead
and the 'new world' had 'already come' (L. 51, 113). Since the Kingdom

5. L. Festinger, H.W. Riecken, and S. Schachter, *When Prophecy Fails* (Minneapolis:
University of Minnesota Press, 1956); J.A. Hardyck and M. Braden, 'Prophecy Fails Again: A
Report of a Failure to Replicate,' *JASP* 65 (1962) pp. 136–141.

6. R. Carroll, *When Prophecy Failed: Cognitive Dissonance in the Prophetic Traditions of
the Old Testament* (New York: The Seabury Press, 1979) p. 126.

7. Carroll, *Prophecy Failed,* p. 110.

now was spread out among them on the earth (L. 113), Jesus would be revealed to them immediately and directly (L. 37).

Such was the new apocalyptic hermeneutic that replaced the previous one. The community members, however, did not perceive this hermeneutic to be new. Rather this was the correct hermeneutic through which Jesus' words should have been understood in the first place. The community members just had not recognized this previously (L. 51). This is a function of communal memory, serving to make the past relevant to the present experience of the group in a seamless way.

A community faced with disconfirming evidence may try to avoid references to it in the future, especially when the belief impinges on reality in a severe way. The community may attempt to create an environment or ideology that avoids the subject completely.[8] Or the community may identify current events with past predictions or traditions, collapsing the expectations as it demonstrates their fulfillment in the present.[9]

Such is the situation in the *Gospel of Thomas*. The community attempted to avoid further problems associated with future disconfirmation by collapsing its expectations in these question and answer units and dialogues, demonstrating the fulfillment of its expectations *in the present*. In this process, its hermeneutic shifted away from an eschatological interpretation of Jesus' sayings to a mystical one.[10] The kingdom, the new world, was not a future event at all, but was realized in their community as the recreation of the beginning of time before the Fall of Adam. It was actualized by individual community members as they tried to transform their bodies, reshaping them into the utopian body of Adam through encratic performance. This was the immediate, rather than future, transformation of the human self into the Image of God, the androgynous primordial Adam (L. 18, 22, 37). In such a paradisial community, visions of Jesus could be anticipated (L. 37).

Thus their interpretative revision shifted the apocalypse from an imminent cosmic event to an immanent personal mystical experience. As the new introduction to the old gospel, L. 1, aptly states, 'The person who finds the meaning (*hermeneia*) of these words will not experience death.' This hermeneutic was not some philosophical or intellectual explanation, but a mystical one. The believer was supposed to apprehend his or her divine Self and God by meditating on the sayings of Jesus in the gospel and practicing the encratic ideal it honored.

This crisis in theology must have been very acute for the Thomas

---

8. Carroll, *Prophecy Failed*, pp. 93–94.

9. Carroll, *Prophecy Failed*, p. 114.

10. For a detailed analysis of the mystical traditions in the *Gospel of Thomas*, refer to my book, *Seek to See Him: Ascent and Vision Mysticism in the Gospel of Thomas*, VCSup 33 (Leiden: E.J. Brill, 1996).

Christians since the sayings tradition in *Thomas* appears to have been drastically reshaped in order to bring the sayings in line with the community's own experience of the Non-Event and its shifting communal memories. In addition to this handful of mitigative question and answer units (L. 18, 20, 22, 37, 51, and 113), we find a series of later accretions serving similar mitigative functions. They directly address the problem of the delayed Eschaton by developing the concept of the *fully* present kingdom on earth (L. 3.1–3), speculating about the primordial Adam and the encratic ideal (L. 4, 11, 16, 19, 21, 23, 27.1, 49, 75, 85, 105, 110, 114), and shifting emphasis to the mystical dimension of apocalypticism away from the eschatological (L. 1, 3.4–5, 7, 19, 24, 28, 29, 38, 50, 56, 59,61, 67, 70, 77, 80, 83, 84, 85, 108, 111.3). Their resolution appears to be a radical hemeneutic that revised the older eschatological traditions preserved in sayings 10, 11.1, 15, 16.1–3, 23.1, 35, 40, 57, 58, 60.1, 61.1, 64, 65, 68.1, 69.2, 71, 74, 79, 81, 82, 98, 103, 107, 111.1. As we saw in the last chapter, these older sayings appear to have been eschatological warnings about an impending cosmic destruction. When these expectations of the community were threatened by the experience of the Non-Event, these traditions underwent a hermeneutical shift within the communal memory, resulting in new material accruing in the gospel, material that reinterpreted the old.

6.2.1 *Accretions that Reconfigured Expectations*

(Kernel in regular type; *accretions in italics*)

1. **The Fully Present Kingdom on Earth**

(3)   *¹((Jesus said, 'If your leaders say to you, "Look! the Kingdom is in heaven," then the birds of heaven will arrive first before you. ²If they say, "It is under the earth," then the fish of the sea will enter it, arriving first before you. ³But the Kingdom of Heaven is inside of you and outside.'*

2. **The Primordial Adam and the Encratic Ideal**

(4)   ¹*Jesus said, 'The old man will not hesitate to ask a little child seven days old about the place of life, and he will live.* ²For many who are first will be last, ³((and the last will be first,)) *⁴and they will become single people.'*

(11)   ¹Jesus said, 'This heaven will pass away, and the one above it will pass away. ²*But the dead are not alive, and the living will not die. ³In the days when you ate what is dead, you made it something living. When you are in the light, what will you become? ⁴On the day when you were one, you became two. When you are two, what will you become?'*

(16)   ¹Jesus said, 'Perhaps people think it is peace that I have come to cast upon the world. ²And they do not know it is division that I have come to cast upon the earth – fire, sword, war! ³For there

will be five people in a house. There will be three people against two, and two against three, father against son, and son against father. *⁴And they will stand as celibates.'*

(19) *¹Jesus said, 'Whoever existed before being born is blessed. ²If you become my disciples and listen to my teachings, these stones will support you. ³For you, there are five trees in Paradise. They do not change, summer and winter, and their leaves do not fall. Whoever knows them will not die.'*

(21) *¹Mary said to Jesus, 'Whom are your disciples like?'*
He said, 'They are like little children sojourning in a field that is not theirs. When the owners of the field come, they will say, "Leave our field!" In front of them, they strip naked in order to abandon it, returning their field to them.'

⁵*'For this reason I say*, If the owner of a house knows that a thief is coming, he will keep watch before he arrives. He will not allow him to break into his house, part of his estate, to steal his furnishings. *⁶You, then, keep watch against the world. ⁷Arm yourselves with great strength so that the robbers do not find a way to come to you, ⁸because the possessions you are looking after, they will find. ⁹There ought to be a wise person among you!'*

¹⁰'When the grain ripened, he came quickly with his sickle in his hand. He harvested it.

¹¹Whoever has ears to hear should listen!'

(23) ¹Jesus said, 'I will select you, one from a thousand, and two from ten thousand. *²And they will stand as single people.'*

(27) *¹((Jesus said)), 'If you do not fast from the world, you will not find the Kingdom.'*

(49) *¹Jesus said, 'Blessed are the celibate people, the chosen ones, because you will find the Kingdom. ²For you are from it. You will return there again.'*

(75) *Jesus said, 'Many people are standing at the door, but those who are celibate are the people who will enter the bridal chamber.'*

(85) *¹Jesus said, 'Adam came into being out of a great power and great wealth. But he was not deserving of you. ²For, had he been deserving, [he would] not [have] died.'*

(105) *Jesus said, 'Whoever is aquainted with (one's) father and mother will be called, "the child of a prostitute."'*

(110) *Jesus said, 'Whoever has found the world and become wealthy, he should disown the world.'*

(114) *¹Simon Peter said to them, 'Mary should leave us because women do not deserve life.' ²Jesus said, 'Look, I myself will impel her in order to make her male, so that she too may become a living spirit – male, resembling you. For every woman who will make herself male will enter the Kingdom of Heaven.'*

3. *Mysticism*

(1) *And he said, 'Whoever finds the meaning of these words will not die.'*

(3)   [4]'((*Whoever knows himself will find it.* [5]*And when you know yourselves, you will understand that you are the children of the Living Father. But if you will not know yourselves, you live in poverty and you are poverty))*.'

(7)   [1]Jesus said, 'Blessed is the lion that the human will eat, and the lion becomes human.
[2]And cursed is the human whom the lion eats, [[and the human becomes a lion]].'

(19)   [1]Jesus said, 'Whoever existed before being born is blessed. [2]If you become my disciples and listen to my teachings, these stones will support you. [3]For you, there are five trees in Paradise. They do not change, summer and winter, and their leaves do not fall. The person who knows them will not die.'

(24)   [1]His disciples said, 'Teach us about the place where you are, because we must seek it.'
[2]He said to them, 'Whoever has ears should listen! [3]There is light inside a person of light. And it lights up the whole world. If it does not shine, it is dark.'

(28)   [1]Jesus said, 'I stood in the midst of the world and I appeared to them in flesh. [2]I found all of them drunk. I found none of them thirsty. [3]And my soul suffered in pain for human beings because they are blind in their hearts and they do not see. For they, empty, came into the world. And they, empty, seek to leave the world. [4]For the moment, they are drunk. When they shake off their wine, then they will repent.'

(29)   [1]Jesus said, 'It would be a miracle if the flesh existed for the sake of the Spirit. [2]It would be a miracle of miracles if the Spirit (existed) for the sake of the body! [3]Nevertheless, I marvel at how this great wealth settled in this poverty.'

(38)   [1]Jesus said, 'The words that I am speaking to you, often you have longed to hear them. And you have no other person from whom to hear them. [2]There will be days when you will seek me, (but) will not find me.'

(50)   [1]Jesus said, 'If they say to you, "Where did you come from?", say to them, "We came from the light" – the place where the light came into being on its own accord and established [itself] and became manifest through their image. [2]If they say to you, "Is it you?", say "We are its children, and we are the chosen people of the living Father." [3]If they ask you, "What is the sign of your Father in you?", say to them, "It is movement and rest."'

(56)   [1]Jesus said, 'Whoever has come to know the world has found a corpse. [2]The world does not deserve the person who has found (that the world is) a corpse.'

(59)   Jesus said, 'Gaze upon the Living One while you are alive, in case you die and (then) seek to see him, and you will not be able to see (him).'

(61) ^{2}*Salome said, 'Who are you, sir? That is, from [[whom]]? You have reclined on my couch and eaten at my table.'*
^{3}*Jesus said to her, 'I am he who comes from the one who is an equal. I was given some who belong to my Father.'*
^{4}*'I am your disciple.'*
^{5}*'Therefore I say, when a person becomes [[equal]] (with me), he will be filled with light. But if he becomes separated (from me), he will be filled with darkness.'*

(67) *Jesus said, 'Whoever knows everything, but needs (to know) himself, is in need of everything.'*

(70) ^{1}*Jesus said, 'When you become what is within you, what is within you will save you. ^{2}If you do not have it within you, what you do not have within you will kill you.'*

(77) ^{1}*Jesus said, 'I am the light which is above all things. I am everything. From me, everything came forth, and up to me, everything reached. ^{2}Split a piece of wood. I am there. ^{3}Lift the stone, and you will find me there.'*

(80) ^{1}*Jesus said, 'Whoever has come to know the world has found the corpse. ^{2}The world does not deserve the person who has found (that the world is) the corpse.'*

(83) ^{1}*Jesus said, 'The images are visible to people, but the light in them is concealed in the image of the Father's light. ^{2}The light will be revealed, but his image is concealed by his light.'*

(84) ^{1}*Jesus said, 'When you see the likeness of yourselves, you are delighted. ^{2}But when you see the images of yourselves which came into being before you – they neither die nor are visible – how much you will suffer!'*

(85) ^{1}*Jesus said, 'Adam came into being out of a great power and great wealth. But he was not deserving of you. ^{2}For, had he been deserving, [he would] not [have] died.'*

(87) ^{1}*Jesus said, 'Miserable is the body, which is crucified by a body. ^{2}Miserable is the soul, which is crucified by these together.'*

(106) ^{1}*Jesus said, 'When you make the two one, you will become children of Man. ^{2}And when you say, "Mountain, go forth!" it will move.'*

(108) ^{1}*Jesus said, 'Whoever drinks from my mouth will become as I am. ^{2}I myself will become that person, ^{3}and what is hidden will be revealed to him.'*

(111) ^{3}*'Does not Jesus say, "The world does not deserve the person who has found himself"?'*

(112) ^{1}*Jesus said, 'Alas to the flesh, which is crucified by the soul. ^{2}Alas to the soul, which is crucified by the flesh.'*

6.3 *A Hermeneutical Shift*

The accumulation of these new sayings in the *Gospel of Thomas* suggests that the message of Jesus which the community had retained over the years in their gospel experienced the type of incremental interpretative shift commonly occurring to traditions subjected to communal memory. As the eschatological coming of the Kingdom of God came to be a Non-Event, these Christians felt pressure to recast their original apocalyptic traditions. The future fulfillment of the eschatological promises of Jesus receded in favor of their present mystical reality. In other words, the temporal dimension of the apocalypticism of Jesus' message was collapsed, refocusing the community's apocalyptic hopes on the atemporal mystical dimension. The cumulative result of the remaking of the traditions was a shift away from understanding the apocalyptic traditions in eschatological terms.

In the final form of the *Gospel of Thomas*, the hermeneutical focus is on the mystical encounter of the individual believer with God and the present transformation of his or her Self, not the eschatological. An analysis of the sayings reveals that the community developed a theology of Paradise regained through encratic performance and mystical practice. The shift from eschatological to encratic and mystical is explicitly developed in the secondary question and answer unit, L. 37.[11] The question expresses concern, and perhaps even disappointment, that the imminent return of Jesus had not yet occurred. The community demands to know when this will happen:

> (37)   [1]His disciples said, 'When will you appear to us? When will we see you?'
> [2]Jesus said, 'When you strip naked without shame, take your garments, put them under your feet like little children, and trample on them. [3]Then [you will see] the Son of the Living One and you will not be afraid.'

The imagery in this secondary unit suggests that, at this time, the ideal conditions necessary to 'see' Jesus were not perceived by the community to include the collapse of the world and the end of history. Rather the ideal condition is the state of each individual person. This ideal state is said to be that of a 'child' who has renounced his body, returning to the pre-fall state of Adam when Adam was not afraid or ashamed to come into God's presence. Jesus will be revealed to the disciples when they, like children, remove their clothes and tread on them without shame or fear, an idea developing out of a certain exegesis of the Genesis story, particularly verses 2.25 and 3.7–10.

Here the community is describing a situation in which the eschatological vision of Jesus is now believed to be achievable in the present, particularly

11. For a complete analysis of the mystical elements of this saying, refer to A.D. DeConick and J. Fossum, 'Stripped Before God: A New Interpretation of Logion 37 in the Gospel of Thomas,' *VC* 45 (1991) pp. 123–150.

when the person renounces his or her body and becomes a 'child' again in the Garden. This is an expression of an encratic ideal as we will see in the next chapter, an ideal which also is expressed in the dialogue unit, L. 22, and several other sayings that accrued in the gospel (4.1, 4.4, 16.4, 21.2–4, 23.2, 75, 114). In fact, in L. 37 achieving this ideal through the practice of celibacy is perceived to be a prerequisite to the vision of God. If a ritual practice is alluded to in this saying, it is likely from an analysis of the imagery that the community had anointing in mind, one of the initiatory rituals that the early Christians performed at baptism.[12] The community may have believed that the performance of the initiatory rituals combined with an encratic lifestyle prepared the human being for visionary experiences of God and his Son.

It is apparent that the addition of this accretion to the Kernel caused problems for the preceding Kernel saying, L. 36, which is preserved in its earliest form in the Greek fragments:

> (36) [1](([Jesus said, 'Do not be anxious] from morning [until evening and] from evening [until] morning, neither [about] your [food] and what [you will] eat, [nor] about [your clothing] and what you [will] wear. [2][You are far] better than the [lilies] which [neither] card nor [spin]. [3]As for you, when you have no garment, what [will you put on]? Who might add to your stature? The same one will give you your garment)).'

The accretive saying, L. 37, was added at this point because of the catchword, 'garment.' Yet it is this very catchword that caused later interpretative problems for the encratic hermeneutic applied to the text. In L. 36, it appeared that the receipt of a 'garment' was a gift from God's grace, while in L. 37, the 'garment' was something to be scorned and renounced. As long as the garment in L. 36 was understood by the interpreters to be clothing while, in L. 37, the body, the logia remained connected in their entirety. But the hermeneutical tension seems to have become too great and, by the time of the Coptic translation, the old Kernel saying, L. 36, had been reduced to a few lines introducing L. 37. All reference to God providing clothing had been eliminated:

> Jesus said, 'Do not be concerned from morning until evening and from evening until morning about what you will wear' (L. 36).

Now the believers are told that they should not be concerned about what they wear. Why? Because Jesus said that it is necessary to remove their garments and renounce them in order for them to return to Paradise and achieve the ultimate mystical vision of the 'Son of the Living One.'

---

12. DeConick and Fossum, 'Stripped Before God,' pp. 123–150.

The mitigative response to the Non-Event is quite pronounced in L. 38.2 where a rationalization of eschatological expectations is made:

> (38)   [1]Jesus said, 'The words that I am speaking to you, often you have
> longed to hear them. And you have no other person from whom
> to hear them. [2]*There will be days when you will seek me, (but) will
> not find me.'*

In this unit, the older saying of Jesus is appended with a startling *'new'* *observation*, 'There will be days when you will look for me and will not find me!' This accretive clause serves to alleviate the disappointment of Jesus' non-appearance eschatologically, noting that Jesus had predicted this. Further, the clause alludes to the disappointment of failed mystical practices. The saying takes on a very practical problem that faces all mystics: there would be days that they sought direct experiences of God, desiring to hear his voice or gaze on his form, only to be faced with failure. In this way, the saying seems to appeal to the preceding saying, L. 37, reminding the believer that even though Jesus did promise the encratite Christian a beatific vision of himself, this would not happen 'on demand.' The believers may desire this experience just as they desire to hear Jesus' words. But as Jesus himself says, there will be times when it will not happen no matter how intense the believers' desire.

The quest for an ecstatic vision of God, a direct experience of the divine, is quite pronounced in L. 59, an accretion that clearly delineates the vision quest as a pre-mortem experience, something that must be achieved during the believer's lifetime rather than after death:

> (59)   Jesus said, 'Gaze upon the Living One while you are alive, in case
> you die and (then) seek to see him, and you will not be able to see
> (him).'

Wilhelm Bousset recognized this mystical distinction in his famous work, 'Die Himmelsreise der Seele.' He understood the ecstatic soul journey as one that occurs during the life of the performer rather than after the body's death. He thought that such a mystic journey could anticipate the moment of death, but it had to be performed in the *present* if it was to bear the hallmark of mysticism.[13] L. 59 bears this very hallmark. Jesus commands his believers to seek visions of God before their own deaths. In fact, if the believers wait for post-mortem visions, they will have waited too long and will suffer severe consequences. They will be denied the vision and its guarantee of immortality. This logion displays the tell-tale signs that this

---

13.   W. Bousset, 'Die Himmelsreise der Seele,' *ARW* 4 (Freiburg: J.C.B. Mohr, 1901) pp. 136–169.

community has recast its original apocalyptic dream based on their present experience.

Add to these sayings, the fragment of ascent lore found in L. 50 and the magnitude of the mystical shift that has occurred in the communal memory becomes even more pronounced:

> (50) [1]Jesus said, 'If they say to you, "Where did you come from?", say to them, "We came from the light" – the place where the light came into being on its own accord and established [itself] and became manifest through their image. [2]If they say to you, "Is it you?", say "We are its children, and we are the chosen people of the living Father." [3]If they ask you, "What is the sign of your Father in you?", say to them, "It is movement and rest." '

The *Sitz im Leben* in which these questions and answers make the *most* sense is that of the ascent of the soul through the heavenly spheres and the interrogation of the soul as it journeys to God.[14] We find such interrogations at death to be characteristic of Egyptian, Orphic, and some gnostic traditions. Since L. 50 gives us no indication that the context is death, we can assume a pre-mortem context based on the fact that *Thomas* advocated mystical ascent before death in L. 37 and 59. For this idea, there is ample evidence in Jewish sources where we discover that the mystic could expect the angelic guards to be hostile and question his right and worthiness to be in heaven (cf. *Asc. Isa.* 10.28–29; *3 Enoch* 2, 4 and 5; *Apoc. Abr.* 13.6; *b. Hag.* 15b; *b. Shab.* 88b–89a; *Shem. Rab.* 42.4; *Pesiq. Rab.* 96b–98a; *Ged. Mos.* 273; *Hekh. Frag.* lines 28–38; *Hist. Rech.* 5.1–2). Moreover, he could anticipate life-or-death tests to be administered by the angels. He had to memorize passwords and hymns in order to appease the guards of heaven and insure his safe passage to the foot of God's throne (*Apoc. Abr.* 17–18; *Hekh. Rabb.* 1.1, 2.5–5.3, 16.4–25.6; *Hekh. Zutt.* 413–415; *b. Hag.* 14b; *M. Merk.* 9, 11, 15).[15]

Even though the language in these sayings describes the ecstatic experience prominently in mythic terms of a heavenly journey and vision of the Father and the glorious Jesus, the Son of the Living One (L. 24.1, 37, 38.2, 50, 59), the transformation itself was understood also to be an interior psychic experience of the soul. This can be clearly seen with the creation of a dialogue between Jesus and his disciples in L. 24. A *newer*

---

14. For complete discussion, refer to DeConick, *Seek to See Him*, pp. 43–96.

15. On this subject refer to the classic work by P. Schäfer, *Rivalität zwischen Engeln und Menschen* (Berlin: De Gruyter, 1975); D.J. Halperin, 'Ascension or Invasion: Implications of the Heavenly Journey in Ancient Judaism,' *Religion* 18 (1988) pp. 47–67; and more recently, the balanced work of R. Elior, 'Mysticism, Magic, and Angelology – The Perception of Angels in Hekhalot Literature,' *JSQ* 1 (1993/94) pp. 3–53.

question, L. 24.1, now introduces and recontextualizes an older saying, L. 24.2–3:

(24)   *¹His disciples said, 'Teach us about the place where you are, because we must seek it.'*
²He said to them, 'Whoever has ears should listen! ³There is light inside a person of light. And it lights up the whole world. If it does not shine, it is dark.'

The disciples' question represents the voice of the community. They ask Jesus to show them where he lives since they must 'seek' this 'place' in order to be redeemed. Here the language of mystical journey to the 'place' where Jesus is, has been connected to a psychic discussion about the interior 'man of light,' the soul. Here the ecstatic 'journey' is an internal one, an encounter with one's own transformed soul, a soul that has recovered its original state of luminosity. The accretive clause has reoriented the thrust of the Kernel saying. Now the disciple is understood to be a person who can seek Jesus by turning inward to his or her own soul, a soul that has been transformed, a soul that is the very reflection of Jesus, the Anthropos, the heavenly Man of Light. As we will see in later chapters, this journey is the subject of several other sayings in *Thomas*, sayings which invoke both the Jewish story of the person's recovery, through mystical encounter, of the original Image of God in which he or she was created (L. 19, 22, 70, 84, 106) and the Hermetic story of the return, through Self-knowledge, of the person's fallen soul (L. 3.4–5, 56, 67, 80, 111.3).

All in all, these sayings represent the voice of a community whose members are no longer waiting for death or the Eschaton in order to enter heaven and achieve immortality. Instead of waiting for heaven to come to them, they are invading Eden, believing the eschatological promises of God fulfilled in the present. Their apocalyptic expectations have collapsed, shifting their theology away from hopes of an imminent Eschaton to achieving mystical pre-mortem experiences of God. They developed an encratic theology and regime, working to transform their bodies into the prelapsarian Adam and Eve and their Church into Paradise even while they lived on earth. In a community where Eden had been regained, mystical visions of Jesus and God directly and immediately were accessible to the practitioner. The believer could experience all the fruits of the New World now, living like an angel on earth, gazing on God like an angel in heaven.

Chapter 7

THE RESTORATION OF EDEN

The charismatic message becomes rationalized. ~ *E. Shils*

In the complete *Gospel of Thomas*, the Thomasine community has redefined its parameters in an intentionally encratic manner, reflecting the building of a *utopian community* whose members 'live' in Paradise even while in the midst of 'this world.' In so doing, the community has stepped forward across the eschatological threshold, so to speak, no longer living in anticipation of the imminent Eschaton, but experiencing it immanently now (Diagram 6). Not only is this shift eschatological in *Thomas*, but also protological since the community perceives that its members have recreated primordial time in this 'new world' and live honorably the prelapsarian single life of Adam.

Encratism was not a Christian sectarian phenomenon *per se*. Rather, it was an attitude toward sexuality adopted by particular early Christian communities for various reasons. Encratic Christians esteemed 'self-control' above all else, honoring a severity of the body that included sexual abstinence even between married partners, dietary restrictions usually prohibiting the intake of meat and wine, and voluntary poverty.[1] This severity toward the body was, in the opinion of Clement of Alexandria, 'too ascetic' since it promoted the belief that sex was sin and marriage, a sinful state (*Strom.* 3.5.40; 3.6.45; 3.7.60; 3.9.66–67; 3.12.85; 3.12.89). According to Clement, the justification for encratic behavior varied from community to community. Some gnostic Christians, like the Marcionites and the Basilidians, renounced the body and sexuality on theological grounds: the body and sexuality supported the created order of the lesser god, an order which should not be perpetuated by the gnostic. Non-gnostic

---

1. G. Blonde, 'Encratisme,' in M. Viller, F. Cavallera, and J. de Guibert (eds.). *Dictionnaire de Spiritualité* 4 (Paris: G. Beauchesne, 1960) pp. 628–642; G. Quispel, 'The Study of Encratism: A Historical Survey,' in U. Bianchi (ed.), *La Tradizione dell'Enkrateia, Atti del Colloquio Internazionale – Milano 20–23 Aprile 1982* (Rome: Edizioni Dell'Ateneo, 1985) pp. 35–81; P. Brown, *The Body and Society: Men, Women, and Sexual Renunciation in Early Christianity*, Lectures on History of Religions 13 (New York: Columbia Univeristy Press, 1988) pp. 83–102.

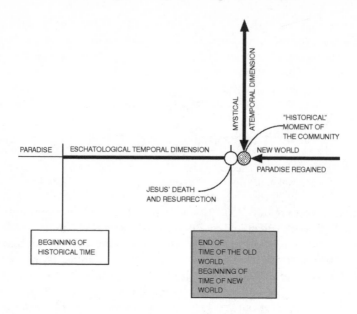

Diagram 6: Utopian Community

groups, however, justified their behavior on different grounds, eschatological and protological, to be sure. The encratic response in the *Gospel of
Thomas* has affinities with these latter non-gnostic encratic Christians.

7.1 *Sexuality in Second Temple Judaism*

This shift to an encratic paradigm is not a deviant development of some
Christian communities as they began to adopt Greco-Roman attitudes
toward the body. Rather, its roots run deep in Jewish attitudes toward
sexuality and toward the scripture, which required, for the Thomasine
Christians, renewed exegesis to recover God's instructions for the present
age when the End did not come.

Recent research about Jewish attitudes toward sexuality in this early
period has shown that the Jews were as conflicted as the Romans when it
came to sex. Sex was a 'good' drive in that it was procreative within
marriage and was necessary for the fulfillment of God's commandment to
be fruitful and multiple (Gen 1.28).[2] This did not lead to a 'positive'
attitude among first-century Jews about sexuality and the body, however,
as some scholars have argued in the past. In fact, we do not have to think

---

2.   J. Cohen, '*Be Fertile and Increase, Fill the Earth and Master It.*' *The Ancient and
Medieval Career of a Biblical Text* (Ithaca: Cornell University Press, 1989).

any longer that the early Christians deviated from Judaism by turning to Platonic philosophy with its negative assessment of corporeality to explain the origins of sexual asceticism.[3] The seeds were planted already in the Jewish soil because the Jews believed that sexual desire was part of the soul's 'evil impulse', the *yeser hara'*. It was the primary threat to self-control, an idea in which the Rabbis, like the Hellenistic philosophers, put great stock.[4]

In fact, such notions are as early as the second century BCE, as can be seen in various passages in the *Testament of the Twelve Patriarchs*. The *Testament of Asher* explains that there are two ways or 'mind-sets,' two 'dispositions', good and evil, within the soul. If the soul follows the 'good way' or 'spirit' all deeds are done in righteousness, wickedness is rejected, and sins are immediately repented. If the 'evil way' or 'spirit' is followed, the soul is disposed to sin. It accepts evil and allows Beliar to become its overlord (*T. Asher* 1). This evil drive or 'spirit' within the soul is explicitly associated with sexuality:

> But you, my children, run from evil, corruption, and hatred of brothers; cling to goodness and love. For the person with a mind that is pure with love does not look on a woman for the purpose of having sexual relations. He has no pollution in his heart, because upon him is resting the spirit of God (*T. Ben.* 8.1–3; cf. *T. Issac.* 4.4).

This dubious attitude toward sexuality also appears in the teaching on this topic from the *Rule of the Community:*

> He created man to rule the world and placed within him two spirits so that he would walk with them until the moment of his visitation: they are the spirits of truth and of deceit...To the spirit of deceit belong greed, frailty of hands in the service of justice, irreverence, deceit, pride and haughtiness of heart, dishonesty, trickery, cruelty, much insincerity, impatience, much insanity, impudent enthusiasm, appalling acts performed in a lustful passion, filthy paths for indecent purposes, blasphemous tongue, blindness of eyes, hardness of hearing, stiffness of neck, hardness of heart in order to walk in all paths of darkness and cunning. And the visitation of those who walk in it will be for a glut of punishments at the hands of all the angels of destruction, for eternal damnation, for the scorching wrath of the God of revenge, for

3. Cf. H. Strathmann, *Geschichte der frühchristlichen Askese* (Leipzig, 1914) pp. 16–40; D. Satran, 'Askese VI: Judentum,' *RGG* 1 (1998) pp. 839–840; S.D. Fraade, 'Ascetical Aspects of Ancient Judaism,' in A. Green (ed.), *Jewish Spirituality From the Bible through the Middle Ages* (New York: Crossroads, 1985) pp. 253–288.

4. M.L. Satlow, 'Rhetoric and Assumptions: Romans and Rabbis on Sex,' in M. Goodman (ed.). *Jews in a Graeco-Roman World* (Oxford: Clarendon Press, 1998) pp. 135–144.

permanent error and shame without end with the humiliation of destruction by the fire of the dark regions (*IQS III.17–IV.13*).

Such speculations about the struggle between the two impulses in the soul is linked, in Second Temple Judaism, to the common Hellenistic discussion of the descent of the *psyche* through the planetary spheres, when it accumulates certain faculties or *dynameis*, some positive and some negative.[5] Thus, according to the *Testament of Reuben*, the person is given seven 'spirits' at creation: 'life' which makes a 'composite' human being; 'seeing' with which comes desire; 'hearing' for instruction; 'smell' to help with breathing; 'speech' so that knowledge can be pursued; 'taste' to aid the nourishment of the body; and finally 'procreation and intercourse, with which come sins through fondness and pleasure. For this reason, it was the last in the creation and the first in youth, because it is filled with ignorance; it leads the young person like a blind man into a ditch and like an animal over a cliff' (*Test. Reuben* 2).

Thus, the ancient Jews viewed sex as 'good' when it was part of marriage and had a procreative purpose. But sex for recreational pleasure was suspect because it easily led to sinful behavior and loss of self-control.[6] So limitations were put into place by the Jews to control this potentially dangerous drive. Regular intercourse between married partners, as well as early marriage, was encouraged to prevent lustful thoughts and immoral behavior (*m. Ketub.* 5.6; *m. 'Abot* 5.21; *b. Qidd.* 29b–30a; *b. Sanh.* 76a–b; *Mek. Nez.* 3.112–114).[7] According to Rabbi Eliezer:

> The duty of marriage enjoined in the Law is: every day for them that are unoccupied; twice a week for laborers; once a week for ass-drivers; once every thirty days for camel-drivers; and once every six months for sailors (*m. Ketub.* 5:6).

However, periods of abstinence were allowed particularly as a prerequisite for mystical encounter and in participation of certain sacred rites such as the Day of Atonement and particular fast days (*m. Ta'an* 1.6; *t. Ta'an* 1.5).[8]

---

5.   Numenius, in Macrobius, *Commentary on the Dream Vision of Scipio* I.12.4 (rational powers at Saturn, active powers at Jupiter, spirited powers at Mars, perceptive powers at the sun, appetitive powers at Venus, linguistic powers at Mercury, nutritive powers at the moon); Macrobius, *In somnium Scipionis* 1.12.13, and Proclus, *Commentary on the Timaeus* 1.148.1–6 and 3.355.12–15 (theoretical, political, spirited, linguistic, appetitive, perceptive, nutritive); Servius, *Commentary on the Aeneid* 6.127 (torpor, desire for absolute power, anger, passion, greed); *Poimandres* 24–26 (falsehood, unlimited appetite, presumptuous audacity, arrogance, appetitive guile, evil devices, nutritive).

6.   D.C. Allison, Jr., 'Divorce, Celibacy and Joseph (Matthew 1.18–25 and 19.1–12),' *JSNT* 49 (1993) pp. 6–9.

7.   H. McArthur, 'Celibacy in Judaism at the Time of Christian Beginnings,' *AUSS* 25 (1987) pp. 164–168.

8.   McArthur, 'Celibacy in Judaism,' pp. 172–173.

Exegesis of Exodus 19.10–15 played into these views and even fostered an ancient tradition that Moses was justified (against his wife's wishes!) to declare permanent celibacy for himself, since God spoke frequently to him but not on a fixed predictable schedule (Philo, *Vita Mos.* 2.68–69; *b. Yebam.* 62a; *b. Shabb.* 87a; *b. Pesah.* 87b; *'Abot R. Nat.* 9.2; *Tg. Num.* 12.1–2; *Sifre Num.* 99; *Deut. Rab.* 11.10; *Exod. Rab.* 46.3; *Cant. Rab.* 4.4).[9] This same passage from Exodus was used to explain what appears to be another well-known Jewish 'limitation' on sexuality: sexual relations would be forbidden in the age to come:[10]

> Still others say that in the time-to-come sexual intercourse will be entirely forbidden. You can see for yourself why it will be. On the day that the Holy One, blessed be he, revealed himself on Mount Sinai to give the Torah to the children of Israel, he forbade intercourse for three days, as it is said … Now since God, when he revealed himself for only one day, forbade intercourse for three days, in the time-to-come, when the presence of God dwells continuously in Israel's midst, will not intercourse be entirely forbidden? (*Midr. Ps.* 146.4; cf. *b. Ber.* 17a; ct. *y. Quidd.* 4.12 [66d]).

Understanding the ambiguity that the Jews felt toward sexuality and the limitations that they placed upon sexual behavior as a result, accounts for the ranges of attitudes toward sex present in the Qumran literature and the secondhand accounts of the Essenes and the Therapeutae. Degrees of restrictions, from temporary to permanent, were placed upon members of these groups, groups that engaged in a mystical praxis of worship while sitting on the threshold of the Eschaton.[11]

---

9.   McArthur, 'Celibacy in Judaism,' p. 171; Allison, 'Divorce,' p. 6; P.W. van der Horst, 'Celibacy in Early Judaism,' *RB* (2002) pp. 396–397; L. Ginzburg, *The Legends of the Jews* (Philadelphia: Jewish Publication Society, 1942) volume 2, p. 316; volume 3, pp. 107, 258; volume 4, p. 90.

10.   McArthur, 'Celibacy in Judaism,' p. 172.

11.   O. Betz, *Offenbarung und Schriftforschung in der Qumransekte* (Tübingen: Mohr, 1960); T.S. Beall, *Josephus' Description of the Essenes Illustrated by the Dead Sea Scrolls* (Cambridge: Cambridge University Press, 1988) pp. 38–41; T.S. Beall, 'Essenes,' in L.H. Schiffmann and J.C. VanderKam (eds.), *Encyclopedia of the Dead Sea Scrolls*, volume 1 (Oxford: Oxford University Press, 2000) pp. 262–269; A. Adam and Chr. Burchard, *Antike Berichte über die Essener* (Berlin: De Gruyter, 1972); J.M. Baumgarten, 'Celibacy,' in L.H. Schiffmann and J.C. VanderKam (eds.), *Encyclopedia of the Dead Sea Scrolls*, vol. 1 (Oxford: Oxford University Press, 2000) pp. 122–125; J.M. Baumgarten, 'Damascus Document,' in L.H. Schiffmann and J.C. VanderKam (eds.), *Encyclopedia of the Dead Sea Scrolls*, vol. 1 (Oxford: Oxford University Press, 2000) pp. 166–170; H. Stegemann, *Die Essener, Qumran, Johannes der Täufer und Jesus* (Leiden: E.J. Brill, 1998) pp. 72–74; F. García Martínez and J. Trebolle Barrera, *The People of the Dead Sea Scrolls. Their Writings, Beliefs and Practices* (Leiden: E.J. Brill, 1993) pp. 139–157; Van der Horst, 'Celibacy in Early Judaism,' pp. 393–396.

This ambiguity in first-century Jewish thought also provides the context for the teachings of Jesus of Nazareth who certainly considered sexual desire very dubious. On the one hand, like his fellow Jews, Jesus supported the institution of marriage (Mk 10.2–12) and understood sexual relations to be for procreative purposes. This understanding is implicit in his popular teaching that humans in the present age marry, but in the age-to-come will not since they will be like the angels who have no need to propagate (Mk 12.18–27//Lk 20.34–36). Jesus, however, is very suspicious of sexuality because it can lead to lust and sin in the present life. So he makes a strong case for self-control in this area, threatening the one who fails to control his lust with terrible images of Judgment (Mt 5.27–30).[12] Jesus' concern about the advanced state of history and the imminence of the Eschaton and the New World brings into question in his mind the necessity for procreation to continue at present. Thus Jesus blessed the barren woman instead of the fertile (Lk 23.29//GTh 79; Mk 13.17–19//Mt 24.19–21//Lk 21.20–24).[13]

7.2 *Sexuality in Earliest Christianity*

The first Christian Jews retain this ambiguous attitude toward sexuality. The teachings from Jerusalem preserved in the letters of James and Peter are cases in point. The believer is supposed to 'guard' himself, especially keeping his desires in check because they can give birth to sin (James 1.14–15, 27). The perfect man is able to 'bridle' his body (James 3.23), reining in his passions which are at war in the 'members' of his body (James 4.1; cf. 1 Peter 2.11). In such a state of 'self-control,' the flesh will no longer be ruled by human passions but the will of God (1 Peter 4.1–2; cf. 2 Peter 1.4–6). Believers are warned that God will punish 'especially those who indulge in the lust of defiling passion' (2 Peter 2.10).

The Christians at Corinth must have been subjected to this kind of early Christian teaching from Jerusalem about the body and sexuality since they ask Paul if it is just better not to touch a woman at all (1 Cor 7.1). Paul responds with the same ambivalence toward sexuality we have noted in other Jewish teachings and places the same limitations on sexual behavior. First, to curb immoral thoughts and activities, marriage is encouraged (1 Cor 7.2). Regular intercourse is suggested so that Satan will not be able to tempt either of the partners to immorality because neither person will have occasion to lose his or her self-control (1 Cor 7.5). Temporary abstinence is allowed for times of prayer (1 Cor 7.5) and permanent abstinence only if the person has mastered completely his desires as Paul claims he himself

---

12. Allison, *Jesus*, pp. 178–182.

13. B.J. Pitre, 'Blessing the Barren and Warning the Fecund: Jesus' Message for Women Concerning Pregnancy and Childbirth,' *JSNT* 81 (2001) pp. 59–80.

has done (1 Cor 7.8–9). In Paul's mind, the reason for this option of permanent abstinence is eschatological, 'in view of the present distress' (1 Cor 7.25–26). The 'appointed time has grown short,' he argues. So 'let those who have had wives live as though they had none... for the form of this world is passing away' (1 Cor 7.29, 31).

So it seems that early Christianity quickly developed a dual approach to the problem of sexuality. On the one hand, marriage was permitted and sexual relations encouraged between partners to subdue lust, control passions and curb immoral activities. Temporary periods of abstinence were built in to the marriage relationship for times of sacred activities like prayer (1 Cor 7.5) or mystical practices (Col 2.18, 23).[14] On the other hand, permanent abstinence was encouraged since the community stood on the threshold of the Eschaton. Not only would it be burdensome for pregnant and nursing mothers in the days of eschatological oppression looming on the horizon, but also procreation itself would soon cease as the angelic life dawned at the start of the new age. So if one had already mastered one's body and its sexual drive, and had no fear of falling into temptation, it was permitted to abstain from sexual relations even within marriage in anticipation of the angelic state and the cessation of procreation. This latter option seems to have been fostered particularly at the leadership levels of early Christianity since Paul claims this option for himself and mentions that the apostles, particularly Jesus' brothers and Peter, had 'sister' relationships with their wives (ἀδελφὴν γυναῖκα) (1 Cor 9.5).

This dual approach to sexuality led to the development of the early Christian accretive dialogue, found in Matthew's version of the divorce pericope, between Jesus and his disciples.[15] The disciples decide that 'it is not expedient to marry' and Jesus supports them:

> Not all men can receive this saying, but only those to whom it is given. For there are eunuchs who have been so from birth, and there are eunuchs who have been made eunuchs by men, and there are eunuchs who have made themselves eunuchs for the sake of the kingdom of heaven. He who is able to receive this teaching, let him receive it (Mt 19.10–12).

---

14. F.O. Francis, 'Humility and Angelic Worship in Col 2:18,' *ST* 16 (1962) pp. 109–134; C. Evans, 'The Colossian Mystics,' *Biblica* 63 (1982) pp. 188–205.

15. The eunuch saying in Matthew 19.10–12 must be a Matthean addition emerging from later Christian teachings rather than from the teachings of Jesus of Nazareth. The most recent arguments for authenticity remain unconvincing to me primarily because Paul does not know it even though he refers to Jesus' teaching about divorce (1 Cor 7.10–11, 25). For these arguments, refer to J.D. Crossan, *The Historical Jesus: The Life of a Jewish Mediterranean Peasant* (San Francisco: HarperCollins, 1991) pp. xxiii, 448; J.P. Meier, *A Marginal Jew: Rethinking the Historical Jesus*, volume 1 (New York: Doubleday, 1991) pp. 342–344; D.C. Allison, *Jesus of Nazareth: Millenarian Prophet* (Minneapolis: Fortress Press, 1998) pp. 182–188.

This dual approach also led to Luke's addition of 'wife' to the list of relatives one must leave behind in order to follow Jesus (cf. Lk 18.29 with Mk 10.29–30 and Mt 19.29) and 'hate' in order to be a disciple (cf. Lk 14.25–27 with Mt 10.37–38 and L. 55, 101). The traditions in these passages testify to the first incremental step taken *toward* the formation of encratic communities by preferencing the unmarried state instead of viewing it as just a viable option to marriage.

7.3 *Encratism and the Role of Eschatology*

Eschatology continued to force the hand of Christians on the subject of sexuality. As history lengthened rather than shortened, a few Christian communities began to inch forward over the apocalyptic threshold and found themselves standing inside the door of the next world. They argued that the resurrection from the dead had already taken place with Jesus' own, and that the new age was upon them (cf. 2 Thess 2.2; 1 Cor 4.8; 15.12–28). Because of this, some even went so far as to conclude that the angelic life should be taken up, permanent abstinence adopted, and marriage suspected of being a state of sin (cf. 1 Tim 4.3). In the End, it would be the virgins who would be redeemed (Rev 14.4).

In fact, Clement of Alexandria's famous treatise *On Marriage* informs us that the leading reason for such encratic behavior among certain Christians he knew in Alexandria was eschatological, justified by reference to Luke 20.34–36.[16]

> The sons of this age marry and are given in marriage; but those who are accounted worthy to attain to that age and to the resurrection from the dead neither marry nor are given in marriage, for they cannot die any more, because they are equal to the angels and are sons of God, sons of the resurrection.

According to the encratic exegesis of this passage, 'the children of the age to come neither marry nor are given in marriage,' time is divided into two eras, before the resurrection and after the resurrection (*Strom.* 3.12.87). During the first era, marriage was a concession of the Law. But now that the resurrection of Jesus had occurred, a new age had dawned. The ' "old things are passed away" ' and ' "new things have happened" ' (*Strom.* 3.8.62). The encratites believed that they themselves represented the 'sons'

---

16. Luke's text is cited because the encratic exegesis relies on a version of this tradition represented by Luke's version rather than Mark's or Matthew's because it speaks of the 'sons' of different ages and implies that the age of the resurrection has already dawned. On this, refer to U. Bianchi, 'The Religio-Historical Relevance of Lk 20.34–36,' in R. van den Broek and M.J. Vermanseren (eds.), *Studies in Gnosticism and Hellenistic Religions, presented to Gilles Quispel on the Occasion of his 65th Birthday*, EPRO 91 (Leiden: E.J. Brill, 1981) pp. 31–37.

of this new age (*Strom.* 3.12.87). They were sons of God because they were the sons of the resurrection of Jesus. They were like the angels who know no death and belong to no marriage. They were already ' "a new creation" no longer inclined to sin' (*Strom.* 3.8.62). They declared that, according to Philippians 3.20, their 'citizenship is in heaven' and not of the earth (*Strom.* 3.14.95). So, 'for the sake of the kingdom of heaven,' they practiced 'abstinence from the world (εἰσιν οἱ τοῦ κόσμου νησεύοντες)' (*Strom.* 3.15.99) and 'from everything' in the world (*Strom.* 3.16.101). Clement tell us that, because of these beliefs, the Alexandrian encratites failed to understand that God's Judgment was still to come and that every person would be judged 'for what he has done with his body, whether it is good or bad' (*Strom.* 3.8.62).

Because these encratites believed that they had attained the body resurrected and immortal, the time had come for them to reject marriage as Jesus told them to do (*Strom.* 3.6.48). The rules had changed. Marriage was no longer a concession of the Law, but was outlawed based on the teachings of Jesus (*Strom.* 3.14.95). Marriage was regarded by them as 'fornification' and the virgin wife, 'a harlot' (*Strom.* 3.17.107). Thus, the 'destruction' of this world had already been accomplished within their communities by their refusal to procreate. Such actions, they argued, dissolved the world as Jesus had proclaimed when he said, 'I came to destroy the works of the female' (*Strom.* 3.9.63). These Alexandrian encratites whom Clement knows additionally argued that death itself was overcome by the believer when he or she gave up procreation. They based their belief on a saying of Jesus from the *Gospel of the Egyptians:*

> When Salome asked the Lord, 'How long will death hold sway?' he answered, 'As long as you women bear children' (*Strom.* 3.6.45).

Many of the accretions in *Thomas* squarely link the Thomasine community with the thought-world of the Alexandrian encratic Christians of whom Clement speaks. The Thomasine accretions present a similar encratic re-action to eschatological disappointment. As we have mentioned previously, they relate the opinion that the resurrection from the dead had already happened and that the New World, the new era, was already in vogue:

> (51) [1]His disciples said to him, 'When will the dead rest, and when will the new world come?'
> [2]He said to them, 'What you look for has come, but you have not perceived it.'

They suggest that the members of the community believed they were living already as citizens of this new world, abiding in God's Kingdom which had been literally and fully established in their midst on earth:

> (3) [1]((Jesus said, 'If your ⟨leaders⟩ say to you, "Look! the Kingdom is in heaven," then the birds of heaven will arrive first before you. [2]If

they say, "It is under the earth," then the fish of the sea will enter it, arriving first before you. [3]But the Kingdom of Heaven is inside of you and outside.'

(113)   [1]His disciples said to him, 'When will the Kingdom come?'
[2]'It will not come by waiting. [3]It will not be said, "Look! Here it is!" or "Look! There it is!" [4]Rather, the Kingdom of the Father is spread out over the earth, but people do not see it.'

Like the Alexandrian encratites, the Thomasine Christians' 'new world' was opposed to the 'old.' They thought that the old world must be guarded against and thoroughly rejected. We can see this hermeneutic in the *Thomas* parable about the thief plundering a house, a kernel parable (L. 21.5) that is given both *a new interpretation* (L. 21.6–9) and a new *interpretive context* (L. 21.1–4).

(21)   [1]*Mary said to Jesus, 'Whom are your disciples like?'*
[2]*He said, 'They are like little children sojourning in a field that is not theirs. [3]When the owners of the field come, they will say, "Leave our field!" [4]In front of them, they strip naked in order to abandon it, returning their field to them.'*
[5]'*For this reason I say*, If the owner of a house knows that a thief is coming, he will keep watch before he arrives. He will not allow him to break into his house, part of his estate, to steal his furnishings. [6]*You, then, keep watch against the world. [7]Arm yourselves with great strength so that the robbers do not find a way to come to you, [8]because the possessions you are looking after, they will find. [9]There ought to be a wise person among you!'*

The old parable (L. 21.5) secondarily developed (L. 21.6–9) now warns people to '*Keep watch against the world! Arm yourselves with great strength!*' – a command for encratic behavior. Prefixed to this old parable is a question and answer unit of some importance (L. 21.1–4) since it further forces the old apocalyptic parable which warned the hearer to be prepared for the lawless last days, to be reinterpreted in this way. In response to Mary's questions about discipleship, Jesus says that his followers are like children who have settled in a field that they do not own. One day, the owners of the field return and demand that the children leave. The children undress and leave the field to the owners (L. 21.2–4). By the manner in which these sayings have been juxtaposed, it is highly likely that the community interpreted the field parable allegorically: they themselves were the 'children,' their clothes were their bodies, the 'field' was the world, and the owners were the ruling demons.[17]

---

17. A discussion of the early Christian use of the garment-body metaphor, see A. DeConick, *Seek to See Him: Ascent and Vision Mysticism in the Gospel of Thomas*, VCSupp 33 (Leiden: E.J. Brill, 1996) pp. 143–145.

According to such an interpretation, when a new Christian joined their utopian community, he or she was supposed to renounce his or her body and leave the world and its rulers behind. They were to take seriously Jesus' warning:

> (27) [1]((Jesus said)), 'If you do not fast from the world, you will not find the Kingdom.'

They were to follow literally Jesus' command:

> (110) Jesus said, 'Whoever has found the world and become wealthy, he should disown the world.'

Living in this 'new world' meant for the Thomasine Christians that the cosmos and death had been overcome, a belief prominently displayed in the accretive *phrase* (L. 111.2) appended to the prophetic prediction of the imminent End of the World (L. 111.1):

> (111) [1]Jesus said, 'The heavens and the earth will roll up in your presence. [2]*And whoever is alive because of the Living One will not see death.'*

The accretion, 'and whoever is alive because of the Living One will not see death,' blunts the original eschatological focus on the imminent destruction of the cosmos by shifting to a discussion of the destruction of death. This new clause forces new meaning back onto the old saying. When the believer comes to experience that the source of life is the Living God, not procreative activity as most people think, death is overcome. When procreation ceases, even the destruction of the cosmos itself is taking place. Those who engage in procreative activities were thought to be committing a grave sin. Like the Alexandrian encratites, the Thomasine Christians believed that the one engaged in procreative activities was a 'son of a harlot' (L. 105) rather than a son of the Living God.

7.4 *Encratism and the Role of Protology*

Clement relates that some of the encratites in Alexandria, like Julius Cassianus, additionally developed a sophisticated protological justification of their beliefs and practices. This development would have been quite reasonable given the fact that the Christians thought that the eschatological New World would be Paradise Regained. So they turned to the Genesis story and speculated about Paradise, the primordial humans, Adam and Eve, and their fall (*Strom.* 3.17.102). Their exegesis centered on the use of the word 'knowledge' in the Genesis story. They noted that the forbidden fruit grew on the tree of 'knowledge' of good and evil (Gen 2.9).

Adam was told by God that, if he ate from the tree of 'knowledge,' he would die (Gen 2.17). Eve was told by the serpent that, if she ate of its fruit, she would 'know' good and evil (Gen 3.5). As the story progressed, after the couple ate the fruit, the exegetes noticed that Adam and Eve 'knew' they were naked (Gen 3.7). Then, after they were expelled from the garden, Adam 'knew' Eve his wife and she conceived and bore a son (Gen 4.1).

For them, this verse, 4.1, was the key to unlocking the secrets of this story. Since the word 'knowledge' was used of Adam having marital relations with Eve in Genesis 4.1, it became evident to these Bible literalists that when Adam and Eve gained 'knowledge' by eating the forbidden fruit, in reality, they had had sex. They concluded that the serpent must have gained knowledge of sexual intercourse through voyeurism, by watching the animals in the garden! The serpent then persuaded Adam to agree to have sexual relations with Eve, to taste the forbidden fruit (*Strom.* 3.17.102). So they identified the primal sin to be sex, and in so doing, figured that abstinence would return them to the prelapsarian state of the human being.

The Alexandrian encratic speculations did not stop here. More thought was put to the problem of Genesis 1.27 and 2.22 as these Christians pondered the nature of the prelapsarian human, whom they hoped to recreate through imitation. According to Genesis 1.27, God created the first human as male *and* female, while according to Genesis 2.22, woman had been taken out of Adam's side. So the pristine state was understood to be androgyny, while the state of sin, sexual differentiation, a position similar to that of other Alexandrians like Philo and the Hermetics (*Opif. mundi* 151–153; *C.H.* 18). This protological justification for encratic behavior owes much to the widely known Platonic myth from the *Symposium* of the androgynous progenitor into which the two sexes wish to reunite themselves.

Since birth and the human body, the 'robe of shame,' the 'garments of skins' given to Adam and Eve by God (Gen 3.16, 20–21), were consequences of the sexual fall, these both must be renounced (*Strom.* 3.3.12; 3.12.86; 3.14.95; 3.16.101). According to Julius Cassianus, Jesus delivered humans from the 'use of the generative organs.' Jesus taught that redemption from sexual differentiation occurs 'when you trample on the robe of shame, and when the two shall be one, and the male with the female, and there is neither male nor female' (*Strom.* 3.13.91). Had not Jesus come to destroy desire and procreation, the works of the 'female?' they asked (*Strom.* 3.6.45; 3.9.63).

Driving the course of this part of their exegesis must have been similar views of procreation found in Hellenistic traditions, which teach that *eros* and birth lead to death:

Once born, they desire to live and that also means to be destined to die, or rather to be absorbed into the eternal cycle of the cosmos. And they leave behind children to die (Heraclitus, *frag.* 20).[18]

In fact, according to Clement of Alexandria, some encratites, particularly the Marcionites, used Greek traditions in order to support these very opinions. He quotes from several Greek authors whom he thinks certain encratites relied on (*Strom.* 3.3.12–24).

For the encratites, return to the prelapsarian state involved a return to androgyny, which was understood to be an asexual state of 'neither male nor female' (*Strom.* 3.13.92) or 'becoming male' (*Strom.* 6.12.100; Hermas, *Vision* 3.8.4; *Acts of Paul and Thecla* 40; *Acts of Philip* 44).[19] These two seemingly contradictory metaphors were used interchangably to refer to the prelapsarian condition because Adam was perceived to be the primordial androgynous 'male' according to Genesis 1.27 where God created the first *man* as male and female. These astute exegetes also noted that, according to Genesis 2.22, woman was taken out of Adam's side. Thus, they concluded that the ideal state could be described as a condition before sexual differentiation when the primordial *man* was neither gender but consisted of both. This *man* appeared in the male form as Adam, with the female, Eve, concealed inside of him. Philo of Alexandria is a contemporary witness to the fact that it was not uncommon for the Genesis story to be read this way. In a single sentence, Philo tells us that the 'heavenly *man*' (emphasis mine) in Genesis 1.27 was 'neither male nor female' (*Opif. mundi* 134). For the Christians who revered the encratic ideal, this meant that their own celibacy was lived in an attempt to imitate the primordial 'genderless' state of Adam, a state which they characterized as 'neither male nor female' as well as 'male.' In this way, their ascetic behavior was a performance act which transformed them into a new Self and which transported them to Paradise.[20]

Many of the accretions in *Thomas* suggest that the later community in Syria had experienced an encratic response to the eschatological delay which included protological speculation practically identical with that developed in Alexandria. Particularly important is the presence of two encratic motifs in the secondary accretions, 'neither male nor female' and 'becoming male':

---

18. H. Diels, *Die Fragmente der Vorsokratiker* 1 (Berlin, 1956) p. 155.

19. K. Vogt, ' "Becoming Male": A Gnostic and Early Christian Metaphor,' in K.E. Børresen (ed.), *The Image of God: Gender Models in Judaeo-Christian Tradition* (Minneapolis: Fortress Press, 1995) pp. 170–186.

20. For more on this topic, see R. Valantasis, 'Constructions of Power in Asceticism,' *JAAR* 63 (1995) pp. 775–821; R. Valantasis, 'Is the Gospel of Thomas Ascetical? Revisiting an Old Problem with a New Theory,' *JECS* 7 (1999) 55–81.

(22) [1]Jesus saw little babies nursing. [2]He said to his disciples, 'These little ones nursing are like those who enter the Kingdom.'
[3]They said to him, 'Will we enter the Kingdom as little babies?'
[4]Jesus said to them, 'When you make the two one, and when you make the inside like the outside, and the outside like the inside, and the above like the below. [5]And when you make the male and the female into a single being, with the result that the male is not male nor the female female. [6]When you make eyes in place of an eye, and a hand in place of a hand, and a foot in place of a foot, and an image in place of an image, [7]then you will enter the Kingdom.'

(114) [1]Simon Peter said to them, 'Mary should leave us because women do not deserve life.'
[2]Jesus said, 'Look, I myself will <<guides> > her in order to make her male, so that she too may become a living spirit – male, resembling you. For every woman who will make herself male will enter the Kingdom of Heaven.'

My past publications have shown that L. 22 especially is steeped in an exegetical tradition of the Genesis story common to early Christian groups that honored the encratic lifestyle.[21] Here, the disciple is required to transform himself or herself into the androgynous ideal, to 'make the two into one (**ⲣ̄-ⲡⲥⲛⲁⲩ ⲟⲩⲁ**),' 'male and female into a single one (**ⲉⲓⲣⲉ ⲙ̄ⲫⲟⲟⲩⲧ ⲙⲛ̄ ⲧⲥϩⲓⲙⲉ ⲙ̄ⲡⲓⲟⲩⲁ ⲟⲩⲱⲧ**), so that the male will not be male nor the female be female.'

In L. 22, this genderless state is further described as a return to childhood, an ideal image for the Thomasine Christians found in several other accretions, all of which reference the Genesis story.

(4) [1]Jesus said, 'The old man will not hesitate to ask a little child seven days old about the place of life, and he will live.'

(21) [1]Mary said to Jesus, 'Whom are your disciples like?'
[2]He said, 'They are like little children sojourning in a field that is not theirs. [3] When the owners of the field come, they will say, "Leave our field!" [4] In front of them, they strip naked in order to abandon it, returning their field to them.'

(37) [1]His disciples said, 'When will you appear to us? When will we see you?'
[2]Jesus said, 'When you strip naked without shame, take your garments, put them under your feet like little children, and trample on them. [3]Then [you will see] the Son of the Living One and you will not be afraid.'

21. Especially, DeConick, *Seek to See Him*, pp. 17–20.

In early Christian literature, there is much interest in the condition of Adam before the Fall and it is quite common to find discussions about him as a 'child.' This expression usually indicates that Adam has not yet engaged in sexual relations or been overcome by sexual desire (cf. Irenaeus, *Adv. haer.* 3.22.4; *Demo.* 12; Theophilus of Antioch, *Ad. Auto.* 2.25; Clement of Alexandria, *Prot.* 11.111.1). This childlike state was an imitative state in which the Thomasine Christians sought to recreate the youth of Adam within the present experience of their community. They were to return to Eden and the seventh day when God rested after creating the world and Adam, to a time when Adam was still a child and had not yet fallen into sexual sin (L. 4.1). This was accomplished through complete renunciation of the body (L. 21.1–4; 37). This return to the prelapsarian Adam was characterized as a state of 'worthiness' that Adam had not achieved:

> (85) ¹Jesus said, 'Adam came into being out of a great power and great wealth. But he was not deserving of you. ²For, had he been deserving, [he would] not [have] died.'

L. 18 invokes similar sentiment. When the disciples ask Jesus to describe what the 'end' will be like for them, he says that their 'end' will not be the experience that they have previously anticipated. He says that their end will be like their beginning. If they will return to the beginning, they will know the end and 'will not experience death.'

> (18) ¹The disciples said to Jesus, 'Tell us, how will our end come about?' ²Jesus said, 'Have you discovered the beginning that you seek the end? Because where the beginning is, the end will be also. ³Whoever will stand in the beginning is blessed. This person will know the end, yet will not die.'

The text literally says that, in order to overcome death, the disciple must 'stand in the beginning' (ΠΕΤΝΑ[2]ωϨΕ ΕΡΑΤϤ ϨΝ ΤΑΡΧΗ). The 'standing' metaphor was commonly used by Jews and Christians to describe the way in which the angels worshiped before the seated and enthroned God. In some of these texts, it was thought to be possible for the righteous human to enter heaven, either ecstatically or at death, and experience a bodily transformation into an angelic-like being. Thus he becomes one who 'stands' in the presence of God, offering praise to God like one of the angels.[22] This interpretation sheds additional light on *the secondary clause* in L. 23:

> (23) ¹Jesus said, 'I will select you, one from a thousand, and two from ten thousand. ²And they will stand as single people.'

---

22. DeConick, *Seek to See Him*, pp. 90–91.

By choosing to live a life characterized by celibacy and singlehood, the Elect have chosen to imitate the angels who 'stand' before God's face and have no need for marriage and procreative activities. The reference to 'the beginning' in L. 18 appears to have been understood by the community as Eden or 'Paradise' as the parallel saying, L. 19, indicates. Their 'end' would not be the death that they anticipated, but would be like living forever in Paradise. The goal for the disciple who wished for immortality was to rediscover and enter Eden before death, to 'stand' before God's throne like one of the angels. This disciple would never die.

Practically, this meant that marriage and sexual relations had to be forsaken. So the single life became the ideal for the Thomasine community. This shift to honoring singlehood over marriage and family is easily seen in L. 16 where an *interpretative clause* (L. 16.4) has been tacked onto the old saying 16.1–3:

> (16) [1]Jesus said, 'Perhaps people think it is peace that I have come to cast upon the world. [2]And they do not know it is division that I have come to cast upon the earth – fire, sword, war! [3]For there will be five people in a house. There will be three people against two, and two against three, father against son, and son against father. [4]*And they will stand as celibate people.*'

The Coptic vocabulary is very important here since it is one of the first times in history that the word ⲙⲟⲛⲁⲭⲟⲥ, which eventually comes to mean 'monk' or 'virgin,' is used as a noun.[23] As M. Harl and F.-E. Morard have shown in their studies, *monachos* in *Thomas* results from the Greek translation of the Syriac term *iḥidaja*, meaning single unmarried person, a celibate living in a holy community. *Ihidaja* is connected to the Hebrew יחיד, signaling a pious or holy person. In fact, the Rabbis understood this word to refer specifically to bachelors, while the Church Fathers to consecrated celibates.[24] Thus, I have rendered *monachos* in my translation

---

23.   The first use as 'monk' is found in P.Coll. Youtie 77, a papyrus dated to June 324 CE

24.   M. Harl, 'A propos des Logia de Jésus: le sens du mot *monachos*', *REG* 73 (1960) 464–474; F.-E. Morard, 'Monachos Moine, Historie du terme grec jusqu'au 4ᵉ siècle', *FZPhTh* (1973) pp. 332–411; F.-E. Morard, 'Monachos: une importation sémitique en Egypte?' in E.A. Livingstone (ed.), *Papers Presented to the Sixth International Conference on Patristic Studies Held in Oxford 1971*, TU 115 (Berlin: Akademie-Verlag, 1975) pp. 242–246; F.-E. Morard, 'Encore quelques réflexions sur monachos,' *VC* 34 (1980) pp. 395–401. See also, A. Adam, 'Grundbegriffe des Mönchtums in sprachlicher Sicht,' *ZKG* 65 (1953–54) pp. 209–239; G. Quispel, 'L'Évangile selon Thomas et les Origines de l'Ascèse Chrétienne,' *Aspects du Judéo-Christianisme. Colloque de Strasbourg 23–25 avril 1964* (Paris: Presses Universitaires de France, 1965) pp. 37–45.

For *ihidaya* in Syrian Christianity, refer to E. Beck, 'Ein Beitrag zur Terminologie des ältesten syrischen Mönchtums,' *SA* 38 (1956) pp. 254–267; A. Vööbus, *History of Asceticism in the Syrian Orient*, volume 1: *The Origin of Asceticisim, Early Monasticism in Persia*, CSCO

'celibate people' in order to get across in our language today the ancient intent rather than obscure it by using the ambiguous English expression 'solitary' favored in other translations. The addition of this phrase to the Kernel changes the meaning of an apocalyptic saying (L. 16.1–3) which originally warned people about the impending Judgment and the dissolution of their families. Now the saying was an injunction from Jesus to abandon their families for the holy life of the single celibate believer.[25]

In *Thomas*, the use of the term ⲙⲟⲛⲁⲭⲟⲥ is synonymous with the Coptic phrase ⲟⲩⲁ ⲟⲩⲱⲧ, a phrase describing a single person.[26] Thus, the interpretative clause appended to L. 23.1 is equally arresting. An old apocalyptic saying about Judgment when the few faithful would be chosen out of the many unfaithful (L. 23.1) has been transformed by this *new final phrase* which highlights the phrase ⲟⲩⲁ ⲟⲩⲱⲧ (L. 23.2):

> (23)   [1]Jesus said, 'I will select you, one from a thousand, and two from
>   ten thousand. [2]*And they will stand as single people.*'

With the extra clause, the saying now points to an election process in which those who have chosen the encratic lifestyle are already counted as Jesus' Elect! In L. 49, Jesus blesses these 'celibate people (ⲙⲟⲛⲁⲭⲟⲥ), the elect' and promises them that they will 'find the Kingdom' because they are from the Kingdom and will return to it. Jesus compares this situation to a wedding in L. 75 – only the 'celibate (ⲙⲟⲛⲁⲭⲟⲥ)' can enter the bridal chamber. Full membership in the Church required celibacy.

7.5 *The Origin of* Thomas' *Encratism*

The early Christian community responsible for the encratic accretions in *Thomas* honored celibacy and encouraged this as the ideal lifestyle. They did so, like the Alexandrian encratites, for eschatological and protological reasons. The performance of celibacy was for them the avenue to

---

184 (Louvain: Van den Bempt, 1958) pp. 106–108; R. Murray, 'The Exhortation to Candidates for Ascetical Vows at Baptism in the Ancient Syriac Church,' *NTS* 21 (1974) pp. 59–80; R. Murray, *Symbols of Church and Kingdom: A Study in Early Syriac Tradition* (Cambridge: Cambridge University Press, 1975) pp. 16–17; S.H. Griffith, 'Asceticism in the Church of Syria: The Hermeneutics of Early Monasticism,' in V.L. Wimbush and R. Valantasis (eds.), *Asceticism* (Oxford: Oxford University Press, 1995) pp. 220–245.

25.   R. Uro has tried to make a case that *monachos* in *Thomas* does not *have to* refer to celibacy. Although he offers his own interpretation, that *monachos* is to be associated with an anti-familial posture instead of celibacy, he does not offer an alternative explanation for this word's clear linguistic heritage with reference to singlehood and celibacy. On this, see R. Uro, 'Is *Thomas* an Encratite Gospel?' in U. Risto (ed.), *Thomas at the Crossroads* (Edinburgh: T&T Clark, 1998) pp. 140–162.

26.   A.F.J. Klijn, 'The "Single One" in the Gospel of Thomas,' *JBL* 81 (1962) pp. 271–272.

immortality because it literally recreated their bodies in the present. They had already returned to the perfect state of the first man and woman in the Garden of Eden. They had already taken their stand in Paradise, overcoming sin and death. For them, the world had come to an end. In so doing, they were stepping across the eschatological threshold and claiming the rewards of the New World for themselves even while bound to earth – the body resurrected and the joys of Paradise. With this incremental step, their community became a Utopian Community (Diagram 6, see p.176).

This brings to mind a group of Christians whom Epiphanius describes. Although this group is *not* our Thomasine community, it is striking the extent to which these Christians performed an encratic theology very similar to what we have described in this chapter, seemingly aware of a tradition of exegesis quite close to that purported in L. 37 and the *Gospel of the Egyptians* (*Strom.* 3.13.92):

> First of all, they say that these people construct their churches or lairs and caverns . . . in hypocausts, and build a fire underneath to warm with vapors those gathered inside the dwelling. As one enters, there are wardrobe attendants at the doors like bath attendants whom they appoint, and each person upon entering, whether man or woman, undresses outside and goes in as completely naked as at birth. Those whom they consider their leaders and teachers, all of them naked as at birth, are seated among the rest, scattered among them with some of them higher up and some lower down. All belonging to their sect are supposedly continent, such at least is their boast, and virgins, or so they deceive themselves. They do their readings and everything else naked. But if they consider that a transgression occurs, as they put it, they no longer receive the one who committed it into their gathering. They say that he <is> Adam, who ate from the tree, and they sentence him to be put out of their church as from paradise. For they consider their church to be paradise, and themselves to be of the company of Adam and Eve . . . Their nakedness is not due to their feeling no shame, even if that is what they think, but because of their insatiable lust (*Pan.* 52.2.1–3.1).

Although a text's mythology may not provide us with a complete map of the community's behavior, it certainly can give us some good directions, especially in the case of Christianity where Jesus' words were not simply philosophical quips, but words to live by. This passage from Epiphanius shows us one community's practical performance of the body of Paradise. Whether the Thomasine community went to such lengths as Epiphanius' community in their performance is doubtful. But it is a stimulating description nonetheless.

The emphasis on encratism in *Thomas* has been traced by some scholars, prominently Han Drijvers, to Tatian in Syria who supposedly influenced the *Gospel of Thomas*.[27] The evidence presented in this chapter, however, supports a very different scenario more akin to Gilles Quispel's reflections. The encratic theology in the accretions is *most* similar to that developed by the Alexandrian encratites like Julius Cassianus whom Clement discusses at length. In other words, *Thomas*' Syrian encratism is familiar with Alexandrian speculations. Saying this, however, does not negate the fact that the first Christian Jewish community established at Edessa already looked upon the sexual drive as dubious or unnecessary because of the advanced state of history, a position they derived from the Jerusalem mission (L. 79). In fact, this attitude would have made the Thomasine community more vulnerable to the Alexandrian theology once it became a topic of discussion in Edessa, a situation facilitated by the interaction between missionaries and teachers from their respective communities.

Although Tatian was a renunciate too, his theology appears to be an advancement of the type of encratic traditions that *Thomas* knows rather than vice versa. For instance, he identifies the serpent specifically with the devil, believing that marriage is fornication *because it was introduced by Satan* (*Strom.* 3.6.49; 3.12.80–81). He also claims that after baptism a person can no longer engage in sexual intercourse *because there is only one baptism. A person cannot 'wash' again after intercourse and be made clean again by God as is commanded in Leviticus 15.18*, he reasons. Neither of these doctrines which are central to Tatian are even alluded to in the accretions. Again, it is better to see Tatian's ideas as a further development of earlier Syrian encratic thought such as we find in *Thomas*' accretions than the reverse.

We might also add that the encratism promoted by the *Gospel of Thomas* was sympathetic to and congruent with early Christianity as it developed in Syria. The early Syrian community took very seriously celibacy, which it required of all its baptizands. 'Spiritual' or virgin marriage was preferred to ordinary marriage because it was considered the only legitimate form of Christian life for full Church members. In the later Syrian Church, from Aphrahat onwards, the expectation of celibacy was relaxed to include only the elect class of Christians, the 'Sons and Daughters of the Covenant.' Celibacy was no longer a requirement for admission to baptism or full membership of the Church. Only at this late date did virginity become a voluntary state for the chosen elite.[28]

---

27. H.J.W. Drijvers, 'Facts and Problems in Early Syriac-Speaking Christianity,' *SecCent* 2 (1982) pp. 172–174.

28. A. Vööbus, *Celibacy: A Requirement for Admission to Baptism in the Early Syrian Church*, Papers of Estonian Theological Society in Exile 1 (Stockholm, 1951); A. Vööbus,

It appears then that the Kernel gospel from Jerusalem allowed for celibacy on the basis of eschatological distress (L. 79). When the Eschaton did not come, the community collapsed its expectations, rediscovered Eden and achieved the body resurrected through the performance of celibacy. This solution to the eschatological collapse was developed as a *tandem enterprise*, as the result of a dialogue between the Thomasine Christians and a circle of Christians from the Alexandrian community. As teachers, prophets, and missionaries traveled between Edessa and Alexandria, visiting the two communities, they involved them in a mutual theological exchange. Thus, in the early second century, the encratic solution to the delayed Eschaton became popular for the same reasons in Syrian Christianity as it did in Alexandrian. In the mid- to late second century, it was more thoroughly and uniquely developed in Syria by Tatian and, in the third century, by the authors of the apocryphal Acts and *Thomas the Contender*. These encratic traditions later provided fertile ground for the cultivation of Manicheism in the East.[29] Not until the time of Aphrahat, when the Syrian Church was becoming more influenced by Roman theology and practices, were the requirements for celibacy relaxed, reserved for the Christian Elect. It appears that only at this time were the married allowed full entrance into the Syrian Church.

History of Asceticism in the Syrian Orient: A Contribution to the History and Culture in the Near East: Early Monasticism in Mesopotamia and Syria, volume 2, CSCO 197, 17 (Louvain: Secretariat du Corpus SCO, 1960).

29.   On the comparison of the *Gospel of Thomas* with Manichean traditions, see H.-Ch. Puech, 'The Gospel of Thomas,' in E. Hennecke and W. Schneemelcher (eds.), *New Testament Apocrypha*, volume 1 (trans. R. McL. Wilson; Philadephia: The Westminster Press, 1963) pp. 278–307.

Chapter 8

A MYSTICAL REVIVAL

Memory is the in-gathering of all the parts of our life history. ~ *E. Casey*

The encratic response to the delayed Eschaton was a movement toward the mystical dimension of apocalyptic. So it is not surprising that, in Clement's treatise *On Marriage*, he notes that the Alexandrian encratites were mystics as well. Clement relates that these encratites disposed of marriage in compliance with Moses' directive in Exodus 19.15, that humans must abstain from sexual intercourse for three days before they would be able to come directly into God's presence. They regarded their celibacy as a primer for these experiences (*Strom.* 3.11.73). As we have already noted, this tradition had been developed in Jewish exegetical circles in order to justify the permanent abstinence of Moses, who was the role-model mystic for many antique Jews.[1] Clement recounts with interest not only the encratites' exegetical traditions regarding Adam which we reviewed in the last chapter, but also the welding of these traditions with the Platonic fall and embodiment of the soul, particularly in the teachings of the Julius Cassianus. In this condition, the encratites argue, the soul 'suffers' punishment for the misdeeds that caused its original plunge to earth where it was buried in the bodily tomb (*Strom.* 3.3.16). Clement even agrees with these encratites that 'to attain the knowledge of God is impossible for those who are still under the control of their passions' (*Strom.* 3.5.43), although their insistence that marriage be disbanded does not fulfil this obligation for Clement.

What we do not know from Clement's accounting are the fuller parameters of the mysticism practiced by these Alexandrian encratites, only the major points as outlined above. Fortunately, this is not the case with *Thomas*' accretions. They provide us with details that allow for a much more complete reconstruction of their mystical theology and praxis. The accretions tell us that the recreation of Eden within the present

---

1. For more on this, see A.D. DeConick, *Seek to See Him: Ascent and Vision Mysticism in the Gospel of Thomas*, VCSup 33 (Leiden: E.J. Brill, 1996) pp. 132–133. This appears to be evidence for a connection between the Alexandrian Christian encratic community and Alexandrian Jews like Philo who had been fostering Jewish mystical traditions long before the Christians.

parameters of their community made the Christian eschatological dream a present reality for the Thomasine Christians.

This shift in their apocalyptic ideology was quite natural for the Thomasine Christians whose communal memory, as we have seen, was already so developed regarding the apocalyptic. Those Kernel sayings reflecting theophanic traditions particularly served as the bridge to the revision of their eschatological past. For instance, the etiquette for mystical visions is prescribed already in L. 15, a Kernel saying which invokes imagery similar to the ecstatic visions of the Jewish heroes who journey to heaven and the divine throne room (*1 Enoch* 14.24; *2 Enoch* 22.4). Common imagery associated with theophanies was already reflected in the Kernel L. 82 where Jesus was identified with the fire of the heavenly realm, the Kingdom. According to this saying, the believer who draws near to Jesus will experience a fiery theophany, while those who do not will remain far from the Kingdom. Application of this hermeneutic to the fire saying was not uncommon, preserved, for instance, also in the *Gospel of the Savior*. There, in the context of a vision of the glorified Jesus, John is told not to touch Jesus because 'if one is [near] to me, he will [burn.] I am the [fire that] blazes; the one who [is near to me, is] near to [the fire]; the one who is far from me, is far from life' (*Gos. Sav.* 107.39–48).

As we will see in the next chapter, the Thomasine accretions that celebrate the mystical quest, are syncretistic, embedding Hermetic tradi-tions within older Jewish mystical ideas. They represent an in-gathering, a revival and adaptation of older stories. On the one hand, these accretions represent Jewish exegetical traditions of the Genesis story in which Adam is a great luminous being who loses his shining Image. The work of the human being is to recover or be reunited with this lost Image, an Image that ultimately is God's own. The transformation into this glorious being can be the result of a journey into heaven and a visionary experience. On the other hand, the story is Hermetic. The soul has fallen into a prison, the body, and remains separated from its divine source. Through an interior ecstatic visionary encounter with one's own divine soul, called 'knowledge of the self,' redemption from this world is achieved.

8.1 *The Jewish Mystical Story*

In the Second Temple period, there emerged a striking Jewish myth supported by a specific exegesis of the scripture, a myth that served a mystical end for some Jews while preserving the old priestly traditions from Israel. The priestly traditions that comprise this myth are embedded in much of the literature produced during the Second Temple period. One could even say that this myth is practically assumed by the authors of this literature, who, if not commenting upon it directly, at least are reacting to it. The implications that this myth held for Jews of the period who were mystically minded, is quite significant, as we will see, especially in regard to their understanding of the human condition and redemption. The meaning of this myth for these mystical Jews is preserved in Jewish and Christian apocalyptic literature,[2] in the writings of the Jewish theologian, Philo of Alexandria,[3] in the Qumran literature,[4] and in the memories of the

2. G. Scholem, *Major Trends in Jewish Mysticism* (Jerusalem: Schocken Publishing House, 1941), pp. 40–79; G. Scholem, *Jewish Gnosticism, Merkavah Mysticism and Talmudic Tradition* (New York: Jewish Theological Seminary of America, 1960); G. Scholem, *On the Kabbalah and its Symbolism* (trans. R. Manheim; New York: Schocken Books, 1965); G. Scholem, *Kabbabah* (Jerusalem and New York: Meridian, 1974) pp. 8–21; G. Scholem, *Origins of the Kabbalah* (ed. R.J.Z. Werblowsky; trans. A. Arkush; Princeton: Princeton University Press, 1987) pp. 18–24; G. Scholem, *On the Mystical Shape of the Godhead: Basic Concepts in the KABBALAH* (ed. J. Chipman; trans. J. Neugroschel; forward by J. Dan; New York: Schocken Books, 1991). I. Gruenwald, *Apocalyptic and Merkavah Mysticism*, AGJU 14 (Leiden: E.J. Brill, 1980); C.R.A. Morray-Jones, *Merkabah Mysticism and Talmudic Tradition* (PhD dissertation, University of Cambridge, 1988); C.R.A. Morray-Jones, *A Transparent Illusion. The Dangerous Vision of Water in Hekhalot Mysticism: A Source-Critical and Tradition-Critical Inquiry*, JSJSup 59 (Leiden: E.J. Brill, 2002).
   A challenge to this view has been proposed by some scholars who believe that Rabbinic traditions about Ezekiel chapter 1 do not presuppose actual endeavors to ascend but are merely exegetical and speculative developments. Moreover, the Hekhalot tradition originates in circles marginal to Rabbinic Judaism during the post-Talmudic era. See D.J. Halperin, *The Merkabah in Rabbinic Literature* (New Haven: American Oriental Society, 1980); J. Halperin, *The Faces of the Chariot* (Tübingen: Mohr, 1988); P. Schäfer, 'Tradition and Redaction in Hekhalot Literature,' *JSJ* 14 (1983); P. Schäfer, 'The Aim and Purpose of Early Jewish Mysticism,' in his *Hekhalot-Studien*, TSAJ 19 (Tübingen: J.C.B. Mohr, 1988); P. Schäfer, 'Merkavah Mysticism and Rabbinic Judaism,' *JAOS* 104 (1984) pp. 537–554; M. Himmelfarb, 'Heavenly Ascent and the Relationship of the Apocalypses and the *Hekhalot* Literature,' *HUCA* 59 (1988), pp. 73–100; Himmelfarb, M., *Ascent to Heaven in Jewish and Christian Apocalypses* (Oxford: Oxford University Press, 1993).
   3. K. Kohler first determined that elements of Merkavah mysticism can be found in Philo: 'Merkabah,' *The Jewish Encyclopedia* 8 (ed. I. Singer; New York: Funk and Wagnalls, 1904) p. 500. H. Chadwick has suggested that agreements between Paul and Philo may be the result of a common background in Jewish mysticism: 'St. Paul and Philo of Alexandria,' *BJRL* 48 (1966) pp. 286–307. See also, the classic work by E.R. Goodenough, *By Light, By Light* (Amsterdam: Philo Press, 1969).
   4. J. Strugnell, 'The Angelic Liturgy,' VTSup 7 (1960) pp. 318–345; Gruenwald, *Merkavah Mysticism*, p. vii; L.H. Schiffman, 'Merkavah Speculation at Qumran: The 4Q Serekh Shirot "Olat ha-Shabbat," in J. Renharz and D. Swetschinski (eds.), *Mystics, Philosophers, and Politicians: Essays in Jewish Intellectual History in Honor of A. Altmann* (Durham, North Carolina: Duke University Press, 1982) pp. 15–47; C. Newsom, *Songs of the Sabbath Sacrifice*, HSS 27 (Atlanta: Scholars Press, 1985); M. Smith, 'Two Ascended to Heaven – Jesus and the Author of 4Q491,' in J.H. Charlesworth (ed.), *Jesus and the Dead Sea Scrolls* (New York: Doubleday, 1992) pp. 290–301; C.H.T. Fletcher-Louis, *All the Glory of Adam: Liturgical Anthropology in the Dead Sea Scrolls*, STDJ 42 (Leiden: E.J. Brill, 2002); R. Elior, *The Three Temples. On the Emergence of Jewish Mysticism* (Oxford: The Littman Library of Jewish Civilization, 2004).

Palestinian Jewish school of Yohanan ben Zakkai.[5] Subsequently, these mystical traditions were absorbed into the Pharisaic and Tannaitic trajectory,[6] some forms of Christianity including Pauline,[7] gnostic schools,[8] Samaritan texts,[9] Merkavah and Hekhalot tracts,[10] and later

5. Cf. Scholem, *Major Trends*, p. 41; J.W. Bowker, 'Merkavah Visions and the Visions of Paul,' *JJS* 16 (1971), pp. 157–173; J. Neusner, *A Life of Yohanan ben Zakkai: Ca. 1–80 CE* (Leiden: E.J. Brill, 2nd rev. edn., 1970); A. Goldberg, 'Der Vortrag des Ma'asse Merkawa: Eine Vermutung zur frühen Merkavamystik,' *Judaica* 29 (1973) pp. 9–12; C. Rowland, *The Influence of the First Chapter of Ezekiel on Jewish and Early Christian Literature* (PhD thesis, Cambridge University, 1974); C. Rowland, *The Open Heaven: A Study of Apocalyptic in Judaism and Early Christianity* (London: SPCK, 1982) pp. 282–283, and 303–305; Gruenwald, *Merkavah Mysticism*, pp. vii, and 73–86; cf. Morray-Jones, *Merkabah Mysticism and Talmudic Tradition*; J.J. Kanagaraj, *'Mysticism' in the Gospel of John*, JSNTSup 158 (Sheffield: Sheffield Academic Press, 1998) pp. 150–158.

6. Cf. Schiffman, 'Merkavah Speculation,' p. 46; Rowland, *Influence of Ezekiel*; Morray-Jones, *Merkavah Mysticism*; Morray-Jones, *A Transparent Illusion*.

7. On Paul's familarity with mystical Judaism, see especially now A.F. Segal, *Paul the Convert: The Apostolate and Apostasy of Saul the Pharisee* (New Haven: Yale University Press, 1990) pp. 34–71; C. Morray-Jones, 'Paradise Revisited (2 Cor. 12.1–12): The Jewish Mystical Background of Paul's Apostolate. Part 1: The Jewish Sources' and 'Part 2: Paul's Heavenly Ascent and its Significance,' *HTR* 86 (1993) pp. 177–217 and 265–292; J. Ashton, *The Religion of Paul the Apostle* (New Haven: Yale University Press, 2000) pp. 198–237. But the old classic, A. Schweitzer, *The Mysticism of Paul the Apostle* (trans. W. Montgomery; Baltimore: The Johns Hopkins University Press, 1931/1998), remains unsurpassed. On John and mysticism, see Kanagaraj, *'Mysticism' in the Gospel of John*; A.D. DeConick, *Voices of the Mystics: Early Christian Discourse in the Gospels of John and Thomas and Other Ancient Christian Literature*, JSNTSup 157 (Sheffield: Sheffield University Press, 2001). On *Thomas* and mysticism, see DeConick, *Seek to See Him*.

8. On this, see especially my articles, 'Heavenly Temple Traditions and Valentinian Worship: A Case for First-Century Christology in the Second Century,' in C.C. Newman, J.R. Davila, and G.S. Lewis (eds.), *The Jewish Roots of Christological Monotheism: Papers from the St. Andrews Conference on the Historical Origins of the Worship of Jesus*, JSJSup 63 (Leiden: E.J. Brill, 1999) pp. 308–341; 'The True Mysteries: Sacramentalism in the *Gospel of Philip*,' *VC* 55 (2002) pp. 225–261.

9. See especially the masterful work by J. Fossum, *The Name of God and the Angel of the Lord*, WUNT 36 (J.C.B. Mohr: Tübingen, 1985).

10. P. Schäfer, *The Hidden and Manifest God: Some Major Themes in Early Jewish Mysticism* (trans. A. Pomerance; New York: SUNY, 1992); Elior, R., 'Mysticism, Magic, and Angelology – The Perception of Angels in Hekhalot Literature,' *JSQ* 1 (1993/94) pp. 3–53; R. Elior, 'From Earthly Temple to Heavenly Shrines. Prayer and Sacred Song in the Hekhalot Literature and Its Relation to Temple Traditions,' *JSQ* 4 (1997) pp. 217–267; R. Elior, 'The Merkavah Tradition and the Emergence of Jewish Mysticism,' in A. Oppenheimer (ed.), *Sino-Judaica, Jews and Chinese in Historical Dialogue, An International Colloquium, Najing 11–19 October 1996* (Tel Aviv: Tel Aviv University, 1999) pp. 101–158; R. Elior, *The Three Temples*; Morray-Jones, *Transparent Illusion*; J.R. Davila, *Descenders to the Chariot: The People Behind the Hekhalot Literature*, JSJSup 70 (Leiden: E.J. Brill, 2001).

Kabbalistic materials.[11] As expected with traditional material, certain aspects of this mythology varied in explanation, emphasis, and evolution from text to text, time to time, and location to location, although the essential ideas remained strikingly constant.

8.1.1 *The Heavenly Man of Light*

At the center of this myth were speculations about the 'body of God,' the 'Glory' or the *Kavod* of Yahweh. These speculations were enhanced by the study of particular Jewish scriptures, especially passages from Ezekiel where the seer has a vision of an enthroned 'likeness as the appearance of a Man (דמות כמראה אדם),' a Man that appeared like 'fire' with 'brightness round about him.' This was 'the appearance of the likeness of the glory (כבוד) of the Lord' (1.28). God's *Kavod*, in fact, was often depicted in the literature as an anthropomorphic figure of fire or light (cf. Ezek 1.27–28; Isa 6.1–4) seated on the *merkavah*, the special throne consisting of two cherubim with wings spread over the *kapporet*, the lid of the Ark of the Covenant in the heavenly Temple (cf. 1 Chron 28.18; cf. 1 Kings 6.23–28, 8.6–7; 2 Chron 3.10–11, 5.7–8).[12] In the Priestly source, the Glory is a light phenomenon associated with the pillar of cloud or fire which surrounded Yahweh as he led the Israelites through the desert or when his presence was at the Tabernacle (Exod 16.10b; 24.16–17, 43–44; 40.34–35, 38; Num 17.7; 1 Kings 8.10–11; Lev 9.23–24; 1 Sam 3.3; 4.21). Later, a luminous bodily form in the appearance of a human being was attributed to the Glory (Exod 33.18–34.8).

This luminous manifestation of God acted, in a way, as a mask or screen that hid God himself from the direct gaze of his creatures. It served to secure the very old belief of the ancient Israelites that no creature could directly see God and live. This tradition is at least as old as the Exodus story where Moses is told that no one can see God face to face and live through the ordeal (Exod 33.20). So there developed the concept that God's manifestation was glorious, characterized by a luminous screen that concealed him while at the same time revealing him in a way that did not instantly kill the onlooker.

This luminosity is, in fact, a common descriptor of the *Kavod* in our ancient Jewish sources. For instance, Enoch relates that the *Kavod* was robed in a gown 'which was shining more brightly than the sun.' This light served to conceal God from direct view as Enoch states: 'None of the angels was able to come in and see the face of the Excellent and the Glorious One; and no one of the flesh can see him' (*1 Enoch 14*). The

---

11. E.R. Wolfson, *Through a Speculum that Shines: Vision and Imagination in Medieval Jewish Mysticism* (Princeton: Princeton University Press, 1994).

12. See the detailed presentation of the *Kavod* by J. Fossum, 'Glory,' *Dictionary of Deities and Demons in the Bible* (ed. K. van der Toorn *et. al.*; Leiden: E.J. Brill, 1996).

reason for this, in Enoch's words, is that 'the flaming fire was round about him, and a great fire stood before him.' Enoch's vision in *2 Enoch* 22 is comparable. Here Michael brings Enoch 'in front of the face of the Lord' and Enoch says that he 'saw the appearance of the face of the Lord' (22.1).[13] What he describes, however, indicates that he did not see God's face directly but through a light screen. Thus the text records that the face of God which Enoch beheld was 'like iron made burning hot in a fire [and] brought out, and it emits sparks and is incandescent.' In *De mutatione nominum* 7, Philo relates Moses' vision of God in Exodus 33 where he 'entered into the darkness.' Even though Moses searched to see God, Philo insists that God himself 'by his very nature cannot be seen' (*Mut.* 9). The reason for this is explained by Philo in *De fuga et inventione* 165: 'the man that wishes to set his gaze upon the Supreme Essence, before he sees him will be blinded by the rays that beam forth all around him.' Consequently, Philo concludes that God said to Moses, 'What is behind Me thou shalt see, but My face thou shalt by no means see (Exod. 33.23).'

Speculations about this luminous figure, called also the heavenly *Anthropos*, can be found dispersed in many traditions that were associated with or grew out of Second Temple thought, particularly in traditions from Ebionism,[14] Valentinianism,[15] Sethianism,[16] Samartianism,[17] Mandaeism,[18] Hekhalot mysticism,[19] the *Shiur Qomah*,[20] and Kabbalism.[21] Second

13.　R.H. Charles, *The Apocrypha and Pseudepigrapha of the Old Testament in English*, volume 2 (Oxford: The Clarendon Press, 1913) p. 442.

14.　Cf. Scholem, *Jewish Gnosticism*, p. 30.

15.　Cf. Scholem, *On the Mystical Shape*, pp. 25–29; DeConick, 'Heavenly Temple Traditions,' pp. 310–341.

16.　Cf. G. Quispel, 'Der gnostische Anthropos und die jüdische Tradition,' *ErJb* 22 (1953) pp. 195–234; H.-M. Schenke, *Der Gott 'Mensch' in der Gnosis: Ein religionsgeschichtlicher Beitrag zur Diskussion über die paulinische Anschauung von der Kirche als Leib Christi* (Göttingen: Vandenhoeck & Ruprecht, 1962); J. Jervell, *Imago Dei*, FRLANT 76 (Göttingen, 1960); N. Dahl, 'The Arrogant Archon and the Lewd Sophia: Jewish Traditions in Gnostic Revolt,' in B. Layton (ed.), *The Rediscovery of Gnosticism*, volume 2: *Sethian Gnosticism*, NumenSup 41 (Leiden: E.J. Brill, 1981) pp. 689–712; Fossum, 'Gen 1,26 and 2,7 in Judaism, Samaritanism, and Gnosticism,' *JSJ* 16 (1985) pp. 202–239; Fossum, *Name*.

17.　Fossum, 'Gen 1,26,' pp. 202–239; Fossum, *Name*.

18.　Cf. C. Kraeling, *Anthropos and Son of Man* (New York: Columbia University Press, 1927); E.S. Drower, *The Secret Adam: A Study of Nasoraean Gnosis* (Oxford: Clarendon Press, 1960); Dan Cohn-Sherbok, 'The Gnostic Mandaeans and Heterodox Judaism,' in *Rabbinic Perspectives on the New Testament* (Lewiston, 1990).

19.　Cf. Wolfson, *Speculum*, pp. 38–39 and 108; for another position, see M. Idel, 'Enoch is Metatron,' *Jerusalem Studies in Jewish Thought* 6 (1987) (Hebrew) p. 157; S. Nidtitch, 'The Cosmic Adam: Man as Mediator in Rabbinic Literature,' *JJS* 34 (1983).

20.　Cf. Scholem, *Major Trends*, pp. 65–66; G. Stroumsa, 'The Form(s) of God: Some Notes on Metatron and Christ,' *HTR* 76 (1983) p. 280.

21.　Cf. E. Wolfson, 'God, the Demiurge, and the Intellect: On the Usage of the Word *Kol* in Abraham ibn Ezra,' *REJ* 149 (1990) pp. 77–111.

Temple Jewish theologians were quick to associate this luminous anthropomorphic 'Man' with the 'light' of Genesis 1.3, 'God said, "Let there be *phos*!"' And *phos* came into being.' This identification was helped due to a pun on the word *phos* which can mean both 'light (τό φῶς)' and 'man (ὁ φώς).'[22] Therefore, they regarded this luminous heavenly Man as God's associate or partner in creation, a concept which the later rabbis reacted against (cf. *b. Sanh.* 38b; *t. Sanh.* 8.7). Thus, it was believed that this Light-Man, sometimes identified with the cosmic Adam, was the image of God, an image that came into existence on the first day of creation and acted as a cosmogonic agent.[23]

Philo works with this tradition when he writes that the primal light came into being and was manifested in creation as the image of the Logos (*Opif. mundi* 31). One of the main functions of the Logos in Philo's mythology is cosmogonic (cf. *Leg. all.* 3.96; *Cher.* 125; 127; *Migr.* 6; *De spec. leg.* 1.81; *Sacr.* 8; *Deus* 57; *Opif. mundi* 20; *Fug.* 94). He claims that the heavenly Man, the Image of God, is the 'eldest son' and 'first-born' of God, titles he also attributes to the Logos. This Man, Philo states, 'imitating his Father's ways, looked to the archetypal models and shaped the forms' (*Conf.* 62–63). The creative activity of the heavenly Man is highlighted in another Jewish Alexandrian source, the story of Adoil found in *2 Enoch*.[24] According to this story, a pre-existent light encompasses God. God commands that the invisible be made visible (Gen 1.3–5), and Adoil, a man-like figure, descends with a great light in his stomach. Upon his disintegration, the light is released, revealing (version J) or carrying (version A) 'all the creation in it' (25.3) and 'the foundation of the higher elements,' the stars and constellations (25.4).

Since the Jews considered this primordial Man to be androgynous, it is not strange that they attributed to Sophia some of these same qualities. She also is identified with the *Phos* of Genesis 1.3 (*Frag. 5* of Aristobulus according to Eusebius, *Praep. ev.* 13.12.9–11). She is either God's associate in creation (Prov 8.30; *Wis. Sol.* 8.4; 9.1–2, 9) or a demiurge herself (*Wis. Sol.* 7.22; 8.1, 5–6; *2 Enoch* 11; *Ps. Clem. Hom.* 16.12.1. In fact, Philo calls

22.   On this, see G. Quispel, 'Ezekiel 1:26 in Jewish Mysticism and Gnosis,' *VC* 34 (1980) p. 6; Fossum, *Name*, p. 280.

23.   See especially J. Fossum, 'The Adorable Adam of the Mystics and the Rebuttal of the Rabbis,' in H. Cancik, H. Lichtenberger, and P. Schäfer (eds.), *Geschichte-Tradition-Reflexion. Festschrift für Martin Hengel zum 70. Geburtstag*, volume 1, *Judentum* (Tübingen: J.C.B. Mohr, 1996) pp. 529–539.

24.   For a summary of interpretations of the etymology of the name Adoil, refer to Fossum, *Name*, pp. 288–289. Since this publication, A. Orlov has suggested a different etymology. For this discussion, refer to his article 'The Secrets of Creation in *2 (Slavonic) Enoch*,' *Hen* 22 (2000) pp. 45–62.

her 'the mother of all' (*Det.* 54, and 115–116; *Leg. all.* 2.49; *Det Ebr.* 30–31).

Later Jewish mystical traditions, in fact, explicitly call the primordial luminous Man the *Yotser Bereshith*, the 'creator in the beginning.'[25] In *3 Enoch*, Metatron, the Light-Man, is given a crown etched with the letters of light by which 'all the necessities of the world and all the orders of creation were created' (13.1–2). Christian texts, Hermetic texts and gnostic texts, all influenced by this old Jewish mythology, also preserve reference to the demiurgic aspect of the Light-Man (cf. Jn 1.1–5, 9–10; *C.H.* 1.6–13; 13.19; *Gos. Egy.* 3.49.10–12; 4.61.8–11).

8.1.2 *The Radiant Image and Its Loss*
The next piece of the myth regards the human being who was created after the likeness of this gigantic cosmic Light-Man (cf. Philo, *Quest. Gen.* 1.32; 2.62; *Opif. mundi* 25; 69; 139; *Leg. all.* 3.96; *Hev.* 230–231; *Apoc. Abr.* 23.4–6; *Abr.* 11.4 rec. A; cf. *Fug.* 68–71).[26] This meant for some Jews that the first man was created in God's image, originally reflecting God's *Kavod*. This aspect of the myth may explain some of the Adamic traditions which depict the veneration of the created Adam (cf. *Life Adam and Eve* 13.2–14.2; *3 Bar.* 4; *2 En.* 22).[27] The image of the first man, in fact, was so bright that it even surpassed the brightness of the sun.[28] His body was so immense that it filled the universe from one end to the other (cf. *Gen. R.* 8.1; 21.3; 24.2; *Lev. R.* 14.1; 18.2; *Pirke R. El.* 11).[29]

But this radiant image (cf. *Gen. R.* 11–12; *b. Moed* 15b; *'Abod. Zara* 8a) or immense body (cf. *Gen. R.* 8.1; *b. Hag.* 12a; *Pesiq. Rab. Kah.* 1.1)[30] was either taken away from Adam or altered as a consequence of his fall. Some

25. On this, see G. Scholem, *Major Trends in Jewish Mysticism* (Jerusalem: Schocken Publishing House, 1941) p. 65.

26. Schenke, *Der Gott 'Mensch' in der Gnosis*; Fossum, *Name*, pp. 266–291; P.B. Munoa III, *Four Powers in Heaven: The Interpretation of Daniel 7 in the Testament of Abraham*, JSPSup 28 (Sheffield: Sheffield Academic Press, 1998) pp. 85–90. The most recent article by A. Orlov brings together descriptions of the luminous Adam and the creation of the first human being after the Image: '"Without Measure and Without Analogy": The Tradition of the Divine Body in *2 (Slavonic) Enoch*,' (forthcoming).

27. M. Stone, 'The Fall of Satan and Adam's Penance: Three Notes on the Books of Adam and Eve,' *JTS* 44 (1993) pp. 142–156.

28. L. Ginzberg, *The Legends of the Jew*, volume 5 (Philadelphia: Jewish Publication Society, 1928). p. 97; n. 69; B. Murmelstein, 'Adam, ein Beitrag zur Messiaslehre,' *WZKM* 35 (1928) p. 255; n. 3; W. Staerk, *Die Erlösererwartung in den östlichen Religionen* (Stuttgart and Berlin, 1938) p. 11.

29. Orlov, '"Without Measure and Without Analogy."'

30. P. Alexander, 'From Son of Adam to Second God: Transformation of the Biblical Enoch,' in M.E. Stone and T.A Bergen (eds.), *Biblical Figures Outside the Bible* (Harrisburg: Trinity Press International, 1998) pp. 102–111.

of this speculation was rooted in discussion about Genesis 3.21 where God made Adam and Eve 'garments of skin, and clothed them.' These Jews concluded that Adam and Eve originally must have worn garments of light which were lost as a consequence of their sin.[31]

Growing out of these Second Temple speculations about the lost Image was the notion that each person had his or her own heavenly image or *eikon*, a perfected double of the person which sometimes also was described as a guardian spirit or angel. This double was pre-existent and pictured as the exact visual counterpart to the person to whom it belonged (cf. *Deut. Rab.* 2.26–27; 4.4; *Midr. Teh.* 55.3 [146b]; *Gen. R.* 78.3 [50a]; *y. Ber.* 9, 13a, 37; *Midr. Qoh.* 87.4; *T. Issac.* 2.3–4; *Bet ha-Midrasch* 6 [A. Jellinek, 21].[32] In later Kabbalistic texts, references to this heavenly double, the צלם, abound. According to G. Scholem, in this literature, the heavenly image refers to the 'unique, individual spiritual shape of each human being' or the 'self.' This 'perfected nature' or 'body' is the celestial garment, the primal celestial image, which is kept in heaven and comes out to meet and envelop the soul when it returns to the upper world.[33]

Early references to the divine double filtered into Christianity and are found embedded, for instance, in the legend of Peter's angel in Acts 12.15, Jesus' saying in Matthew 18.10, the *Hymn of the Pearl*, and the Valentinian doctrine of the *mysterium conjunctionis* (cf. *Gos. Phil.* 58.10–14; 65.1–26; *Exc. Theo.* 15; 21–22; 79–80; Iren. *Adv. haer.* 1.7.1). Paul's idea that people have heavenly bodies which are images of the heavenly Man, bodies that will be donned at the resurrection, appears to be a development of this Jewish mythology too. According to 1 Corinthians 15.35–49, the 'glory' of the heavenly body differs from the earthly in the same way that the illumination of the sun differs from the moon and the stars. 'As we have

---

31. See A.D. DeConick and J. Fossum, 'Stripped Before God: A New Interpretation of Logion 37 in the Gospel of Thomas,' *VC* 45 (1991) p. 124 n. 8. For later Rabbinic reports, see M. Idel, 'Enoch is Metatron,' *Immanuel* 24/25 (1990) pp. 220–240. There is also a tradition that understands the verbs in Genesis 3.21 to be pluperfects, referring to the status of Adam and Eve *before* the Fall. Thus *Gen. R.* 20.12 states that the scroll of R. Meir read אור, 'light,' instead of עור, 'skin.' The Targums presuppose this wording since they read 'garments of glory (יקאר).'

32. To explain the origins of this tradition, Quispel argues that the Jews combined their ideas about God's image and lore about angels with the Greek concept of the *daimon*; G. Quispel, 'Das Ewige Ebenbild des Menschen. Zur Begegnung mit dem Selbst in der Gnosis,' *Gnostic Studies*, Nederlands Historisch-Archaeologisch Instituut te Istanbul 34.1 (Leiden: E.J. Brill, 1974) pp. 140–157; G. Quispel, *Markarius, das Thomasevangelium, und von der Perle*, NovTSup 15 (Leiden: E.J. Brill, 1967) pp. 39–64; G. Quispel, 'Markarius und das Lied von der Perle,' in U. Bianchi (ed.), *Le Origini dello Gnosticismo, Colloquio di Messina 13–18 Aprile 1966*, Studies in the History of Religions, NumenSup 12 (Leiden: E.J. Brill, 1967) pp. 625–644.

33. Scholem, *Mystical Shape*, pp. 251–273.

worn the image of the earthly,' Paul states, 'so also shall we wear the image of the heavenly.' This heavenly image corresponds to the heavenly Man who Paul identifies with Christ while the earthly with Adam (v. 48). This tradition seems to be a development from the exegesis of Genesis 5.3 where, after the Fall, Adam begot a son in his 'likeness' (ἰδέα) and 'image' (εἰκών). Thus, from that time forward, the earthly bodies as images of the fallen Adam have been reproduced, while the heavenly bodies as images of the heavenly Man, the Christ, must be put on at the resurrection (v. 53; cf. 2 Cor 5.1–10).

8.1.3 *The Restoration of the Lost Image*

The consequences of this type of exegesis meant for some Second Temple Jews that human beings were in something of a predicament. They had lost or been separated from their original radiance or body of cosmic proportions. How was restoration possible? Most Jews believed in some type of a 'righteous life' soteriology: if a person lived his or her life in obedience to God's commandments, at death or the Eschaton, he or she would be returned to the glorious state Adam had lost. Some Jews, accommodating their older monistic anthropology with that of the dualistic one of the Greeks, characterized this state as a reconstruction and glorification of the whole person, a perfected body resurrected and reunited with the soul. Other Jews, like Philo and Josephus, adopted the Hellenistic anthropology with less accommodation to the older monistic schema. They felt that the soul had become incarcerated in the body. Because of this imprisonment in a mortal body, it was 'dead.' Once released at death, it had the chance of being restored to the divine sphere and its 'pure' condition (cf. Jos., *Wars* 7.8.7; Philo, *Opif. mundi* 27, 66, and 134–135). So 'resurrection' was a matter of the restoration of the soul to its original glorious state (though also understood to be some type of 'body') rather than the resuscitation, reconstitution and glorification of the whole person, physical body and soul.[34]

Another type of soteriology seems to have emerged in the Second Temple period as well – the way of 'mystical apprehension.' Apparently, some Jews felt that the lost Image could be restored, at least provisionally, through mystical experience, particularly by means of a heavenly journey that culminated in a vision of God or his *Kavod*. This began the process of the person's transformation whereby his or her body became 'angelic' or

---

34. For an overview of ideas about resurrection of the body, see A. Segal, *Life After Death: A History of the Afterlife in the Religions of the West* (New York: Doubleday, 2004).

was 'glorified.'[35] Since some early Christians identified Jesus with the *Kavod*, the Glory of God, they talk about visionary journeys to see Jesus as well as the Father. Avenues for mystical transformation other than the visionary were also popular in Judaism, including spirit possession,[36] the consumption of 'divine' food or drink,[37] and anointing the body with a 'divine' oil or dew.[38] Whatever the avenue, these mystically-minded Jews hoped to achieve in the present the Jewish eschatological dream: resurrection and transformation into glorious bodies of angels.[39]

The mechanism for vision *apotheosis*, with which we are concerned primarily, is Greek in origin.[40] It was based on an ancient physiology that suggested that the 'seen' image enters the seer through his eye and transforms his soul: 'The pleasure which comes from vision enters by the eyes and makes its home in the breast; bearing with it ever the image . . . it impresses it upon the mirror of the soul and leaves there its image' (Achilles Tatius, *Clitophon and Leucippe* 5.13). This idea is as old as Plato who suggested that the vision of the object touched the eye and was transmitted to the soul. In fact, he uses the image of the soul as a block of wax upon which a vision received is imprinted like a stamp of a signet ring (*Theaetetus* 191a–196c). The Stoics as well as most ancient physicians attributed sight to the stretching of the person's 'innate' *pneuma* in the eye. As it was impressed with the object of vision, the *pneuma* along the nerves carried this communication to the soul where it was then imprinted (i.e. Herophilius, ed. von Staden, 204).[41]

For these mystical Jews, this must have meant that a vision of the *Kavod*, the Image of God, literally resulted in the 're-stamping' of God's image on the soul, restoring it to its original Form and Glory. In the ancient

---

35.   Regarding the Rabbinic ambiguity about whether or not one can see God, refer to Gruenwald, *Apocalyptic and Merkavah Mysticism*, pp. 93–97, who proposes that the negative opinion on seeing God in this literature, rules out 'the possibility of a direct visual encounter with God;' I. Chernus, 'Visions of God in Merkabah Mysticism,' *JSJ* 13 (1982) pp. 123–146, outlines all of the passages in mystical literature where visions of God are mentioned and concludes that the majority of mystics 'did think it possible for certain individuals, both human and celestial, to see God' (p. 141); N. Deutsch, *The Gnostic Imagination: Gnosticism, Mandaeism, and Merkabah Mysticism*, Jewish Studies 13 (Leiden: E.J. Brill, 1995) pp. 75–79.

36.   J.R. Levison, *The Spirit in First-Century Judaism* (Leiden: E.J. Brill, 2002); Ashton, *The Religion of Paul the Apostle*, pp. 198–237.

37.   H. Lewy, *Sobria Ebrietas*, BZNW 9 (Berlin: Alfred Töpelmann, 1929); A. Lieber, *God Incorporated: Feasting on the Divine Presence in Ancient Judaism* (PhD dissertation: Columbia University, 1998).

38.   A. Orlov, 'Resurrection of Adam's Body: The Redeeming Role of Enoch-Metatron in 2 Enoch 46 and Sefer Hekhalot 48C,' forthcoming.

39.   Morray-Jones, 'Transformational Mysticism'; Himmelfarb, *Ascent to Heaven*, pp. 47–71.

40.   For a broader discussion, see DeConick, *Voices of the Mystics*, pp. 34–67.

41.   F. Solmsen, 'Greek Philosophy and the Discovery of Nerves,' *MH* 18 (1961) pp. 150–197.

language of their mythology, the Jews said that they would become 'glorified,' 'exalted,' or 'angelic.' They would be clothed in shining white garments, become 'standing' angels worshiping God before his throne, be transformed into beings of fire or light, be 'enthroned,' regain their cosmic-sized bodies, or be invested with God's Name or Image.[42] Many of these ideas are preserved in sum in the Samaritan traditions about Moses. When Moses ascended Mt Sinai, he received the image which Adam had lost, being reinvested with the Light. So in *Memar Marqa* 5.4, we find the passage, 'He [Moses] was vested with the Form which Adam cast off in the Garden of Eden; and his face shone up to the day of his death.'[43] How was the reinvestment effected? Through vision of the Image of God, as *Memar Marqa* 6.3 relates: 'He [Moses] drew near to the holy deep darkness where the Divine One was, and he saw the wonders of the unseen – a sight no one else could see. His Image dwelt on him. How terrifying to anyone who beholds and no one is able to stand before it!'[44]

8.2 *The Hermetic Story*

The *Thomasine* accretions not only reflect Jewish mystical mythology. They also tell the Hermetic story of the Fall and recovery of the soul. Hermetism is an ancient tradition that is not well understood by scholars today because our information about it has been clouded by Renaissance representations of the traditions and scholarly distinctions made in the 1900s between philosophical and magical *Hermetica*.[45] Neither the antiquity nor the living religious essence of Hermetism has been appreciated until very recently even though the Hermetic texts insist that Hermetism is a religion that contemplates and praises (cf. *Asc.* 13–14; 37–38).[46] Two discoveries in the mid- and late 1900s have led to a renewed interest in antique Hermetism and a reawakening to the significance of this tradition for the development of early Christianity and certain gnostic

42. Cf. Wolfson, *Speculum*, pp. 84–85 and n. 46; E. Wolfson, '*Yeridah la-Merkavah*: Typology of Ecstasy and Enthronement in Ancient Jewish Mysticism,' in R. Herrera (ed.), *Mystics of the Book: Themes, Topics, and Typologies* (New York: Lang, 1993) pp. 13–44.

43. Macdonald, J., *Memar Marqa. The Teaching of Marqua* 2, BZW 83 (Berlin: A. Töpelmann, 1963) p. 209.

44. Macdonald, *Memar Marqa*, 223.

45. P. Kingsley, 'An Introduction to the Hermetica: Approaching Ancient Esoteric Tradition,' in R. van den Broek and C. van Heertum, *From Poimandres to Jacob Böhme: Gnosis, Hermetism and the Christian Tradition* (Amsterdam: Bibliotheca Philosophica Hermetica, 2000) pp. 17–40.

46. R. van den Broek, 'Religious Practices in the Hermetic "Lodge": New Light from Nag Hammadi,' in R. van den Broek and C. van Heertum, *From Poimandres to Jacob Böhme: Gnosis, Hermetism and the Christian Tradition* (Amsterdam: Bibliotheca Philosophica Hermetica, 2000) pp. 78–113.

systems:[47] the discovery of several Hermetic texts from Nag Hammadi (*Discourse on the Eighth and Ninth; Prayer of Thanksgiving; Asclepius* 21–29) which clearly integrate theurgic and theosophical elements, demonstrating Hermetism's integrity as a *living religious tradition*; and the discovery of the *Definitions of Hermes Trimegistos* in Armenian, a first-century CE collection of sayings of Hermes uttered to Asclepius, a collection that functioned as a manual for meditation![48]

Thoth, the Egyptian god of knowledge and wisdom, 'the intelligence [literally, heart] of Re,' was understood by the Hermetics to be the primoridal source of wisdom and revelation, Poimandres [ⲡ-ⲉⲓⲙⲉ ⲛⲧⲉ ⲣⲉ] himself.[49] The Greek god Hermes was identifed with Thoth while at the same time was also understood to be a descendant of Thoth and recipient of the mysteries of God. Hermes Trismegistos was the thrice-great revealer of God's mysteries to worthy humans seeking immortalization, seeking 'to become god' (*C.H.* 1.18–19; 20–26; 10.6–7; 11.20; Lat. *Asc.* 5–6; 28).[50] He came to extremely pious humans in visions with this revelatory knowledge.

8.2.1 *The Fallen Soul*

Contemporary studies are demonstrating that ancient Egyptian religion, especially its magical arts and astrological speculations, were central to antique Hermetism and can be identified as early as the astrological lore attributed to the Hermetic Panaretos (*ca.* 200 BCE).[51] Also integral to Hermetism are Middle Platonic theories akin to those promoted by the Alexandrians Eudorus and Numenius about God, the soul, and human life. They believed that a spiritual world existed beyond time and space, a world of ideas or archetypes of the things below. The world below was an image of the world of Reality above.[52] The human psyche had descended from this upper world. In the process of passing through the planetary

47. G. Fowden, *The Egyptian Hermes: A Historical Approach to the Late Pagan Mind* (Princeton: Princeton University Press, 1986) pp. 179–180.

48. J.-P. Mahé, *Hermès en Haute-Egypte*, BCNH 7 (Québec: Presses de l'Université Laval, 1982); see also J.-P. Mahé, 'Preliminary Remarks on the Demotic *Book of Thoth* and the Greek *Hermetica*,' *VC* 50 (1996) pp. 353–363, a first-century BCE Egyptian pre-Hermetic text.

49. P. Kingsley, 'Poimandres: The Etymology of the Name and the Origins of the Hermetica,' in R. van den Broek and C. van Heertum, *From Poimandres to Jacob Böhme: Gnosis, Hermetism and the Christian Tradition* (Amsterdam: Bibliotheca Philosophica Hermetica, 2000) pp. 39–76.

50. J.-P. Mahé, 'La voie d'immortalité á la lumière des *Hermetica* de Nag Hammadi et de découvertes plus récentes,' *VC* 45 (1991) pp. 347–375.

51. G. Quispel, 'Hermes Trismegistos and the Origins of Gnosticism,' in R. van den Broek and C. van Heertum, *From Poimandres to Jacob Böhme: Gnosis, Hermetism and the Christian Tradition* (Amsterdam: Bibliotheca Philosophica Hermetica, 2000) p. 155.

52. J. Dillon, *The Middle Platonists: A Study of Platonism 80 BC to AD 220* (Ithaca: Cornell University Press, 1977) pp. 115–135.

realms, certain faculties or *dynamis* had accumulated in the soul. Some of these powers were positive while others were negative. Numenius, for instance, attributes to Saturn the rational powers of the soul, to Jupiter the active, to Mars the spirited, to the Sun the perceptive, to Venus the appetitive, to Mars the linguistic, and to the Moon the nutritive (Macrobius, *Commentary on the Dream Vision of Scipio* 1.12.4). Similar lists were given by Macrobius, Proclus and Servius.[53] In the Hermetic tradition, these accumulations to the soul were considered largely negative: falsehood, unlimited appetite, presumptuous audacity, arrogance, appetitive guile, evil devices, nutritive (*C.H.* 1.24–26). The return of the soul to the upper world required that the soul slough off its negative faculties.

In the lodges of the Hermetics, religious seekers of many ancient faiths, including Jews who brought with them the Genesis story and speculations about the heavenly *Anthropos* (*C.H.* 1),[54] would gather to receive initiation into the mysteries of God, overcoming the tyranny of Fate and the planets in the process. The journey began with an individual awakening from indifference and ignorance to an awareness that God exists and wishes to be known (*C.H.* 1.31). This is characterized by the Hermetics as a state of '*nous*' or 'mindfulness,' the stirring of the consciousness from drunkenness or sleep (*Prayer of Thanksgiving* 64.8–15). Next the neophyte would receive instruction, called '*logos*' or 'speech,' from the master about the origins of humans and the world (*Prayer of Thanksgiving* 64.8–15). These 'discourses' explain the reality of the Self and God to the neophyte. He or she learns that the human being originates with the archetypal *Anthropos* who had leapt down from heaven as Nature's lover. This *Anthropos*, the Image of God the Father or Mind, falls into material bodies that Nature had created in the shape or *eidos* of *Anthropos* (*C.H.* 1.17). Thus the human being has two natures: the immortal and the mortal, the psychic and the material.

The psychic aspect housed the *logos* as well as the lower appetites, so it existed in a rather precarious predicament. If the soul gave in to the cravings of the appetites and allowed the bodily passions to rule, it became a 'wretched thing,' a 'slave' to evil demons (*C.H.* 10.8–9; cf. *C.H.* 10.15; 11.21; *Asc.* 22). In such a state, it was impossible for the soul at death to rise beyond the planets and become god. It would continue to

---

53. Macrobius, *In somnium Scipionis* 1.12.13, and Proclus, *Commentary on the Timaeus* 1.148.1–6 and 3.355.12–15 (theoretical, political, spirited, linguistic, appetitive, perceptive, nutritive); Servius, *Commentary on the Aeneid* 6.127 (torpor, desire for absolute power, anger, passion, greed).

54. The interplay between Hermetism and Judaism in Alexandria was quite pronounced even as early as Philo of Alexandria. On this, see H.D. Betz, 'The Delphic Maxim ΓΝΩΘΙ ΣΑΥΤΟΝ in Hermetic Interpretation,' *HTR* 63 (1970) pp. 477–479 (465–484); DeConick, *Seek to See Him*, pp. 120–122.

exist in a state of ignorance about its true nature and would be embodied again.

8.2.2 *The Recovery of the Soul*

To achieve liberation from this cycle of reincarnation, the person had to be 'reborn.' This meant for the Hermetics that, in this life, the person had to thoroughly cleanse him or herself of the appetites that had been given to the soul in its original descent into the body (*C.H.* 1.24–26; *C.H.* 13.7). In order to be led to the 'portals of knowledge,' the person had first to rip off 'the tunic that you wear, the garment of ignorance, the foundation of vice, the bonds of corruption, the dark cage, the living death, the sentient corpse, the portable tomb, the resident thief' (*C.H.* 7.2) since this 'odious tunic' dragged the person down and made it impossible for him or her to 'look up and see the fair vision of truth and the good that lies within' (*C.H.* 7.3). The appetites which blocked the immortalization process had to be brought under control.

Once this happened, the appetites were replaced with the powers of God: knowledge of God, knowledge of joy, continence, perserverance, justice, liberality, truth, good, light, and life (*C.H.* 13.8). In so doing, the powers of God set in order 'a birth of mind' that 'expels' the appetites. The person has been 'divinized by this birth' (*C.H.* 13.10). This experience means that the person no longer is what he or she 'was before' because he or she has been 'born in mind' (13.3). The new Self which has been birthed does not have color or mass, nor can it be touched or seen with the eyes (13.3). The person rejoices in the Self-vision: 'Father, I see the universe and I see my Self in mind' (13.13). This Self cannot be dissolved because, unlike the sensible body, it is 'immortal' (13.14).

Thus, it is the quest of the human to gain knowledge of his or her true Self or divine nature (*C.H.* 1.18, 19, 21; 4.4; 13.10; 14.2). The famous Delphic maxim, in Hermetism, becomes a slogan to apprehend one's divine Self, one's true nature.[55] Such is the refrain of a saying from the *Definitions of Hermes Trismegistos to Asklepios*:

Whoever knows himself, knows everything.[56]

To aid the soul in its struggle, God, through grace, sends to the reverent seeker a holy spirit, Mind or *Nous* (*C.H.* 4.3–6). *Nous* not only helps the person truly comprehend or experience God (*C.H.* 4.5–6), it also serves as a spirit guardian or gatekeeper, keeping out demons who try to steal into the soul and turn it to fulfilling its own appetites (*C.H.* 1.22–23; 9.3–4; 12.3–4; 16.15–16). The Hermetics believed that *Nous* was a spirit that was

---

55. Betz, 'The Delphic Maxim,' pp. 465–484.
56. J.-P. Mahé, 'Les définitions d'Hermès Trismégiste à Asclépius,' *RSR* 50 (1976) p. 203.

received during a special water immersion ceremony, a ceremony which included a prayer petitioning God to send this holy spirit into the initiate's soul (*C.H.* 4.3–6; 10.22).

After the initiate had acquired *Nous* through baptism and received instruction from the master, he or she was finally prepared for the mystical ascent journey. The Hermetics believed that reasoned discourse itself could not attain the truth, that it was instead necessary for them to possess *Nous* in order to achieve a state of 'rest' within 'belief' (*C.H.* 9.10). Like the Jewish mystics, according to the Hermetics, the pinnacle of the spiritual quest, understanding God, is completely different from 'thinking' about him or even living piously, although these conditions are part of that journey. It comes from direct experience or '*gnosis*' of the Ultimate Reality (*Prayer of Thanksgiving* 64.8–65.2) , a Reality beyond the concept or idea of that Reality, an experience of transformative proportions.

This mystical experience was achieved through communal contemplation and prayer led by the master of the lodge. The prayers included pious petitions to the Father (*Prayer of Thanksgiving; C.H.* 5.2; 13.16–17; *Asc.* 11; 41) as well as hymns and meditative intonations of the Name of God.[57] The guided contemplations included travel through the created order of the universe (*C.H.* 5.3–7, 9–10; 11.22; 12.21) where the harmony of God was discovered, and visions of the Good (*C.H.* 10.4–6) and the person's true Self (*C.H.* 5.10; 13.13; *Disc.* 57.29–59.29).

The *Discourse on the Eighth and Ninth* appears to be a transcript of one such contemplative journey. Significantly, it combines mythic language of an exterior ascent journey with the psychic language of Self-encounter. It begins with the initiate's request to the master for guidance (52.3–53.27). The master then offers a communal prayer, intoning God's Name, and requesting the great vision 'to see the Form of the Image that has no deficiency' (57.6–7) through the guidance of the spirit (53.27–57.25). Master and initiate embrace and kiss (57.26–27). Following this, the master receives a vision of Mind which he understands to be a vision of his own Self, a vision which unites him with the universal Mind:

> How shall I tell you, my son?... How [shall I describe] the universe? I [am Mind and] I see another Mind, the one that [moves] the soul! I see the one that moves me from pure forgetfulness. You give me power! I see myself! I want to speak! Fear restrains me! I have found the beginning of the power that is above all powers, the one that has no beginning. I see a fountain bubbling with life. I have said, my son, that I am Mind. I have seen! Language is not able to reveal this. For the entire eighth, my son, and the souls that are in it, and the angels, sing a hymn in silence. And I, Mind, understand (57.33–58.22).

---

57. Quispel, 'Reincarnation,' pp. 206–210.

The initiate ascends into the eighth sphere, following the instruction of the master to hymn 'in silence' (58.23–60.1). The initiate exclaims, 'Father Trismegistos! What shall I say? We have received this light. And I myself see this same vision as in you' (59.25–29). Like the master, he then sees the choir of angels singing in the eighth to the powers of the ninth (59.30–60.1). Both master and initiate 'keep silence in a reverent posture,' singing a hymn 'within' themselves, 'resting' in their praise (60.1–61.18). As the initiate sings, he glories, 'No hidden word will be able to speak about you, Lord. Therefore my mind wants to sing a hymn to you daily. I am the instrument of your spirit; Mind is your plectrum. And your counsel plucks me. I see my Self! I have received power from you. For your love has reached us' (60.25–61.2). The hymn ends with another intonation of the divine Name that is now 'hidden' within the initiate (61.9–15). The initiate has been transformed and is guaranteed that, upon death, his soul will be able to make its way along the path of immortality and be absorbed into God.

The Thomasine community appears to have turned to these stories when they experienced a memory crisis, when its past was threatened, when the End did not come. In the accretions, we will find that clusters of ideas from these two stories merged as the result of a confluence of two streams of traditions, the Jewish mystical and the Hermetic. The consequence was an in-gathering of stories which regrouped or reconfigured both the community's memories, traditions, and gospel – indeed, all parts of their life history – into a new unity. This in-gathering and reinterpretation allowed the community to honor, preserve, and even cherish its old memories while, at the same time, aligning it with its common present. Although this sounds like a conscious project on the part of the community, it rather was a function of its communal memory which served to revise and validate its past for the needs of its present, transforming the traditions of its past and present into a seamless narrative.

Chapter 9

THE IMMANENT APOCALYPSE

Whatever is written demonstrates a will to be remembered. ~ *P. Connerton*

There has been increasing interest in reconstructing *Thomas'* mythology over the last decade. I began initially mapping *Thomas'* mythology when writing my doctorate in 1992 and 1993 at the University of Michigan. At that same time, S. Davies published his version of *Thomas'* protology, which hinted at some similar themes.[1] By 1996, my dissertation was rewritten and published as my monograph, *Seek to See Him: Ascent and Vision Mysticism in the Gospel of Thomas*. Drawing on the mythology presented largely in Davies' article and *Seek to See Him*, E. Pagels turned to the task of comparing this *Thomas* mythology to that of the Gospel of John, first as an article in the *Journal of Biblical Literature*, and then as a Random House book.[2] My continued reflection on *Thomas'* story confirms that, ultimately, the story which the accretions tell is one that has fused the Jewish and Hermetic mythologies described in the last chapter with the community's memories of Jesus.

9.1 Thomas' *Mysticism*

This fusion of Jewish and Hermetic mythologies meant that within the memory of the community elements from both the Jewish mystical and Hermetic stories were welded into a new whole, a new story with its own distinctive pervasive themes. In this synthesis, the new story embraced elements from the older independent stories. It is a new Christian apocalyptic story that has shifted emphasis from the eschatological dimension to the mystical, to the immediate apprehension of the person's true divine Self, Jesus and God through direct experience rather than

---

1. S. Davies, 'The Christology and Protology of the Gospel of Thomas,' *JBL* 111 (1992) pp. 663–683.
2. E. Pagels, 'Exegesis of Genesis 1 in the Gospels of Thomas and John,' *JBL* 118 (1999) pp. 477–496; E. Pagels, *Beyond Belief: The Secret Gospel of Thomas* (New York: Vintage Books, 2003).

rational discourse or cosmic events. That is, it is a story that has interiorized the apocalyptic, shifting perspectives from cosmic transformation to the individual soul. Ultimately, it is within the individual that God is to be sought and found. This is the message of Jesus in the full *Gospel of Thomas*.

9.1.1 *The Image of God and the Divine Double*

Thomas' story commences with the Heavenly Man of Light which L. 77 identifies with Jesus.

> (77) [1]Jesus said, 'I am the light which is above all things. I am everything. From me, everything came forth, and up to me, everything reached. [2]Split a piece of wood. I am there. [3]Lift the stone, and you will find me there.'

This saying is one of our earliest references to the fact that the Christians quickly read Jesus into these ancient Jewish traditions about the *Anthropos*, identifying him with the *Kavod*. It should not be surprising that L. 13 implies that this community, in their accretions, also had invested Jesus with the unutterable Name of God, an investiture which the *Kavod*, in Jewish tradition, also possessed.[3] The *Kavod* is referenced again in L. 83.2. According to this saying, the light of the Father 'will become manifest' to the mystic while the Father's 'image will remain concealed by his light.' The mystic would be able to see only the light surrounding God's Image, the *Kavod*, not God directly:

> (83) [2]'The light will be revealed, but his image is concealed by his light.'

It probably was the vision of the 'Son of the Living One' (L. 37) that the Thomasine Christians had in mind here.

The main function of this Light-Man was cosmogonic according to L. 77. Creation came out of his light and he infused creation with his light. His light was believed by the Thomas Christians to have become manifest particularly as human beings through the image of the angels, an allusion made in L. 50, 'through their image.' How is this to be explained? The phrase, 'the place where the light came into being on its own accord and established [itself] and became manifest through their image', is a later explanation appended to the saying's original answer, 'We came from the light.' This signifies that 'their' must refer to the interrogators themselves,

---

3. B. Gärtner, *The Theology of the Gospel According to Thomas* (trans. E. Sharpe; New York: Harper & Bros., 1961) p. 123; A.D. DeConick, *Seek to See Him: Ascent and Vision Mysticism in the Gospel of Thomas*, VCSup 33 (Leiden: E.J. Brill, 196) pp. 111–113.

the angels. The Light therefore manifests itself through the images of the angels into human beings according to L. 50.

It is not a unique motif to *Thomas* that the human being was created in the image of the angels.[4] There is a Rabbinic tradition to this effect. According to *Exodus Rabbah* 30.16, 'man was created in the form of the angels.' This must be the meaning behind *Numbers Rabbah* 16.24, where the statement that humans are like the immortal angels is prooftexted by Genesis 3.22 *and* Genesis 1.27:

> I said: Ye are godlike beings, and all of you sons of the Most High (Ps 82.6), like the ministering angels, who are immortal... Behold, the man was as one of us (Gen 3.22). Similarly, And God created man in His own image (Gen 1.27)...[5]

The Samaritan Targum on Genesis 9.6, 'for God made man in his own image,' helps to explain the meaning of this peculiar exegesis. It states: 'Have I not created man in the image of the angels?' This is a reference to the plural '*elohim*' in Genesis 1.26 where God commands, 'Let *us* make man in *our* image' as well as an association with Genesis 3.22 where the human being is said to have become 'like one of us.'

We find a similar exegesis as the basis for the theology of Valentinus' pupil, Marcus, where we find the Heavenly Man manifested through 'forms' or 'angels.' It was recognized in the 1920s by M. Gaster that Marcus' theology is intimately related to the Jewish mystical traditions and represented an early second-century form of *Shiur Komah* speculation.[6] Marcus describes the genesis of human beings by stating that God who is 'neither man nor woman' made himself visible through sounding out

---

4. Refer to J. Fossum, 'Gen. 1,26 and 2,7 in Judaism, Samaritanism, and Gnosticism,' *JSJ* 16 (1985) pp. 202–239, esp. 214–215 and n. 39. Other discussions of Genesis 1.26 include E. Sjöberg, 'אדם בן und אנש בר im Hebräischen und Aramäischen.' *AcOr* 21 (1950–1951) pp. 57–65 and 91–107; R. McL. Wilson, 'The Early History of the Exegesis of Gen. 1.26,' *Studia Patristica*, TU 63 (Berlin: Akademie-Verlag, 1957) pp. 420–437.

5. The Targum *Onkelos* Gen 1.27b, 5.1, and 9.6, seems to be teaching that man was created in the image of the angels since 'Elohim' is not paraphrased, as is usually the case in *Onkelos*. Thus 'Elohim' here is probably designating the angels. Man was created with four attributes of the angels according to *Genesis Rabbah* 8.11; these attributes of the ministering angels include standing upright, speech, understanding, and sight. Moreover, we are told that the angels were 'created in the image and likeness [of God].' Likewise the Holy One said, 'Behold, I will create him [man] in [my] image and likeness, [so that he will partake] of the [character of the] celestial beings.' Cf. *Mekhilta Bashallah* 7.73ff.

6. M. Gaster, 'Das Shiur Komah,' *Studies and Texts in Folklore, Magic, Mediaeval Romance, Hebrew Apocrypha and Samaritan Archaeology 2* (New York, 1971) pp. 1343–1348; on this, see also G. Scholem, *On the Mystical Shape of the Godhead: Basic Concepts in the KABBALAH* (ed. J. Chipman; trans. J. Neugroschel; forward by J. Dan; New York: Schocken Books, 1991) pp. 25–28; Stroumsa, G. 'The Form(s) of God: Some Notes on Metatron and Christ,' *HTR* 76 (1983) pp. 280–281.

particular letters of the alphabet (Iren., *Adv. Haer.* 1.14.1; Epiph., *Pan.* 34.4.3). So this *Anthropos*, also called the 'body of truth,' is said to consist of the 'letters' or 'forms' of the alphabet. These forms are the 'angels' who are 'continually beholding the Father's face' (Iren., *Adv. Haer.* 1.14.1; Epiph., *Pan.* 34.4.7). When this primal being pronounced 'a word which resembled him,' the divine name of God, the invisible became manifest. The *Anthropos* manifested sounds which were the forms of the angels. Thus humans were said to be emitted 'in their image' (Iren., *Adv. Haer.* 1.13.6; Epiph., *Pan.* 34.3.7)!

These examples demonstrate that, during the Second Temple period, there was an exegetical tradition that was a variation of the more common interpretation that the Light-Man was manifested directly into human beings. The tradition that the human being was a manifestation of the Light-Man through an angelic interface of some sort represents this exegetical variation on the myth. The reason for this mythic variation was further reflection on the plural '*elohim*' in Genesis 1.26 and God's commandment 'Let *us* make man in *our* image.' The late Thomasine Christians seem to have been familiar with just such a teaching.

It is not surprising that the concept of the divine double is prominent in the accretions of *Thomas*. L. 84 mentions that each person has a heavenly eternal *eikon*, an Image which came into existence before the human body, the *eine* or 'resemblance' of the person. This heavenly image is concealed from the person because the person is living in a fallen condition, separated from his or her transcendent self.

> (84) [1]Jesus said, 'When you see the likeness of yourselves, you are delighted. [2]But when you see the images of yourselves which came into being before you – they neither die nor are visible – how much you will suffer!'

Likewise, according to L. 83.1, within each human being there exists 'an image' that has become 'manifest' on earth, the fallen *eikon* or soul that has become separated from its original radiance. The original 'light' of this image, however, remains concealed in the light enveloping God's *Kavod*:

> (83) [1]Jesus said, 'The images are visible to people, but the light in them is concealed in the image of the Father's light.'

Thus, according to this saying, the primal radiance of the fallen soul awaits the soul's return to heaven.

9.1.2 *The Fallen Condition of the Soul*
Thomas is certain that human beings are from the 'light,' are 'children of the light,' and will 'return' to the light (L. 24, 50).[7] The aspect of the human

---

7. For a larger discussion of L. 50, see DeConick, *Seek to See Him*, pp. 64–96.

being that is worth this redemption is the soul, the separated or altered image that hopes for restoration to its original radiance. So *Thomas* teaches about the soul within the body, calling it the 'light inside a person of light' (L. 24; cf. L. 61.2), indicating that it dwells within the body of 'poverty' (L. 3.5). We should note that this anthropology has adopted the dualistic Greek model, shifting away from the earlier Jewish concept of a monistic 'person,' a living *nefesh*, to the Greek anthropology of a body and soul.

How did the soul come into this fallen condition, separated from its original radiance? As we saw in the last chapter, L. 85 provides *Thomas'* answer: Adam is said to have come from a 'great power and great wealth,' although he showed himself unworthy and brought death upon himself. Since 'Great Power' or 'Power' are alternative names of 'Great Glory' or the 'Adam of Light' who is God's image (cf. Justin Martyr, *1 Apol.* 33.6; *Silv.* 106.21–28; 112.8–10; *Eugn.* 75.5–6; 76.19–24; 81.12), we have in L. 85 another reference to this story of the original radiant image of God that experienced an altercation, a separation because of Adam's sin. So, the soul had become separated from its original brilliance. It had fallen into the body, been covered with 'garments of skins' and was subjected to death (L. 37, 85). Now it exists separated from its original Image or Glory, fallen and entombed in the material body, living in a condition of poverty and intoxication (L. 3.5, 28).

This condition is further characterized as one of immense suffering, misery and torture, as two other accretions indicate:

(87)   [1]Jesus said, 'Miserable is the body, which is crucified by a body. [2]Miserable is the soul, which is crucified by these together.'

(112)   [1]Jesus said, 'Woe to the flesh, which is crucified by the soul. [2]Woe to the soul, which is crucified by the flesh.'

Past translators and interpreters of the *Gospel of Thomas* have failed to understand these two sayings because they have translated the Coptic ⲉⲓⲱⲉ, 'to depend.' This verb, however, also means 'to crucify' by hanging or suspension and is used in this manner throughout the Coptic gospel tradition when referring to Jesus' crucifixion (cf. Mt 20.19 *B*; Mk 15.14 *BF*; Lk 23.39 *S*; Gal 5.24 *B*; Heb 6.6 *SB*; Acts 2.23 *SB*). The translation, 'to depend,' although technically possible, does not make good sense of these sayings, especially when taken along with ⲧⲁⲗⲁⲓⲡⲱⲣⲟⲥ which is derived from ⲧⲁⲗⲁⲡⲉⲓⲣⲟⲥ, indicating an extreme condition of suffering or misery.

These sayings, far from suggesting that the soul and body are interdependent, comment on the terrible predicament facing the human being. According to L. 87, the human body by its own nature is a vessel of suffering akin to crucifixion, while the soul is subjected to this same misery because it exists embodied in this material vessel of suffering. The doublet

L. 112 similarly finds the human situation unbearable. Not only is the soul suffering its own state of embodiment, but also the flesh of the believer is tortured by the awakening and repentance of the soul. The awakened soul crucifies the body of passions. As Jesus says in another accretion:

(69)   [1]'Blessed are those who have been persecuted in their hearts. They are the people who truly have known the Father.'

When these sayings are heard or read in conjunction with the old kernel saying L. 55.2, 'And whoever does not hate his brothers and sisters and carry his cross as I do will not be worthy of me,' we find the community's reinterpretation of Jesus' crucifixion: it is understood by them to have been the ultimate model of the soul conquering the passions and the miserable state of embodiment! Like Jesus, these believers attempted to bring their bodies and their appetites under the control of their awakened souls. This was the beginning of their path of liberation.

9.1.3 *The Path of Liberation*

The believer achieved this passionless state when he or she had destroyed his or her personal appetites, as L. 7 metaphorically states, when he or she had 'eaten' the 'lion,' when the lion had become a 'man.'[8] For this particular community, such a state was achieved through a severe encratic regime. As we saw in chapter 7, the community members imitated the prelapsarian Adam by honoring celibacy, the asexual state of the child before concupiscence brought about the Fall of the soul into the body and its subjugation to the appetites. The members of the community had literally returned to Paradise. By ending the cycle of birth and death, they were destroying the cosmos itself. The world had ended for them and Paradise had been regained.

Here the accretions in the *Gospel of Thomas* clearly bear influence from the Hermetic tradition, not so much in the way of amalgamation or incorporation of Hermetic ideas, but rather as a fusion of Hermetic mythology with the Jewish mystical patterns discussed in the last chapter. As we have already seen, several of the accretions in *Thomas* reflect Jewish mystical traditions, investing the acquisition of immortality to flights to heaven and visionary encounters with the Father and the glorious Jesus, the Son of the Living One (L. 24.1; 37; 38.2; 50; 59). L. 84, however, develops the mystical vision of God in a 'new' way, influenced by the Hermetic story of the Self-encounter. It mentions a terrifying gaze at one's *own* pre-existent Image, the Divine Double, the Perfect Self.

---

8.   H.M. Jackson, *The Lion Becomes Man: The Gnostic Leontomorphic Creator and the Platonic Tradition*, SBLDS 81 (Atlanta: Scholars Press, 1985) pp. 175–213.

(84)   ¹Jesus said, 'When you see the likeness of yourselves, you are
        delighted. ²But when you see the images of yourselves which came
        into being before you – they neither die nor are visible – how
        much you will suffer!'

The language in this logion is that of mystical apprehension, a direct
experience of the divine serving the soteriological goal of immediate
transformation. Through gaze upon the soul's divine Image, the soul is
reunited with its original Image. It has become perfected. Such an
experience is described in terrifying terms. Like the terrified Jewish mystic
who comes into the presence of God's Image and falls trembling and
prostrate on the ground, 'how much the person will have to suffer' when he
or she gazes upon the Perfect Self, the Image created after the *Kavod* from
which the person had been separated for so long!

The unification of the individual believer with the divine is mentioned by
Jesus in L. 61.1–5, an accretion that reflects a tradition it holds in common
with the Gospel of John, that Jesus comes from the Father and that the
Father and Jesus are equal (John 5.18b; 10.29–30, 38b; cf. Phil 2.6):

(61)   ²Salome said, 'Who are you, sir? That is, from [[whom]]? You
        have reclined on my couch and eaten at my table.'
        ³Jesus said to her, 'I am he who comes from the one who is an
        equal. I was given some who belong to my Father.'
        ⁴'I am your disciple.'
        ⁵'Therefore I say, when a person becomes [[equal]] (with me), he
        will be filled with light. But if he becomes separated (from me), he
        will be filled with darkness.'

In L. 61.3, it is claimed that Jesus is from the Father, his 'equal.' This
notion is a development of the early Christian understanding of Jesus as
the one who bears God's unutterable Name, having his Form or Glory, his
illuminous *Kavod*.[9] Those who come into Jesus' presence have actually
come into the very presence of God Himself. And this experience is
transformative. Comparable to John 17.11–12, Jesus was given the
disciples by the Father, 'some who belong to my Father.' According to
this logion, once a person becomes Jesus' disciple, through his or her
relationship with Jesus, he or she gains a share in this divine equality. In
the language of the Jewish-Hermetic story, the illuminous image of God
has been recreated within the person as the result of his or her experience
of God's presence. He or she is filled with light.

The reunification of the separated soul with its divine Image also is
heard in the refrain, 'make the two into one,' found in the accretions L. 22
and 106. According to L. 22, a person will only enter the heavenly

---

9.   On the development of *kavod* Christology, see DeConick, *Voices*, pp. 113–117.

Kingdom when he or she has made the two into one, when his or her human image has been recreated into his or her heavenly Image, the primordial Adam:

> (22)   ⁴Jesus said to them, 'When you make the two one, and when you make the inside like the outside, and the outside like the inside, and the above like the below. ⁵And when you make the male and the female into a single being, with the result that the male is not male nor the female female. ⁶When you make eyes in place of an eye, and a hand in place of a hand, and a foot in place of a foot, and an image in place of an image, ⁷then you will enter the Kingdom.'

Salvation is granted only to the person who has been reunited with his or her divine Image, when he or she has made 'an Image in place of an image,' recreating his or her eyes, hands, and feet. 'When you make the two into one, you will become children of Man,' states L. 106. In the context of this myth, it makes perfect sense that, when the separation is rectified and the person reunites with his or her Image of the heavenly Man, he or she regains the original condition, becoming a 'child' of the heavenly *Anthropos* or Man!

The accretions also describe this transformative journey as a psychic journey into the person's true Self. So Self-knowledge is a recurring theme in the accretions. According to L. 3.4–5:

> (3)   ⁴'((Whoever knows himself will find it. ⁵And when you know yourselves, you will understand that you are the children of the Living Father. But if you will not know yourselves, you live in poverty and you are poverty)).'

In this saying, the Hermetic theme that the true Self is embodied in poverty is fused with elements of the Jewish story. Self-knowledge now is redemptive in the sense that it becomes the means of finding the kingdom, of becoming 'children of the Living Father.' Those who remain in ignorance will continue to live in an impoverished condition, duped into thinking that the material body is the person's true nature.

Perhaps the most interesting accretion in this regard is L. 111.3:

> (111)   ³Does not Jesus say, '"The world does not deserve the person who has found himself"'?

This accretion is a second addition to the original eschatological saying, L. 111.1: 'Jesus said, "The heavens and earth will roll up in your presence."' As we saw in the last chapter, the Thomasine Christians first shifted the eschatological understanding of this saying by applying an encratic hermeneutic: 'And whoever is alive because of the Living One will not see death' (L. 111.2). The saying then indicated to the Thomasine Christian that the source of life was the Living God, not procreative activity. If the procreation process, the cycle of birth and death, would cease, the cosmos would be destroyed. Death would be overcome!

L. 111.3, however, now serves to fuse the Hermetic tradition with the encratic. The two previous sayings are now combined with a third, introduced by a gloss, 'Does not Jesus say?' His words in this third saying are those of Hermes, promoting Self-knowledge as a way to overcome the world and death. The person who truly has apprehended his or her divine nature is to be counted superior to the material world. The cosmos is destroyed and death is overcome since the awakened soul will be able to return to its place of rest beyond the cosmos rather than remaining attached to this world and incarnating in another body. Thus, Self-knowledge in the accretions includes not only apprehension of the divine Self, but also the recognition that the material body and the world are only 'corpses' or death-traps:

(56)   [1]*Jesus said, 'Whoever has come to know the world has found a corpse. [2]The world does not deserve the person who has found (that the world is) a corpse.'*

(80)   [1]*Jesus said, 'Whoever has come to know the world has found the corpse. [2]The world does not deserve the person who has found (that the world is) the corpse.'*

Jesus' voice in all these accretions is very similar to that in L. 67. Like Hermes who says in the *Definitions*, 'Whoever knows himself, knows everything,' Jesus says:

(67)   Jesus said, 'Whoever knows everything, but needs (to know) himself, is in need of everything.'

It appears that the voices of Hermes and Jesus have been welded in these accretions. In L. 28, Jesus' mission is stated in terms of his descent and revelation of God's mysteries to humans. He finds them living in a state of intoxication, in need of sobriety and the revelation he has to give:

(28)   [1]Jesus said, 'I stood in the midst of the world and I appeared to them in flesh. [2]I found all of them drunk. I found none of them thirsty. [3]And my soul suffered in pain for human beings because they are blind in their hearts and they do not see. For they, empty, came into the world. And they, empty, seek to leave the world. [4]For the moment, they are drunk. When they shake off their wine, then they will repent.'

Redemption means that the person has to turn from his or her intoxication with the world to thirst for Jesus' message, that he or she must repent and live piously. This mirrors the first steps in the Hermetic process of return: the individual awakening, the stirring of the consciousness from drunkenness followed by the renunciation of the world and its appetites.

According to L. 19, it is further necessary for the person to apprehend 'five trees' in Paradise in order to overcome death:

(19)   [1]Jesus said, 'Whoever existed before being born is blessed. [2]If you become my disciples and listen to my teachings, these stones will support you. [3]For you, there are five trees in Paradise. They do not change, summer and winter, and their leaves do not fall. Whoever knows them will not die.'

This saying implies an ascent to Paradise and an encounter with the unmoving and undying trees there. The language is that of Jewish mysticism. The meaning of this encounter, however, is infused with Hermetic astrological speculations that the soul suffers certain appetitive accumulations that must be sloughed off and replaced with their virtuous counterparts in order for the soul to return back to its heavenly home at death.[10] The number of virtues and vices vary in different texts, but they are all based on two numerical systems: the twelve divisions of the zodiac and the five planetary spheres (excluding the sun and the moon) and the list of elements (breeze, wind, earth, water, and fire).[11]

Philo had already adapted such a theme to the Jewish mythology of Paradise. According to Philo's allegory, the trees of Paradise are virtues that God planted for the nourishment of the soul and the acquisition of immortality (*Leg. all.* 1.97–98; *Conf.* 61; *Mig.* 36–37; *Quaest. Gen.* 1.6, 1.56; *Agr.* 8.19). This 'garden of virtues' brings 'the soul to perfect happiness' and 'immortality.'[12] Christians seem to have been quick to adapt this tradition to their own mythology as can be seen in the Syrian *Odes of Solomon*. According to an ancient hymn recorded there, the person who ascends to Paradise, dons a garment of light. In Eden, he 'contemplates' the 'blooming and fruit-bearing trees' with 'flourishing' branches and 'shining' fruit. These trees are identified with the righteous and virtuous people who have been 'planted' in God's immortal land and

10.   On this see especially R. Reitzenstein, 'Appendix XIII: Virtues and Vices as Members,' *Hellenistic Mystery-Religions: Their Basic Ideas and Significance* (Pittsburgh Theological Monograph Series 15; trans. J.E. Steely; Pittsburg: Pickwick Press, 1978) pp. 47–51, 209–212, and 338–351; G. Mussies, 'Catalogues of Sins and Virtues Personified (NHC II,5),' in R. van den Broek and M.J. Vermaseren, *Studies in Gnosticism and Hellenistic Religions presented to Gilles Quispel on the Occasion of his 65th Birthday*, (EPRO 91; Leiden: E.J. Brill, 1981) pp. 315–335. For lists of vices in Jewish-Christianity and Judaism, refer to J. Zandee, '"The Teachings of Silvanus" (NHC VII,4) and Jewish Christianity,' in R. van den Broek and M.J. Vermaseren, *Studies in Gnosticism and Hellenistic Religions, Presented to Gilles Quispel on the Occasion of his 65th Birthday*, ERPO 91 (Leiden: E.J. Brill, 1981) pp. 502–503.

11.   On these lists, see Reitzenstein, *Hellenistic Mystery-Religions*, pp. 279–288.

12.   See also *3 Baruch* 4:7 which tells of five archangels in Eden who planted five trees.

who have taken their place in Paradise. They 'grow in the growth of the trees' and are 'blessed' having passed from 'darkness into light' (*Ode Sol.* 11.16–19). This traditional context suggests that the five trees referred to in L. 19.3 represent five virtues which the righteous person takes up upon his or her ascent. The effect is transformative, bringing with it immortalization.

According to L. 70, the process of this mystic transformation was not something achieved by the power of the human soul alone. Although salvation was considered by these Thomasine mystics to involve a metamorphosis of the soul into its original Glory, the transformation did not happen without the possession of a divine element *in addition to the soul*:

> (70)   [1]Jesus said, 'When you become what is within you, what is within you will save you. [2]If you do not have it within you, what you do not have within you will kill you.'

The divine 'thing' referred to in this saying cannot be the soul since ancient anthropology held that *all* humans consisted of a body and a *psyche*. So this saying implies that the Christians in this community were not so different from other early Christians. In addition to a soul, they believed that each of them had been possessed by a holy 'spirit,' a 'great wealth' (L. 29). As L. 70 assumes, this spirit acted as a 'helper' for their souls, aiding their mystical journey and the process of their transformation so that their souls not only were able to regain their original radiance, but also were able to illuminate the world with God's Glory (L. 24). It may be that they believed, like other Christians, that this spirit was granted them during the initiation ceremony when they were baptized and anointed, although there is no saying in *Thomas* which explicitly states this.

Finally, the accretions reflect the Hermetic goal, 'rest,' the ultimate achievement of the soul after its laborious journey home (cf. *C.H.* 9.10; *Disc.* 60.1–61.18), a reincorporation into God who exists at 'rest' (cf. *C.H.* 2.6; 2.12; 6.1; *Asc.* 7, 32). Like the beautiful hymn sung following a Hermetic intitiation, 'From your eternity I have won praise, and in your counsel I have found the rest I seek; I have seen, as you wished it' (*C.H.* 13.20), the accretions in *Thomas* tell the story of the soul which has sought the divine within and 'seen,' the soul which has journeyed home and found rest (L. 50, 60.6).[13]

---

13. On the theme of rest in *Thomas*, see E. Haenchen, *Die Botschaft des Thomas-Evangeliums*, TBT 6 (Berlin: Verlag Alfred Töpelmann, 1961) p. 73; Gärtner, *Theology of the Gospel According to Thomas*, pp. 265–267; R. Kasser, *L'Évangile selon Thomas: Présentation et commentaire theologique*, Bibliotèologique (Neuchâtel: Delachaux & Nestlé, 1961) p. 79; P. Vielhauer, 'ΑΝΑΠΑΥΣΙΣ. Zum gnostischen Hintergrund des Thomasevangeliums,' *Apophoreta. Festschrift für Ernst Haenchen*, BZNW 30 (ed. W. Eltester and F. Kettler; Berlin: Alfred

9.1.4 *The Mystical Praxis*

The mystical story recovered from the accretions hints at the praxis which guided believers to the fabulous apprehension of God, 'gnosis.' Gnosis was not understood by these Christians to be intellectual, philosophical or ontological knowledge. It had nothing to do with the left brain. Quite to the contrary, the point of the gospel is that God is Beyond-Thinking. God is an Experience. This is the gnosis that brings life eternal. Because this aspect of the *Gospel of Thomas* has been so misunderstood in the Academy, I wish to emphasize this point. The 'gnosis' sought by the Thomasine Christians was mystical knowledge, not philosophical or otherwise. It was the ultimate God-Experience.

In order to achieve this God-Experience, the Thomasine Christians taught that one first had to achieve a personal state of passionlessness. Complete control over their bodies garnered for the Thomasine Christians the condition necessary to storm the gates of Eden. Thus their encratic praxis and theology which I described in chapter 7 was a serious companion to their mystical leanings. As we have seen, they worked hard to recreate their bodies into the glorious Image of Adam, the primal Man through permanent celibacy. Moreover, we find that they tried to imitate Jesus' crucifixion which they understood to be the crucifixion of the flesh and its appetites (L. 55, 56, 58, 80, 87, 112) by 'fasting from the world' (L. 27) and guarding against temptations and worldliness (L. 21.6–8, 110). With the help of the Holy Spirit received at baptism (L. 29, 70), they fought the apocalyptic battle internally, overpowering their inner demons (L. 21). Furthermore, because several sayings refer to the transforming power of divine food and drink rendering the person 'equal' to Jesus (L. 13, 61, 108), the Thomasine Christians may have placed great stock in the power of the eucharist which worked to further transfigure their bodies into the divine body they sought to personally remake on earth.

The gospel suggests particularly in L. 1 that, once the passionless body in imitation of Jesus had been achieved, the believer was encouraged to study and meditate on the sayings of Jesus:

(1)   And he said, 'Whoever finds the interpretation of these sayings will not die.'

Topelmann, 1964) 294–296; J. Ménard, *L'Évangile selon Thomas*, NHS 5 (Leiden: E.J. Brill, 1975) p. 154; R.M. Grant and D.N. Freedman, *The Secret Sayings of Jesus* (New York: Doubleday, 1960) pp. 160–161. S. Patterson, *The Gospel of Thomas and Jesus* (Sonoma: Polebridge Press, 1993) pp. 133–134. Also refer to the exhaustive study on the theme of rest in the *Gospel of Truth*, J. Helderman, *Die Anapausis im Evangelium Veritatis*, NHS 18 (Leiden: E.J. Brill, 1984).

What did the Thomasine Christians hope to achieve by hearing, reciting, reading and contemplating the sayings of Jesus in their gospel? The accretions are very clear that the experience they sought was revelatory and visionary, as I described in chapter 6. This God-Experience included journeys into the heavenly realms to see Jesus (L. 37) and worship before God's throne (L. 15). Knowledge of the passage through the spheres was learned (L. 50) so that the believer could gaze upon God before death in order not to die (L. 59). In heaven, they would meet their lost Images, apprehending their divine Selves (L. 84). They would directly encounter the Living God, Jesus the Son and God the Father. These mystical experiences brought with them the complete reunification of the believers with their lost Images, the final transformation of the believers into their original bodies of Glory. In other words, immortalization. They would no longer 'die.'

Just as the Hermetics used books of Hermes' sayings as contemplative tools for ascent and vision, the later Thomasine Christians were attempting to apprehend their divine Selves and God by meditating on the sayings of Jesus in their little gospel. No longer was their gospel being used primarily as an oral teaching tool, as the basis for the reperformance of the speeches of Jesus the Prophet. Now it was understood to be a book which provided the mystic with rich fodder for contemplation. It contained the secret truths of Jesus, the master who provided the initiate with the necessary teaching in order to prepare him or her for the ascent and visionary journey. The old Kernel sayings, L. 2, 5, 92, 93, and 94, must have taken on new meanings in this new communal environment – the voice of the true Prophet became a voice akin to Hermes, the great Teacher and Mystagogue.

9.2 *The Origin of* Thomas' *Mysticism*

This particular form of Christian mysticism, this Jewish-Hermetic hybrid, is not unique to the accretions in *Thomas*. In fact, across our extant literature, we find it developed in Alexandrian traditions where it emerges in the second century, bursting forth in 'gnostic' and 'orthodox' teachings alike. Julius Cassianus, Basilides, Valentinus, Pantaenus, Clement, and Origen are all familiar with it and, in one way or another, rely on it as the basis for their own religious speculations and peculiar theological systems. Of these various theologians, Clement's theological discussions are most similar to *Thomas*' accretions, preserving many aspects of this very old stream of mysticism. Although his speculations represent significant developments of this old mythology, they reveal striking parallels to the Jewish-Hermetic mysticism recovered from our study of the accretions, parallels that further strengthen a historical connection between early

Alexandrian Christianity and the majority of the accretions of *Thomas*. It suggests that Clement's writings can be read as a second-century philosopher's reconsideration and development of the older brand of Alexandrian mysticism which had been familiar also to *Thomas*.[14]

9.2.1 *Alexandrian Christian Mysticism*

Naturally, Jesus is characterized by Clement as the great luminous *Anthropos*. He is called by Clement the 'archetypal Light of Light,' the Image of God, the Form of God, the Son of *Nous*, the divine *Logos* (*Exh.* 10: *Strom.* 7.3; *Inst.* 1.2). 'by whom the visible and invisible things of the world were created' (*Rich Man* 36). His Light, *Logos*, or *Nous* is said to be 'always everywhere, and being contained nowhere' (*Strom.* 7.2; cf. *Strom.* 7.3). The '*nous* which is human' is the 'Image of the *Logos*,' since the human being is said to have been created '"in the image and likeness of God," assimilated to the Divine *Logos* in the affections of the soul' (*Exh.* 10; cf. *Rich Man* 36). The human *Nous* is 'the Image of the Image' (*Strom.* 5.14).

This perfect creation was Adam. He had been stamped with the distinctive characteristics of the Form of *Anthropos*, so that he was wanting nothing. Since 'the individual person is stamped according to the impression produced in the soul by the objects of his choice,' Adam altered this Form when he made the bad choice to disobey God (*Strom.* 4.23). Thus, this 'first man' in Paradise 'sported free' because he was 'a child of God.' But he lost his childlike stature when he 'succumbed to pleasure' and was 'seduced by lusts.' He 'grew old in disobedience' and was 'fettered to sins.' So the first man lost his 'original' Image (cf. *Exh.* 12; *Inst.* 1.2; 1.3; 1.12; 3.1; *Strom.* 4.22; 6.14) which was understood by Clement to be genderless (*Strom.* 6.12; *Exh.* 11) and 'fell from heaven' (*Exh.* 11).

Not surprisingly, Clement associates this fall with the descent of the soul into the body, its engendering and attachment to various faculties including the appetites. The 'Intellect' or reasoning faculty is the 'inner man' which Clement thinks should 'rule' the person since it can be 'guided' by God. The other two parts of the soul include the 'irascible brutal' aspect that can draw a person to the brink of insanity, and the 'appetites' that can allure the person to acts of adulteries, licentiousness, and seductions (*Inst.* 3.1). According to *Stromateis* 6.16, although a tenth aspect, the Holy

---

14. For discussion of early Christianity in Alexandria, see C.H. Roberts, *Manuscript, Society and Belief in Early Christian Egypt* (London: Oxford University Press, 1979); G. Quispel, 'African Christianity Before Minucius Felix and Tertullian,' in J. den Boeft and A.H.M. Kessels (eds.), *Studies in Honour of H.L.W. Nelson* (Utrecht: Instituut voor Klassieke Talen, 1982) pp. 271–274; B.A. Pearson and J.E. Goehring (eds.), *The Roots of Egyptian Christianity* (Philadelphia: Fortress Press, 1986); C.W. Griggs, *Early Egyptian Christianity from its Origins to 451 CE* (Leiden: E.J. Brill, 1988).

Spirit, can enter the soul 'through faith,' the soul accumulates in its descent to earth nine aspects: the five senses, the power of speech, the power of reproduction, the vital force of nutrition and growth, and the ruling faculty.

In this condition, the soul is weakened, existing 'enfeebled' (*Strom.* 5.1), 'drunken,' and 'asleep,' unable to ascend back to heaven on its own (*Exh.* 10). To make matters worse, since the soul was not created 'naturally immortal,' it exists in a state of death (*Frags.* 1.1). The only remedy, according to Clement, was an act of God's grace, the sending of Jesus, the great 'Teacher,' the *Logos* who awakens the sleeping or drunken soul with his voice (*Strom.* 5.1). Clement exhorts those who have been 'overpowered with sleep and drunkenness' to 'awake!' and listen to their 'Commander' Jesus (*Exh.* 10). He prays for humans who live as if they have 'drunk mandrake or some other drug' that God may grant them the strength to 'awake from this slumber, and know God' (*Exh.* 10). This awakening is the beginning of faith, along with a 'readiness for adopting a right mode of life, the impulse toward the truth, a movement of inquiry, a trace of knowledge' (*Strom.* 1.1).

Thus, one of the most frequently referenced and theologically developed of Jesus' sayings by Clement is the admonition, 'Seek and find.' In fact, it is in Clement's writings that we find a direct parallel to the Kernel saying, L. 2, an early Jesus saying that appears to have made its way first to Alexandria in the *Gospel of the Hebrews*:

> He who seeks will not stop until he finds, and having found, he will wonder, and wondering, he will reign, and reigning, he will rest (*Strom.* 5.14).

For Clement, this saying encapsulated the progressive life of the enlightened human being from his or her initial awakening, to the discovery of the Teacher, Jesus, to his or her conquest of the appetites, to the attainment of the soteriological dream, rest. Elsewhere, Clement writes:

> The knowledge of ignorance is, then, the first lesson in walking according to the *Logos*. An ignorant man has sought, and having sought, he finds the Teacher; and finding has believed, and believing has hoped; and hence toward having loved, is assimilated to what was loved, endeavoring to be what he first loved (*Strom.* 5.3; cf. *Strom.* 8.1).

The movement of the soul from sleep or drunkenness to wakefulness and discovery 'leads the kingly man near to God the King.' Seeking is 'an effort' on the part of the awakened person to 'grasp,' while discovery is the attainment of this knowledge, the direct 'apprehension of the object of search' (*Strom.* 6.15).

Not surprisingly, this mystical search for '*gnosis*,' the direct apprehension of God, is, for Clement, the search for Self-knowledge. He calls the 'greatest of all lessons,' 'to know one's Self.' For 'if one knows himself, he will know God, and knowing God, he will be made like God' (*Inst.* 3.1). It is, of course, Jesus the Teacher who shows people 'how we are to know ourselves' (*Strom.* 1.28). This search for the divine Self, this pursuit of knowledge, includes the study of 'the genesis of the universe, that thereby we may be able to learn the nature of the human being' (*Strom.* 1.14). Thus he expounds in *Stromateis* 5.4 (cf. *Strom.* 7.3):

> The maxim 'know yourself' shows many things. That you are mortal, and that you were born a human being...And it says, 'Know for what you were born, and whose Image you are. And what is your essence and what your creation, and what your relation to God, and the like.'

Jesus is the 'Perfect Man,' according to Clement, the one who provides the ultimate example of the rationally ruled human being whom others must emulate. He does this not only as a Teacher who cures the 'unnatural passions of the soul by means of exhortations' (*Inst.* 1.2), but also because he is a person 'with a soul devoid of passion.' He is 'wholly free from human passions,' God in 'human form,' 'stainless.' He has 'the Form of God' and, therefore, 'is God.' He is to people 'a spotless Image' to whom 'we are to try with all our might to assimilate our souls' (*Inst.* 1.2). During his life, Jesus had trained his flesh to impassibility (*Strom.* 7.2) because his hope was to 'restore' people to 'the original model, that you may become also like me' (*Exh.* 12). He does this by providing the original model for humans to imitate, both in terms of practical living and contemplative practices (*Inst.* 1.3). Clement states, 'We must, so far as we can, imitate the Lord' (*Strom.* 1.1) whose incarnation and life 'enacted the drama of human salvation' (*Exh.* 10).

In so doing, the human being will fulfill 'what Scripture says as to our being made in his image and likeness' (*Inst.* 1.3). Thus humans are commanded to conform themselves to Jesus' Image (*Inst.* 1.12; 3.1) and to attain to the 'Perfect Man,' the Image of the Lord (*Strom.* 6.14). The 'flesh is dead' to the person who is able to do this. Having 'consecrated the sepulchre,' the body, into 'a holy temple,' such a person reaches 'a state of passionlessness, waiting to put on the divine Image' (*Strom.* 4.22). One finds 'the divine likeness and the holy Image in the righteous soul' (*Strom.* 7.5) because the righteous person has adorned and arranged his or her soul before Jesus, his or her mirror (*Rich Man* 21). Just as wax is softened or copper purified 'to receive the stamp applied to it,' so those people who have endeavored to imitate Jesus' passionlessness will be 'assimilated to the impress given by him' (*Strom.* 7.12;. cf. *Frags.* 1.11), and will be 'formed perfectly in the likeness of the Teacher' (*Strom.* 7.16). Since the soul of the righteous person has been embossed with the divine Image, it not only 'resembles God,' but also 'enshrines' Jesus, the 'express Image of the Glory of the universal King and Almighty Father' so that 'there is now a third divine Image, made as far as possible like the Second Cause, the Essential Life, through which we live the true life' (*Strom.* 7.3)!

The soul's divine Image is recognized by Clement to be genderless. According to Clement, the righteous person spends the early part of his life married, but after the conception of his own children, he lives with his wife 'as a sister and is judged as if of the same father.' At this later point in his life, he prefers 'neither children, nor marriage, nor parents to love for God and righteousness in life.' When the spouses live as siblings, they have 'put off the flesh which separates and limits the knowledge of those who are spiritual by the peculiar characteristics of the sexes. For souls, themselves by themselves, are equal. Souls are neither male nor female, when they no longer marry nor are given in marriage. Is not woman translated into man, when she is become equally unfeminine and manly and perfect?' (*Strom.* 6.12; cf. 7.12; *Exh.* 11).

For Clement, the ultimate example of the achievement of passionlessness was not so much Jesus' life as his crucifixion and death, when he completely separated the passions from his soul. Relying on Plato's imagery, Clement understands that the soul normally exists in a state of crucifixion, each pleasure and pain 'nailing' the soul to the body (*Strom.* 2.20). The soul is 'tortured and corrected, being in a state of sensation lives, though said to suffer' (*Strom.* 5.14). Paradoxically, the crucifixion of Jesus' body, separated the pleasures from the soul. This is 'what the cross means.' In overcoming his passions, he struggled with the 'spiritual powers,' demons who influence or invade the soul, who impress their images of passion upon it (*Strom.* 2.20;. cf. *Rich Man* 29). And he conquered.

In this way, 'our life was hung on' the wood of the tree' so that 'we might believe' (*Strom.* 5.11). The person who sees Jesus' victory over his passions, is to emulate him. 'Bearing about the cross of the Savior,' this person 'will follow the Lord's footsteps, as God, having become a holy of holies' (*Strom.* 2.20). Central to Clement's theology is the notion that we humans 'have to crucify our own flesh' just as Jesus did his flesh (*Frags.* 1.4; *Strom.* 7.3). There is no salvation by nature, only by obedience when the person voluntarily separates his or her passions from the soul, when he or she crucifies himself or herself (*Strom.* 4.3–4; 4.6; 7.3; 7.12). When the person is victorious, not just moderating his or her passions, but becoming passionless, he or she will be able to bear a natural death and ascend to one of the reserved mansions in heaven (*Strom.* 4.3; 6.14; 7.3; 7.12). The person who has 'in the body devoted himself to a good life, is being sent on to the state of immortality' (*Strom.* 4.4). Thus, the person who loses his or her life shall find it, and finding it will ' "know one's Self" ' (*Strom.* 4.6). For Clement, the eucharist is the mystery that embodies this separation of the passions from the soul, 'enshrining the Savior in our souls' so we too may 'correct the affections of our souls' (*Inst.* 1.6; cf. 2.1; 2.2; *Strom.* 5.10–

11). Because this person masters his or her body, he or she is said to 'rule' or 'be king' (*Strom.* 6.15; 6.17; 7.3; 7.4; 7.7).

Such a transformation occurs not only because the person is emulating Jesus practically, but also because he or she has taken up a regime of contemplation. Virtuous living by imitation of Jesus coupled with intellectual study eventually unfolds into a contemplative praxis that leads the person to immediate mystical apprehension of God and the divine Self. This is, of course, the goal of human life in Clement's eyes (*Inst.* 1.1; 1.7; 1.12; *Strom.* 1.9; 2.2). This praxis includes meditation and study of scripture (*Strom.* 1.1; 1.6; 2.11), a master's notes such as Clement's own (*Strom.* 6.1; cf. 1.6; 1.9), and knowledge 'transmitted unwritten' (*Strom.* 6.7; 6.8). In this way, 'the soul studies to be God.' The person regards 'nothing bad but ignorance' and any action 'contrary to right reason.' He or she gives thanks to God for all things, entering into contemplation 'by righteous *hearing* and divine *reading*, by true investigation, by holy oblation, by blessed prayer: lauding, hymning, blessing, praising' (*Strom.* 6.14; *Exh.* 11). Clement believes that baptism and anointing help the success of this praxis by drawing the Holy Spirit into the person's soul. This 'wealth within' the 'carcasse' (*Rich Man* 33–34) is essential, strengthening the soul to withstand the onslaught of demons and guiding the soul's ascent to heaven (cf. *Rich Man* 40; *Strom.* 5.12; 7.7; 7.11).

Devotion to contemplation of the divine allows the person directly to 'commune' with God so that he or she can enter 'more nearly into the state of impassible identity' (*Strom.* 4.6). Clement understands passionless people to have drawn God 'towards themselves,' imperceptibly bringing 'themselves to God.' For the person who 'reverences God, reverences himself.' The contemplative life in which one worships God continuously, results in the person attending to himself or herself: through his or her own 'spotless purification,' he or she 'beholds the holy God.' He of she is 'as far as possible assimilated to God' (*Strom.* 4.23).

Thus Clement speaks of the standard mystical visions on high and their transformative powers. He speaks of these visions as the result of 'initiations into the most blessed mystery' which the perfected celebrate before their own deaths even though they are bound to their bodies like oysters to their shells. These initiations 'introduce' them to 'the knowledge of perfect and tranquil visions,' contemplations of 'pure sunlight' (*Strom.* 5.14; cf. *Exh.* 11). Since the person has become 'pure in heart through knowledge,' he or she may be 'initiated into the beatific vision face to face' (*Strom.* 6.12). To accomplish this requires ascent to heaven where the initiate surpasses 'each of the holy ranks . . . reaching places better than the better places, embracing the divine vision not in mirrors or by means of mirrors, but in the transcendently clear and absolutely pure insatible vision which is the privilege of intensely loving souls.' The result is 'converse with God . . . being made like the Lord' (*Strom.* 7.3; cf. 7.10; 7.11; *Exh.* 11).

Clement asks, 'Who is he who pursues his way to Erebus, when it is in his power to be a citizen of heaven and to cultivate Paradise, and walk about in heaven, and partake of the tree of life and immortality, and cleaving his way through the sky in the track of the luminous cloud, behold, like Elias, the rain of salvation?' (*Exh.* 10).

Clement describes this ascent as the movement of the soul past the planets and sun, discarding the accumulated faculties in the process: the five senses, speech, and the power of reproduction. The soul must ascend above these to *Nous*, to the ninth and then tenth abode where it will meet the Creator of the universe (*Strom.* 2.11). This is the place of rest, described elsewhere in connection with a particular exegesis of Genesis 1, as beyond the seventh heaven (*Strom.* 4.25; 5.6; 6.14; 6.16). The person who has not achieved a state of passionlessness will be subject to the demons who 'demand toll.' They will be detained by them. The person 'full of knowledge,' however, they 'pass on with good wishes, blessing the person.' This person's life will 'not fall away' because its leaves are those of the 'living tree that is nourished "by the water-courses." So, Clement says, righteous people 'are likened to fruit-bearing trees, and not only to such as are of the nature of tall-growing ones' (*Strom.* 4.18) while the 'trees of autumn' that do not bear fruit are likened to unbelievers (*Frags.* 1.2).

Clement struggles with eschatology in relation to these concepts and, out of this struggle, he creates an eschatological opinion more nuanced than what we found in *Thomas*' accretions. He clearly understands that the righteous person who bears the Image of Jesus in his soul has experienced an immediate transformation. He compares such a person to Moses who was 'glorified in face and body.' So the righteous person's body 'bears the stamp' of his or her soul even while here on earth (*Strom.* 6.12). He or she 'is here [on earth] equal to the angels. Luminous already, and like the sun shining in the exercise of beneficence, he speeds by righteous knowledge through the love of God to the sacred abode' (*Strom.* 6.13). Like Moses whose face and body were glorified from his 'righteous conduct' and 'uninterrupted intercourse with God who spoke to him,' so 'a divine power of goodness clinging to the righteous soul in contemplation ... impresses on it something, as it were, of intellectual radiance ... uniting the soul with light, through unbroken love, which is God-bearing and God-born.' Thence the person is 'assimilated to the Savior' 'as far as permitted to human nature.' In this way the person is 'being made perfect' as 'the Father who is in heaven' (*Strom.* 6.12; cf. *Inst.* 1.6).

The key here is Clement's emphasis on 'process.' The enlightened person is one who has achieved as far as he or she possibly can, *as a human being*, a transformation into the glorious Image of God: through imitation of the Lord, 'as far as allowed to human beings,' the person receives 'a sort of quality akin to the Lord himself, in order to be assimilated to God' (*Strom*

6.17). This is a very important point for Clement, a modification or correction of an earlier Alexandrian position more akin to the opinion expressed in *Thomas*' accretions. Clement argues against this opinion, disagreeing wholeheartedly with those who believe that their mystical transformation into the Image is complete now while they still are living on earth, that they have experienced the End. Thus he states in this regard:

> The end is reserved until the resurrection of those who believe. It is not the reception of some other thing, but the obtaining of the promise previously made. For we do not say that both take place together at the same time, that is both the arrival at the end and the anticipation of that arrival. For eternity and time are not the same thing, neither is the attempt and the final result. But both have reference to the same thing, and one of the same person is concerned in both ... As far as possible in this world, which is what he means by last day, and which is preserved until the time that it shall end, we believe that we are made perfect ... having in anticipation grasped by faith that which is future, after the resurrection we receive it as present (*Inst.* 1.6).

According to Clement, even though the pure person is already singing in the choirs of angels (*Strom.* 7.12), this condition is not eternal yet. The righteous person 'prays in the society of angels, as being already of angelic rank, and he is never out of their holy keeping. Though he pray alone, he has the choir of angels standing with him' (*Strom.* 7.12). He 'lives in Spirit with those who are like him, among the choirs of angels, though still detained on earth' (*Strom.* 7.12).

For Clement, this transformation, although as complete as possible while in human form, cannot be fully or eternally completed until after death when the soul is guided by the Spirit back to heaven (*Exh.* 11) and is restored to 'everlasting contemplation,' to 'the crowning place of rest.' The pre-mortem visions have been preparatory, teaching the person how 'to gaze on God, face to face,' a gaze that will become permanent in the afterlife. Once the person flies back after death to 'the ancestral hall, through the holy septenniad to the Lord's own mansion,' he or she becomes 'a light, steady and continuing eternally, entirely and in every part immutable' (*Strom.* 7.10). Thus, the pre-mortem transformation makes it possible for the person, after death, to eternally gaze on the 'splendors of truth' face to face (*Strom.* 6.15).

9.2.2 *The Adaptation of the Kernel*

Certainly Clement's expression of Alexandrian mysticism is very developed when compared to the accretions of *Thomas*. But core themes and even details are held in common, something which we expect when viewing two distinct currents that flowed out of an earlier stream of tradition. So it is reasonable to postulate a connection between the mystical story presented in *Thomas'* accretions and a late first-century form of Alexandrian Christian mysticism, a form of mysticism that was developed and adapted to second-century forms of Alexandrian thought in the writings of Clement and other Alexandrian teachers.

But how did the Kernel come to be adapted in this way? There are two distinct possibilities. First, the Kernel gospel might have been carried to Alexandria where it was adapted to the mystical theology of a Christian community there. Or second, these peculiar Jewish-Christian-Hermetic mystical traditions from Alexandria may have traveled northeast to Syria along the missionary route. Once in Syria, the traditions were reinterpreted and reused by the community of Thomasine Christians to update the Kernel text, answering probing questions in the wake of the destruction of the Jerusalem church center, the death of the eyewitnesses, and the influx of Gentile converts. Since the community's apocalyptic consciousness was already developed in terms of its eschatological and mystical dimensions based on the teachings of the Jerusalem mission, the community would have been very receptive to the Alexandrian theology. It would have represented to them a small but meaningful shift in reconfiguring their memories and expectations.

Even though both of these scenarios are possibilities, the second offers the better explanation, not only as far as the *Gospel of Thomas* is concerned, but also in relation to our broader knowledge of early Syrian Christianity. Reviewing past studies of the Semitisms in many of the logia has convinced me that the *Gospel of Thomas* was composed in an Aramaic dialect(s) rather than Greek, particularly A. Guillamont's identification of specific logia whose translation into Greek and Coptic are best explained with a Semitic substratum (L. 3, 4, 9, 12, 14, 16, 23, 27, 30, 33, 36, 39, 43, 45, 48, 49, 55, 56, 64, 75, 78, 79, 80, 85, 91, 97, 98, 102, 104, 107, 113).[15]

---

15. A. Guillaumont, 'Sémitismes dans les logia de Jésus retrouvés à Nag-Hammâdi,' *JA* 246 (1958) pp. 113–123; A. Guillamont, 'Les "Logia" d'Oxyrhynchus sont-ils traduits du copte?' *Mus* 73 (1960) pp. 325–333; A. Guillaumont, 'ΝΗΣΤΕΥΕΙΝ ΤΟΝ ΚΟΣΜΟΝ (P. Oxy. 1, verso, 1.5–6),' *BIFAO* 61 (1962) pp. 15–23; A. Guillamont, 'Les sémitismes dans l'Évangile selon Thomas: Essai de classement,' in R. van den Broek and M.J. Vermaseren (eds.), *Studies in Gnosticism and Hellenistic Religions presented to Gilles Quispel on the Occasion of his 65th Birthday*, EPRO 91 (Leiden: E.J. Brill, 1981) pp. 190–204; H. Quecke, 'Sein Haus seines Königreiches: Zum Thomasevangelium 85,9f.,' *Mus* 76 (1963) pp. 51–53; A. Strobel, 'Textgeschichtliches zum Thomas-Logion 86 (Mt 8,20/Luk 9,58),' *VC* 17 (1963) p. 224; K. Rudolph, 'Gnosis und Gnostizismus: Ein Forschungsbericht,' *TRu* 34 (1969) p. 194; P. Nagel, 'Erwägungen zum Thomas-Evangelium,' in F. Altheim and R. Stiehl (eds.), *Der Araber in der alten Welt*, volume 2 (Berlin: De Gruyter, 1969) pp. 368–392; J.-E. Ménard, 'Der syrische Synkretismus und das Thomasevangeliuum,' in A. Dietrich (ed.), *Synkretismus im syrisch-persischen Kulturrgebist* (Göttingen: Vandenhoeck and Ruprecht, 1975) pp. 65–79; F. Morard, 'Encore quelques réflexions sur monachos,' *VC* 34 (1980) p. 397; H.J.W. Drijvers, 'Facts and Problems in Early Syriac-Speaking Christianity,' *SecCent* 2 (1982) pp. 173–175.

Based on the results of his research, Guillaumont preferred to talk about two levels of tradition prior to the Greek and Coptic. The first and earliest is a Palestinian or Western Aramaic level while the second and latest is a Syriac or Eastern Aramaic stage that has fused with the early tradition.[16]

W. Schrage, K.H. Kuhn, and B. Dehandschutter have offered a qualifier to this opinion, maintaining that some of these Semitisms are explained best as biblicisms or Coptic idioms.[17] Even if they may be correct in some of the limited cases they present, these objections do not supplant the weight of the counter-evidence. They do not overturn the fact that there remain a substantial number of Semitisms in *Thomas* which cannot be explained on these grounds, expressions which occur frequently in other literature produced in Syria. Particularly noteworthy are those logia that contain Semitic syntax such as the expression 'fast from the world' found in L. 27. This expression is not native to Greek but is a Semitic construction and occurs frequently in Syriac literature.[18] The strongest evidence for a Semitic substratum, in my opinion, however, lies not with arguments about syntax but with translation errors. A fine example is L. 30, a particularly troublesome aphorism that makes no sense in the Coptic. The Greek is very fragmentary and scholars have struggled to understand the aphorism by reconstructing the Greek in such a way to make it sensible but completely different from the Coptic. My own analysis of the papyrus in the Bodleian Library, however, has led me to a reconstruction similar to the Coptic: 'Where there are three people, gods are there. Where there is one alone, [I say,] I am with him.' In this case, neither the Greek nor the Coptic makes sense, *but* the nonsense can be easily explained, as Guillaumont did years ago, by understanding 'gods' (θεοί) to be a mistranslation of Elohim which is, of course, both a name of God in Judaism as well as the plural form 'gods.' This is a case where we are not dealing with a simple Semitism retained in a Greek or Coptic translation, but a translation error from an Aramaic 'original' into Greek.

Although N. Perrin's recent reconstruction of a Semitic substratum is hypothetical, it additionally offers a substantial challenge to the theory of

16. Guillaumont, 'Èvangile selon Thomas,' p. 201.

17. W. Schrage, 'Evangelienzitate in den Oxyrhynchus-Logien und im koptischen Thomas-evangelium,' in W. Eltester and F.H. Kettler, *Apophoreta. Festschrift für Ernest Haenchen*, BZNW 30 (Berlin: Alfred Töpelmann, 1964) pp. 251–268; K.H. Kuhn, 'Some Observations on the Coptic Gospel according to Thomas,' *Mus* 73 (1961) 317–323; B. Dehandschutter, 'Le lieu d'origine de l'Èvangile selon Thomas,' *Orientalia Lovaniensia Periodica* 6/7 (1975) pp. 129–130.

18. Guillaumont, 'ΝΗϹΤΕΥΕΙΝ,' pp. 18–23; Baker, A., 'Fasting to the World,' *JBL* 84 (1965) pp. 291–294.

Greek composition since it provides significant evidence that the composition of the text may have been based on Syriac catchwords and puns.[19] If this is the case, this would mean that the accretions, like the Kernel, would have accrued largely based on catchwords and puns in an Aramaic dialect rather than Greek.[20] The weight of the evidence favors a Palestinian-Syrian environment of recomposition rather than Alexandrian.

Additionally, the complete *Gospel of Thomas* was known by later Syrian texts and authors who reference many Thomasine sayings, predominately accretions: Pseudo-Macarius (L. 3, 11, 22, 27, 37, 51, 112, 113),[21] the *Liber Graduum* (L. 6, 18, 19, 22, 27, 37, 75, 85, 105, 106),[22] the *Acts of Thomas* (L. 2, 22, 37, 52, 76),[23] *Thomas the Contender* (L. 2, 3.2, 5, 6, 7, 67, 73),[24] and the *Odes of Solomon* (L. 13, 61, 108, 111, 113).[25] The textual variants of *Thomas'* canonical parallels have been shown to be part of the Western

19.   On this, see N. Perrin, *Thomas and Tatian: The Relationship between the Gospel of Thomas and the Diatessaron*, AcadBib 5 (Atlanta: Society of Biblical Literature, 2002) pp. 49–170. He thinks that the dialect is Syriac.

20.   A.F.J. Klijn discusses the bilingual character of Edessa and argues that a Greek text would not have been unusual: A.F.J. Klijn, 'Christianity in Edessa and the Gospel of Thomas,' *NovT* 14 (1972) pp. 70–77. Perhaps it existed also in Greek translation.

21.   See G. Quispel, 'The Syrian Thomas and the Syrian Macarius,' *Gnostic Studies* 2, Nederlands Historisch-Archaeologisch Instituut te Istanbul 34(2) (Leiden, 1975) pp. 113–121; G. Quispel, *Makarius, das Thomasevangelium, und das Lied von der Perle*, NovTSup 15 (Leiden: E.J. Brill, 1967); and A. Baker, 'Pseudo-Macarius and the Gospel of Thomas,' *VC* 18 (1964) pp. 215–225.

22.   See D.A. Baker, 'The "Gospel of Thomas" and the Syriac "Liber Graduum,"' *NTS* 12 (1965/66) pp. 49–55; G. Quispel, 'Gnosis and the New Sayings,' in *Gnostic Studies* 2 (Leiden: Nederlands Historische-Archaeologisch Instituut te Istanbul, 1975) p. 198.

23.   H.-Ch. Puech, *En Quête de la Gnose*, volume 2 (Paris: Gallimard, 1978) pp. 44 and 76, who argues that *Acts* 14 and 92 have storified L. 37 and L. 22 of *Thomas*; H.-Ch. Puech, 'The Gospel of Thomas,' in E. Hennecke and W. Schneemelcher (eds.), *New Testament Apocrypha*, volume 1 (trans. R. McL. Wilson; Philadelphia: Westminster, 1963) pp. 278–307, where he points to dependence between *Acts of Thomas* c. 136 and *Thomas* L. 2, c. 147 and L. 22, c. 170 and L. 52; G. Quispel, 'Gnosticism and the New Testament,' in *Gnostic Studies I* (Leiden: Nederlands Historisch-Archaeologisch Instituut, 1974) p. 201, who points out that the Hymn of the Pearl is probably a poetical amplification of Logion 76 of *Thomas*; H. Attridge, 'Intertextuality in the *Acts of Thomas*,' in R.F. Stoops, Jr. and D.R. MacDonald (eds.), *The Apocryphal Acts of the Apostles in Intertextual Perpectives*, Semeia 80 (Atlanta: Scholars Press, 1997) pp. 87–124.

24.   *Thom. Cont.* 140.41–141.2 parallels L. 2; 138.8–10 parallels L. 3.2; 138.25–40 parallels L. 5 and 6b; 138.40–139.11 parallels L. 7; 138.7–19 parallels L. 67; 138.35 parallels L. 73. J. Turner mentions a few of these in his book, *The Book of Thomas the Contender from Codex II of the Cairo Gnostic Library from Nag Hammadi (CG II,7): The Coptic Text with Translation, Introduction, and Commentary*, SBLDS 23 (Missoula: Scholars Press, 1975) p. 136.

25.   J. Liebart, 'Les "Odes de Salomon" et l'Èvangile selon Thomas,' *Les Enseignements Moraux des Peres Apostoliques* (Gembloux: J. Duculot, 1970) pp. 227–253; Quispel, 'The Gospel of Thomas Revisited,' in B. Barc (ed.), *Colloque International sur les Textes de Nag Hammadi. Québec, 22–25 août 1978*, BCNH 1 (Louvain: Peeters, 1981) pp. 255–256; Quispel,

Text type in Syria, localizing the text there.[26] Moreover, the Syrian writings like *Thomas the Contender* and the *Acts of Thomas* which are explicitly linked with traditions about Judas Thomas, the Twin, especially hold in common with the *Gospel of Thomas* essential theological, anthropological, Christological, and encratic elements, although they have been substantially developed in these later texts.

Unfortunately, to date, very little has been written on the Thomasine tradition as it develops in the Syrian literature, so this remains a very fertile area for future investigation.[27] Here, however, we might note simply that in this literature, the human being regains Paradise through his or her own effort of righteous living as revealed by Jesus rather than through some act of atonement on Jesus' part. The Christian should become as self-controlled as possible, particularly overcoming the passions. He or she should abandon marriage, abstaining from sexual intercourse in order to return to the prelapsarian condition of 'singleness.' In so doing, gender differences are abolished. Once this is accomplished, the person becomes united with his or her divine double in the 'bridal chamber.' This divine double, the person's new spouse, is none other than Jesus himself. Judas Thomas, in fact, becomes a metaphor for all believers since Jesus is described as his very own divine Twin. Since the theology of the accretions seems to have been known and developed by these authors, becoming the basis for later Syrian traditions, it is more likely than not that the full text of *Thomas* was completed in Syria before being translated and traveling to Egypt where the Greek fragments and Coptic translation were found.

Finally, the mystical theology of the *Gospel of Thomas* represents a precursor to that which was developed by later Syrian Fathers and the Byzantine Church.[28] It was part of the fabric of Syrian Christianity as early

'The Study of Encratism: A Historical Survey,' in U. Bianchi (ed.), *La Tradizione dell'Enkrateia, Atti del Colloquio Internazionale – Milano 20–23 Aprile 1982* (Rome: Edizioni Dell'Ateneo, 1985) p. 55.

26. G. Quispel, 'L'Évangile selon Thomas et le Diatessaron,' *VC* 13 (1959) pp. 87–117; T. Baarda, 'Thomas and Tatian,' in *Early Transmission of Words of Jesus: Thomas, Tatian and the Text of the New Testament* (Amsterdam: VU Boekhandel/Uitgeverij, 1983) pp. 37–49.

27. R. Uro provides a succinct summary of the little work that has been done so far in his book *Thomas. Seeking the Historical Context of the Gospel of Thomas* (London: T&T Clark, 2003) pp. 8–30.

28. For a general overview of this theology, see V. Lossky, *The Mystical Theology of the Eastern Church* (Crestwood: St Vladimir's Seminary Press, 1976); V. Lossky, *The Vision of God* (trans. A. Moorhouse Crestwook: St Vladimir's Seminary Press, 1983); G.I. Mantzaridis, *The Deification of Man* (trans. L. Sherrad; Crestwood: St Vladimir's Seminary Press, 1984); V. Lossky, *In the Image and Likeness of God* (Crestwood: St Vladimir's Seminary Press, 1985); T. Spidlik, *The Spirituality of the Christian East: A Syematic Handbook* (trans. A.P. Gythiel; Kalamazoo: Cistercian Publications, 1986); P. Nellas, *Deification in Christ: Orthodox Persepctives on the Nature of the Human Person* (trans N. Russell; Crestwood: St Vladimir's

as 60–100 CE when the apocalyptic theology of the *Thomas* community began shifting from an emphasis on the eschatological to the mystical in response to the delayed Eschaton. It is discovered developed, for instance, in Pseudo-Macarius who focuses on the interiorization of the apocalyptic battle, the fight within the individual soul of the indwelt Christ and Holy Spirit against the demons who would otherwise corrupt the soul with passion. The human soul 'lost' its glorious Image when Adam disobeyed God (*Hom.* 1.7). This meant that the Image was covered over with a garment (*Hom.* 4.3) or veil (*Hom.* 14.2), or it was a gold coin now mixed with alloy (*Hom.* 12.1), but it was not 'totally lost' so as to have been 'blotted out of existence and died,' according to Macarius (*Hom.* 12.2). It can be recovered gradually by imitating Jesus, especially his crucifixion by crucifying the passions of the flesh (*Hom.* 1.6; 12.5), and becoming one with him through the indwelling of his Spirit (*Hom.* 4.10; 10.4). This indwelling works as a stamp, repressing on the soul its original luminous beauty and glory, or a fire restoring the lost inner light (*Hom.* 11.2–3; 15:35). The driving force of this process of divinization is the individual's experience of God's presence as a mystical transforming vision of light, an experience prepared for through contemplative and ascetic practices but achieved through God's grace. It is a vision of the 'divine light,' the 'image of the soul,' the angelic-like 'form' of the 'inner man' (*Hom.* 7.5–7). And, as Macarius frequently comments, it results in 'rest.'

The evidence – linguistic, thematic, and textual – mounts a case for an early Aramaic Kernel gospel from Jerusalem. This Kernel, apocalyptic in orientation, was used and later adapted in Syria as time lengthened and the End did not come. The adaptation included two shifts which developed earlier aspects of the community's thought and praxis, aspects which the Thomasine Christians had learned from the Jerusalem mission. One was the radicalization of the ideal of self-control to the extent that marriage became a state of sin for the ordinary Christian. The other was the interiorization of the apocalyptic drama, the isolation of the mystical dimension. This mystical dimension was further developed to include not only the God-Experience, but also the Self-Experience where Self-knowledge became redemptive.

This peculiar adaptation of the Kernel was the result of mutual discourse between the Syrian and Alexandrian Christian communities since it is in first-century Alexandria that the prior fusion of Jewish

Seminary Press, 1987); M. Børtnes, *Visions of Glory: Studies in Early Russian Hagiography* (trans. J. Børtnes and P.L. Nielsen; New Jersey: Humanities Press International, 1988); T. Ware, *The Orthodox Church* (New York: Penguin Books, new edition, 1993). For discussion of earlier Syrian traditions, see F.C. Burkitt, *Early Christianity Outside the Roman Empire* (Cambridge: Cambridge University Press, 1899); R. Murray, *Symbols of Church and Kingdom: A Study of Early Syriac Tradition* (Cambridge: Cambridge University Press, 1975).

mystical and Hermetic theologies was first being adapted to the Christian story. We learn from Clement about encratic Christians living in Alexandria for some time past and their mystical leanings. Clement not only preserves in his own teaching a very developed form of the mysticism we find in the Thomasine accretions, but also takes issue with other Alexandrian mystics who, like those responsible for the Thomasine accretions, had insisted that the End had been actualized. So these old Alexandrian mystics appear to have developed their brand of mystical Christianity in response to the delayed Eschaton just as we find also in *Thomas*. That the Syrian and Alexandrian communities were sharing ideas and texts should not be surprising to us. At moments of community crises such as these Christian communities were experiencing particularly between 60–100 CE as the End did not materialize, dialogue across similar communities increases, bolstering the faith, and ultimately refashioning it out of their dialogue.

In this particular case, as the Alexandrian Christians and the Thomasine Christians exchanged ideas and the Jewish-Christian-Hermetic story accrued in the Kernel, the imminent apocalypse became immanent. By 120 CE, the focus of this theology turned away from cosmic endings to the human being who, with the aid of the Holy Spirit, conquered his or her body of passions and recreated, in its place, the virtuous body of the prelapsarian Adam. He or she took his or her place in Paradise, preparing for the great transformative visions of Jesus and God through an encratic regime and meditative praxis. By so doing, the person came face to face with his or her own Image or God-Self, a vision which restored his or her soul to its original glorious Image.

Chapter 10

THOMAS AND CHRISTIAN ORIGINS

There is much at stake with the study of the *Gospel of Thomas*, where we situate it historically and how we translate its meaning, whether it be early or late, sapiential or 'gnostic,' independent or dependent. Scholarly careers and reputations are staked on how these questions are answered. Even Jesus' historical reputation is at stake, as a philosopher or otherwise, how Christianity began and what we are left with. I myself began to study the *Gospel of Thomas* in graduate school because I was enchanted with H. Koester's arguments for an early non-apocalyptic *Thomas* and J.D. Crossan's arguments for the Sage Jesus. These reconstructions gave me hope as I questioned the place of the Cross in my own faith experience. At the time, I never suspected that years later, after intense training and dedicated study, I would find myself in the uncanny position of unraveling what I had hoped to build upon as a scholar in my own right.

Be that as it may, the answers to the questions of *Thomas* have become very clear to me. They are answers that have developed out of a sophisticated historical-critical method welded with Social Memory theory, studies in orality and specific literary tools which I described in the first three chapters of this monograph. The answers turn out to be much more complex and nuanced than I expected, and have implications for Christianity beyond any scope I had originally envisioned.

10.1 *The* Gospel of Thomas *Rediscovered*

What I discovered is that the *Gospel of Thomas* is neither early nor late, but both. The *Gospel* began as a smaller collection of sayings attributed to Jesus, sayings organized into a speech gospel similar to the speech gospels mentioned by Clement in the *Pseudo-Clementine* corpus. In chapters 4 and 5, I argued that this Kernel gospel contained at least five rhetorical speeches of Jesus, speeches which were meant to be used to reperform his teachings. Analysis of these speeches points to their origin in the Jerusalem mission prior to 50 CE. They were organized around eschatological themes, emphasizing the urgency of the times, discipleship and exclusive commitment to Jesus. The christology is very old, pre-dating Quelle. Jesus is both

Prophet who exclusively voices God's Truth, and his Angel of Judgment who already is casting fire upon the earth. These descriptors are comparable to those commonly associated with very early Christian Judaism.

What the development of this early speech gospel tells us about Christian origins is that Jerusalem turned to missionize Syria very early in the movement and that the words of Jesus the missionaries left with the Syrian community quickly developed within an oral environment of reperformance. So the text of this old gospel was not stable. As time progressed, the Kernel was adapted during oral performances to the changing needs, demands, and ideologies of the Christian community in Syria. Accretions entered the speeches of Jesus when Gentile converts came to dominate this community and questions about dietary laws and circumcision were agreed upon.

My analysis of the gospel in chapter 6 revealed that it contains traditions and references to hermeneutics that serve to reconfigure older traditions and hermeneutics no longer relevant to the experience of the community. The community's original eschatological expectations were disconfirmed by its contemporary experience of the Non-Event. When the Kingdom did not come, rather than discarding their gospel and closing the door of their church, the Thomasine Christians responded by reinterpreting Jesus' sayings, believing themselves to have previously misunderstood Jesus' intent, to have applied the wrong hermeneutic to his words. So they aligned their old traditions with their present experience, rationalizing the Non-Event, shifting their theology to the mystical, and creating a new hermeneutic through which the old traditions could be viewed. This response is visible in the way in which they revised their gospel, adding question and answer units and dialogues that addressed the subject specifically along with a series of new sayings that worked to instruct the believer in the new theology and guide him or her hermeneutically through the gospel. Thus we find in the accretions echoes of the community's response. Between 60 and 100 CE, the Thomasine Christians began to collapse their apocalypticism, shifting its focus from the eschatological to the mystical dimension, from the imminent Kingdom to the immanent one. This response does not seem to be unique, but at least underpins the experience of the community at Corinth and the Johannine Gospel. This conclusion is in line with my previous argument in *Voices of the Mystics*, that some of the theology in John's Gospel is a direct response to the visionary mystical traditions such as we find preserved in *Thomas*.[1]

---

1. A.D. DeConick, *Voices of the Mystics: Early Christian Discourse in the Gospels of John and Thomas and Other Ancient Christian Literature*, JSNTSup 157 (Sheffield: Sheffield Academic Press, 2001).

In chapter 7, I argued that the Non-Event appears to have become very pronounced for the Thomasine community since its members continued to reinterpret their traditions in terms of mysticism. Between 80 and 120 CE, the community became an advocate for a fully present Kingdom, the New World of Eden which members recreated among themselves in their utopian community. Their church was Paradise. They were Adam and Eve before the Fall. Through encratic performance and visionary experiences, they came to believe that they had achieved the eschatological promises of God in the present, including the ultimate transformation of their bodies into the original luminous Image of God. The Non-Event became for them the fulfillment of the Event. Jesus' promise of the imminent End had been actualized within the boundaries of their community!

This reading of the *Gospel of Thomas* suggests that the scholarly consensus that this gospel exemplifies an early Christian non-apocalyptic gospel preserving the message of a philosophical Jesus is highly suspect. In fact, the opposite appears to be the case. The earliest version of the *Gospel of Thomas* was an apocalyptic speech gospel emphasizing the imminent End and its demands. It is only in the face of a communal memory crisis, which also was experienced by other Christian communities in the late first century and early second century, that the text's emphasis was shifted away from the eschatological interpretation of Jesus' sayings to the mystical. The person no longer waited for the End to arrive and Jesus to return. His or her transformation or immortalization was achieved immediately through imitative performance and direct mystical apprehension of God and his Son.

This hermeneutical shift was achieved seamlessly because teachings about self-control and the mystical dimension of apocalyptic were already known to the community through the Jerusalem mission. Further, missionary routes between Syria and Alexandria allowed for the exchange of ideas and texts between these two hubs of Christianity so that the Syrian and Alexandrian Christian communities developed compatible theologies and practices in response to the Non-Event. Both promoted the encratic ideal and a mystical praxis with an emphasis on complete pre-mortem transformation as the result of a vision of God and Self-Knowledge as I outlined in chapters 8 and 9. In both geographical locations, this early encratism and mysticism continued to be discussed: in Syria by Tatian, the author of the *Liber Graduum*, the authors of the apocryphal Acts, Pseudo-Macarius, and so on; in Alexandria by Julius Cassianus, Basilides, Valentinus, Clement, Origen, and so on.

This places the complete *Gospel of Thomas* at a date no later than 120 CE, making the accretions contemporary to the composition of the Johannine literature and the Pastoral Epistles. It also grounds *Thomas'* theology *inside* early orthodoxy rather than outside. The *Gospel of Thomas*, far from representing the voice of some late generic 'gnostic' heresy or some early unique sapiential Christianity, is quite cogent with early Syrian Christianity as described in the oldest literature from the area. As A. Vööbus taught us long ago, Christianity in Syria in the first couple of hundred years demanded celibacy for admission into the Church. The literary evidence shows that it was encratic, honoring the solitary life. This position appears to have shifted with Aphraates when the demands for celibacy were relaxed, required only of the privileged class of the Church, the 'sons and daughters of the Covenant.'[2] Moreover, G. Quispel demonstrated years ago that *Thomas*' mystical theology had great affinity with Pseudo-Macarius, the Messalian from Syria.[3]

I would go further to state that, in fact, it has an even greater affinity with the later teachings of the Orthodox Church, as even a superficial reading of that catechism reveals, that it appears to represent a precursor to this theology. This fact was pointed out to me by the Orthodox Hieromonk and Professor Alexander Golitzin who, upon reading my first book *Seek to See Him*, wrote a letter to me introducing himself and thanking me for discovering the origins of his religion. At the time, I had no idea that this is what I had done since I had been raised in rural Michigan in the Protestant tradition. My graduate school training at the University of Michigan had been in Antiquity, so Orthodoxy was hardly touched upon. But Alexander's remark spurred me on to investigate, and I discovered that indeed he was correct. My historical reconstructions of the mystical Christianity in *Thomas* looked very much like an early version of Orthodox spirituality.

The spirituality of the Christian East grew upon the traditions of a mysticism of the heart indwelled by the Holy Spirit and the progressive transformation of the soul into its glorious Image. Unlike the West which carries on the Augustinian position that Adam's sin had completely severed the Image of God from the human being, leaving him dark, lost, and helpless, the East teaches that the glorious Image had only been diminished by Adam's decision, that it is recoverable. While the West focuses on sin and atonement through the Cross which is completed in the eucharist, a sacrificial meal, the East focuses on the progressive transformation of the person through at-one-ment with God which is realized in the eucharist when the divine body is ingested and as the person lives a life imitating Jesus. The emphasis in Orthodoxy is on the Incarnation when the human and divine united and the transformation

2. A. Vööbus, *Celibacy: A Requirement for Admission to Baptism in the Early Syrian Church*, Papers of Estonian Theological Society in Exile 1 (Stockholm, 1951); A. Vööbus, *History of Asceticism in the Syrian Orient. A Contribution to the History and Culture in the Near East: Early Monasticism in Mesopotamia and Syria* 2, CSCO 197, 17 (Louvain, 1960).

3. G. Quispel, *Makarius, das Thomasevangelium und das Lied von der Perle*, NovTSup 15 (Leiden: E.J. Brill, 1967).

of the human soul into the glorious Image was rekindled. In Orthodoxy, the believer is called to self-knowledge, renunciation of the flesh through temperance in marriage or the Eremitic life, spiritual warfare and purification of the passions, the path of virtue, contemplation and glorification through Gnosis and Theoria, the great vision.[4]

It may be that the unfamiliarity of scholars from the West with the teachings of the Orthodox Church has failed them in respect to understanding this gospel, resulting in years of misdirection and confusion about the teachings contained in *Thomas*. My studies have made it very clear to me that this gospel does not represent some 'new' or 'unique' or 'lost' Christianity, some Christianity previously unknown to us, nor some late 'heresy' that can be dismissed by scholars who wish to work out Christian origins. Nor is the Thomasine community some previously unknown school, deviant group, or self-identifying church. Rather it represents a current in the stream of Christian traditions that ultimately became Eastern Orthodoxy. It is the voice of eastern Syrian Christianity in its earliest recoverable form.

When the sayings that make up the Kernel gospel are compared to other ancient sources, some fascinating connections emerge. First, when aligned with both G. Quispel's and T. Baarda's work on Tatian's *Diatessaron*, in every case that Tatian's version parallels *Thomas*' version, the saying is located in the Kernel gospel rather than in any of the later accretions with the exception of L. 113 (Quispel: 6, 8, 9, 16, 21, 25, 32, 33, 35, 36, 39, 40, 44, 45, 46, 47, 48, 55, 57, 63, 64, 66, 68, 74, 79, 86, 89, 90, 91, 94, 95, 96, 98, 100, 104, 109, 113; Baarda: 4, 8, 9, 10, 16, 20, 21, 26, 32, 33,34, 35, 38, 39, 40, 44, 45, 46, 47, 48, 54, 55, 56, 57, 61, 63, 64, 65, 68, 69, 72, 73, 76, 78, 79, 86, 89, 91, 93, 94, 96, 99, 100, 104, 107, 113).[5]

Second, every logion in *Thomas* that has a distinctive parallel in the *Pseudo-Clementine* corpus is also located only in the Kernel (L. 9, 16, 32, 39, 40, 54, 62, 64, 68, 76, 93, 95). Even more striking are the clusters of sayings and hermeneutics known in the *Pseudo-Clementine* literature which have the same cluster and hermeneutic as we find in the Kernel *Thomas* (L. 38, 39, 40, 45, 46//*Rec.* 1.54, 59–60, 2.30; L. 92, 93, 94//*Rec.* 2.3, 3.1; L. 62.1, 62.2//*Hom.* 18.17–10, 13; L. 39 and 42//*Hom.* 2.9; L. 9, 10, 11, 14.4,

---

4. For an introduction to the subject, see T. Spidlik, *The Spirituality of the Christian East: A Systematic Handbook* (trans. A. Gythiel; Kalamazoo: Cistercian Publications, 1986).

5. Both Quispel and Baarda have included L. 1 which they indicate parallels John 8.52. I do not find this parallel to be convincing so I have not included it in my discussion. See, G. Quispel, 'L'Évangile selon Thomas et le Diatessaron', *VC* 13 (1959) pp. 87–117; *Tatian and the Gospel of Thomas* (Leiden: E.J. Brill, 1975); T. Baarda, 'Thomas and Tatian,' in his *Early Transmission of Words of Jesus: Thomas, Tatian and the Text of the New Testament* (VU Boekhandel: Uitgeverij, 1983) pp. 37–49.

15//*Hom.* 11.2–7). Especially noteworthy is the fact that in all of these cases, the Synoptic parallels do not show familiarity with the cluster or hermeneutic.

This striking agreement between Tatian, the *Pseudo-Clementina* and the Kernel *Thomas* cannot be coincidence especially since other Syrian witnesses seem to be aware of many of the later accretions. For instance, the *Liber Graduum* seems to be familiar with at least Logia 6, 18, 19, 22, 27, 37, 75, 85, 105, 106[6] while Macarius minimally with Logia 3, 11, 22, 27, 37, 51, 112, 113.[7] The accumulation of this evidence lends weight to the possibility that an early form of the *Gospel of Thomas* similar to the one I have reconstructed was known in Syria to Tatian and may have been one of the sources for the *Pseudo-Clementina*.

Third, just over fifty percent of the sayings in the Kernel gospel are paralleled in Q. Not even one saying with a Q parallel, however, can be found among the later accretions. This also cannot be coincidence. It suggests to me that the sayings in the Kernel *Thomas* are some of our oldest witnesses to the Jesus traditions. Additionally, my initial analysis of the Kernel gospel seems to indicate that neither Q nor the Kernel *Thomas* were literarily dependent upon the other although the exact relationship is something which I expect to work out in the sister commentary to this monograph.[8] The sequence, language, and use of the parallel sayings suggests that Q and *Thomas* were familiar with a very old (pre-50 CE) set of sayings which were largely apocalyptic in nature and which each text developed in its own way – the apocalyptic expectations were intensified in Q while they were deintensified by the addition of the later accretions of *Thomas*. The vogue thesis that the early stratifications of Quelle were non-apocalyptic may need to be reassessed.

As for the original language of *Thomas*, it certainly appears to me to have been Semitic. My initial probing into this matter reveals that all sayings which, in my judgment, can be explained as Aramaisms are located in the Kernel (L. 9, 16, 30, 33, 36, 39, 45, 48, 55, 76, 78, 79, 97, 98, 102, 104, 107) except one (L. 91.2). The accretions, however, reveal sayings that are better explained as references to Syriac (L. 3, 4.4, 14.1–3, 16.4, 23, 27, 49, 56, 75, 80, 85, 113) except two (L. 12, 43). Could the Kernel have been

---

6. A. Baker, '"The Gospel of Thomas" and the Syriac "Liber Graduum,"' *NTS* 12 (1965/1966) pp. 49–55.

7. G. Quispel, 'The Syrian Thomas and the Syrian Macarius,' *Gnostic Studies* 2, Nederlands Historisch-Archaeologisch Instituut te Istanbul 34(2) (Leiden, 1975) pp. 113–121; *Makarius, das Thomasevangelium, und das Lied von der Perle*, NTSup 15 (Leiden: E.J. Brill, 1967); and A. Baker, 'Pseudo-Macarius and the Gospel of Thomas,' *VC* 18 (1964) pp. 215–225.

8. A.D. DeConick, *The Original* Gospel of Thomas *in Translation, with a Commentary and New English Translation of the Complete Gospel* (London: T&T Clark, forthcoming).

written in Aramaic, the Western dialect from Palestine? Once taken to Syria, could it have been adapted to and modified in the dialect of the east, Syriac? This appears to be quite plausible given the evidence, although a more thorough discussion in my forthcoming commentary will be necessary to confirm this opinion.

Finally, the rolling corpus model has implications for the issue of literary dependence on other early Christian literature, in particular dependence on the Synoptic Gospels. In my opinion, we can no longer make the case for the literary independence of the whole *Gospel of Thomas* because it is quite possible that the accretions particularly may reflect knowledge of one or more of the Synoptic Gospels. In fact, dependence is especially likely at this stage in the development of *Thomas* given the fact that these communities created their ideologies in response to the opinions and stances of other Christians.[9] Certainly I am not suggesting that the entire gospel is dependent on the Synoptics, and I wish to work out the relationship more fully in my companion commentary. But, I support the position that recognizes that the time has come for us to temper the arguments for independence and develop a new model for mapping the problem.

10.2 *Implications for the Study of Christian Origins*

This study of the *Gospel of Thomas* does not only bring into question the position that has been worked out in numerous studies by previous scholars, that this gospel is evidence for a unique non-apocalyptic philosophical form of early Christianity rooted in Jesus' historical teachings.[10] It also means that the recent Seminar, 'Ancient Myths and Modern Theories of Christian Origins,' is misdirected.[11] The Seminar consists of a circle of scholars chaired by Ron Cameron who are

9. DeConick, *Voices of the Mystics*, pp. 9–18.

10. Proponents of this view rely heavily on the work of J. Robinson and H. Koester in their pioneering volume, *Trajectories through Early Christianity* (Philadelphia: Fortress Press, 1971). This view is most dominant in American scholarship, particularly among those scholars who belong to the Jesus Seminar. For examples of this position, see S.L Davies, *The Gospel of Thomas and Christian Wisdom* (New York: Seabury Press, 1983) pp. 13–17; J.D. Crossan, *The Historical Jesus: The Life of a Mediterranean Jewish Peasant* (New York: HarperCollins, 1991) pp. 227–302; M. Meyer, *The Gospel of Thomas: The Hidden Sayings of Jesus* (San Francisco: HarperSanFrancisco, 1992); R. Cameron, 'The *Gospel of Thomas* and Christian Origins,' in B. Pearson (ed.), *The Future of Early Christianity: Essays in Honor of Helmut Koester* (Minneapolis: Fortress Press, 1991) pp. 381–392; S.J. Patterson, *The Gospel of Thomas and Jesus* (Sonoma: Polebridge Press, 1993) pp. 94–112; R.W. Funk, *Honest to Jesus* (New York: HarperCollins, 1996) pp. 121–139.

11. R. Cameron and M.P. Miller, *Redescribing Christian Origins*, Symposium Series 28 (Atlanta: Society of Biblical Literature, 2004). See also R. Cameron's earlier argument for this

attempting to reinvent Christian Origins as a plurality of 'social experiments.' In order to accomplish their task, they have relied heavily on an interpretation of the *Gospel of Thomas* which suggests to them that we possess a very early Christian text devoid of death and resurrection theology and apocalypticism. To them, it represents a collection of sayings of the Sage, Jesus, a teacher of wisdom whose authority does not reside in the 'mythology of the risen Christ' but is 'localized in sayings that offer contemporizing wisdom,' sayings in which salvation resides directly.[12]

As a historian, I am particularly sympathetic to their insistence that Protestant and Catholic perspectives have controlled past reconstructions of Christian origins, a point well articulated by Jonathan Z. Smith in his famous *Drudgery Divine*.[13] I also am thoroughly grateful to them for liberating this project from the bonds of 'canonism.' The canon is anachronistic to our early period and its boundaries must be broken if we are ever to move forward with a historically honest reconstruction that accounts for the varieties in early Christianity.[14] But here my agreement with this circle of reinvention ceases.

First, I find the annihilation of a 'singular' point of origin in favor of (spontaneous?) varieties naïve and disconcerting since this position does not seem to me to take into account the complexity of the situation nor other possible solutions to the problem. The members of the Seminar are of the expressed opinion that the traditional scenario of Christian Origins which begins with the historical Jesus as the ultimate point of origin of free-floating traditions which were understood eschatologically as a response to Jesus' death and resurrection and which gave rise to the Jerusalem Church is wrong. They point out that Christianity beyond the New Testament yields varieties of early Christianity rather than Luke's myth of a singular form. They believe that Christianity's origin can only be constructed by appealing to anthropological methods grounded in social theory because appeals to religious experience are impenetrable to

position in his articles, 'Alternate Beginnings, Different Ends: Eusebius, Thomas, and the Construction of Christian Origins,' in L. Bormann, K. Del Tredici, and A. Standhartinger (eds.), *Religious Propaganda and Missionary Competition in the New Testament World: Essays Honoring Dieter Georgi*, NovTSup 74 (Leiden: E.J. Brill, 1994) pp. 507–521; 'Mythmaking and Intertextuality in Early Christianity,' in E. Castelli and H. Taussig (eds.), *Reimagining Christian Origins* (Valley Forge: Trinity Press International, 1996) pp. 37–50; 'Ancient Myths and Modern Theories of the *Gospel of Thomas* and Christian Origins,' *MTSR* 11 (1999) pp. 236–257.

12. Cameron, 'Ancient Myths,' pp. 250–251.

13. J.Z. Smith, *Drudgery Divine: On the Comparison of Early Christianities and the Religions of Late Antiquity*, Jordan Lectures in Comparative Religion 14 (Chicago: University of Chicago Press, 1990).

14. R. Cameron and M.P. Miller, *Redescribing Christian Origins*, Symposium Series 28 (Atlanta: Society of Biblical Literature, 2004).

ordinary human understanding. Thus Christianity is better explained in terms of reflexive social experiments than as responses to Jesus or forces set in motion by personal revelations or singular events.[15]

In my view, the presence of varieties of early Christianities (canonical *and* extra-canonical) in and of themselves does not mean that Christianity could not have developed out of a singular point of origin. There are other paradigms which can explain this and which, in my own study of the problem, are better equipped to do so. But before I can comment on that, it must be decided how early these varieties of Christianity are. The Seminar members assume that *Thomas* and Q1 represent a pre-Synoptic philosophical variety of early Christianity that has no reference to the Cross or eschatology. This leads the Seminar members to the further assumption that there existed in the foundational moments a very old Christian mythology which did not develop as a response to Jesus' death.

But now my analysis of *Thomas* shows these assumptions to be suspect. Knowledge of Jesus' death, in fact, is not only assumed by the later Thomasine Christians who appear to be responsible for accretions which pun the Cross (L. 87 and 112) but also in the Kernel gospel in L. 55. The Cross is not here a philosophical metaphor 'for the ultimate test of a philosopher's integrity' as Cameron imagines.[16] It is not a generic reference to crucifixion in the ancient world. The gospel explicitly tells the believer that he or she must carry his or her cross *in imitation of Jesus*, 'as I do.' The reference cannot be more direct or pointed to the story of Jesus' death. In fact, the reference to Jesus' death is even more pronounced in L. 55 than in its Quelle or Synoptic counterparts which do not mention imitation at all (Matthew 10.37–38; Luke 14.26–27; Mark 8.34; Matthew 16.24; Luke 9.23). As for the presence of eschatological mythology, it also is found in the earliest form of *Thomas*, and the complete gospel is best described as a communal response to the Eschaton's delay and dashed expectations as I have described in the chapters of this monograph.

My research has led me to the opinion that an early philosophical form of Christianity is a romance of the modern (or post-modern) mind. There is no evidence for it in our earliest texts, or our later ones for that matter. To some extent, be it supportive or reactionary, all our early Christian texts appear familiar with the story of Jesus' death as well as apocalyptic mythology, eschatological as well as mystical. The interpretations applied

15. R. Cameron and M.P. Miller, 'Introduction: Ancient Myths and Modern Theories of Christian Origins,' in *Redescribing Christian Origins*, Symposium Series 28 (Atlanta: Society of Biblical Literature, 2004) pp. 1–30.

16. R. Cameron, 'Ancient Myths and Modern Theories of the *Gospel of Thomas* and Christian Origins,' in *Redescribing Christian Origins*, Symposium Series 28 (Atlanta: Society of Biblical Literature, 2004) p. 101.

to the Cross and the apocalyptic worldview or the emphasis on them may vary from text to text, but all appear to assume familiarity with them.

This leads me to wonder whether our varieties of early Christianity formed pre- or post-Jerusalem. From the literary evidence, it looks like most if not all are post-Jerusalem, *Thomas* and Quelle included. The only references I know which *might* marshal some evidence for pre-Jerusalem varieties of early Christianity are found in Mark 9.38–41 and Acts 18.24–19.7. The first is a reference to a non-disciple casting out demons in Jesus' name and presumes an apocalyptic worldview, in my opinion. In Acts, we are told about Apollos, a native Jew from Alexandria, who had brought a version of Christianity to Ephesus which taught a baptism for cleansing of sins, not for the reception of the Holy Spirit in the name of Jesus. This form of Christianity also seems to be known and criticized by the author of the Gospel of John. This is *very* interesting and may be evidence for an early variety of pre-Jerusalem Christianity. *Or* it may represent a very early moment in the mission of the Jerusalem Church before baptism with the Holy Spirit had developed in their praxis. The latter appears to me to be the better solution, especially given John's familiarity with it and indirect references to it in Mark 1.8, Matthew 3.11, and Luke 3.16.

So the best solution to the problem of Christian Origins is to describe the complexity of the situation. It is certainly *possible* that early pre-Jerusalem forms of Christianity took root, but if they did, they did not leave a big enough imprint in our texts to recover their footsteps with any certainty. It looks like the formation of Christianity in Jerusalem took place very early and, since mission work appears to have been a large part of its agenda, the Christian message and praxis was dispersed geographically where it then was translated under a number of other influences into the varieties we find in our literature. For several decades following Jesus' death, as Paul's letters indicate, Jerusalem was powerful enough and respected enough to be considered the authority on all matters Christian. In many ways, Jerusalem controlled the discourse, something which Paul found himself up against as he broke away and began developing his own agenda and brand of Christianity.

As for the actual beginning of Christianity, certainly there was never a singular point of origin nor one event that caused everything to swing into motion. Nor was the development linear or romantic as Luke would have it. A complex of impulses worked together to bring about the formation of Christianity, social forces being only one of many. Certainly the teachings of Jesus *as they were remembered* played a big role given the reliance of the missionaries on the books of Jesus' speeches. The impulse to give meaning to the troubling death of Jesus was also foundational given the allusions and interpretations of his death across the early literature. This process, fueled largely by exegesis, led to Christological developments very early in the tradition. Furthermore, religious experience came into play, whether or not modern minds want to admit it. It does not matter to me as a historian whether or not Paul or any of the disciples actually experienced visions or that their visions point to some divine reality beyond my human comprehension. What matters to me is that they believed that they experienced these things and that they interpreted the visions in very specific ways, ways which helped to give rise to the Christian movement. Certainly they used these visions to legitimate their religious authority and consolidate their social positions, but they also used these visions to grow ideology and religious praxis from piety and belief in religious experience. We should never forget that the ancients understood themselves to be part of a living religious tradition. They had never heard of the death of God. The search for Christianity's origins does not have to be either ecstatic experience or 'social anthropology' as Cameron and his Seminar frame the problem. Rather it is a complex interplay of the two. It is this interplay that is worth understanding, not dismissing one at the cost of the other.

For me, any reconstruction of the origins of the Christian religion should be primarily historical; based on the literature and the material remains of the ancients. Certainly we should not preference the canonical version of these origins. We must work out a paradigm that explains the literature and its ideas, both similar and unique, canonical and non-canonical, within the historical contexture of Second Temple Judaism. We must be able to explain each and every facet of the literature *from* the literature. This is not circular reasoning as Cameron has suggested, but concrete historical analysis. To extrapolate our texts from their historical context in order to subject them solely to literary critical theory and social method runs the terrible risk of imposing our 'post-modern' imaginations on the ancients and creating a new 'history' defunct of history.

10.3 *Final Remark*

The perspective of the rolling corpus certainly solves the persistent problem of the existence of sayings within *Thomas* which promote contradictory ideologies, such as in the case of sayings favoring early Christian Jewish perspectives and those clearly promulgating later Gentile views. Since the text reflects decades of ideological struggles and shifting constituencies, we would expect to see just what we find in the gospel: sayings of contradictory natures along with attempts to reinterpret them. The process of oral reperformance and recontextualization might include creating dialogues out of older sayings, adding interpretative glosses to problematic sayings, framing difficult sayings with a new saying or group of sayings, or building question and answer pericopes, or inserting new material. In all of these cases, the reperformance forces new meaning onto the older problematic sayings. In addition, the reinterpretation might take place at the level of the audience. Over time, this shifting constituency of the community would have provided alternative ways to hear, read and exegete the gospel.

Does this shifting constituency and remodeling of ancient Jesus traditions mean that the later accretions represent less 'historical' Jesus material? Only if we forget that our understanding of the 'historical Jesus' is a product of our era. The Christians responsible for the *Gospel of Thomas* were a charismatic community, believing that Jesus, through his spirit, continued to communicate with its members. One must imagine that, for them, not only were all of the sayings in their original gospel sayings of the Prophet himself, but every saying that was added to their gospel over the course of time as well. The 'historical' Jesus for them was the 'living' Jesus who was ever-present in their community. As he continued to guide and teach them as their community grew and encountered problems and changing needs, they continued to update their gospel with new sayings which they believed were answers from Jesus himself.

BIBLIOGRAPHY

Ableson, R.P., *et al.* (eds.), *Theories of Cognitive Constitency: A Sourcebook* (Chicago: Rand McNally, 1968).

Adam, A., 'Grundbegriffe des Mönchtums in sprachlicher Sicht,' *ZKG* 65 (1953–54) pp. 209–239.

Adam, A. and Burchard, C., *Antike Berichte über die Essener*, KTVU 182 (Berlin: de Gruyter, 1972).

Afzal, C., 'The Communal Icon: Complex Cultural Schemas, Elements of the Social Imagination (Matthew 10:32//Luke 12:8 and Revelation 3:5, A Case Study,' in V. Wiles, A. Brown, and G. Synder (eds.), *Putting Body and Soul Together: Essays in Honor of Robin Scroggs* (Valley Forge: Trinity Press International, 1997) pp. 58–79.

Akagi, T., *The Literary Development of the Coptic Gospel of Thomas* (PhD dissertation; Western Reserve University, 1965).

Alexander, P., 'From Son of Adam to Second God: Transformation of the Biblical Enoch,' in M.E. Stone and T.A. Bergen (eds.), *Biblical Figures Outside the Bible* (Harrisburg: Trinity Press International, 1998) pp. 87–122.

Allison, D.C., *Jesus of Nazareth: Millenarian Prophet* (Minneapolis: Fortress Press, 1998).

Allison, Jr., D.C., 'Divorce, Celibacy and Joseph (Matthew 1.18–25 and 19.1–12),' *JSNT* 49 (1993) pp. 3–10.

Appadurai, A., 'The Past as a Scarce Resource,' *Man* 16 (1981), pp. 201–219.

Arnal, W., 'The Rhetoric of Marginality: Apocalypticism, Gnosticism, and Sayings Gospels,' *HTR* 88 (1995) pp. 471–494.

Aronson, E., *The Social Animal* (San Francisco: W.H. Freeman, 1976).

Asgeirsson, J.A., 'Arguments and Audience(s) in the Gospel of Thomas (Part I),' *SBL Seminar Papers 1997*, SBLSP 36 (Atlanta: Scholars Press, 1997) pp. 47–85.

Asgeirsson, J.A., 'Arguments and Audience(s) in the Gospel of Thomas (Part II),' *SBL Seminar Papers 1998*, SBLSP 37 (Atlanta: Scholars Press, 1998) pp. 325–342.

Ashton, J., *The Religion of Paul the Apostle* (New Haven: Yale University Press, 2000).

Assman, J., *Das kulturelle Gedächtnis: Schrift, Erinnerung und politische Identität in frühen Hochkulturen* (München: D.H. Beck, 1992).

Assmann, J., *Religion und kulturelles Gedächtnis: zehn Studien* (München: Beck, 2000).

Attridge, H., 'Intertextuality in the *Acts of Thomas*,' in R.F. Stoops, Jr. and D.R. MacDonald (eds.), *The Apocryphal Acts of the Apostles in Intertextual Perpectives*, Semeia 80 (Atlanta: Scholars Press, 1997) pp. 87–124.

Aune, D.E., *The Cultic Setting of Realized Eschatology in Early Christianity* (Leiden: E.J. Brill, 1972).

Baarda, T., 'Jesus said: Be Passersby. On the Meaning and Origin of Logion 42 of the Gospel of Thomas,' in J. Helderman and S. Noorda (eds.), *Early Transmission of Words of Jesus* (Amsterdam: Uitgeverij, 1983) pp. 179–206.

Baarda, T., 'Thomas and Tatian,' in J. Helderman and S. Noorda (eds.), *Early Transmission of Words of Jesus: Thomas, Tatian and the Text of the New Testament* (Amsterdam: Uitgeverij, 1983) pp. 37–49.

Baarda T., ' "Chosen" or "Collected": Concerning an Aramaism in Logion 8 of the Gospel of Thomas and the Question of Independence,' *HTR* 84 (1991) pp. 373–397.

Bagatti, B., *Church from the Circumcision* (Jerusalem: Franciscan, 1971).

Bailey, K., 'Informal Controlled Oral Tradition and the Synoptic Gospels,' *AsiaJT* 5 (1991) pp. 34–54.

Bailey, K., 'Middle Eastern Oral Tradition and the Synoptic Gospels,' *ExpTim* 106 (1995) pp. 363–367.

Baker, A., 'Pseudo-Macarius and the Gospel of Thomas,' *VC* 18 (1964) pp. 215–225.

Baker, A., 'Fasting to the World,' *JBL* 84 (1965) pp. 291–294.

Baker, A., 'The "Gospel of Thomas" and the Syriac "Liber Graduum",' *NTS* 12 (1965/66) pp. 49–55.

Barbour, R.S., *Tradition-Historical Criticism of the Gospels* (London: SPCK, 1972).

Barr, J., *Old and New in Interpretation: A Study of the Two Testaments* (London: SCM Press, 1966).

Bastian, A., *Ethnische Elementargedanken in der Lehre vom Menschen* (Berlin: Weidmannsche Buchhandlung, 1895).

Bauckman, R.J., 'The Delay of the Parousia,' *TynBul* 31 (1980) pp. 3–36.

Baumgarten, J.M., 'Celibacy,' in L.H. Schiffmann and J.C. VanderKam (eds.), *Encyclopedia of the Dead Sea Scrolls*, vol. 1 (Oxford: Oxford University Press, 2000) pp. 122–125.

Baumgarten, J.M., 'Damascus Document,' in L.H. Schiffmann and J.C. VanderKam (eds.), *Encyclopedia of the Dead Sea Scrolls*, vol. 1 (Oxford, 2000) pp. 166–170.

Beall, T.S., *Josephus' Description of the Essenes Illustrated by the Dead Sea Scrolls* (Cambridge, 1988).

Beall, T.S., 'Essenes,' in L.H. Schiffmann and J.C. VanderKam (eds.), *Encyclopedia of the Dead Sea Scrolls*, vol. 1 (Oxford: Oxford University Press, 2000) pp. 262–269.

Beck, E., 'Ein Beitrag zur Terminologie des ältesten syrischen Mönchtums,' *SA* 38 (1956) pp. 254–267.

Berger, P. and Luckmann, T., *The Social Construction of Reality: A Treatise in the Sociology of Knowledge* (New York: Doubleday, 1966).

Betz, H.D., 'The Delphic Maxim ΓΝΩΘΙ ΣΑΥΤΟΝ in Hermetic Interpretation,' *HTR* 63 (1970) pp. 465–484.

Betz, H.D., 'The Sermon on the Mount and Q: Some Aspects of the Problem,' in J. Goehring, C. Hedrick, J. Sanders and H.D. Betz, *Gospel Origins and Christian Beginnings in Honor of James M. Robinson* (Sonoma: Polebridge Press, 1990) pp. 19–34.

Betz, O., *Offenbarung und Schriftforschung in der Qumransekte* (Tübingen: Mohr, 1960).

Bianchi, U., 'The Religio-Historical Relevance of Lk 20.34–36,' in R. van den Broek and M.J. Vermanseren (eds.), *Studies in Gnosticism and Hellenistic Religions, presented to Gilles Quispel on the Occasion of his 65th Birthday*, EPRO 91 (Leiden: E.J. Brill, 1981) pp. 31–37.

Blonde, G., 'Encratisme,' in M. Viller, F. Cavallera, and J. de Guibert (eds.). *Dictionnaire de Spiritualité* 4 (Paris: G. Beauchesne, 1960) pp. 628–642.

Bodnar, J., 'Power and Memory in Oral History: Workers and Managers at Studebaker,' *JAH* 74 (1989) pp. 1201–1221.

Bodnar, J., *Remaking America: Public Memory, Commemoration, and Patriotism in the Twentieth Century* (Princeton: Princeton University Press, 1992).

Børtnes, M., *Visions of Glory: Studies in Early Russian Hagiography* (trans. J. Børtnes and P.L. Nielsen; New Jersey: Humanities Press International, 1988).

Botha, P., 'Mark's Story as Oral Traditional Literature: Rethinking the Transmission of Some Traditions About Jesus,' *HvTSt* 47 (1991) pp. 304–331.

Boussett, W., 'Die Himmelsreise der Seele,' *ARW* 4 (1901) pp. 136–169, 229–273.

Boussett, W., *Die Religion des Judentums im späthellenistischen Zeitalter*, HNT 21 (3rd edn. H. Gressmann; Tübingen: J.C.B. Mohr, 1966).

Bowker, J.W., 'Merkavah Visions and the Visions of Paul,' *JJS* 16 (1971), pp. 157–173.

Brehm, J.W. and Cohen, A.R., *Explorations in Cognitive Dissonance* (New York: Wiley, 1962).

Brown, P., *The Body and Society: Men, Women, and Sexual Renunciation in Early Christianity*, Lectures on History of Religions 13 (New York: Columbia University Press, 1988).

Brown, R., *Social Psychology* (New York: Free Press, 1965).

Bultmann, R., 'ζάω,' *TDNT* 2, pp. 832–872.

Bultmann, R., *History of the Synoptic Tradition* (trans. J. Marsh; New York: Harper and Row, revised edition, 1963).

Bultmann, R. and Kundsin, K., *Form Criticism: Two Essays on New Testament Research* (trans. by F.C. Grant; New York: Harper Torchbook, 1962).

Burkett, D., *The Son of Man Debate: A History and Evaluation*, SNTSMS107 (Cambridge: Cambridge University Press, 1999).

Burkitt, F.C., *Early Christianity Outside the Roman Empire* (Cambridge: Cambridge University Press, 1899).

Burridge, K., *New Heaven, New Earth: A Study of Millenarian Activities* (New York: Schocken Books, 1969).

Butts, J., *The 'Progymnasmata' of Theon: A New Text with Translation and Commentary* (Ann Arbor: University Microfilms International, 1987).

Cameron, R., 'The *Gospel of Thomas* and Christian Origins,' in B. Pearson (ed.), *The Future of Early Christianity: Essays in Honor of Helmut Koester* (Minnapolis: Fortress Press, 1991) pp. 381–392.

Cameron, R., 'Alternate Beginnings, Different Ends: Eusebius, Thomas, and the Construction of Christian Origins,' in L. Bormann, K. Del Tredici, and A. Standhartinger (eds.), *Religious Propaganda and Missionary Competition in the New Testament World: Essays Honoring Dieter Georgi*, NovTSup 74 (Leiden: E.J. Brill, 1994) pp. 507–521.

Cameron, R., 'Mythmaking and Intertextuality in Early Christianity,' in E. Castelli and H. Taussig (eds.), *Reimagining Christian Origins* (Valley Forge: Trinity Press International, 1996) pp. 37–50.

Cameron, R., 'Ancient Myths and Modern Theories of the *Gospel of Thomas* and Christian Origins,' *MTSR* 11 (1999) pp. 236–257.

Cameron, R. and Miller, M.P., *Redescribing Christian Origins*, Symposium Series 28 (Atlanta: Society of Biblical Literature, 2004).

Cameron, R. and Miller, M.P., 'Introduction: Ancient Myths and Modern Theories of Christian Origins,' in *Redescribing Christian Origins*, Symposium Series 28 (Atlanta: Society of Biblical Literature, 2004).

Carroll, J.T., *The Return of Jesus in Early Christianity* (Peabody: Hendrickson Publishers, 2000).

Carroll, R., *When Prophecy Failed: Cognitive Dissonance in the Prophetic Traditions of the Old Testament* (New York: The Seabury Press, 1979).

Casey, E., *Remembering: A Phenomemological Study* (Bloomington: Indiana University Press, 1987).

Catchpole, D.R., 'Tradition History,' in I.H. Marshall (ed.), *New Testament Interpretation: Essays on Principles and Methods* (Grand Rapids: Eerdmans Publishing Company, 1977) pp. 165–180.

Chadwick H., 'St. Paul and Philo of Alexandria,' *BJRL* 48 (1966), pp. 286–307.

Charles, R.H., *The Apocrypha and Pseudepigrapha of the Old Testament in English*, volume 2 (Oxford: The Clarendon Press, 1913).

Chernus, I., 'Visions of God in Merkabah Mysticism,' *JSJ* 13 (1982) pp. 123–146.

Clanchy, M.T., *From Memory to Written Record: England, 1066–1307* (Cambridge, MA: Harvard University Press, 1979).

Cohen, A.R., *Attitude Change and Social Influence* (New York: Basic Books, 1964).

Cohen, J.D., *From the Maccabees to the Mishnah* (Philadelphia: The Westminster Press, 1987).

Cohen, J., *'Be Fertile and Increase, Fill the Earth and Master It.' The Ancient and Medieval Career of a Biblical Text* (Ithaca: Cornell University Press, 1989).

Cohen, S., *The Beginnings of Jewishness: Boundaries, Varieties, Uncertainties* (Berkeley: University of California Press, 1999).

Cohn-Sherbok, D., *Rabbinic Perspectives on the New Testament*, Studies in the Bible and Early Christianity 28 (Lewiston: E. Mellen Press, 1990).

Connerton, P., *How Societies Remember* (Cambridge: Cambridge University Press, 1989).

Coote, R.B., *The Bible's First History* (Philadelphia: Fortress Press, 1989).

Coser, L., *The Functions of Social Conflict* (New York: Free Press, 1956).

Crossan, J.D., *The Historical Jesus: The Life of a Mediterranean Jewish Peasant* (New York: HarperSanFrancisco, 1991).

Culley, R.C., 'Oral Tradition and Biblical Studies,' *OT* 1 (1986) pp. 30–65.

Cullmann, O., 'Das Thomasevangelium und die Frage nach dem Alter der in ihm enthaltenen Tradition,' *TLZ* 85 (1960) pp. 321–334.

Cullmann, O., 'The Gospel of Thomas and the Problem of the Age of the Traditions Contained Therein: A Survey,' *Int* 16 (1962) pp. 418–438.

Dahl, N., 'The Arrogant Archon and the Lewd Sophia: Jewish Traditions in Gnostic Revolt,' in B. Layton (ed.), *The Rediscovery of Gnosticism*, vol. 2: *Sethian Gnosticism*, NumenSup 41 (Leiden: E.J. Brill, 1981) pp. 689–712.

Dalman, G., *The Words of Jesus Considered in the Light of Post-Biblical Jewish Writings and the Aramaic Language* (trans. D.M. Kay; Edinburgh: T&T Clark, 1902).

Danielou, J., *The Development of Christian Doctrine before the Council of Nicaea, Volume I: The Theology of Jewish Christianity* (trans. J. Baker; Chicago: The Henry Regnery Company, 1964).

Danielou, J., *The Theology of Jewish Christianity* (London: Darton, Longman and Todd, 1964).

Davies, S.L., *The Gospel of Thomas and Christian Wisdom* (New York: Seabury, 1983).

Davies, S., 'The Christology and Protology of the Gospel of Thomas,' *JBL* 111 (1992) pp. 663–683.

Davila, J.R., *Descenders to the Chariot: The People Behind the Hekhalot Literature*, JSJSup 70 (Leiden: E.J. Brill, 2001).

Davis, N. and Starn, R. (eds.), *Memory and Counter-memory*, Special Edition of *Representations* 26 (1989).

DeConick, A.D., *Seek to See Him: Ascent and Vision Mysticism in the Gospel of Thomas*, VCSup 33 (Leiden: E.J. Brill, 1996).

DeConick, A.D., 'Heavenly Temple Traditions and Valentinian Worship: A Case for First-Century Christology in the Second Century,' in C.C. Newman, J.R. Davila, and G.S. Lewis (eds.), *The Jewish Roots of Christological Monotheism: Papers from the St. Andrews Conference on the Historical Origins of the Worship of Jesus*, JSJSup 63 (Leiden: E.J. Brill, 1999), pp. 308–341.

DeConick, A.D., *Voices of the Mystics: Early Christian Discourse in the Gospels of John and Thomas and Other Ancient Christian Literature*, JSNTSup 157 (Sheffield: Sheffield Academic Press, 2001).

DeConick, A.D., 'The True Mysteries: Sacramentalism in the *Gospel of Philip*,' *VC* 55 (2002) pp. 225–261.

DeConick, A.D., *The Original Gospel of Thomas in Translation, with a Commentary and New English Translation of the Complete Gospel* (London: T&T Clark, forthcoming).

DeConick, A.D. and Fossum, J., 'Stripped Before God: A New Interpretation of Logion 37 in the Gospel of Thomas,' *VC* 45 (1991) pp. 123–150.

Dehandschutter, B., 'Le lieu d''origine de l''Èvangile selon Thomas,' *Orientalia Lovaniensia Periodica* 6/7 (1975) pp. 125–131.

Deutsch, M. and Krauss, R.M., *Theories in Social Psychology* (New York: Basic Books, 1965).

Deutsch, N., *The Gnostic Imagination: Gnosticism, Mandaeism, and Merkabah Mysticism*, Jewish Studies 13 (Leiden: E.J. Brill, 1995).

Dewey, J., 'Oral Methods of Structuring Narrative in Mark,' *Int* 53 (1989) pp. 32–44.

Dewey, J., 'Mark as Interwoven Tapestry: Forecasts and Echoes for a Listening Audience,' *CBQ* 53 (1991) pp. 221–236.

Dewey, J., 'Mark as Aural Narrative: Structures as Clues to Understanding,' *STRev* 36 (1992) pp. 45–56.

Diels, H., *Die Fragmente der Vorsokratiker* 1 (Berlin, 1956).

Dillon, J., *The Middle Platonists: A Study of Platonism 80 BC to AD 220* (Ithaca: Cornell University Press, 1977) pp. 115–135.

Doresse, J., *The Secret Books of the Egyptian Gnostics* (New York: Viking, 1960).

Drijvers, H.J.W., 'Facts and Problems in Early Syriac-Speaking Christianity,' *SecCent* 2 (1982) pp. 157–175.

Drower, E.S., *The Secret Adam: A Study of Nasoraean Gnosis* (Oxford: Clarendon Press, 1960).

Dunn, J.D.G., *Unity and Diversity in the New Testament: An Inquiry Into the Character of Earliest Christianity* (Philadelphia: Westminster Press, 1977).

Elior, R., 'Mysticism, Magic, and Angelology – The Perception of Angels in Hekhalot Literature,' *JSQ* 1 (1993/94) pp. 3–53.

Elior, R., 'From Earthly Temple to Heavenly Shrines. Prayer and Sacred Song in the Hekhalot Literature and Its Relation to Temple Traditions,' *JSQ* 4 (1997) pp. 217–267.

Elior, R., 'The Merkavah Tradition and the Emergence of Jewish Mysticism,' in A. Oppenheimer (ed.), *Sino-Judaica, Jews and Chinese in Historical Dialogue, And International Colloquium, Najing 11–19 October 1996* (Tel Aviv: Tel Aviv University, 1999) pp. 101–158.

Elior, R., *The Three Temples: On the Emergence of Jewish Mysticism* (trans. D. Louvish; Oxford: The Littman Library of Jewish Civilization, 2004).

Elliot, J., *A Home for the Homeless: A Social-Scientific Criticism of 1 Peter: Its Situation and Strategy* (Philadelphia: Fortress Press, 1990).

Elliot, J.H., *Social-Scientific Criticism of the New Testament and its Social World*, Semeia 35 (1986).

Elman, Y., 'Orality and the Redaction of the Babylonian Talmud,' *OT* 14 (1999) pp. 52–99.

Evans, C., 'The Colossian Mystics,' *Biblica* 63 (1982) pp. 188–205.

Everding, H., *The Living God: A Study in the Function and Meaning of Biblical Terminology* (PhD dissertation, Harvard, 1968).

Fallon, F.T. and Cameron, R., 'The Gospel of Thomas: A Forschungsbericht and Analysis,' *ANRW* 2:25.6 (New York, 1988) pp. 4195–4251.

Ferguson, E., *Backgrounds of Early Christianity* (Grand Rapids: Eerdman's Publishing Company, 2nd edn. 1993).

Festinger, L., *A Theory of Cognitive Dissonance* (Stanford: Stanford University Press, 1957).

Festinger, L., Riecken, H.W., and Schachter, S., *When Prophecy Fails* (Minneapolis: University of Minnesota Press, 1956).

Finnegan, R., *Literacy and Orality: Studies in the Technology of Communication* (Oxford: Blackwell, 1988).

Fish, S., *Is There a Text in this Class? The Authority of Interpretative Communities* (Cambridge, MA: Harvard University Press, 1980).

Fletcher-Louis, C.H.T., *All the Glory of Adam: Liturgical Anthropology in the Dead Sea Scrolls*, STDJ 42 (Leiden: E.J. Brill, 2002).

Foley, J.M., *The Theory of Oral Composition: History and Methodology* (Bloomington: Indiana University Press, 1988).

Foley, J.M., *Immanent Art: From Structure to Meaning in Traditional Oral Epic* (Bloomington: Indiana University, 1991).

Foley, J.M., *The Singer of Tales in Performance*, Voices in Performance and Text (Bloomington: Indiana University Press, 1995).

Fossum, J., 'Gen 1,26 an d 2,7 in Judaism, Samaritanism, and Gnosticism,' *JSJ* 16 (1985) pp. 202–239.

Fossum, J., *The Name of God and the Angel of the Lord*, WUNT 36 (Tübingen: J.C.B. Mohr, 1985).

Fossum, J., 'Glory,' *Dictionary of Deities and Demons in the Bible* (ed. K. vander Toorn *et al.*: Leiden: E.J. Brill, 1996) pp. 1486–1498.

Fossum, J., 'The Adorable Adam of the Mystics and the Rebuttal of the Rabbis,' in H. Cancik, H. Lichtenberger, and P. Schäfer (eds.), *Geschichte-Tradition-Reflexion. Festschrift für Martin Hengel zum 70. Geburtstag*, volume 1, *Judentum* (Tübingen: J.C.B. Mohr, 1996) pp. 529–539.

Fowden, G., *The Egyptian Hermes: A Historical Approach to the Late Pagan Mind* (Princeton: Princeton University Press, 1986).

Fraade, M., *From Tradition to Commentary: Torah and Its Interpretation in the Midrash Sifre to Deuteronomy* (Albany: State University of New York Press, 1991).

Fraade, S.D., 'Ascetical Aspects of Ancient Judaism,' in A. Green (ed.), *Jewish Spirituality From the Bible through the Middle Ages* (New York: Crossroads, 1986) pp. 253–288.

Fraade, S., 'Literary Composition and Oral Performance in Early Midrashim,' *OT* 14 (1999) pp. 33–51.

Francis, F.O., 'Humility and Angelic Worship in Col 2.18,' ST 16 (1962) pp. 109–134.

Frend, W.H.C., 'Is Rehabilitation Possible?' *JTS* 18 (1967) pp. 13–26.

Funk, R.W., *Honest to Jesus* (New York: HarperCollins, 1996) pp. 121–139.

Gager, J., *Kingdom and Community: The Social World of Early Christianity* (Englewood Cliffs: Prentice-Hall, 1975).

Gärtner, B., *The Theology of the Gospel of Thomas* (trans. E. Sharpe; London: Collins, 1961).

Gaster, M., 'Das Shiur Komah,' *Studies and Texts in Folklore, Magic, Mediaveal Romance, Hebrew Apocrypha and Samaritan Archaeology* 2 (New York: Ktav Publishing House, 1971) pp. 1343–1348.

Georgi, D., *The Opponents of Paul in Second Corinthians* (Philadelphia: Fortress Press, 1986).

Gerhardsson, B., *Memory and Manuscript: OT and Written Transmission in Rabbinic Judaism and Early Christianity* (Lund: Gleerup, 1961).

Gieschen, C.A., *Angelomorphic Christology: Antecedents and Early Evidence, AGAJU 42* (Leiden: E.J. Brill, 1998).

Gillis, R., *Commemorations: The Politics of National Identity* (Princeton: Princeton University Press, 1994).

Ginzberg, L., *The Legends of the Jews*, volumes 1–5 (Philadelphia: Jewish Publication Society, 1913–1928).

Goldberg, A., 'Der Vortrag des Ma'asse Merkawa: Eine Vermutung zur frühen Merkavamystik,' *Judaica* 29 (1973) pp. 9–12.

Goodenough, E.R., *By Light, By Light* (Amsterdam: Philo Press, 1969).

Goodwin, M.J., *Paul, Apostle of the Living God* (Harrisburg: Trinity Press International, 2001).

Goody, J., *The Domestication of the Savage Mind* (Cambridge: Cambridge University Press, 1977).

Goody, J., *The Interface between the Written and the Oral* (Cambridge: Cambridge University Press, 1987).

Goulder, M., 'The Visionaries of Laodicea,' *JSNT* 43 (1991) pp. 15–39.

Goulder, M., 'Vision and Knowledge,' *JSNT* 56 (1994) pp. 53–71.

Grant, R.M. and Freedman, D.N., *The Secret Sayings of Jesus* (Garden City: Doubleday & Company, 1960).

Grässer, E., *Das Problem der Parusieverzögerung in den synoptischen Evangelien und in der Apostelgeschichte* (Berlin: A. Töpelmann, 1960).

Grenfell, B.P. and Hunt, A.S., ΛΟΓΙΑ ΙΗΣΟΥ. *Sayings of Our Lord from an Early Greek Papyrus* (London: Henry Frowde, 1897).

Griffith, S.H., 'Asceticism in the Church of Syria: The Hermeneutics of Early Monasticism,' in V.L. Wimbush and R. Valantasis (eds.), *Asceticism* (Oxford: Oxford University Press, 1995) pp. 220–245.

Griggs, C.W., *Early Egyptian Christianity from its Origins to 451 CE* (Leiden: E.J. Brill, 1988).

Grobel, K., 'How Gnostic is the Gospel of Thomas?' *NTS* 8 (1961/1962) pp. 367–373.

Gruenwald, I., *Apocalyptic and Merkavah Mysticism*, AGJU 14 (Leiden: E.J. Brill, 1980).

Guillaumont, A., 'Sémitismes dans les logia de Jésus retrouvés à Nag-Hammâdi,' *JA* 246 (1958) pp. 113–123.

Guillamont, A., 'Les "Logia" d'Oxyrhynchus sont-ils traduits du copte?' *Mus* 73 (1960) pp. 325–333.

Guillaumont, A., 'ΝΗΣΤΕΥΕΙΝ ΤΟΝ ΚΟΣΜΟΝ (P. Oxy. 1, verso, 1.5–6),' *BIFAO* 61 (1962) 15–23.

Guillamont, A., 'Les sémitismes dans l'Évangile selon Thomas: Essai de classement,' in R. van den Broek and M.J. Vermaseren (eds.), *Studies in Gnosticism and Hellenistic Religions presented to Gilles Quispel on the Occasion of his 65th Birthday*, EPRO 91 (Leiden: E.J. Brill, 1981) pp. 190–204.

Gunkel, H., *Zum religionsgeschichtlichen Verständnis des Neuen Testaments*, FRLANT 1 (Göttingen: Vandenhoeck & Ruprecht, 1903).

Haenchen, E., *Die Botschaft des Thomas-Evangeliums*, Theologische Bibliothek Töpelmann 6 (Berlin: Töpelmann, 1961).

Haenchen, E., 'Literatur zum Thomasevangelium,' *TRu* 27 (1961/1962) pp. 147–178, 306–338.

Halbwachs, M., *On Collective Memory* (trans. L.A. Coser; Chicago: University of Chicago Press, 1992 [1925]).

Halbwachs, M., *The Legendary Topography of the Gospels in the Holy Land* (trans. L. Coser; Chicago: Chicago University Press, 1992 [1941]).

Halbwachs, M., *The Collective Memory* (trans. F. Ditter and V. Ditter; New York: Harper and Row, 1980 [1950]).

Halperin, D.J., *The Merkabah in Rabbinic Literature* (New Haven: American Oriental Society, 1980).

Halperin, D.J., 'Ascension or Invasion: Implications of the Heavenly Journey in Ancient Judaism,' *Religion* 18 (1988) pp. 47–67.

Halperin, D.J., *The Faces of the Chariot* (Tübingen: Mohr, 1988).

Handler, R. and Linnekin, J., 'Tradition, Genuine or Spurious,' *JAF* 97 (1984) pp. 273–290.

Hardyck, J.A. and Braden, M., 'Prophecy Fails Again: A Report of a Failure to Replicate,' *JASP* 65 (1962) pp. 136–141.

Harl, M., 'A propos des Logia de Jésus: le sens du mot *monachos*,' *REG* 73 (1960) pp. 464–474.

Havelock, E.A., *Origins of Western Literacy*, The Ontario Institute for Studies in Education, Monograph Series 14 (Toronto, 1976).

Havelock, E.A., *Preface to Plato* (New York: Grosset and Dunlap, 1967).

Heidegger, M., *Being and Time* (trans. J. Macquarrie and E. Robinson; New York: Harper & Row, 1962).

Helderman, J., *Gospel of Truth, Die Anapausis im Evangelium Veritatis*, NHS 18 (Leiden: E.J. Brill, 1984).

Hengel, M., *Judaism and Hellenism*, 2 vols. (trans. J. Bowden; Philadelphia: Fortress Press, 1974).

Herder, J.G. and Suphan, B., (ed.), *Herders sämmtliche Werke*, 33 vols. (Berlin: Weidmann, 1877–1913).

Heschel, S., 'Jewish Studies as Counterhistory,' in D. Biale, M. Galchinsky, and S. Heschel (eds.), *Insider/Outsider: American Jews & Multiculturalism* (Berkeley: University of California Press, 1998) pp. 101–115.

Hiers, R.H., 'The Delay of the Parousia in Luke-Acts,' *NTS* 20 (1973–1974) pp. 145–155.

Higgins, A.J.B., 'Non-Gnostic Sayings in the Gospel of Thomas,' *NovT* 4 (1960) pp. 292–306.

Himmelfarb, M., 'Heavenly Ascent and the Relationship of the Apocalypses and the *Hekhalot* Literature,' *HUCA* 59 (1988) pp. 73–100.

Himmelfarb, M., *Ascent to Heaven in Jewish and Christian Apocalypses* (Oxford: Oxford University Press, 1993).

Hirshman, M., *Jewish and Christian Biblical Interpretation in Late Antiquity* (trans. B. Stein; Albany: State University of New York, 1996).

Hock, R.F. and O'Neil, E.N., *The Chreia in Ancient Rhetoric: The Progymnasmata*, vol. 1 (Atlanta: Scholars Press, 1986).

Horsley, R., *Hearing the Whole Story: The Politics of Plot in Mark's Gospel* (Louisville: Westminster/John Knox Press, 2001).

Horsley, R.A. and Draper, J.A., *Whoever Hears You Hears Me: Prophets, Performance, and Tradition in Q* (Harrisburg: Trinity Press International, 1999).

Howard, G., *The Teaching of Addai*, Texts and Translations 16, Early Christian Literature 4 (Chico: Scholars Press, 1981).

Hutton, P., 'Collective Memory and Collective Mentalities: The Halbwachs–Aries Connection,' *Rhist* 15 (1988) pp. 311–322.

Irwin-Zarecka, I., *Frames of Remembrance: The Dynamics of Collective Memory* (New Brunswick: Transaction Publishers, 1994).

Jackson, H.M., *The Lion Becomes Man: The Gnostic Leontomorphic Creator and the Platonic Tradition*, SBLDS 81 (Atlanta: Scholars Press, 1985).

Jackson, J., 'The Resurrection Belief of the Earliest Church: A Response to the Failure of Prophecy?' *JR* 55 (1975) pp. 414–425.

Jaffee, M., 'A Rabbinic Ontology of the Written and Spoken Word: On Discipleship, Transformative Knowledge, and the Living Texts of Oral Torah,' *JAAR* 65 (1997) pp. 525–549.

Jaffee, M., 'Oral Tradition in the Writings of Rabbinic Oral Torah: On Theorizing Rabbinic Orality,' *OT* 14 (1999) pp. 3–32.

Jaffee, N., 'How Much Orality in Oral Torah? New Perspectives on the Composition and Transmission of Early Rabbinic Tradition,' *Shofar* 10 (1992) pp. 53–72.

Janssens, Y., 'L'Évangile selon Thomas et son caractère gnostique,' *Mus* 75 (1962) 301–325.

Jarvie, I.C., *The Revolution of Anthropology* (Chicago: Henry Regnery, 1967).

Jeremias, G., *Der Lehrer der Gerechtigkeit*, SUNT 2 (Göttingen: Vandenhoeck & Ruprecht, 1963).

Jeremias, J., ''Ηλ(ε)ιας,' *TDNT* 2.928–941.

Jeremias, J., *Unbekannte Jesusworte* (Zurich: Zwengli-Verlag, 1948).

Jervell, J., *Imago Dei*, FRLANT 76 (Göttingen: Vandenhoeck & Ruprecht, 1960).

Kanagaraj, J.J., *'Mysticism' in the Gospel of John*, JSNT Supplement 158 (Sheffield: Sheffield Academic Press, 1998).

Kasser, R., 'Les manuscrits de Nag Hammâdi: faits, documents, problèmes,' *RTP* 9 (1959) pp. 357–370.

Kasser, R., *L'Évangile selon Thomas*, Bibliothèque théologique (Neuchâtel: Delachaux et Niestlé, 1961).

Kelber, W.H., *The Oral and the Written Gospel* (Philadephia: Fortress Press, 1983).

Kelber, W.H., 'Scripture and Logos: The Hermeneutics of Communication,' (paper presented at the annual meeting of the Society of Biblical Literature, Kansas City, November 1991).

Kennedy, G.A., *New Testament Interpretation through Rhetorical Criticism* (Chapel Hill: University of North Carolina Press, 1984).

Kingsley, P., 'An Introduction to the Hermetica: Approaching Ancient Esoteric Tradition,' in R. van den Broek and C. van Heertum, *From Poimandres to Jacob Böhme: Gnosis, Hermetism and the Christian Tradition* (Amsterdam: Bibliotheca Philosophica Hermetica, 2000) pp. 17–40.

Kingsley, P., 'Poimandres: The Etymology of the Name and the Origins of the Hermetica,' in R. van den Broek and C. van Heertum, *From Poimandres to Jacob Böhme: Gnosis, Hermetism and the Christian Tradition* (Amsterdam: Bibliotheca Philosophica Hermetica, 2000) pp. 39–76.

Klijn, A.F.J., 'The "Single One" in the Gospel of Thomas,' *JBL* 81 (1962) pp. 271–278.

Klijn, A.F.J., 'Christianity in Edessa and the Gospel of Thomas,' *NovT* 14 (1972) pp. 70–77.

Klijn, A.F.J., 'The Study of Jewish Christianity,' *NTS* 20 (1974) pp. 419–431.

Kloppenberg, J.S., *The Formation of Q: Trajectories in Ancient Wisdom Collections*, Studies in Antiquity and Christianity (Philadelphia: Fortress Press, 1987).

Kloppenborg, J.S., Meyer, M., *et al.*, *Q Thomas Reader* (Sonoma: Polebridge Press, 1990).

Knight, D.A., *Rediscovering the Traditions of Israel*, SBLDS 9 (Missoula: Scholars Press, 1975).

Koch, K., *The Growth of the Biblical Tradition* (trans. S.M. Cupitt; New York: Charles Scribner's Sons, 1969).

Koester, H., 'GNOMAI DIAPHOROI: The Origin and Nature of Diversification in the History of Early Christianity,' *HTR* 58 (1965) pp. 297–318.

Koester, H., 'One Jesus and Four Primitive Gospels,' *HTR* 61 (1968) pp. 203–247.

Koester, H., 'Apocryphal and Canonical Gospels,' *HTR* 73 (1980) pp. 105–130.

Koester H., 'Three Thomas Parables,' in A.H.B. Logan and A.J.M. Wedderburn, *The New Testatment and Gnosis, Essays in Honour of Robert McLachlan Wilson* (Edinburgh: T&T Clark, 1983) pp. 195–203.

Koester, H., *Ancient Christian Gospels: Their History and Development* (Philadelphia: Trinity Press International, 1990).

Koester H., *Introduction to the New Testament*, volume 2 (New York: Walter de Gruyter, 2000).

Kohler K., 'Merkabah,' *The Jewish Encyclopedia* 8 (ed. I. Singer; New York: Funk and Wagnalls, 1904) p. 500.

Kraeling, C., *Anthropos and Son of Man* (New York: Columbia University Press, 1927).

Kraft, R.A., 'In Search of "Jewish Christianity" and its "Theology,"' *RSR* 60 (1972) pp. 81–92.

Kraus, H.J., 'Der lebendige Gott,' *EvT* 27 (1967) pp. 169–201.

Kuhn, K.H., 'Some Observations on the Coptic Gospel According to Thomas,' *Mus* 73 (1960) pp. 317–323.

Layton, B., *The Facsimile Edition of the Nag Hammadi Codices, Codex II* (Leiden: E.J. Brill, 1974) p. 55.

Layton, B., *Nag Hammadi Codex II,2-7, NHS* 20 (Leiden: E.J. Brill, 1989) p. 70.

Leipoldt, J., *Das Evangelium nach Thomas*, TU 101 (Berlin: Akademie-Verlag, 1967).

Lelyveld, M., *Les Logia de la Vie dans L'Évangile selon Thomas*, NHS 34 (Leiden: E.J. Brill, 1987).

Lentz, T.M., *Orality and Literacy in Hellenic Greece* (Carbondale: Southern Illinois University Press, 1989).

Levison, J.R., *The Spirit in First-Century Judaism* (Leiden: E.J. Brill, 2002).

Lewis, B., *History: Remembered, Recovered, Invented* (Princeton: Princeton University Press, 1975).

Lewy, H., *Sobria Ebrietas*, BZNW 9 (Berlin: Alfred Töpelmann, 1929).

Liebart, J., *Les Enseignements Moraux des Peres Apostoliques* (Gembloux: J. Duculot, 1970).

Lieber, A., *God Incorporated: Feasting on the Divine Presence in Ancient Judaism* (PhD dissertation: Columbia University, 1998).

Lindemann, A., 'Zur Gleichnisinterpretation im Thomas-Evangelium,' ZNW 71 (1980) pp. 214–243.

Longenecker, R., *The Christology of Early Jewish Christianity: Studies in Biblical Theology* (Naperville: Alec R. Allenson, 1970).

Lord, A., *The Singer of Tales*, Harvard Studies in Comparative Literature 24 (Cambridge: Harvard University Press, 1960, 2nd edn 2000).

Lossky, V., *The Mystical Theology of the Eastern Church* (Crestwood: St Vladimir's Seminary Press, 1976).

Lossky, V., *The Vision of God* (trans. A. Moorhouse: Crestwook: St Vladimir's Seminary Press, 1983).

Lossky, V., *In the Image and Likeness of God* (Crestwood: St Vladimir's Seminary Press, 1985).

Lovejoy, A.O., *The Great Chain of Being* (Cambridge, MA: Harvard University Press, 1954).

Lowenthal, D., *The Past is a Foreign Country* (Cambridge: Cambridge University Press, 1985).

Luedemann, G., *Opposition to Paul in Jewish Christianity* (trans. M. Eugene Boring; Philadelphia: Fortress Press, 1989).

Macdonald, J., *Memar Marqa. The Teaching of Marqua* 2, BZAW 83 (Berlin: A. Töpelmann, 1963).

Mack, B.L., *A Myth of Innocence: Mark and Christian Origins* (Philadelphia: Fortress Press, 1988).

Mack, B.L. and Robbins, V.K., *Patterns of Persuasion in the Gospels* (Sonoma: Polebridge Press, 1989).

Mack, B.L., *Rhetoric and the New Testament* (Minneapolis: Fortress Press, 1990).

MacRae, G.W., 'The Gospel of Thomas – LOGIA IESOU?' *CBQ* 22 (1960) pp. 56–71.

Mahé, J.-P., 'Les définitions d'Hermès Trismégiste à Asclépius,' *RSR* 50 (1976) pp. 193–214.

Mahé, J.-P., *Hermés en Haute-Egypte*, BCNH 7 (Québec: Presses de l''Université Laval, 1982).

Mahé, J.-P., 'La voie d'immortalité á la lumière des *Hermetica* de Nag Hammadi et de découvertes plus récentes,' *VC* 45 (1991) pp. 347–375.

Mahé, J.-P., 'Preliminary Remarks on the Demotic *Book of Thoth* and the Greek *Hermetica*,' *VC* 50 (1996) pp. 353–363.

Manns, F., *Bibliographie du Judeo-Christianisme* (Jerusalem: Franciscan, 1978).

Mantzaridis, G.I., *The Deification of Man* (trans. L. Sherrad; Crestwood: St Vladimir's Seminary Press, 1984).

Marjanen, A., '*Thomas* and Jewish Religious Practices,' in U. Risto (ed.), *Thomas at the Crossroads* (Edinburgh: T&T Clark, 1998) pp. 163–182.

Marshall, J.W., 'The *Gospel of Thomas* and the Cynic Jesus,' in W.E. Arnal and M. Desjardins (eds.), *Whose Historical Jesus?*, Studies in Christianity and Judaism 7 (Waterloo: Wilfrid Laurier University Press, 1997) pp. 37–60.

Martinez, F.G. and Barrera, J.T., *The People of the Dead Sea Scrolls. Their Writings, Beliefs and Practices* (Leiden: E.J. Brill, 1993) pp. 139–157.

McArthur, H.K., 'The Gospel According to Thomas,' in *New Testament Sidelights: Essays in Honor of Alexander Converse Purdy, Hosner Professor of New Testament, Dean of the Hartford Theological Seminary, the Hartford Seminary Foundation* (Hartford: Hartford Seminary Foundation, 1960) pp. 43–77.

McArthur, H., 'Celibacy in Judaism at the Time of Christian Beginnings,' *AUSS* 25 (1987) pp. 163–181.

McKane, W., *A Critical and Exegetical Commentary on Jeremiah*, The International Critical Commentary, volume 1 (Edinburgh: T&T Clark, 1986).

McKane, W., *Proverbs: A New Approach*, The Old Testament Library (Philadelphia: The Westminster Press, 1977).

Meier, J.P., *A Marginal Jew: Rethinking the Historical Jesus*, volume 1 (New York: Doubleday, 1991).

Ménard, J.-E., 'Der syrische Synkretismus und das Thomasevangeliuum,' in A. Dietrich (ed.), *Synkretismus im syrisch-persischen Kulturrgebist* (Göttingen: Vandenhoeck and Ruprecht, 1975) pp. 65–79.

Ménard, J.-E., *L'Évangile selon Thomas*, NHS 5 (Leiden: E.J. Brill, 1975).

Meyer, M., *The Gospel of Thomas: The Hidden Sayings of Jesus* (San Francisco: HarperSanFrancisco, 1992).

Montefiore, H., 'A Comparison of the Parables of the Gospel According to Thomas and the Synoptic Gospels,' *NTS* 7 (1960/61) pp. 220–248.

Moore, A.L., *The Parousia in the New Testament* (Leiden: E.J. Brill, 1966).

Morard, F.-E., 'Monachos Moine, Historie du terme grec jusqu''au 4e siècle,' *Freiburger Zeitschrift für Philosophie und Theologie* (1973) pp. 332–411.

Morard, F.-E., 'Monachos: une importation sémitique en Egypte?' in E.A. Livingstone (ed.), *Papers Presented to the Sixth International Conference on Patristic Studies Held in Oxford 1971*, TU 115 (Berlin: Akademie-Verlag, 1975) pp. 242–246.

Morard, F.-E., 'Encore quelques réflexions sur monachos,' *VC* 34 (1980) pp. 395–401.

Morray-Jones, C.R.A., *Merkabah Mysticism and Talmudic Tradition* (PhD dissertation, University of Cambridge, 1988).

Morray-Jones, C.R.A., 'Transformational Mysticism in the Apocalyptic-Merkabah Tradition,' *JJS* 48 (1992) pp. 1–31.

Morray-Jones, C.R.A., 'Paradise Revisited (2 Cor. 12.1–12): The Jewish Mystical Background of Paul's Apostolate. Part 1: The Jewish Sources' and 'Part 2: Paul's Heavenly Ascent and its Significance,' *HTR* 86 (1993), pp. 177–217 and 265–292.

Morray-Jones, C.R.A., *A Transparent Illusion. The Dangerous Vision of Water in Hekhalot Mysticism: A Source-Critical and Tradition-Critical Inquiry*, JSJSup 59 (Leiden: E.J. Brill, 2002).

Munck, J., 'Bemerkungen zum koptischen Thomasevangelium,' *ST* 14 (1960) pp. 130–147.

Munoa III, P.B., *Four Powers in Heaven: The Interpretation of Daniel 7 in the Testament of Abraham*, JSP Supplement 28 (Sheffield: Sheffield Academic Press, 1998).

Murmelstein, B., 'Adam, ein Beitrag zur Messiaslehre,' *WZKM* 35 (1928) pp. 242 ff.

Murphy, F., *Early Judaism: The Exile to the Time of Jesus* (Peabody: Hendrickson Publishers, 2002).

Murray, R., 'Defining Judeo-Christianity,' *HeyJ* 13 (1972) pp. 303–310.

Murray, R., 'On Early Christianity and Judaism: Some Recent Studies,' *HeyJ* 13 (1972) pp. 441–451.

Murray, R., 'The Exhortation to Candidates for Ascetical Vows at Baptism in the Ancient Syriac Church,' *NTS* 21 (1974) pp. 59–80.

Murray, R., *Symbols of Church and Kingdom: A Study in Early Syriac Tradition* (Cambridge: Cambridge University Press, 1975).

Murray, R., 'Jews, Hebrews and Christians: Some Needed Distinctions,' *NovT* 24 (1983) pp. 194–208.

Mussies, G., 'Catalogues of Sins and Virtues Personified (NHC II,5),' in R. van den Broek and M.J. Vermaseren, *Studies in Gnosticism and Hellenistic Religions Presented to Gilles Quispel on the Occasion of his 65th Birthday*, EPRO 91 (Leiden: E.J. Brill, 1981) pp. 315–335.

Nagel, P., 'Erwägungen zum Thomas-Evangelium,' in F. Altheim and R. Stiehl (eds.), *Der Araber in der alten Welt*, v. 2 (Berlin: De Gruyter, 1969) pp. 368–392.

Namer, G., *Mémoire et société* (Paris: Méridiens Lincksieck, 1987).

Nellas, P., *Deification in Christ: Orthodox Perspectives on the Nature of the Human Person* (trans. N. Russell: Crestwood: St Vladimir's Seminary Press, 1987).

Neusner, J., *OT in Judaism: The Case of the Mishnah* (New York: Garland, 1987).

Neusner, J., *A Life of Yohanan ben Zakkai: Ca. 1–80 CE* (Leiden: E. J. Brill, 2nd rev. edn., 1970).

Newsom, C., *Songs of the Sabbath Sacrifice*, HSS 27 (Atlanta: Scholars Press, 1985).

Niditch, S., 'The Cosmic Adam: Man as Mediator in Rabbinic Literature,' *JJS* 34 (1983).

Niditch, S., *Oral World and Written Word: Ancient Israelite Literature* (Louisville: Westminster/John Knox Press, 1996).

O'Keeffe, K., O'Brien *Visible Song: Transitional Literacy in Old English Verse*, Cambridge Studies in Anglo-Saxon England 4 (Cambridge: Cambridge University Press, 1990).

Olick, J., 'Genre Memories and Memory Genres: A Dialogical Analysis of May 8, 1945 Commemorations in the Federal Republic of Germany,' *ASR* 64 (1999) pp. 381–402.

Ong, W., *Interfaces of the Word* (Ithaca: Cornell University Press, 1977).

Ong, W., *Orality and Literacy: The Technologizing of the Word* (New York: Methuen, 1982).

Ong, W., *Rhetoric, Romance, and Technology: Studies in the Interaction of Expression and Culture* (Ithaca: Cornell University Press, 1971).

Ong, W., *The Presence of the Word* (New Haven: Yale University Press, 1967).

Orlov, A., 'The Secrets of Creation in 2 (Slavonic) Enoch,' *Henoch* 22 (2000) pp. 45–62.

Orlov, A., '"Without Measure and Without Analogy": The Tradition of the Divine Body in *2 (Slavonic) Enoch*,' (forthcoming).

Orlov, A., 'Resurrection of Adam's Body: The Redeeming Role of Enoch-Metatron in 2 Enoch 46 and Sefer Hekhalot 48C,' (forthcoming).

Osiek, C., 'The New Handmaid: The Bible and the Social Sciences,' *TS* 50 (1989) pp. 260–278.

Pagels, E., 'Exegesis of Genesis 1 in the Gospels of Thomas and John,' *JBL* 118 (1999) pp. 477–496.

Pagels, E., *Beyond Belief: The Secret Gospel of Thomas* (New York: Vintage Books, 2003).

Parry M., *The Making of Homeric Verse: The Collected Papers of Milman Perry*, ed. by A. Parry (Oxford, 1971).

Patterson, S.J., 'The Gospel of Thomas and the Synoptic Tradition: A Forschungsbericht and Critique,' *FFF* 8 (1992) pp. 45–97.

Patterson, S., 'Wisdom in Q and Thomas,' in L.G. Perdue, B.B. Scott, and W.J. Wiseman (eds.), *In Search of Wisdom: Essays in Memory of John G. Gammie* (Louiseville: Westminster/John Knox, 1993) pp. 187–221.

Patterson, S., *The Gospel of Thomas and Jesus* (Sonoma: Polebridge Press, 1993).

Pearson, B.A. and Goehring, J.E. (eds.), *The Roots of Egyptian Christianity*, (Philadelphia: Fortress Press, 1986).

Perrin, N., *Thomas and Tatian: The Relationship between the Gospel of Thomas and the Diatessaron*, Academia Biblica 5 (Atlanta: Society of Biblical Literature, 2002).

Person, Jr., R., *The Deuteronomic School: History, Social Setting, and Literature*, Studies in Biblical Literature 2 (Atlanta: Society of Biblical Literature, 2002).

Peterson, E., *Frühkirche, Judentum und Gnosis* (Rome: Herder, 1959).

Pitre, B.J., 'Blessing the Barren and Warning the Fecund: Jesus'' Message for Women Concerning Pregnancy and Childbirth,' *JSNT* 81 (2001) pp. 59–80.

Pritz, N., *Nazarene Jewish Christianity: From the End of the New Testament Period until Its Disappearance in the Fourth Century* (Leiden: E.J. Brill, 1988).

Puech, H., 'The Gospel of Thomas,' in E. Hennecke and W. Schneemelcher (eds.), *New Testament Apocrypha*, volume 1 (trans. by R. McL. Wilson; Philadelphia: Westminster, 1963) pp. 278–307.

Puech, H., *En Quête de la Gnose*, volume 2 (Paris: Gallimard, 1978).

Quecke, H., 'Sein Haus seines Königreiches: Zum Thomasevangelium 85,9f.,' *Mus* 76 (1963) pp. 47–53.

Quispel, G., 'Der gnostische Anthropos und die jüdische Tradition,' *ErJb* 22 (1953) pp. 195–234.

Quispel, G., 'The Gospel of Thomas and the New Testament,' *VC* 11 (1957) pp. 189–207.

Quispel, G., 'L'Évangile selon Thomas et les Clémentines,' *VC* 12 (1958) pp. 181–196.

Quispel, G., 'L'Évangile selon Thomas et le Diatesssaron,' *VC* 13 (1959) pp. 87–117.

Quispel, G., 'Some Remarks on the Gospel of Thomas,' *NTS* 5 (1958/1959) pp. 276–290.

Quispel, G., 'L'Évangile selon Thomas et les Origines de l''Ascèse Chrétienne,' *Aspects du Judéo-Christianisme. Colloque de Strasbourg 23–25 avril 1964* (Paris: Presses Universitaires de France, 1965) pp. 35–52.

Quispel, G., 'The "Gospel of Thomas" and the "Gospel of the Hebrews",' *NTS* 12 (1966) pp. 371–382.

Quispel, G., *Makarius, das Thomasevangelium, und das Lied von der Perle*, NovTSupp 15 (Leiden: E.J. Brill, 1967).

Quispel, G., 'Markarius und das Lied von der Perle,' in U. Bianchi (ed.), *Le Origini dello Gnosticismo, Colloquio di Messina 13–18 Aprile 1966*, Studies in the History of Religions, NumenSup 12 (Leiden: E.J. Brill, 1967) pp. 625–644.

Quispel, G., 'The Discussion of Judaic Christianity,' *VC* 22 (1968) pp. 81–93.

Quispel, G., 'Gnosticism and the New Testament,' in *Gnostic Studies* 1 (Leiden: Nederlands Historisch-Archaeologisch Instituut, 1974) pp. 196–212.

Quispel, G., 'Das Ewige Ebenbild des Menschen. Zur Begegnung mit dem Selbst in der Gnosis,' *Gnostic Studies*, Nederlands Historisch-Archaeologisch Instituut te Istanbul 34.1 (Leiden: E.J. Brill, 1974) pp. 140–157.

Quispel, G., 'Gnosis and the New Sayings,' in *Gnostic Studies* 2 (Leiden: Nederlands Historische-Archaeologisch Instituut te Istanbul, 1975) pp. 180–209.

Quispel, G., 'L'Evangile selon Thomas et les Clementines,' in *Gnostic Studies 2* (Leiden: Nederlands Historisch-Archaeologisch Instituut te Istanbul, 1975) pp. 24–25.

Quispel, G., 'The Gospel of Thomas and the New Testament,' in *Gnostic Studies 2* (Leiden: Nederlands Historisch-Archaeologisch Instituut te Istanbul, 1975) pp. 13–14.

Quispel, G., 'The Syrian Thomas and the Syrian Macarius,' *Gnostic Studies* 2, Leiden: Nederlands Historisch-Archaeologisch Instituut te Istanbul 34(2) (1975) 113–121.

Quispel, G., *Tatian and the Gospel of Thomas* (Leiden: E.J. Brill, 1975).

Quispel, G., 'Ezekiel 1:26 in Jewish Mysticism and Gnosis,' *VC* 34 (1980) pp. 1–13.

Quispel, G., 'The *Gospel of Thomas* Revisited,' in B. Barc (ed.), *Colloque International sur les Textes de Nag Hammadi. Québec, 22–25 août 1978*, BCNH 1 (Louvain: Peeters, 1981) pp. 218–266.

Quispel, G., 'African Christianity Before Minucius Felix and Tertullian,' in J. den Boeft and A.H.M. Kessels (eds.), *Studies in Honour of H.L.W. Nelson* (Utrecht: Instituut voor Kassieke Talen, 1982) pp. 257–335.

Quispel, G., 'The Study of Encratism: A Historical Survey,' in U. Bianchi (ed.), *La Tradizione dell'Enkrateia, Atti del Colloquio Internazionale – Milano 20–23 Aprile 1982* (Rome: Edizioni Dell''Ateneo, 1985) pp. 35–81.

Quispel, G., 'Reincarnation and Magic in the Asclepius,' in R. van den Broek (ed.), *From Poimandres to Jacob Böhme: Gnosis, Hermetism and the Christian Tradition* (Amsterdam: Bibliotheca Philosophica Hermetica with E.J. Brill, 2000) pp. 167–232.

Quispel, G., 'Hermes Trismegistos and the Origins of Gnosticism,' in R. van den Broek and C. van Heertum, *From Poimandres to Jacob Böhme: Gnosis, Hermetism and the Christian Tradition* (Amsterdam: Bibliotheca Philosophica Hermetica, 2000) pp. 146–165.

Randolph, Tate, W., *Biblical Interpretation: An Integrated Approach* (Peabody: Hendrickson Publishers, 1997, revised edition).

Rast, W.E., *Tradition History and the Old Testament*, Guides to Biblical Scholarship (Philadelphia: Fortress Press, 1972).

Rehm, B., *Die Pseudoklementinen I. Homilien* (Berlin: Akademie Verlag, 1953).

Reiser, M., *Jesus and Judgment: The Eschatological Proclamation in Its Jewish Context* (trans. L. Maloney; Minneapolis: Fortress Press, 1997).

Reitzenstein, R., *Hellenistic Mystery-Religions: Their Basic Ideas and Significance* (Pittsburgh Theological Monograph Series 15; trans. J.E. Steely; Pittsburg: Pickwick Press, 1978).

Riesenfeld, H., 'The Gospel Tradition and Its Beginning,' in *The Gospel Tradition* (Philadelphia: Fortress Press, 1970) pp. 1–29.

Robbins, V., '*The Chreia,*' in D.E. Aune (ed.), *Greco-Roman Literature and the New Testament: Selected Forms and Genres*, SBLSBS 21 (Atlanta: Scholars Press, 1988) pp. 1–23.

Robbins, V., 'Writing as a Rhetorical Act in Plutarch and the Gospels,' in D.F. Watson (ed.), *Persuasive Artistry: Studies in New Testament Rhetoric in Honor of George A. Kennedy* (Sheffield: JSOT, 1991) pp. 142–168.

Robbins, V., 'Progymnastic Rhetorical Composition and Pre-Gospel Traditions: A New Approach,' in C. Focant (ed.), *The Synoptic Gospels: Source Criticism and the New Literary Criticism*, BETL 110 (Leuven: University Press, 1993) pp. 111–147.

Robbins, V., 'Oral, Rhetorical, and Literary Cultures,' *Semeia* 65 (1994) pp. 75–91.

Robbins, V., *Exploring the Texture of Texts: A Guide to Socio-rhetorical Interpretation* (Valley Forge: Trinity Press International, 1996).

Robbins, V., 'Rhetorical Composition and Source in the Gospel of Thomas,' *SBL 1997 Seminar Papers*, SBLSP 36 (Atlanta: Scholars Press, 1997) pp. 86–114.

Robbins, V., 'Enthumemic Texture in the Gospel of Thomas,' *SBL Seminar Papers 1998*, SBLSP 37 (Atlanta: Scholars Press, 1998) pp. 343–366.

Roberts, C.H., *Manuscript, Society and Belief in Early Christian Egypt* (London: Oxford University Press, 1979).

Robinson, J., 'LOGOI SOPHON: On the Gattung of Q,' in J. Robinson and H. Koester (eds.), *Trajectories through Early Christianity* (Philadelphia: Fortress Press, 1971) pp. 71–113.

Rordorf, W., *Sunday. The History of the Day of Rest and Worship in the Earliest Centuries of the Christian Church* (trans. A.A.K. Graham; Philadelphia: Westminster Press, 1968).

Rosenzweig, R. and Thelen, D., *The Presence of the Past: Popular Uses of History in American Life* (New York: Columbia University Press, 1988).

Rowland, C., *The Influence of the First Chapter of Ezekiel on Jewish and Early Christian Literature* (PhD thesis, Cambridge University, 1974).

Rowland, C., *The Open Heaven: A Study of Apocalyptic in Judaism and Early Christianity* (London: SPCK, 1982).

Rowland, C., *Christian Origins: An Account of the Setting and Character of the Most Important Messianic Sect of Judaism* (London: SPCK, 2nd edn, 2002).

Rudolph, K., 'Gnosis und Gnostizismus, ein Forschungsbericht,' *TRu* 34 (1969) pp. 185–187.

Russell, D.S., *The Method and Message of Jewish Apocalyptic* (Philadelphia: Westminster Press, 1964).

Sanders, E.P., *The Tendencies of the Synoptic Tradition*, SNTSMS 9 (Cambridge: Cambridge University Press, 1969).

Sanders, E.P., *Jewish Law From Jesus to the Mishnah: Five Studies*, Philadelphia: Trinity Press International, 1990).

Sanders, E.P., *Judaism: Practice & Belief 63 BCE–66CE* (Philadelphia: Trinity Press International, 1992).

Sanders, J.T., *Schismatics, Sectarians, Dissidents, Deviants: The First One Hundred Years of Jewish–Christian Relations* (Valley Forge: Trinity Press International, 1993).

Satlow, M.L., 'Rhetoric and Assumptions: Romans and Rabbis on Sex,' in M. Goodman (ed.). *Jews in a Graeco-Roman World* (Oxford: Clarendon Press, 1998) pp. 135–144.

Satran, D., 'Askese VI: Judentum,' *RGG* 1 (1998) pp. 839–840.

Schäfer, P., *Rivalitat zwischen Engeln und Menschen* (Berlin: De Gruyter, 1975).

Schäfer, P., 'Tradition and Redaction in Hekhalot Literature,' *JSJ* 14 (1983) pp. 172–181.

Schäfer, P., *Hekhalot-Studien*, TSAJ 19 (Tübingen: J.C.B. Mohr, 1988).

Schäfer, P., 'Merkavah Mysticism and Rabbinic Judaism,' *JAOS* 104 (1984), pp. 537–554.

Schäfer, P., *The Hidden and Manifest God: Some Major Themes in Early Jewish Mysticism* (trans. A. Pomerance; New York: SUNY, 1992).

Schenke, H.-M., *Der Gott 'Mensch' in der Gnosis: Ein religionsgeschichtlicher Beitrag zur Diskussion über die paulinische Anschauung von der Kirche als Leib Christi* (Göttingen: Vandenhoeck & Ruprecht, 1962).

Schenke, H.-M., 'On the Compositional History of the Gospel of Thomas,' *FFF* 10 (1994) pp. 9–30.

Schiffman, L.H., 'Merkavah Speculation at Qumran: The 4Q Serekh Shirot "Olat ha-Shabbat,' in J. Renharz and D. Swetschinski (eds.), *Mystics, Philosophers, and Politicians: Essays in Jewish Intellectual History in Honor of A. Altmann* (Durham, North Carolina: Duke University Press, 1982) pp. 15–47.

Schiffman, L.H., *From Text to Tradition: A History of the Second Temple and Rabbinic Judaism* (Hoboken: KTAV, 1991).

Schippers, R., *Het Evangelie van Thomas* (Kampen: J.H. Kok, 1960).

Schoedel, W.R., 'Naassene Themes in the Coptic Gospel of Thomas,' *VC* 14 (1960) pp. 225–234.

Schoeps, H.-J., *Theologie und Geschichte des Judenchristentums* (Tübingen: Mohr, 1956).

Schoeps, H.-J., *Jewish Christianity: Factional Disputes in the Early Church* (trans. D.R.A. Hare; Philadelphia: Fortress Press, 1969).

Scholem, G., *Major Trends in Jewish Mysticism* (Jerusalem: Schocken Publishing House, 1941).

Scholem, G., *Jewish Gnosticism, Merkavah Mysticism and Talmudic Tradition* (New York: Jewish Theological Seminary of America, 1960).

Scholem, G., *On the Kabbalah and its Symbolism* (trans. R. Manheim; New York: Schocken Books, 1965).

Scholem, G., *Kabbabah* (Jerusalem and New York: Merdian, 1974).

Scholem, G., *Origins of the Kabbalah* (ed. R.J.Z. Werblowsky; trans. A. Arkush; Princeton: Princeton University Press, 1987).

Scholem, G., *On the Mystical Shape of the Godhead: Basic Concepts in the KABBALAH* (ed. J. Chipman; trans. J. Neugroschel; forward by J. Dan; New York: Schocken Books, 1991).

Schrage, W., *Das Verhältnis des Thomas-Evangeliums zur synoptischen Tradition und zu den koptischen Evangelienübersetzungen*, BZNW 29 (Berlin: Töpelmann, 1964).

Schrage, W., 'Evangelienzitate in den Oxyrhynchus-Logien und im koptischen Thomas-evangelium,' in W. Eltester and F.H. Kettler, *Apophoreta. Festschrift für Ernest Haenchen*, BZNW 30 (Berlin: Alfred Töpelmann, 1964) pp. 251–268.

Schröter, J., *Erinnerung an Jesu Worte: Studien zur Rezeption der Logienüberlieferung in Markus, Q und Thomas* (WMANT 76; Neukirchen-Vluyn: Neukirchener, 1997).

Schürmann, H., 'Das Thomasevangelium und das lukanische Sondergut,' *BZ* 7 (1963) pp. 236–260.

Schwartz, B., 'Postmodernity and Historical Reputation: Abraham Lincoln in Late Twentieth-Century American Memory,' *SF* 77 (1998) pp. 63–103.

Schwartz, S., *Imperialism and Jewish Society: 200 BCE to 640 CE* (Princeton: Princeton University Press, 2001).

Schweitzer, A., *The Mysticism of Paul the Apostle* (trans. W. Montgomery; Baltimore: The Johns Hopkins University Press, 1931, reprinted 1998).

Segal, A., *Rebecca's Children: Judaism and Christianity in the Roman World* (Cambridge: Harvard University Press, 1986).

Segal, A.F., *Paul the Convert: The Apostolate and Apostasy of Saul the Pharisee* (New Haven: Yale University Press, 1990).

Segal, A., 'Jewish Christianity,' in H. Attridge and G. Hata (eds.), *Eusebius, Christianity, and Judaism* (Leiden: E.J. Brill, 1992) pp. 326–351.

Segal, A., *Life After Death: A History of the Afterlife in the Religions of the West* (New York: Doubleday, 2004).

Shils, E., *Tradition* (Chicago: University of Chicago Press, 1981).

Sieber, J.H., 'The Gospel of Thomas and the New Testament,' in J.E. Goehring, C.W. Hedrick and J. Sanders, with H.D. Betz, *Gospel Origins and Christian Beginnings. In Honor of James M. Robinson* (Sonoma: Polebridge Press, 1990) pp. 64–73.

Simon, M., *Verus Israel* (Paris: Boccard, 1948).

Simon, M., 'Réflexions sur le Judeo-Christianisme,' in J. Neusner (ed.), *Christianity, Judaism and Other Greco-Roman Cults: Studies for Morton Smith at Sixty*, Part 2: *Early Christianity* (Leiden: E.J. Brill, 1975) pp. 53–76.

Sjöberg, E., 'בך אדם und בר אנש im Hebräischen und Aramäischen,' *AcOr* 21 (1950–1951) pp. 57–65 and 91–107.

Smith, J.Z., *Drudgery Divine: On the Comparison of Early Christianities and the Religions of Late Antiquity*, Jordan Lectures in Comparative Religion 14 (Chicago: University of Chicago Press, 1990).

Smith, M., 'Two Ascended to Heaven – Jesus and the Author of 4Q491,' in J.H. Charlesworth (ed.), *Jesus and the Dead Sea Scrolls* (New York: Doubleday, 1992) pp. 290–301.

Solages, B. de, 'L'Évangile de Thomas et les Évangiles Canoniques: L'order des Péricopes,' *BLE* 80 (1979) pp. 102–108.

Spidlík, T., *The Spirituality of the Christian East: A Sytematic Handbook* (trans. A.P. Gythiel; Kalamazoo: Cistercian Publications, 1986).

Staerk, W., *Die Erlösererwartung in den östlichen Religionen* (Stuttgart and Berlin, 1938).

Stegemann, H., *Die Essener, Qumran, Johannes der Täufer und Jesus* (Leiden: E.J. Brill, 1998).

Stenger, W., 'Die Gottesbezeichnung "lebendiger Gott" im Neuen Testament,' *TTZ* 87 (1978) pp. 61–69.

Stock, B., *The Implications of Literacy: Written Language and Models of Interpretation in the Eleventh and Twelfth Centuries* (Princeton: Princeton University Press, 1983).

Stock, B., *Listening for the Text: On the Uses of the Past* (Baltimore: Johns Hopkins University Press, 1990).

Stone, M., 'The Fall of Satan and Adam's Penance: Three Notes on the Books of Adam and Eve,' *JTS* 44 (1993) pp. 142–156.

Strathmann, H., *Geschichte der frühchristlichen Askese* (Leipzig, 1914).

Strecker, G., *Das Judenchristentum in den Pseudoclementinen* (Berlin: Akademie, 1958).

Strecker, G., 'On the Problem of Jewish Christianity,' in W. Bauer, *Orthodoxy and Heresy in Earliest Christianity* (ed. R. Kraft and G. Krodel; Philadelphia: Fortress Press, 2nd edn. 1971) pp. 241–285.

Strobel, A., *Untersuchungen zum eschatologischen Verzögerungsproblem*, SNT 2 (Leiden: E.J. Brill, 1961).

Strobel, A., 'Textgeschichtliches zum Thomas-Logion 86 (Mt 8,20/Luk 9,58),' *VC* 17 (1963) pp. 211–224.

Stroumsa, G., 'The Form(s) of God: Some Notes on Metatron and Christ,' *HTR* 76 (1983) pp. 269–288.

Strugnell, J., 'The Angelic Liturgy,' VTSup 7 (1960) pp. 318–345.

Swartz, B., *Abraham Lincoln and the Forge of National Memory* (Chicago: University of Chicago Press, 2000).

Teeple, H.M., *The Mosaic Eschatological Prophet* (Philadelphia: Society of Biblical Literature, 1957).

Terdiman, R., *Present Past: Modernity and the Memory Crisis* (Ithaca: Cornell University Press, 1993).

Thelen, D., 'Memory and American History,' *JAH* 75 (1989) pp. 1117–1129.

Thomas, R., *Oral Tradition and Written Records in Classical Athens* (Cambridge: Cambridge University Press, 1989).

Tripp, D.H., 'The Aim of the Gospel of Thomas,' *ExpTim* 92 (1980/1981) pp. 41–44.

Turner, V.W., *The Ritual Process* (Chicago: Aldine Publishing Company, 1969).

Uro, R., 'Is *Thomas* an Encratite Gospel?' in U. Risto (ed.), *Thomas at the Crossroads* (Edinburgh: T&T Clark, 1998) pp. 140–162.

Uro, R., '*Thomas* and Oral Gospel Tradition,' in R. Uro (ed.), *Thomas at the Crossroads: Essays on the Gospel of Thomas* (Edinburgh: T&T Clark, 1998) pp. 8–32.

Uro, R., *Thomas: Seeking the Historical Context of the Gospel of Thomas* (London: T&T Clark, 2003) pp. 8–30.

Valantasis, R., 'Constructions of Power in Asceticism,' *JAAR* 63 (1995) pp. 775–821.

Valantasis, R., 'Is the Gospel of Thomas Ascetical? Revisiting an Old Problem with a New Theory,' *JECS* 7 (1999) 55–81.

Van den Broek, R., 'Religious Practices in the Hermetic "Lodge": New Light from Nag Hammadi,' in R. van den Broek and C. van Heertum (eds.), *From Poimandres to Jacob Böhme: Gnosis, Hermetism and the Christian Tradition* (Amsterdam: Bibliotheca Philosophica Hermetica, 2000) pp. 78–113.

Van der Horst, P.O., 'Celibacy in Early Judaism,' *RB* (2002) pp. 390–402.

Van Gennep, A., *The Rites of Passage* (trans. M.B. Vizedom and G.L. Caffe; London: Routledge & Kegan Paul, 1960).

Vansina, J., *OT: A Study in Historical Methodology* (London: Routledge and Kegan Paul, 1965); *OT as History* (Madison: University of Wisconsin, 1985).

Vermes, G., *Jesus the Jew: A Historian's Reading of the Gospels* (Philadelphia: Fortress Press, 1973).

Vielhauer, P., 'ΑΝΑΠΑΥΣΙΣ. Zum gnostischen Hintergrund des Thomasevangeliums,' *Apophoreta. Festschrift für Ernst Haenchen*, BZNW 30 (ed. W. Eltester and F. Kettler; Berlin: Alfred Topelmann, 1964) pp. 281–299.

Vogt, K., '"Becoming Male": A Gnostic and Early Christian Metaphor,' in K.E. Børresen (ed.), *The Image of God: Gender Models in Judaeo-Christian Tradition* (Minneapolis: Fortress Press, 1995) pp. 170–186.

Vööbus, A., *Celibacy: A Requirement for Admission to Baptism in the Early Syrian Church*, Papers of Estonian Theological Society in Exile 1 (Stockholm, 1951).

Vööbus, A., *History of Asceticism in the Syrian Orient*, 2 volumes: *The Origin of Asceticisim, Early Monasticism in Persia*, CSCO 184, and *A Contribution to the History and Culture in the Near East: Early Monasticism in Mesopotamia and Syria* CSCO 197 (Louvain: Secretariat du Corpus SCO, 1960).

Wachtel, N., 'Memory and History: Introduction,' *HA* 12 (1986) pp. 207–224.

Ware, T., *The Orthodox Church* (New York: Penguin Books, new edition, 1993).

Werner, M., *The Formation of Christian Dogma* (New York: Harper, 1957).

Wernik, U., 'Frustrated Beliefs and Early Christianity,' *Numen* 22 (1975) pp. 96–130.

William, M., 'Gnosticism' *Rethinking 'Gnosticism': An Argument for Dismantling a Dubious Category* (Princeton: Princeton University Press, 1996).

Wilson, R. McL., 'The Early History of the Exegesis of Gen. 1.26', *Studia Patristica*, TU 63 (Berlin: Akademie-Verlag, 1957) pp. 420–437.

Wilson, R. McL., '"Thomas" and the Growth of the Gospels,' *HTR* 53 (1960) pp. 231–250.

Wilson, R. McL., *Studies in the Gospel of Thomas* (London: Mowbray, 1960).

Wolfson, E., 'God, the Demiurge, and the Intellect: On the Usage of the Word *Kol* in Abraham ibn Ezra,' *REJ* 149 (1990) pp. 77–111.

Wolfson, E., '*Yeridah la-Merkavah*: Typology of Ecstasy and Enthronement in Ancient Jewish Mysticism,' in R. Herrera (ed.), *Mystics of the Book: Themes, Topics, and Typologies* (New York: Lang, 1993) pp. 13–44.

Wolfson, E., *Through a Speculum that Shines: Vision and Imagination in Medieval Jewish Mysticism* (Princeton: Princeton University Press, 1994).

Wuthnow, R., 'Introduction: The Problem of Articulation,' *Communities of Discourse* (Cambridge, Massachusetts: Harvard University Press, 1989).

Yerushalmi, Y., *Zakhor: Jewish History and Jewish Memory* (Seattle: University of Washington Press, 1982).

Zandee, J., ' "The Teachings of Silvanus" (NHC VII,4) and Jewish Christianity,' in R. van den Broek and M. J. Vermaseren, *Studies in Gnosticism and Hellenistic Religions, Presented to Gilles Quispel on the Occasion of his 65th Birthday*, ERPO 91 (Leiden: E.J. Brill, 1981) pp. 498–584.

Zelizer, B., 'Reading the Past Against the Grain: The Shape of Memory Studies,' *CSMC* 12 (1995) pp. 214–239.

Zerubavel, E., 'Social Memories: Steps to a Sociology of the Past,' *QS* 19 (1996) pp. 238–299.

Zerubavel, Y., *Recovered Roots: Collective Memory and the Making of Israeli National Tradition* (Chicago: University of Chicago Press, 1997).

Zoeckler, T., *Jesu Lehren im Thomasevangelium*, NHMS 47 (Leiden: E.J. Brill, 1999).

Zonabend, F., *The Enduring Memory: Time and History in a French Village* (trans. A. Forster; Manchester: Manchester University Press, 1984).

INDEX

INDEX OF REFERENCES

OLD TESTAMENT

New Testament

OLD TESTAMENT APOCRYPHA AND PSEUDEPIGRAPHA

New Testament Apocrypha and Nag Hammadi Codices

OTHER ANCIENT SOURCES

INDEX OF AUTHORS